Joey Green's
Kitchen
Magic

Other Books by Joey Green

Hellbent on Insanity

The Gilligan's Island Handbook

The Get Smart Handbook

The Partridge Family Album

Polish Your Furniture with Panty Hose

Hi Bob!

Selling Out

Paint Your House with Powdered Milk

Wash Your Hair with Whipped Cream

The Bubble Wrap Book

Joey Green's Encyclopedia of Offbeat Uses for
    Brand-Name Products

The Zen of Oz

The Warning Label Book

Monica Speaks

The Official Slinky Book

You Know You've Reached Middle Age If . . .

The Mad Scientist Handbook

Clean Your Clothes with Cheez Whiz

The Road to Success Is Paved with Failure

Clean It! Fix It! Eat It!

Joey Green's Magic Brands

The Mad Scientist Handbook 2

Senior Moments

Jesus and Moses: The Parallel Sayings

Joey Green's Amazing Kitchen Cures

Jesus and Muhammad: The Parallel Sayings

Joey Green's Gardening Magic

How They Met

Joey Green's Incredible Country Store

Potato Radio, Dizzy Dice

Joey Green's Supermarket Spa

Weird Christmas

Contrary to Popular Belief

Marx & Lennon: The Parallel Sayings

Joey Green's Rainy Day Magic

The Jolly President

Champagne and Caviar Again?

Joey Green's Mealtime Magic

The Bathroom Professor: Philosophy on the Go

Famous Failures

Lunacy: The Best of the Cornell Lunatic

Joey Green's Fix-It Magic

Too Old for MySpace, Too Young for Medicare

You Know You Need a Vacation If . . .

Sarah Palin's Secret Diary

Joey Green's Cleaning Magic

Joey Green's Amazing Pet Cures

Dumb History

Joey Green's
Kitchen Magic

1,882 QUICK COOKING TRICKS, CLEANING HINTS,
AND KITCHEN REMEDIES USING
YOUR FAVORITE BRAND-NAME PRODUCTS

BY **JOEY GREEN**

AUTHOR OF *JOEY GREEN'S AMAZING KITCHEN CURES*

RODALE.

Direct and trade editions are both being published in 2012.
Rodale books may be purchased for business or promotional use or for special sales. For information, please write to: Special Markets Department, Rodale Inc., 733 Third Avenue, New York, NY 10017.

Printed in the United States of America
Rodale Inc. makes every effort to use acid-free ∞, recycled paper ♲.

Book design by Chris Rhoads
Illustrations by Scott Burroughs

Library of Congress Cataloging-in-Publication Data

Green, Joey.
    Joey Green's kitchen magic : 1,882 quick cooking tricks, cleaning hints, and kitchen remedies using your favorite brand-name products / by Joey Green.
        p.   cm.
    Includes index.
    ISBN 978–1–60961–702–8 direct hardcover
    ISBN 978–1–60961–703–5 trade paperback
    1. Home economics.   2. House cleaning.   3. Brand name products—United States.
4. Consumer education.   I. Title.   II. Title: Kitchen magic.
TX321.G74   2012
648—dc23   2012002369

Distributed to the trade by Macmillan
2   4   6   8   10   9   7   5   3   1   direct hardcover
2   4   6   8   10   9   7   5   3   1   trade paperback

We inspire and enable people to improve their lives and the world around them.
www.rodalebooks.com

For Michael and Audrey

Ingredients

But First, a Word from Our Sponsor   xiii

CHAPTER 1: Shopping and Storing

Dairy and Eggs   1

Fruits   5

Grains   10

Herbs and Spices   13

Leftovers   14

Meat, Chicken, and Fish   15

Shopping Supplies   19

Sweets and Treats   20

Vegetables   23

CHAPTER 2: Cookware and Tableware

Aprons   32

Cake Pans   32

Cake Plates   32

Cast-Iron Cookware   33

China   34

Cutting Boards   35

Dishwashing Liquid   35

Funnels   35

Garbage Pails   36

Glassware   37

Graters   37

Jar Labels   37

Jar Opener   38

Knives   38

Measuring Cups   38

Measuring Spoons   39

Meat Mallets   39

Napkins   40

Nonstick Cookware   40

Oven Mitts   40

Plastic Containers   40

Plastic Wrap   41

Pot Holders   41

Pots and Pans   41

Rolling Pins   42

Rubber Gloves   43

Salt and Pepper Shakers   44

Scissors   44

Serving Spoons   44

Shelf Liners   45

Silverware   45

Steel Wool Pads   46

Sifters and Strainers   46

Teapots   46

Whisks   47
Wok   47

Wooden Salad Bowls   47
Wooden Spoons   48

CHAPTER 3: Appliances and Gadgets

Barbecue   49
Blender   52
Bread Machine   52
Can Opener   53
Coffee Filters   53
Coffee Grinder   54
Coffeemaker   54
Coffee Percolator   55
Dehydrator   56
Dishwasher   56
Eggbeater   59
Electric Skillet   59
Fire Extinguisher   60
Food Processor   60
Freezer   61
Garbage Disposer   63
Juicer   64
Meat Grinder   65

Microwave Oven   65
Mixer   67
Oven   68
Oven Racks   69
Pressure Cooker   71
Range Hood   72
Refrigerator   72
Refrigerator Drip Trays   75
Rice Cooker   75
Slow Cooker   76
Stove   76
Stove Burner Drip Plates and
    Burner Grates   77
Stove Knobs   78
Teakettle   78
Toaster   79
Toaster Oven   80
Waffle Iron   81

CHAPTER 4: Food Secrets

Apples   82
Artichokes   83
Asparagus   84
Avocados   85
Bacon   86
Baking Powder   87

Baking Soda   87
Bananas   88
Barbecue Sauce   89
Beans   89
Beets   91
Berries   91

Beverages   91

Biscuits   92

Bratwurst   92

Bread   92

Breadcrumbs   98

Broccoli   99

Brown Sugar   100

Brownies   101

Brussels Sprouts   101

Butter   102

Cabbage   102

Cake   104

Candy   117

Cantaloupe   118

Carrots   118

Cauliflower   120

Celery   121

Cereals   122

Cheese   123

Chicken   128

Chocolate   136

Clams   139

Coffee   140

Collard Greens   141

Cookies   141

Corn   145

Corn Syrup   146

Crab   147

Cranberries   147

Crêpes   147

Cucumbers   148

Cupcakes   149

Custard   150

Doughnuts   150

Dried Fruit   150

Eggplant   151

Eggs   152

Fish   160

Flour   168

Frozen Food   169

Fruit   169

Garlic   171

Gelatin   172

Grapefruit   173

Grapes   174

Gravy   174

Ham   176

Hamburgers   177

Herbs and Spices   181

Honey   182

Honeydew Melon   183

Hot Chocolate   183

Ice Cream   185

Jams and Jellies   185

Juices   186

Ketchup   186

Kiwi   186

Lamb   187

Lemons and Limes   187

Lettuce   188

Lima Beans   189

Liver   190

Mangoes   190
Mayonnaise   190
Meatloaf   191
Meats   193
Meringues   203
Milk and Cream   204
Molasses   207
Muffins   208
Mushrooms   209
Mussels   210
Mutton   210
Nuts   210
Oil   212
Onions   213
Oranges   216
Oysters   217
Pancakes   217
Pasta   219
Pastry   222
Peaches   222
Pears   223
Peppers   224
Pies   224
Pineapple   227
Popcorn   227
Pork Chops   229
Potatoes   229
Poultry   236
Pudding   236
Pumpkins   236
Raisins   237

Rice   237
Salad Dressing   241
Salads   241
Salsa   243
Salt   243
Sauces   245
Sausages   247
Scallops   247
Shrimp   247
Snow Cones   248
Soufflés   249
Soups   250
Sour Cream   254
Spinach   255
Strawberries   255
String Beans   256
Stuffing   257
Sugar   258
Sweet Potatoes   259
Sweetbreads   259
Syrup   259
Tacos   260
Tea   260
Tomatoes   261
Turkey   262
Turnips   263
Vegetables   264
Waffles   265
Watermelon   266
Wine   267
Yogurt   268

CHAPTER 5: Astonishing Kitchen Remedies

Arthritis   269

Athlete's Foot   269

Backache   270

Bad Breath   270

Blisters   271

Body Odor   271

Bruises   272

Burns   272

Chapped Lips   273

Colds and Flu   273

Constipation   275

Cuts and Scrapes   275

Dandruff   276

Diarrhea   276

Eyes   277

Facials   278

Feet   279

Food Poisoning   280

Gum in Hair   280

Hands   281

Headache   281

Heartburn   282

Hiccups   282

Ice Packs   282

Indigestion   283

Insect Bites   284

Insomnia   284

Itchy Skin   284

Nausea   285

Shaving   285

Skin   286

Smoking   286

Sore Throat   286

Tongue Burn   287

Ulcers   287

CHAPTER 6: Cleaning Up the Mess

Aluminum Cookware   289

Bottles   289

Broiler Pan   290

Broken Glass   291

Brooms   291

Butcher Block   292

Cabinets   292

Candle Wax   293

Carpet Stains   293

Casserole Dishes   296

Cast-Iron Cookware   297

China   299

Cleanser Cans   299

Coffee and Tea Cups   300

Coffeepots   300

Cooktops   301

Coolers   302

Copper   303

Countertops   304

Crystal Glassware   305

Crystal Vases   306

Cutting Boards   308

Dishes   309

Drain Boards   310

Drains   310

Eggs   312

Enamel Pots and Pans   312

Flatware   313

Floors   313

Garbage Pails   315

Glassware   316

Graters   316

Hands   316

Highchairs   317

Kitchen Magnets   317

Lunch Boxes   317

Mops   318

Nonstick Cookware   319

Odors   319

Oil   320

Pewter   321

Plastic Containers   321

Pot Scrubber   322

Pots and Pans   323

Scouring Powder   326

Silverware   326

Sink Mats   327

Sinks   327

Spilled Milk   330

Sponges   330

Sports Bottles   330

Stainless-Steel Appliances   331

Tablecloths and Napkins   332

Teapots   334

Thermos Bottles   334

Waffle Iron   335

Walls and Wallpaper   336

Wine Stains   336

Wooden Spoons   337

Acknowledgments   339

The Fine Print   341

Trademark Information   345

Index   353

About the Author   370

But First,
a Word from Our Sponsor

Cooking is an art, but like any art, there are amazingly simple tricks of the trade, clever shortcuts, and ingenious secrets that can turn cooking from a humdrum chore into an invigorating and riveting adventure. You can make beef melt in your mouth by marinating the meat in Coca-Cola. You can save burned gravy with a tablespoon of Jif Peanut Butter. You can substitute Mott's Applesauce for butter when baking a cake. You can give spaghetti sauce a zesty flavor by adding Maxwell House Coffee. If you don't have any buttermilk for a recipe, you can substitute the same amount of Dannon Plain Nonfat Yogurt. Over the years, I've discovered literally hundreds and hundreds of astonishing cooking tips using everyday brand-name products sitting in your pantry right now. These simple yet inventive tips not only save time and money in the kitchen, but they also make you feel like an ingenious mad scientist and a master chef all rolled into one.

Why slave away over a hot stove when you can be cooking up fun in your kitchen? With this book, you'll discover how to revive hardened brown sugar with a slice of Wonder Bread, how to slice cake with Oral-B Dental Floss, and how to make light and fluffy pancakes with Canada Dry Club Soda. You'll learn how to enrich potato salad with French's Mustard, bread chicken croquettes with Lay's Potato Chips, and marinate fish with Wish-Bone Robusto Italian Dressing. You'll find out how to prevent pasta from boiling over with Pam Cooking Spray, prolong the life of lettuce with Bounty Paper Towels, and stop pastry dough from sticking with Kingsford's Corn Starch. I'll share secret tips on how to shop for the freshest fruits and vegetables, like how to choose apples and pick the best asparagus. You'll learn the tricks to storing spices and pasta in the pantry so they stay fresh. I'll teach you how to keep appliances running smoothly by defrosting a jammed ice maker with a Conair Hair Dryer or deodorizing your microwave oven with McCormick Pure Vanilla Extract. And I'll explain how to get your dishes sparkling clean with Heinz White Vinegar and remove stubborn stains from cookware with Efferdent. I've also included some astonishing kitchen remedies (like how to soothe burns with French's Mustard and soothe tired feet with Cool Whip) and quick, easy recipes (like Classic Meatloaf, Glazed Walnuts, and Candied Fruit Peels) that you can whip up in a snap.

How did I come up with all these magical ways to use ordinary products in the kitchen? I contacted dozens of companies to get their secret files, I waded through thousands of cooking tips, I experimented with scores of brand-name products we all know and love, I spoke with numerous chefs and homemakers, I locked myself in the library for days at a time, I slaved over a hot stove, and I sifted through all the e-mails sent to me through my Web site by ingenious cooks sharing their innovative uses for brand-name products. I mastered the best way to cook rice. I learned the trick to hard-boiling an egg without cracking the shell. And I finally figured out how to cut onions without shedding any tears.

With this book, I share all these secrets so you can use everyday products—like L'eggs Sheer Energy Panty Hose, Jell-O, Heinz Ketchup, and Quaker Oats—in ways you never imagined to cook up a storm and make the kitchen your favorite room in the house.

CHAPTER 1

Shopping and Storing

Dairy and Eggs

Cheese

- **Domino Sugar Cubes** and **Ziploc Storage Bags.** To prevent mold from forming on a block of cheese, place the cheese and a few Domino Sugar Cubes in a Ziploc Storage Bag, seal the bag partially shut, suck out the excess air from the bag, and seal tightly. The sugar cubes attract the mold spores away from the cheese. Change the sugar cubes every few days.

- **Heinz Apple Cider Vinegar.** To prevent a chunk of cheese from getting moldy, dampen a soft, clean piece of cheesecloth with Heinz Apple Cider Vinegar, wrap it around the block of cheese, seal it in a Ziploc Storage Bag or airtight container, and refrigerate. The acetic acid in the vinegar helps prevent the growth of mold without affecting the flavor of the cheese. Refresh the cheesecloth with more vinegar when necessary.

- **Morton Salt.** To prevent cheese from molding in the refrigerator, dissolve two tablespoons Morton Salt in three cups of water, dampen a cloth with the salt water, and wrap the block of cheese in the damp cloth before refrigerating.

WHAT'S COOKING

SAY CHEESE

- The best places to buy cheese: a specialty market, a cheese shop, or a gourmet food store that specializes in cheeses.

- Check the label to ensure that the cheese is well within its expiration date. Question whether any cheese offered at a bargain price has passed its expiration date.

- Before buying cheese, check the aroma, appearance, and flavor. Avoid any cheese that smells like ammonia, sour milk, or a barnyard. Make sure the cheese appears free of cracks, discoloration, and mold (except for blue cheese). If possible, taste a sample of the cheese before you buy.

- If you have any dietary restrictions or concerns, check the label on the cheese or ask the cheesemonger to determine whether the cheese was made from pasteurized or raw cow, goat, or sheep milk and whether the cheesemaker used animal, vegetal, or microbial rennet.

- Avoid buying more cheese than you will consume within a few days.

- If you accidentally purchase a spoiled cheese, return the cheese to the store for an exchange or refund.

- Don't be repulsed by the unsightly appearance of some types of cheese. Many cheeses taste wonderful even though they look hideous.

- To prolong the shelf life of cottage cheese or ricotta cheese, store the container upside down in the refrigerator.

- Store packages of blue cheese and Roquefort cheese in the freezer. To prepare a salad, use a paring knife to scrape the cheese, causing it to crumble beautifully.

- **Reynolds Cut-Rite Wax Paper** and **Saran Wrap.** Natural cheese contains enzymes and bacteria that require air and moisture to survive. Rewrap cheese in a sheet of Reynolds Cut-Rite Wax Paper, followed

- The following cheeses can be frozen and will remain fresh: Cheddar, French, Greek, Italian, Swiss, and processed cheese. Cream-cheese dips can also be frozen. If the cream cheese appears grainy after being thawed, simply whip the dip thoroughly.

- If a blue-green mold forms on the outside of hard cheeses (with the exception of fresh cheese or blue cheese), cut it off roughly one-half inch below the mold. The remaining cheese is safe to eat.

- Cottage cheese can be frozen. However, when thawed, it breaks down. Whip it until creamy and use it in cooking.

- Processed cheese sold in jars does not require refrigeration until opened.

- Store cheese in the vegetable or fruit bin (where the humidity is highest) of a refrigerator set between 35 and 45 degrees Fahrenheit. Keep cheese away from the freezer compartment and the meat bin, where the cheese might accidentally freeze.

- Place strong, pungent cheeses in airtight containers to prevent the aroma of the cheese from permeating other foods stored in your refrigerator.

- Store cheeses separately to prevent them from acquiring each other's flavors.

- Freezing natural cheeses may turn the texture dry and crumbly and may alter the flavor. To defrost frozen cheese, place the cheese in the refrigerator, so it thaws slowly. You can still use the defrosted cheese for cooking or for topping salads.

- If any cheese becomes excessively dry, develops a slimy texture, or exudes an ammoniated or peculiar odor, throw it away.

- Soft cheeses tend to spoil before aged cheeses because they contain more moisture, making them more prone to bacterial growth.

by a sheet of Saran Wrap and refrigerate to create a healthy microenvironment. After using some of the cheese, rewrap the remaining cheese in fresh waxed paper and fresh plastic wrap.

- **Ziploc Storage Bags.** Store grated cheese in a Ziploc Storage Bag in the freezer to prevent mold from forming. Seal the bag partially shut, suck out the excess air from the bag, and seal tightly.

Eggs

- **Crayola Crayons.** To differentiate hard-boiled eggs from raw eggs in the refrigerator, mark the hard-boiled eggs with a Crayola Crayon.

- **Morton Salt.** To store unbroken egg yolks intact for up to one week, dissolve one-eighth teaspoon Morton Salt into one-half cup of cool water, and pour the salty solution into a jar. Carefully slide the yolk into the jar without breaking the membrane, making certain the salt water covers the yolk completely. Seal the lid and refrigerate. Before using the yolk, simply drain out the salt water.

Food for Thought
SURE AS EGGS

- Always buy eggs from a refrigerated case. Eggs stored at room temperature lose the same quality in one day that a refrigerated egg loses in a week.

- Medium eggs weigh at least twenty-one ounces per dozen, large eggs weigh at least twenty-four ounces per dozen, extra-large eggs weigh at least twenty-seven ounces per dozen, and jumbo eggs weigh at least thirty ounces per dozen.

- Two medium eggs, unbeaten, yield approximately one-quarter cup of egg.

- Eggs stored in the carton remain fresh longer than eggs stored in the refrigerator egg shelf. The snug carton prevents the eggs from losing moisture quickly and absorbing odors from the refrigerator.

- Eggs stored with the large end up remain fresh longer than eggs stored with the large end down. With the large end up, the air pocket inside the egg rises to the top, keeping the yolk centered.

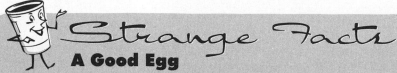
A Good Egg

Brown eggs are neither tastier nor more nutritious than white eggs. Brown eggs and white eggs are equally nutritious. The only difference between different colored eggs is the breed of the hen that lays it.

Milk and Cream

- **Morton Salt.** To extend the shelf life of milk and cream and prevent spoilage, add a pinch of salt to the milk or cream. The small amount of salt does not affect the taste of the milk or cream.

Fruits

Apples

- **Ziploc Storage Bags.** One bad apple can indeed spoil the whole bunch. The excessive ethylene gas produced by the bad apple triggers the healthy apples to rot. Instead of storing apples in a brown paper bag, store the fruit in a Ziploc Storage Bag so you can see whether any apples are going bad and remove the rotten apples before they contaminate the good fruit. Using a hole puncher, perforate a few holes in the Ziploc Storage Bag. The holes permit air movement, while allowing the bag to retain the ethylene that hastens ripening.

Food for Thought
AN APPLE A DAY

- When buying apples, look for a light green color at the bottom of each fruit—an indication that the apple is sufficiently ripe.

- Buy firm, hard apples that look fresh and crisp, without any soft spots or bruises.

- For eating, the best apples are Baldwin, Delicious, Fuji, Gala, Golden Delicious, Granny Smith, Jonathan, McIntosh, Opalescent, Pippin, Red Delicious, Stayman, and Winesap.

- For baking, the best apples are Granny Smith, Jonathan, Northern Spy, and Rome Beauty.

- For pies, the best apples are Cortland, Granny Smith, Gravenstein, Greening, Northern Spy, and Pippin.

- Store apples in the fruit bin in your refrigerator, but make sure they do not touch each other—to prevent bad apples from spoiling good apples.

Avocados

- **Forster Toothpicks.** To test whether an avocado is ripe, insert a Forster Toothpick into the fruit near the stem. If the toothpick goes in and slides back out easily, the avocado is ripe.

Food for Thought
A QUICK PIT STOP

- When buying an avocado, make sure the green skin is spotted with brown, and press the leathery skin to make sure the flesh underneath is soft.

- An unripe avocado is green, shiny, and hard. To ripen avocados, place them in a brown paper bag and store in a warm, dark place. Adding a ripe apple inside the bag speeds the ripening by releasing ethylene gas.

- Store ripe avocados in the refrigerator.

Bananas

- **Bounty Paper Towels.** To ripen green bananas, wrap them in a damp sheet of Bounty Paper Towels and place them in a bag, and store in a dark, cool place. Adding an overripe banana to the bag speeds up the ripening by releasing ethylene gas.

- **Ziploc Storage Bags.** Place ripe, unpeeled bananas in a Ziploc Storage Bag, remove as much air as possible before sealing, and store in the refrigerator. The cold turns the skin dark brown but preserves the banana color and flavor inside, impeding further ripening.

Berries

- **Saran Wrap** and **Ziploc Storage Bags.** To freeze berries, spread the berries on a cookie sheet, cover with a sheet of Saran Wrap, and place in the freezer for twenty minutes. Then place the frozen berries in a Ziploc Storage Bag, remove as much air as possible, seal securely, and freeze.

Cherries

- **Ziploc Storage Bags.** To freeze cherries, rinse well, pat dry, pit, place inside a Ziploc Storage Bag, and store in the freezer for up to one year.

Cranberries

- **Saran Wrap** and **Ziploc Storage Bags.** To freeze cranberries, spread the cranberries on a cookie sheet, cover with a sheet of Saran Wrap, and place in the freezer for twenty minutes. Then place the frozen berries in a Ziploc Storage Bag, remove as much air as possible, seal securely, and freeze. Stored in the freezer, fresh cranberries last for months.

Dried Fruit

- **Ziploc Storage Bags.** To store dried fruit fresh for a longer period, seal the dried fruit in a Ziploc Storage Bag and place it in the freezer.

Eggplant

- **Ziploc Storage Bags.** Using a hole puncher, perforate a few holes in a Ziploc Storage Bag. Place the eggplant in the bag and store in the refrigerator for up to one week.

Food for Thought
PUTTING ALL YOUR EGGPLANTS IN ONE BASKET

- When buying eggplant, choose small, heavy ones, which tend to be sweeter and meatier.

- To determine whether an eggplant is overripe, gently press the skin. If the dent quickly pops out and vanishes, the eggplant is ripe. If the dent remains, the eggplant is overripe.

Fruits

- **Scotch Tape.** To remove sticker labels from fruit without damaging the peel, place a small strip of Scotch Tape over the sticker, and then peel off the tape and sticker together as one.

Food for Thought
FORBIDDEN FRUIT

- Do not wash fruits before storing them. The moisture will cause them to decay faster. Instead, store fruits unwashed and wash them before eating or preparing.

- To buy the juiciest grapefruits, do not judge grapefruits by the yellowness of their skin. Instead, choose the grapefruits with the thinnest skins.

Pineapple

- **Saran Wrap.** To store a whole pineapple in the refrigerator for up to three days, wrap the pineapple below the crown in Saran Wrap.

Food for Thought
PINING FOR PINEAPPLE

- To determine whether a pineapple is ripe, pull out one of the inner leaves from the crown. If it comes out easily, the pineapple is ripe.

Strawberries

- **Mr. Coffee Filters.** To keep unwashed strawberries fresh in an airtight container, place a folded Mr. Coffee Filter on top of the strawberries, secure the lid shut, and store upside-down in the refrigerator. The coffee filter absorbs any excess moisture that might otherwise turn the strawberries soggy.

- **Saran Wrap** and **Ziploc Storage Bags.** To freeze strawberries, spread the berries on a cookie sheet, cover with a sheet of Saran Wrap, and place in the freezer until they freeze solid. Then place the frozen berries in a Ziploc Storage Bag, remove as much air as possible, seal securely, write the date on the bag, and freeze.

Food for Thought
STRAWBERRY FIELDS FOREVER

- Buy strawberries with bright green caps.

- Storing strawberries in a colander in the refrigerator allows the cold air to circulate around the strawberries, keeping them fresh for several days.

Watermelon

- *USA Today* and **Scotch Tape.** When taking a refrigerated whole watermelon on a picnic, wrap the cool watermelon in pages from *USA Today* secured in place with Scotch Tape. The newsprint seals in the coolness.

Food for Thought
WHEN THE TIME IS RIPE

- To determine whether a watermelon is ripe, rap the hard skin with your knuckles. You should hear a low, deep echo.

Grains
Bread

- **Forster Clothespins.** To seal a bread bag firmly shut, use a Forster Clothespin to clip the bag closed.

- **Reynolds Wrap.** If you do not intend to serve French or Italian bread within a few hours, wrap the bread in Reynolds Wrap and keep it in the freezer. Otherwise, within a few hours, these breads, made without oil or fat, dry out and get crusty. When you're ready to serve the bread, let it thaw (still in the aluminum foil) at room temperature and then heat the foil-wrapped bread in a 350 degree Fahrenheit oven for ten minutes.

- **Saran Wrap.** To store sliced or unsliced bread in the freezer, wrap the bread as airtight as possible in Saran Wrap to prevent any moisture from escaping and drying out the bread.

Food for Thought
LIVING BY BREAD ALONE

- Slices of frozen bread will thaw at room temperature within fifteen minutes, or insert frozen slices into a toaster and heat them up.

- A frozen, unsliced loaf of bread is much easier to slice (and into thinner slices, too) than a defrosted loaf of bread.

Breadcrumbs

- **Pringles** and **Con-Tact Paper.** To store breadcrumbs in an airtight container, cover a clean, empty Pringles can with Con-Tact paper and label.

Grains

- **Quaker Oats.** Store grains in a clean, empty Quaker Oats canister, appropriately labeled.

Pasta

- **Pringles.** Store uncooked spaghetti in a clean, empty Pringles can, which can be sealed properly.

- **Wrigley's Spearmint Gum.** To keep mealworms out of pasta, spaghetti, or macaroni, place a few wrapped sticks of Wrigley's Spearmint Gum nearby on the panty shelf. Spearmint repels mealworms.

Food for Thought
USING YOUR NOODLE

- After opening a box of pasta, store the leftover pasta in an opaque airtight glass or plastic container. Light breaks down the vitamin content in fortified pasta.

- Fresh raw pasta looks smooth and shiny. Stale pasta looks dusty and feels brittle.

Types of Pasta

PASTA	NICKNAME	LOOKS LIKE
Italian		
Capellini	Angel Hair Pasta	Long, thin strings
Capelletti		Crescent filled with cheese
Conchiglie	Sea Shell Noodles	Miniature conch shells
Farfalle	Bowtie Noodles	Little bowties
Fettuccine	Ribbons	Long, flat noodles
Fusilli	Corkscrews	Corkscrew noodle
Gnochi	Dumplings	Small lump
Lasagna		Long, flat noodle with ridged edges
Linguine	Little Tongues	Long, flattened noodles
Orzo		Long, large grains of rice
Penne		Hollow tubes cut diagonally
Ravioli		Square pillows filled with cheese or meat
Spaghetti	Little Strings	Long strings
Tortellini		Crescent filled with meat
Vermicelli	Little Worms	Long, thin strings
Ziti		Short, hollow tubes
Asian		
Mein		Long, thin strings
Ramen		Curly thick strings
Soba		Long, thin strings
German		
Potato Dumplings		Balls
Spaetzle		Dumplings

Rice

- **Gatorade.** Store rice in a clean, empty Gatorade bottle with the lid sealed securely.

- **Maxwell House Coffee.** Another great place to store rice is in a clean, empty Maxwell House Coffee can with the plastic lid tightly sealed.

- **Pringles** and **Con-Tact Paper.** To store rice in an airtight container, cover a clean, empty Pringles can with Con-Tact paper and label.

Food for Thought
MAKE NICE WITH RICE

- White rice stored in an airtight container on a cupboard shelf lasts up to one year. Brown rice stored in an airtight container on a shelf lasts only six months because the oily bran layer makes brown rice more vulnerable to rancidity. You can store brown rice in the refrigerator for up to one month.

Herbs and Spices

Chives

- **Ziploc Storage Bags.** To freeze chives, wash the stems well and shake vigorously. Then put them in a Ziploc Storage Bag and store in the freezer. They'll keep their green color if you use them without defrosting as soon as you remove them from the freezer.

Garlic

- **L'eggs Sheer Energy Panty Hose.** To store garlic cloves, use a pair of scissors to snip off the foot from a clean, used pair of L'eggs Sheer Energy Panty Hose, fill it with garlic cloves, tie a loose knot, and hang it high to keep the contents dry.

Herbs and Spices

- **Bounty Paper Towels.** To dry fresh herbs, place the herbs on a sheet of Bounty Paper Towels and heat them in the microwave oven for approximately one minute. Repeat for thirty-second intervals if necessary. Store the dried herbs in Ziploc Storage Bags, labeled appropriately, in the pantry for up to one year.

- **Ziploc Storage Bags.** To freeze fresh herbs, wash the herbs, slice them into small pieces, and fill each compartment in an ice-cube tray with one teaspoon of cut herbs. Fill the rest of each compartment with water, and place the ice-cube tray in the freezer. After the herb-filled ice cubes freeze solid, remove the cubes from the tray, place them in a Ziploc Freezer Bag, label with the name of the herb, and store in the freezer. Whenever a recipe calls for that herb, place one ice cube for each teaspoon required in a small strainer and run hot water over it to melt away the ice and defrost the herb.

Food for Thought
THE SPICE OF LIFE

- Stored in an airtight container in a cool, dry place, whole spices retain their potency for up to four years, ground spices last two to three years, and leafy herbs keep their flavor for one to three years.

- Store spices in covered jars in a cool place away from heat and light.

- Store bottled herbs and spices—particularly chili powder, curry, and paprika—in the refrigerator.

Leftovers

- **Cool Whip.** Store leftovers in a clean, empty, airtight Cool Whip canister.

- **Post-it Notes.** To avoid leaving leftovers in the refrigerator until they spoil, put Post-it Notes on containers of leftovers to remind you to eat them by a certain day.

- **Reynolds Wrap.** To keep leftovers fresh in the refrigerator or freezer, wrap them tightly in a sheet of Reynolds Wrap.

- **Saran Wrap.** To preserve a bowl of leftover food fresh in the refrigerator, stretch a sheet of Saran Wrap across the top the bowl, making certain it clings securely around the rim.

- **Ziploc Storage Bags.** Keep leftovers for single servings in Ziploc Storage Bags for quick, easy-to-prepare meals.

Meat, Chicken, and Fish

Bacon

- **Reynolds Cut-Rite Wax Paper** and **Ziploc Storage Bags.** To store cooked bacon, line a cookie sheet with a piece of Reynolds Cut-Rite Wax Paper, place the bacon strips on the waxed paper, and freeze. Once the bacon strips have frozen, place them in a Ziploc Storage Bag in the freezer.

- **Reynolds Wrap** and **Ziploc Storage Bags.** For another way to freeze bacon strips, place the strips side by side on a sheet of Reynolds Wrap, roll up the sheet lengthwise (so each strip of bacon is essentially rolled into a curl without touching any other strip of bacon), and place the roll in a Ziploc Storage Bag.

Chicken

- **Reynolds Cut-Rite Wax Paper.** To keep fresh chicken fresh, the moment you get home from the store, remove the polyethylene wrapper, loosely wrap the chicken in Reynolds Cut-Rite Wax Paper, and refrigerate. Cook the refrigerated chicken within three days.

- **Reynolds Cut-Rite Wax Paper.** When wrapping chicken parts for storage in the freezer, place sheets of Reynolds Cut-Rite Wax Paper between the pieces to prevent them from freezing together. Later, when you retrieve the items from the freezer, the pieces will separate easily and defrost faster.

Food for Thought
COUNTING YOUR CHICKENS

- To avoid spreading diseases from raw chicken—like *Salmonella* or *Staphylococcus aureus*—do not store uncooked chicken next to any food typically eaten raw, like fresh fruit or vegetables.

- Before handling any other food, use hot, soapy water to wash everything that came into contact with raw chicken—including your hands, the cutting board, knives, the countertop, and any dishes—to avoid spreading any bacteria from the chicken.

- In a freezer set at 0 degrees Fahrenheit, frozen chicken (raw or cooked) will stay good for up to nine months to one year. Freeze cooked chicken within one or two days.

- Thaw frozen chicken in its original package on a plate set on the lowest shelf in the refrigerator. In the refrigerator, the chicken retains its own moisture, and the cool temperature impedes the growth of harmful bacteria.

Fish

- **Bounty Paper Towels.** Before wrapping fish for the freezer, use a sheet of Bounty Paper Towel to pat dry any moist surfaces.

Food for Thought
SOMETHING FISHY

● When buying fish, examine the eyes, scales, and gills. Fresh fish have bright, clear eyes that protrude slightly. If the eyes appear cloudy, pink, or sunken, the fish is likely stale.

● The scales should appear shiny and tight against the skin, and the gills should look red or pink—not gray.

● If you're unable to determine the freshness of a fish, place the fish in cold water. A recently caught fish will float.

Freezing

● **Band-Aid Bandages.** In a pinch, you can use a Band-Aid Bandage as a label that adheres to aluminum foil wrapped around food for the freezer. Write a description of the food on the Band-Aid, peel off the paper backing from the adhesive, and apply to the foil.

● **Bounty Paper Towels.** Before wrapping meats, chicken, or fish for the freezer, use a sheet of Bounty Paper Towel to pat dry any moist surfaces.

● **Glad Flexible Straws.** To remove as much air as possible from a Ziploc Storage Bag filled with food to be frozen, seal the bag shut, leaving a small opening, and insert a Glad Flexible Straw into the hole. Suck out the excess air through the straw, remove the straw, and seal the bag securely.

● **Saran Wrap, Reynolds Wrap,** or **Ziploc Storage Bags.** Before placing foods in the freezer, wrap them airtight in Saran Wrap, Reynolds Wrap, or a Ziploc Storage Bag, Otherwise, the water molecules in the food escape, resulting in freezer burn—ruining the texture and flavor of the item. To be completely safe, wrap the food in Saran Wrap followed by Reynolds Wrap.

Food for Thought
COLD HARD FACTS

- Never freeze fresh caviar, celery, liquid cream, cream pies, custards, hard-boiled egg whites, mayonnaise, meringue pie topping, cooked pasta, raw or boiled potatoes, or raw tomatoes.

- Do not season food that you intend to freeze. When frozen, most seasonings lose their flavor. After defrosting the food, add the seasonings while reheating.

- To store sliced or unsliced bread in the freezer, wrap the bread as airtight as possible to prevent dehydration.

- To minimize leakage while defrosting frozen food (especially meat and fish), let the item thaw slowly in the refrigerator.

- If you plan to freeze a turkey or chicken, whether cooked or uncooked, do not fill it with stuffing first. Stuffing absorbs the juices.

- Thaw the entire frozen turkey or chicken before cooking to prevent the flesh from becoming stringy.

- To sauté frozen chicken breasts and legs without thawing, cook them with the pan covered until the flesh has defrosted.

- A frozen container of milk generally requires two days to defrost in the refrigerator or roughly six hours at room temperature.

- When frozen, yeast lasts indefinitely.

Meat

- **ReaLemon.** Before storing steaks or large cuts of meat in the refrigerator, squeeze some lemon juice over them to enhance their flavor and tenderness and ward off bacteria. The cuts will stay fresh in the refrigerator for up to two days.

- **Reynolds Cut-Rite Wax Paper.** When wrapping pork chops for storage in the freezer, place sheets of Reynolds Cut-Rite Wax Paper between the pieces to prevent them from freezing together. Later, when you retrieve the items from the freezer, the pieces will separate easily and defrost faster.

- **Reynolds Cut-Rite Wax Paper** and **Ziploc Freezer Bags.** When you buy ground beef, press the meat into patties, place a piece of Reynolds Cut-Rite Wax Paper between each patty, put the stack in a Ziploc Freezer Bag, and freeze.

- **Ziploc Storage Bags.** To store a package of ground beef in your freezer, remove the meat from the package, place it in a Ziploc Freezer Bag, and flatten with a rolling pin. Label the bag with the date you purchased the ground beef and freeze. When you're ready to use the ground beef, the flattened beef will thaw quickly.

Shopping Supplies

Coupons

- **Forster Clothespins.** To make shopping with coupons more efficient, bring a Forster Clothespin along to the supermarket and clip it to the shopping cart. When you add an item for which you have a coupon to your shopping cart, clasp the coupon in the Forster Clothespin so when you're ready to check out, you'll have all your coupons neatly prepared.

- **Ziploc Storage Bags.** If you don't own a coupon organizer, store your coupons in one or more Ziploc Storage Bags to keep them together, dry, and easy to tote to the grocery store.

Grocery Lists

- **Post-it Notes.** Keep a Post-it Note stuck to your refrigerator door so you can immediately jot down any items you need to purchase the next time you make a trip to the grocery store.

Plastic Grocery Bags

- **Kleenex Tissues.** Stuff plastic grocery bags inside a clean, empty Kleenex Tissue box for convenient space-saving storage.

Recipe Cards

- **Aqua Net Hair Spray.** To laminate homemade recipe cards, simply spray the cards with Aqua Net Hair Spray. The fixative in the hairspray gives the recipe cards a protective gloss.

- **Forster Clothespins.** To keep a recipe card within easy view while preparing food, use a Forster Clothespin to clip the recipe card to a cabinet door. To make a permanent holder, glue or screw the clothespin to an appropriate surface.

- **Scotch Packaging Tape.** For a simple way to laminate recipe cards and make them waterproof, cover the card with several strips of Scotch Packaging Tape.

- **Scotch Tape.** To save recipes clipped from magazines or newspapers, simply use Scotch Tape to adhere the clipped recipes to index cards.

Sweets and Treats

Brown Sugar

- **Jet-Puffed Marshmallows.** To prevent brown sugar from hardening, place a few Jet-Puffed Marshmallows in the bag, box, or jar of sugar.

- **Wonder Bread.** Another way to prevent brown sugar from hardening is to place the sugar in an airtight container and add a slice of Wonder Bread. The bread absorbs the excess moisture.

- **Ziploc Freezer Bags.** Storing brown sugar inside a sealed Ziploc Freezer Bag kept in the freezer prevents the brown sugar from hardening.

Cake

- **Wonder Bread** and **Forster Toothpicks.** To keep leftover cake fresh in an airtight storage container, attach a slice of Wonder Bread to the open side of the cake with Forster Toothpicks. The bread helps the cake retain its freshness without drying out.

Food for Thought
A PIECE OF CAKE

- To keep a cake moist and fresh, place half an apple in the airtight storage container alongside the cake.

Chocolate

- **Ziploc Storage Bags.** Store extra chocolates (for eating) in a Ziploc Storage Bag (or in its unopened plastic-wrapped packaging) in the freezer.

Food for Thought
SWEET NOTHINGS

- Store cooking chocolate in a cool, dry place, such as a cupboard away from a heat source.

- The best times to get the best deals on chocolate are the days after Valentine's Day, Easter, Halloween, or Christmas, when stores put it on sale for half price. You can cut up those chocolate bunnies or any piece of chocolate to use in recipes calling for chocolate.

Cookies

- **Kleenex Tissues.** To keep cookies crisp when storing them in an airtight Rubbermaid or Tupperware container, place a Kleenex Tissue on the bottom of the container and then place the cookies on top of the tissue. The tissue will absorb excess moisture.

- **Pringles** and **Con-Tact Paper.** To store cookies in an airtight container, cover a clean, empty Pringles can with Con-Tact paper and label.

- **Wonder Bread.** To keep cookies moist, add a slice of Wonder Bread to the cookie jar.

Flour

- **Pringles** and **Con-Tact Paper.** To store flour in an airtight container, cover a clean, empty Pringles can with Con-Tact paper and label.

- **Maxwell House Coffee.** Another great place to store flour is in a clean, empty Maxwell House Coffee can.

- **McCormick Bay Leaves.** To repel insects from your flour canister, place a McCormick Bay Leaf in the flour. The mere smell of bay leaves wards off insects.

- **Wrigley's Doublemint Gum.** To keep weevils out of flour, place an unwrapped stick of Wrigley's Doublemint Gum inside the flour canister. Mint repulses weevils, and the stick of gum does not add any flavor to the flour.

Honey

- **Blue Bonnet Margarine.** To prevent honey jars and bottles from dripping honey on pantry shelves, use clean, used lids from empty canisters of Blue Bonnet Margarine as coasters for the honey jars and bottles.

- **Maxwell House Coffee.** The lids from empty cans of Maxwell House Coffee also make excellent coasters for honey jars and bottles.

Marshmallows

- **Wonder Bread** and **Ziploc Storage Bags.** To revitalize hardened, stale marshmallows, place the marshmallows and two fresh slices of Wonder Bread in a gallon-size Ziploc Storage Bag, seal securely shut, and let sit for a few days. The bread absorbs the excess moisture from the marshmallows, returning them to their original condition.

Oil

- **French's Mustard.** To make a bottle of cooking oil easier to use, pour it into a clean, empty French's Mustard squeeze bottle and label appropriately.

- **Maxwell House Coffee.** To avoid cleaning oil drips from pantry shelves and countertops, use lids from used Maxwell House Coffee cans as coasters for storing bottles of oil in the pantry and when placing bottles of oil on the countertop when cooking.

Potato Chips and Pretzels

- **Forster Clothespins.** To seal open bags of potato chips or pretzels, use a Forster Clothespin to clip the bags closed.

- **Scotch Packaging Tape.** Seal an open potato chip bag with Scotch Packaging Tape, which adheres and re-adheres.

Sugar

- **Gatorade.** Store sugar in a clean, empty Gatorade bottle. The sealed jug will prevent insects and moisture from getting into the sugar.

- **Maxwell House Coffee.** Another great place to store sugar is in a clean, empty Maxwell House Coffee can, appropriately labeled.

- **Nabisco Original Premium Saltine Crackers.** Placing a few Nabisco Original Premium Saltine Crackers inside a canister of sugar absorbs any excess moisture and prevents the sugar from clumping together.

- **Pringles** and **Con-Tact Paper.** To store sugar in an airtight container, cover a clean, empty Pringles can with Con-Tact paper and label.

Vegetables

Artichokes

- **Bounty Paper Towels** and **Ziploc Storage Bags.** Wrap a damp sheet of Bounty Paper Towels around unwashed artichokes and store in a Ziploc Storage Bag placed in the refrigerator. Stored this way, artichokes will retain their freshness for nearly a week.

Food for Thought
ALL CHOKED UP

- When buying artichokes, choose firm artichokes with closed leaves.

Asparagus

- **Bounty Paper Towels.** To store asparagus, trim the ends of the stalks slightly, wet a sheet of Bounty Paper Towel, and wrap the paper towel around the cut ends of the asparagus. Refrigerate, but do not store for more than a day or two.

- **Ziploc Storage Bags.** To keep prepared asparagus fresh before cooking or to revitalize flaccid uncooked asparagus, cut one inch from the bottom of the spear, fill a tall drinking glass with one inch of ice water, stand the asparagus upright in the glass, cover with a Ziploc Storage Bag, place in the refrigerator for thirty minutes, and then cook as usual.

Food for Thought
STALKING THE WILD ASPARAGUS

- Buy asparagus spears with firm green stalks and compact, tightly closed tips.

- Asparagus can be frozen. However, when thawed and cooked, it will go limp.

Beans

- **Maxwell House Coffee.** Store dried beans in a clean, empty Maxwell House Coffee can with the plastic lid tightly sealed.

Canned Vegetables

● **Blue Bonnet Margarine.** To prevent cans of food from leaving rust rings on a pantry shelf, use clean, used lids from empty canisters of Blue Bonnet Margarine as coasters for cans.

● **Dawn Dishwashing Liquid.** Grocery stores and food warehouses tend to spray their shelves with insecticide. Before storing cans of foods, use a few drops of Dawn Dishwashing Liquid in a sink full of water to wash the cans clean. Rinse with water and dry well.

Carrots

● **Ziploc Storage Bags.** To store carrots, put the unwashed carrots in a Ziploc Storage Bag, remove as much air as possible from the bag, seal tightly, and place in the coolest part of the refrigerator.

Celery

- **Reynolds Wrap.** To prolong the shelf life of celery, wrap the stalks in Reynolds Wrap and store in the refrigerator.

- **Ziploc Storage Bags.** To store celery and keep it fresh, cut one inch from the bottom of the spear, fill a tall drinking glass with one inch of ice water, stand the celery upright in the glass, cover with a Ziploc Storage Bag, and place in the refrigerator.

Lettuce

- **Bounty Paper Towels** and **Ziploc Storage Bags.** To prolong the life of lettuce heads, wrap the lettuce heads in sheets of Bounty Paper Towel, seal in a gallon size Ziploc Storage Bag, and store in the refrigerator. The paper towel absorbs excess moisture, which would otherwise cause the lettuce to rust quickly.

- **Wonder Bread** and **Ziploc Storage Bags.** Toast a slice of Wonder Bread and store it with a head of lettuce in a large Ziploc Storage Bag in the refrigerator. The toast absorbs the excess moisture, keeping the lettuce crisp and firm. If the piece of toast gets soggy, replace it with another freshly toasted slice of Wonder Bread.

- **Ziploc Storage Bag.** To fit a head of lettuce into a Ziploc Storage Bag with ease, turn the bag inside out, insert your hand into the bag, grab the lettuce head through the plastic, and pull the bag right-side out over the lettuce head.

Mushrooms

● **Ziploc Storage Bags.** If refrigerated in a sealed plastic bag, mushrooms can become gooey and slimy. To avoid this, use a hole puncher to perforate a few holes in a Ziploc Storage Bag, seal unwashed mushrooms inside, and refrigerate. The unwashed mushrooms will stay fresh for three to four days. To freeze mushrooms, wash and dry them, slice them if desired, and place in a Ziploc Storage Bag and freeze. Use the frozen mushrooms without defrosting them.

Onions

- **L'eggs Sheer Energy Panty Hose.** To store onions, use a pair of scissors to cut off one of the legs from a pair of clean, used L'eggs Sheer Energy Panty Hose, drop an onion into the foot of the leg, tie a knot above the onion, and continue adding onions and tying knots between them. Hang the onion-filled panty hose leg from a hook on the back of a door. When you need an onion, simply cut one off from the bottom—just under the knot. The nylon hose allows air to circulate around the onions, keeping them fresh longer.

- **Reynolds Wrap.** To prolong the life of green onions, wrap them in Reynolds Wrap aluminum foil.

Food for Thought
KNOW YOUR ONIONS

- One pound onions yields roughly four cups sliced or chopped onion.

- Spanish (golden) onions have a sweet flavor, white onions have a soft flavor, and red (Italian) onions have a light flavor.

- Store cut onions in a sealed glass jar—not a plastic container—in the refrigerator. Plastic containers absorb onion odor.

Potatoes

- **L'eggs Sheer Energy Panty Hose.** To store potatoes, use a pair of scissors to cut off one of the legs from a pair of clean, used L'eggs Sheer Energy Panty Hose, drop a potato into the foot of the leg, tie a knot above the potato, and continue adding potatoes and tying knots between them. Hang the potato-filled panty hose leg from a hook on the back of a door. When you need a potato, simply cut one off from the bottom—just under the knot. The nylon hose allows air to circulate around the potatoes, keeping them fresh longer.

Salad Mix

● **Bounty Paper Towels.** Excess moisture will cause an open bag of salad mix to wilt and brown. To avoid this and keep the salad mix crisp for as long as possible, place a sheet of Bounty Paper Towels inside the open bag of salad mix and seal tightly.

Spinach

● **Ziploc Storage Bags.** Spinach will retain its moisture and stay fresh longer if sealed in a Ziploc Storage Bag before storing in the refrigerator.

Tomatoes

● *USA Today.* To accelerate the ripening of tomatoes, put the fruit (erroneously listed in this section on vegetables for your convenience) in a box, cover the tomatoes with a copy of *USA Today*, and close the box. The newspaper keeps the ethylene, the natural gas produced by tomatoes that causes them to ripen, close to the fruit.

Vegetables

- **Arm & Hammer Baking Soda.** To clean pesticides and insects from vegetables, wet the vegetables slightly, sprinkle with a little Arm & Hammer Baking Soda, scrub gently, and rinse thoroughly.

- **Bounty Paper Towels.** To keep vegetables fresh in the refrigerator, line the bottom of the vegetable crisper with a sheet of Bounty Paper Towels to absorb any excess moisture. Or wrap the vegetables in a sheet of Bounty Paper Towels.

- **Bounty Paper Towels.** To dehydrate fresh vegetables for use in soups and stews, wash the vegetables and cut them into thin slices or dice them. Place a sheet of Bounty Paper Towels on a cookie sheet, spread the sliced or diced vegetables across the paper towel, and place in the oven set on as low heat as possible, occasionally using a wooden spoon or spatula to gently stir the vegetables. When the moisture dries from the vegetables and they attain the thinness of paper, remove from the oven, and store in covered jars or airtight containers in the pantry.

- **Clorox Bleach.** To rinse pesticides and insects from vegetables, add one-half cup Clorox Bleach in a sink filled with enough water to cover the vegetables. Soak the vegetables for ten minutes, and then rinse clean. The bleach disinfects the vegetables and kills any pesky bugs.

- **Heinz White Vinegar.** To wash insecticides from vegetables, fill your kitchen sink with cold water and add one cup Heinz White Vinegar. Immerse the vegetables in the solution for ten minutes, and scrub them gently with a clean sponge to loosen any residue. Rinse clean with cold water.

- **Morton Salt** and **ReaLemon.** Another way to remove pesticides from vegetables: Fill the skin with cold water, add four tablespoons Morton Salt and two tablespoons ReaLemon lemon juice, and soak the vegetables for five to ten minutes or leafy greens for two to three minutes. Rinse with clean water and dry.

Watercress

- **Ziploc Storage Bag.** To store watercress and keep it fresh, wash it well, fill a tall drinking glass with cold water, stand the watercress upright in the glass, cover with a Ziploc Storage Bag, and place in the refrigerator for up to one week.

CHAPTER 2

Cookware and Tableware

Aprons

- **Glad Trash Bags.** To make an inexpensive homemade apron, cut holes in a Glad Trash Bag for your head and arms to go through, pull the bag over your head, and put your arms through the holes.

Cake Pans

- **Crisco All-Vegetable Shortening.** To break in a new cake pan, grease the tin with Crisco All-Vegetable Shortening and warm in an oven set on moderate heat for fifteen minutes. Conditioning the pan this way will prevent the bottom of the cake from burning.

Cake Plates

- **Reynolds Wrap.** To make a disposable cake plate, cover an old vinyl record album with Reynolds Wrap.

Cast-Iron Cookware

- **Bounty Paper Towels.** To prevent cast-iron pots and pans from rusting, place a sheet of Bounty Paper Towels inside each cast-iron pot and pan in the cupboard. The paper towel absorbs excess moisture that would otherwise rust the skillets. Replace the paper towel after each use.

- **Crisco All-Vegetable Shortening.** To season a new cast-iron pot or pan, rub Crisco All-Vegetable Shortening into the cookware to create a thin coating, and bake the cookware in an oven heated to 200 degrees Fahrenheit for two hours. After using the new cookware a few times, repeat this procedure.

- **Crisco All-Vegetable Shortening** and **Bounty Paper Towels.** To reseason a cast-iron pot or pan after each use, use a sheet of Bounty Paper Towels to run a dab of Crisco All-Vegetable Shortening on the inside and outside of the pot or pan. Wipe off the excess.

- **Mr. Coffee Filter.** To store cast-iron pots or pans, place a Mr. Coffee Filter inside the cookware. The paper filter absorbs excess moisture, preventing rust. Replace the coffee filter after each use.

- **Pam Cooking Spray** and **Bounty Paper Towels.** To reseason cast-iron cookware, coat the inside with Pam Cooking Spray, and then wipe clean with a sheet of Bounty Paper Towels.

- **Reynolds Cut-Rite Wax Paper.** To prevent moisture from rusting a stored cast-iron pot or pan, place a sheet of Reynolds Cut-Rite Wax Paper in the pot or pan.

- **Wesson Oil.** To reseason a cast-iron pot or pan, saturate a paper towel with Wesson Oil, rub the inside of the cookware after each use, and wipe off the excess oil.

- **Wesson Oil** and **Bounty Paper Towels.** To season a new cast-iron pot or pan, rub a few drops of Wesson Oil into the inside of the cookware with a sheet of Bounty Paper Towel, and warm the skillet in an oven heated to 200 degrees Fahrenheit for two hours. Repeat after washing the skillet for several weeks.

China

- **Dixie Paper Plates.** Place a Dixie Paper Plate between each piece of fine china when stacking dishes to prevent scratches to the decorated surfaces.

- **Kleenex Tissues.** To protect china when storing in the cupboard, place a sheet of Kleenex Tissue between each dish.

- **Mr. Coffee Filters.** To prevent damage to the decorated surfaces of your fine china dishes, place a Mr. Coffee Filter between each plate when stacking the dishes.

- **Nestlé Carnation Evaporated Milk.** To make a hairline crack in a china cup or dish magically disappear, place the dish or cup in a pan, cover it with Nestlé Carnation Evaporated Milk, bring to a boil, and then simmer for 30 minutes at low heat. The milk protein casein fills the crack, and the fissure seems to disappear. Let cool, rinse clean, and dry.

- **Playtex Living Gloves.** Use a pair of scissors to snip off a finger from a clean, used pair of Playtex Living Gloves, and put the fingertip over the spout of your china teapot to protect it from unsightly chips.

Cutting Boards

- **Crisco All-Vegetable Shortening** and **Bounty Paper Towels.** To preserve a wooden cutting board, rub a few dabs of Crisco All-Vegetable Shortening into all sides of the board, let sit overnight to allow the wood to absorb the shortening, and then wipe off the excess shortening with a sheet of Bounty Paper Towels.

- **Pam Cooking Spray** and **Bounty Paper Towels.** If you don't have any Crisco All-Vegetable Shortening (see above), preserve a wooden cutting board by spraying the entire board with Pam Cooking Spray, use a sheet of Bounty Paper Towels to rub the oil into the wood, and then wipe clean.

- **Wesson Oil** and **Bounty Paper Towels.** For another way to preserve a wooden cutting board, put a few drops of Wesson Oil on a sheet of Bounty Paper Towel, rub it into the wood, and then wipe clean.

Dishwashing Liquid

- **Arm & Hammer Baking Soda.** To improve the effectiveness of your regular dishwashing liquid, dissolve two tablespoons Arm & Hammer Baking Soda in the hot water in your dishpan along with the usual amount of dishwashing liquid you use.

- **Heinz White Vinegar.** To stretch your dishwashing liquid five times further and enhance its disinfecting power, mix one part Heinz White Vinegar, one part of your regular dishwashing liquid, and three parts water in a plastic squeeze bottle. Shake well before using.

- **Johnson's Baby Shampoo.** If you're all out of dishwashing liquid, in a pinch you can use Johnson's Baby Shampoo to wash the dishes.

Funnels

- **Clorox Bleach.** To devise a funnel, cut a clean, empty Clorox Bleach jug in half horizontally, turn the upper half upside down, and remove the cap.

- **Dixie Cups.** To make a funnel in a pinch, punch a hole in the bottom of a Dixie Cup near the outer edge.

- **Reynolds Wrap.** To make an impromptu funnel, cut off a square sheet of Reynolds Wrap aluminum foil, fold it in half, and then fold it in half a second time. Snip off the folded corner, open one of the flaps, and—presto—you've got a funnel.

- **Ziploc Storage Bags.** In a pinch, you can make an impromptu funnel by simply using a pair of scissors to snip off one of the bottom corners from a Ziploc Storage Bag.

Garbage Pails

- **Arm & Hammer Baking Soda.** To deodorize smelly garbage in the kitchen trash pail, sprinkle a handful of Arm & Hammer Baking Soda into the pail every time you add food scraps.

- **Bounce.** To neutralize odors in a kitchen garbage pail, place a sheet of Bounce in the bottom of the pail before lining it with a plastic trash bag.

- **Bounty Paper Towels.** Place a sheet of Bounty Paper Towels on the bottom of the kitchen garbage pail to absorb moisture and prevent mold and mildew odors.

- **Tidy Cats.** To absorb moisture from the bottom of a kitchen garbage pail and prevent odors, pour a one-inch layer of Tidy Cats on the bottom of the trash pail.

- **20 Mule Team Borax.** To inhibit mold and bacteria from growing in a garbage pail, sprinkle one-half cup 20 Mule Team Borax onto the bottom of the pail.

Glassware

- **Pam Cooking Spray.** To pry apart two glasses stuck inside each other, spray a little Pam Cooking Spray between the two glasses, wait a few seconds for the oil to seep in, and gently tug the glasses apart.

- **Q-tips Cotton Swabs.** To clean gunk or debris from inside the hollow stem of a drinking glass, insert a Q-tips Cotton Swab into the opening, and then rinse under hot running water. Drain upside-down in a rack and air dry.

- **Wesson Oil.** When one drinking glass gets stuck inside another, trickle a few drops of Wesson Oil between the two glasses, wait a few seconds, and pull them apart slowly and carefully.

Graters

- **Pam Cooking Spray.** Before grating food, spray the grater with a thin coat of Pam Cooking Spray to make cleaning the grater easier. Reapply as needed.

- **Wesson Vegetable Oil.** To make cleaning the grater less cumbersome, use a pastry brush to paint a thin coat of Wesson Vegetable Oil on the grater before grating any food.

- **Ziploc Storage Bags.** To avoid making a mess when grating food, hold the grater inside a large Ziploc Storage Bag, and then grate the food item inside the bag—so when you finish, the bag contains the grated food.

Jar Labels

- **Jif Peanut Butter.** After peeling a label from a jar, remove any remaining glue residue from the jar by covering it with Jif Peanut Butter, waiting ten minutes for the oils in the peanut butter to dissolve the gums in the glue, and washing the jar clean with soapy water.

- **Kraft Real Mayo.** To remove a label from a jar, rub a thin coat of Kraft Real Mayo over the label, let sit for ten minutes, and soak the jar in hot water for another ten minutes. The mayonnaise dissolves the gums in the glue, and the label peels off with relative ease.

- **Pam Cooking Spray.** You can also remove labels and any glue residue from jars with Pam Cooking Spray, following the same directions for Jif Peanut Butter and Kraft Real Mayo above.

Jar Opener

- **Playtex Living Gloves.** To open a stubborn jar, simply put on a pair of Playtex Living Gloves and twist off the lid. The rubber gloves give your hands the traction they need to unscrew the top.

- **Vaseline Petroleum Jelly.** After opening a jar of a sticky food like honey, jam, maple syrup, or molasses, rub a thin coat of Vaseline Petroleum Jelly around the rim of the jar to make the lid easy to screw on and off.

Knives

- **3M Sandpaper** and **Elmer's Glue-All.** To sharpen a knife blade, use Elmer's Glue-All to glue a sheet of 3M Sandpaper to a block of wood, let dry, and carefully slide the blade of the knife back and forth along the sheet of sandpaper. For best results, use silicon carbide sandpaper.

Measuring Cups

- **Dannon Yogurt.** A clean, empty Dannon Yogurt container makes an excellent measuring cup.

- **Pam Cooking Spray.** To prevent gooey ingredients from sticking inside a measuring cup, spray the inside of the measuring cup with a fine coat of Pam Cooking Spray.

- **Revlon Red Nail Polish.** If the incremental markings on your measuring cup have faded, repaint the lines and numbers with Revlon Red Nail Polish.

- **Saran Wrap.** To avoid having to clean sticky ingredients like honey, molasses, or chocolate syrup from inside a measuring cup, line the inside of the cup with a piece of Saran Wrap. After pouring the gooey ingredient from the cup, discard the sticky sheet of Saran Wrap.

Measuring Spoons

- **Pam Cooking Spray.** To prevent gooey ingredients like honey, molasses, chocolate syrup, or peanut butter from sticking inside the bowl of a measuring spoon, spray the measuring spoon with a fine coat of Pam Cooking Spray.

- **Revlon Red Nail Polish.** To highlight the raised markings on your measuring spoons, paint them with Revlon Red Nail Polish, making them easier to read.

Food for Thought
FOR GOOD MEASURE

● Before following a recipe, measure all of the dry ingredients and place them in separate bowls. Then measure all the wet ingredients and place them in separate bowls as well. Arrange the bowls in the order you will need the ingredients for the recipe. With this method, you avoid cleaning the measuring cup repeatedly, and you have the measured ingredients easily accessible when cooking.

Meat Mallets

- **Reynolds Cut-Rite Wax Paper.** If you don't own a special mallet for flattening pieces of meat, place the meat between two sheets of

Reynolds Cut-Rite Wax Paper and hammer it with the bottom of a cast-iron frying pan.

Napkins

- **Mr. Coffee Filters.** If you run out of napkins, in a pinch use a Mr. Coffee Filter, which is equally absorbent.

Nonstick Cookware

- **Dixie Paper Plates.** To prevent nonstick cookware from getting scratched, place a Dixie Paper Plate inside the bottoms of nonstick cookware before stacking the pots and pans on top of each other.

- **Mr. Coffee Filters.** Place a Mr. Coffee Filter between each nonstick pot and pan before stacking to avoid scratching the delicate surfaces.

Oven Mitts

- **Niagara Spray Starch.** To prevent oven mitts from getting soiled with grease and oil stains from cooking, spray the oven mitt with a protective coat of Niagara Spray Starch. The starch prevents the fabric from absorbing stains.

Plastic Containers

- **Pam Cooking Spray.** To prevent tomato sauce stains on plastic containers, spray the insides of the containers with Pam Cooking Spray before filling the container with any food containing tomatoes. The lecithin in the cooking spray repels the pigments that would otherwise stain the plastic.

- **Saran Wrap.** To avoid staining the inside of a plastic container or permeating the plastic with foul odors, line the container with a sheet of Saran Wrap before adding the food item.

Plastic Wrap

- **Scotch Tape.** If you can't find the starting point on a roll of plastic wrap, tap the roll with a strip of Scotch Tape until it picks up the loose end.

Pot Holders

- **Niagara Spray Starch.** To prevent potholders from getting soiled with grease and oil stains from cooking, spray the potholders with a protective coat of Niagara Spray Starch. The starch prevents the fabric from absorbing stains.

Pots and Pans

- **Morton Salt.** To improve the efficiency of a double boiler, dissolve one teaspoon Morton Salt in the water in the bottom half of the double boiler. The salt raises the boiling point of water, transmitting more heat to the food in the upper half of the boiler.

- **Pam Cooking Spray.** To prevent food from sticking to the inside of a pot or pan, before you start frying, sautéing, or stewing, spray Pam Cooking Spray on the inside of the metal, glass, or enamel cookware (unless you intend to boil a liquid).

- **Reynolds Cut-Rite Wax Paper.** If the lid of your pot or pan does not make a tight seal over the cookware, cover the open pot with a sheet of Reynolds Cut-Rite Wax Paper, and place the lid over the waxed paper to contain the heat and moisture. If you wish for a little steam to escape, simply punch a small hole in the center of the waxed paper.

Rolling Pins

- **Arm & Hammer Baking Soda.** To clean and deodorize a wooden rolling pin, sprinkle Arm & Hammer Baking Soda on a damp sponge, rub the rolling pin, and rinse clean.

- **Clorox Bleach.** To disinfect a wooden rolling pin, wash the rolling pin with hot sudsy water and rinse clean. Then apply a solution of three tablespoons Clorox Bleach per gallon of water, wait two minutes, and then rinse clean.

- **Coca-Cola** and **L'eggs Sheer Energy Panty Hose.** To improvise a rolling pin, insert a full, cold bottle of Coca-Cola (any size) into one leg cut from a pair of clean, used L'eggs Sheer Energy Panty Hose.

- **Crisco All-Vegetable Shortening** and **Bounty Paper Towels.** To preserve a wooden rolling pin, rub a few dabs of Crisco All-Vegetable Shortening into the wood, let sit overnight, and then wipe off the excess shortening with a sheet of Bounty Paper Towels.

- **Heinz White Vinegar.** To disinfect a wooden rolling pin, apply Heinz White Vinegar to the surface, let sit for ten minutes, rinse clean, and dry well.

- **Listerine.** To sanitize a wooden cutting board, apply Listerine antiseptic mouthwash to the wood, let sit for ten minutes, rinse clean, and dry thoroughly. Listerine disinfects and deodorizes.

- **Pam Cooking Spray.** To prevent foods from sticking to a rolling pin, spray the roller with a fine coat of Pam Cooking Spray.

- **ReaLemon** and **Morton Salt.** To deodorize pungent odors and remove stains from a wooden rolling pin, rub ReaLemon lemon juice over the rolling pin, and then roll the pin through a mountain of Morton Salt.

Wash in warm, soapy water, rinse clean, and dry. The lemon juice helps bleach out the stains and deodorizes, and the abrasive salt absorbs odors and grease.

- **Wesson Oil** and **Bounty.** To preserve a wooden rolling pin, put a few drops of Wesson Oil on a sheet of Bounty Paper Towels, rub it into the wood, and then wipe clean.

Rubber Gloves

- **Arm & Hammer Baking Soda.** To help rubber gloves slide on and off easily, dust your hands with Arm & Hammer Baking Soda before putting on the gloves.

- **Johnson & Johnson Cotton Balls.** To prevent your fingernails from tearing through the fingertips of Playtex Living Gloves, stuff a Johnson & Johnson Cotton Ball into each fingertip of the gloves.

- **Johnson's Baby Powder.** To prevent rubber gloves from irritating your skin while washing the dishes, sprinkle Johnson's Baby Powder on your hands before putting on the gloves to reduce friction and to help the gloves slip on and off easily.

- **Kingsford's Corn Starch.** Sprinkle Kingsford's Corn Starch inside a pair of rubber gloves before putting them on to absorb moisture and enable your fingers to slide into and out of the gloves almost effortlessly.

- **Ziploc Storage Bags.** To answer the telephone while you're preparing food without getting the receiver messy, keep a Ziploc Storage Bag next to the phone. When the phone rings, simply slip your hand inside the plastic bag and pick up the receiver.

- **Ziploc Storage Bags** and **Pam Cooking Spray.** To improvise plastic gloves when spreading sticky foods, put each hand inside its own Ziploc Storage Bag, coat the outside of the bag with Pam Cooking Spray, and spread the messy ingredients.

Salt and Pepper Shakers

- **Revlon Clear Nail Enamel.** To prevent a salt or pepper shaker from sprinkling too much salt or pepper, empty the shaker, plug up a few of the holes with Revlon Clear Nail Enamel, and let dry.

- **Uncle Ben's Converted Brand Rice.** To prevent salt from clumping together in a salt shaker, add a few grains of Uncle Ben's Converted Brand Rice in the salt shaker. The rice absorbs the moisture that would otherwise cause the salt to clump together. Replace the rice once a year.

Scissors

- **Cutex Nail Polish Remover.** To clean a gunked-up pair of kitchen scissors, saturate a cotton ball with Cutex Nail Polish Remover and carefully wipe the blades clean.

- **Reynolds Wrap.** To sharpen a pair of kitchen scissors, fold a sheet of Reynolds Wrap in half and then fold it in half again. Using the scissors, cut through the aluminum foil a dozen or more times.

- **Smirnoff Vodka.** To clean any sticky residue from the blades of scissors, soak a cotton ball with Smirnoff Vodka and carefully rub the blades clean.

- **3M Sandpaper.** If cutting through a folded sheet of Reynolds Wrap fails to sufficiently sharpen a pair of kitchen scissors, use the scissors to cut up a sheet of 3M Sandpaper.

Serving Spoons

- **Pam Cooking Spray.** To prevent sticky foods from clinging to a serving spoon, spray a light coat of Pam Cooking Spray on the serving spoon before dishing out the fare.

Shelf Liners

- **Conair Hair Dryer.** To lift old Con-Tact Paper from pantry shelves, aim a Conair Hair Dryer set on high at the Con-Tact Paper to melt the adhesive backing, enabling you to peel up the paper with ease.

Silverware

- **Alberto VO5 Conditioning Hairdressing.** To prevent tarnish on clean silverware, silver serving pieces, and silver candlestick holders, apply a thin coat of Alberto VO5 Conditioning Hairdressing with a soft cloth and wipe off the excess, leaving a thin, undetectable protective coating. The organic protectants in VO5 prevent tarnishing. Simply wash the silverware with soapy water and rinse clean before using.

- **Arm & Hammer Baking Soda.** To clean tarnish from silver, mix a thick paste of Arm & Hammer Baking Soda with water, and then apply to the silver with a damp sponge. Scrub, rinse, and buff dry. For more ways to clean silverware, see page 326.

- **Crayola Chalk.** To prevent tarnish from forming on silverware, place a few sticks of Crayola Chalk in your silverware chest to absorb moisture, which causes tarnish.

Steel Wool Pads

- **Arm & Hammer Baking Soda.** To prevent a steel wool pad from rusting, dissolve three tablespoons Arm & Hammer Baking Soda in a jar filled halfway with water, and store the steel wool pad in the solution.

- **Maxwell House Coffee.** To prevent steel wool pads from leaving rust marks on your sink or kitchen counter, use the lid from an empty Maxwell House Coffee can as a coaster.

- **Playtex Living Gloves.** To protect your hands from metal splinters, wear a pair of Playtex Living Gloves when using steel wool.

- **Ziploc Freezer Bags.** To prevent a steel wool pad from rusting, place the steel wool pad in a Ziploc Freezer Bag and store it in the freezer after each use. To defrost the frozen pad, simply hold it under warm running water.

Sifters and Strainers

- **L'eggs Sheer Energy Panty Hose.** To improvise a food strainer, cut off one leg from a clean pair of L'eggs Sheer Energy Panty Hose, stretch the opening across the mouth of a pot or bowl, and pour the food into the leg. Lift up the panty hose leg and squeeze the food through the nylon mesh into the pot or bowl.

- **Ziploc Storage Bags.** To avoid having to clean your flour sifter after every use, keep the flour sifter in a Ziploc Storage Bag.

Teapots

- **Playtex Living Gloves.** Use a pair of scissors to snip off a finger from a clean, used pair of Playtex Living Gloves, and put the fingertip over the spout of your china teapot to protect it from unsightly chips.

Whisks

- **Pam Cooking Spray.** To prevent sticky ingredients from clogging up a whisk, spray a light coat of Pam Cooking Spray on the whisk before whipping sticky foods.

Woks

- **Crisco All-Vegetable Shortening** and **Bounty Paper Towels.** To season a wok before cooking, use a sheet of Bounty Paper Towels to run a dab of Crisco All-Vegetable Shortening on the inside of the wok. Wipe off the excess.

- **Morton Salt.** To help prevent the oil in a wok from splattering while cooking, mix one-half teaspoon Morton Salt into the oil before cooking and reduce the amount of salt called for by the recipe by one-half teaspoon.

Wooden Salad Bowls

- **Crisco All-Vegetable Shortening** and **Bounty Paper Towels.** To revitalize and seal a wooden salad bowl, rub Crisco All-Vegetable Shortening all over the inside and outside of the bowl. Let sit overnight to give the wood time to absorb the shortening, and then use a sheet of Bounty Paper Towels to remove the excess shortening and buff.

- **Pam Cooking Spray** and **Bounty Paper Towels.** To preserve a wooden salad bowl, spray the bowl with Pam Cooking Spray, rub the oil into the wood with a sheet of Bounty Paper Towels, and then wipe clean.

- **Reynolds Cut-Rite Wax Paper.** To restore the shine to a wooden salad bowl, wash the bowl with soapy water, dry thoroughly, and then rub the entire bowl with a sheet of Reynolds Cut-Rite Wax Paper. The wax gives the wood a rich luster.

- **Wesson Oil** and **Bounty Paper Towels.** To preserve a wooden salad bowl, saturate a Bounty Paper Towel with Wesson Oil and rub the oil into the wood until the bowl cannot absorb any more. Let sit overnight, and in the morning, wipe off the excess oil. The oil moisturizes and seals the wood. Rub the bowl with oil every three months.

Wooden Spoons

- **Crisco All-Vegetable Shortening** and **Bounty Paper Towels.** To prevent tomato sauce and other foods from staining new wooden spoons, rub a dollop of Crisco All-Vegetable Shortening into the wood and buff well with a sheet of Bounty Paper Towels. The shortening seals the wood.

- **Pam Cooking Spray** and **Bounty Paper Towels.** If you don't have any Crisco All-Vegetable Shortening (see above), seal new wooden spoons by spraying them with Pam Cooking Spray, use a sheet of Bounty Paper Towels to rub the oil into the wood, and then wipe clean.

- **Wesson Oil** and **Bounty Paper Towels.** For another way to preserve wooden spoons, put a few drops of Wesson Oil on a sheet of Bounty Paper Towel, rub it into the wood, and then wipe clean.

CHAPTER 3

Appliances and Gadgets

Barbecue

- **Arm & Hammer Baking Soda.** To clean burned-on food and grease from a barbecue grill, mix equal parts Arm & Hammer Baking Soda and water to make a thick paste, apply with a wire brush, and scrub. Wipe clean, and dry with a cloth.

- **Conair Hair Dryer.** To fan the flames of a recently ignited charcoal fire in a barbecue grill, point the nozzle of a Conair Hair Dryer set on cool at the flames until the charcoal briquettes catch fire.

- **Crisco All-Vegetable Shortening** and **Bounty Paper Towels.** To season cast-iron grates or a griddle on a barbecue, spread a thin coat of Crisco All-Vegetable Shortening over the entire surface of the grates or griddle with a sheet of Bounty Paper Towels. Preheat the gas grill for fifteen minutes, place the cast-iron grates or griddle in the grill, and heat on medium with the lid closed for one hour. Turn off all the burners and let the grates or griddle cool.

- **Dawn Dishwashing Liquid.** To clean grease from a barbecue grill rack, mix one-half cup Dawn Dishwashing Liquid and one gallon of water in a bucket. Apply the soapy solution to the grill rack, scrub with a wire brush, and rinse clean. Dawn cuts through grease.

- **Easy-Off Oven Cleaner.** To clean a barbecue grill rack, place the grill rack on the ground outside, and, wearing protective eyewear and rubber gloves, spray the rack thoroughly with Easy-Off Oven Cleaner. Let sit for one hour, and then rinse well with a garden hose.

- **Gillette Foamy.** Before placing pots or pans on a barbecue grill, coat the bottom of the cookware with Gillette Foamy shaving cream. When you finish grilling, the black soot will wash off of the bottom of the pots and pans with ease.

- **Maxwell House Coffee.** To clean grease from a barbecue griddle quickly and efficiently, pour a pot of hot Maxwell House Coffee on the cool rack and wipe dry with a clean cloth. This trick is used by short-order cooks to clean griddles.

- **Maxwell House Coffee.** To ignite a charcoal barbeque, use a can opener to remove the top and bottom of an empty Maxwell House Coffee can. Use tin snips to cut a few one-inch-tall triangular slots around the bottom rim of the coffee can to allow for air flow. Stand the can with the tabs downward in the center of your barbecue grill and place one sheet of crumpled newspaper inside the can. Fill the rest of the can with charcoal briquettes, add lighter fluid, and light the newspaper through one of the triangular slots. When the coals glow orange, use a pair of tongs to carefully remove the hot can and set it in a safe place until it cools.

- **Morton Salt.** After barbecuing in a charcoal grill, sprinkle Morton Salt over the smoldering charcoal to prevent a grease fire from suddenly bursting into flames.

- **Pam Cooking Spray.** To make cleaning a barbecue grill effortless, before igniting the barbecue, coat the grill with Pam Cooking Spray.

- **Parsons' Ammonia, Bounty Paper Towels,** and **Glad Trash Bags.** To clean a barbecue grill rack, wrap Bounty Paper Towels around the rack, place it inside a Glad Trash Bag, and saturate the paper toweling with one cup Parsons' Ammonia—being careful not to breath the ammonia fumes. Close the bag securely with a twist tie and let sit overnight outside or in a well-ventilated garage. The ammonia fumes loosen the baked-on food and grease from the grill rack. The next morning, open the bag outdoors (again being careful to avoid breathing the fumes), and remove the rack, leaving the paper towels in the bag. Discard the bag. Rinse the rack with a garden hose, and then bring it back inside the house to wash thoroughly with soapy water, rinse clean, and dry.

- **Purell Instant Hand Sanitizer.** To clean the glass window on the barbecue grill, rub a dollop of Purell Instant Hand Sanitizer on the glass and buff with a soft, clean cloth.

- **Reynolds Wrap.** To clean burned-on food and grease from a barbecue grill with ease, carefully place a sheet of Reynolds Wrap on the hot grill immediately after you finish barbecuing, and close the lid. The next time you use the barbecue, peel off the foil, crumple it into a ball, and scrub the grill clean. The burnt food falls right off.

- **Tidy Cats.** To prevent grease fires in a charcoal barbecue grill, cover the bottom of the pan with an even layer of unused Tidy Cats cat box filler to absorb grease and fat drippings.

- **Vaseline Petroleum Jelly.** To ignite a fire in a charcoal barbecue, apply a thick coat of Vaseline Petroleum Jelly to a cotton ball, place it among the charcoal, and light it.

- **WD-40.** If you don't have any lighter fluid, spray the charcoal with WD-40 and ignite—making sure to let the charcoal fire burn off the WD-40 before cooking food on the grill.

Blender

- **Clorox Bleach.** To clean the outside of a blender, mix three-quarters cup Clorox Bleach and a gallon of water, apply with a sponge, and let sit for ten minutes. Rinse and dry thoroughly.

- **Colgate Regular Flavor Toothpaste** and **Oral-B Toothbrush.** To clean tight crevices on the outside of a blender, scrub with a dollop of Colgate Regular Flavor Toothpaste on a clean, old Oral-B Toothbrush.

- **Dawn Dishwashing Liquid.** To clean the blender jar and blades, carefully fill the blender halfway with boiling water, add a few drops of Dawn Dishwashing Liquid, and let sit until the water cools. Add a handful of ice cubes, secure the lid in place, and blend for thirty seconds. Rinse clean and dry thoroughly.

- **Huggies Baby Wipes.** To clean grease and grime from the outside of a blender, wipe clean with a Huggies Baby Wipe.

- **Q-tips Cotton Swabs.** To clean tight crevices between the push buttons on the outside of a blender, dip a Q-tips Cotton Swab in alcohol and run it along the tight spaces.

- **Wesson Oil.** To clean caked-on food from the blades of a blender, immerse the blades in Wesson Oil overnight, and in the morning wash them clean with hot soapy water.

Bread Machine

- **Canada Dry Club Soda.** Dampen a sponge with Canada Dry Club Soda and wipe down the exterior of the bread machine to keep it clean and shiny. Buff dry with a soft cloth.

- **Forster Toothpicks.** If the hole in the kneading blades gets clogged, carefully clean it out with a Forster Toothpick, being careful not to scratch the nonstick coating on the blade or get the toothpick stuck in the blades.

- **Huggies Baby Wipes.** To clean grease and grime from the exterior of a bread machine, wipe clean with a Huggies Baby Wipe. Dry thoroughly with a soft, clean cloth.

Can Opener

- **Arm & Hammer Baking Soda** and **Oral-B Toothbrush.** To clean food particles from the cutting wheel and lid holder on an electric can opener, unplug the appliance, wet a clean, old Oral-B Toothbrush with water, dip the bristles into an open box of Arm & Hammer Baking Soda, and scrub the blade and visible gears. Rinse well.

- **Pam Cooking Spray.** To lubricate an electric or hand-held can opener, spray the cutting wheel and gears with a quick blast of Pam Cooking Spray, let sit for five minutes, and then wipe off the excess oil.

- **Reynolds Cut-Rite Wax Paper.** To lubricate an electric or hand-held can opener, place a sheet of Reynolds Cut-Rite Wax Paper over the top of an unopened can, hold it securely in place, and run the can through the opener. The wax from the paper will lubricate the can opener. Repeat several times.

Coffee Filters

- **Bounty Paper Towels.** If you run out of coffee filters, use two sheets of Bounty Paper Towels as an impromptu filter. Add the coffee grounds and brew the coffee as usual.

- **Cool Whip.** To keep coffee filters folded in pristine condition, store them in a clean, empty Cool Whip canister.

Coffee Grinder

- **Uncle Ben's Converted Brand Rice.** To flush coffee residue from a coffee grinder and simultaneously sharpen the blades, run one cup Uncle Ben's Converted Brand Rice through the grinder.

- **Wonder Bread.** To clean out a coffee grinder, grind two or three slices of Wonder Bread.

Coffeemaker

- **Arm & Hammer Baking Soda** and **ReaLemon.** To clean the coffee residue from inside a glass coffeepot, pour equal parts Arm & Hammer Baking Soda and ReaLemon lemon juice into the pot and scrub with a sponge. (For more ways to clean a glass coffeepot, see page 300.)

- **Calgon Water Softener.** To clean calcium buildup from the heating element inside a coffeemaker, pour two tablespoons Calgon Water Softener into the water tank, fill the rest with water, let sit overnight, and then run the solution through the coffeemaker's regular cycle with the coffeepot in place. Run clean water through the cycle, wash the coffeepot with soapy water, and rinse clean.

- **Canada Dry Club Soda.** Dampen a sponge with Canada Dry Club Soda and wipe down the exterior of the coffeemaker to keep it clean and shiny. Buff dry with a soft cloth.

- **Clorox Bleach.** To clean the outside of a white coffeemaker, mix three-quarters cup Clorox Bleach and a gallon of water, apply with a sponge, and let sit for ten minutes. Rinse clean and dry thoroughly.

- **Heinz White Vinegar.** To clean the coffee filter basket, remove the basket, fill the kitchen sink with soapy water, add one-quarter cup Heinz White Vinegar, and soak the basket in the solution for thirty minutes. Rinse clean.

- **Heinz White Vinegar.** To clean mineral deposits from the heating elements of a coffeemaker, fill the water reservoir with Heinz White Vinegar and run it through the regular brewing cycle—with the coffeepot in place. The acetic acid in the vinegar dissolves the mineral deposits. Repeat if necessary, and then run water through the cycle to rinse out any lingering vinegar. Wash the coffeepot with soapy water and rinse clean.

- **Huggies Baby Wipes.** To clean coffee stains from the outside of a coffeemaker, wipe the exterior clean with a Huggies Baby Wipe.

- **Jet-Dry.** To clean calcium buildup from a coffeemaker, pour four ounces Jet-Dry into the water tank, fill the rest with water, and let sit overnight. In the morning, run the solution through the coffeemaker's regular cycle with the coffeepot in place. Afterward, run clean water through the cycle, and wash the coffeepot with soapy water and rinse clean.

- **Tang.** To clean mineral deposits from the heating element inside a coffeemaker, fill the coffeepot with water, add two tablespoons Tang powdered drink mix, and pour the orange drink into the water tank. Run the coffeemaker through its regular cycle with the coffeepot in place—allowing the citric acid in the Tang to dissolve the mineral deposits. Run fresh water through the machine twice to eliminate any Tang residue, and then wash the coffeepot with soapy water and rinse clean.

Coffee Percolator

- **Arm & Hammer Baking Soda** and **Dawn Dishwashing Liquid.** To clean and deodorize the inside of a coffee percolator, add two tablespoons Arm & Hammer Baking Soda and one teaspoon Dawn

Dishwashing Liquid and fill with water. Percolate the soapy solution for ten minutes. Drain, refill with hot water, and percolate for an additional five minutes. Rinse clean and dry.

- **Morton Salt.** For another way to clean a percolator, fill the percolator with water, add five tablespoons Morton Salt, and percolate for fifteen minutes. Rinse clean and dry.

Dehydrator

- **Dawn Dishwashing Liquid** and **Oral-B Toothbrush.** To clean dehydrator drying racks caked with food or juices, add one teaspoon Dawn Dishwashing Liquid to a sink filled with hot water, soak the trays in the hot soapy water, and use a clean, old Oral-B Toothbrush to scrub the food stains from the racks.

- **Pam Cooking Spray.** To prevent food from sticking to and staining dehydrator drying racks, spray the racks with a thin coat of Pam Cooking Spray before drying any food.

- **Reynolds Parchment Paper.** Another simple way to prevent food from sticking to and staining dehydrator drying racks is to line the racks with Reynolds Parchment Paper.

Dishwasher

- **Arm & Hammer Baking Soda.** To soften and loosen caked-on food from dirty dishes that have been sitting in the dishwasher overnight, sprinkle one-quarter cup Arm & Hammer Baking Soda on the floor of the dishwasher before running the machine.

- **Arm & Hammer Baking Soda.** Prevent streaks on dishes and glassware by adding two tablespoons Arm & Hammer Baking Soda to the dishwasher soap in the receptacle dish.

- **Arm & Hammer Baking Soda.** To deodorize a stinky dishwasher, sprinkle one-half cup Arm & Hammer Baking Soda on the floor of the dishwasher, let sit overnight, and then run the baking soda through the machine with your next load of dishes to clean the interior walls of the machine and the dishes.

- **Arm & Hammer Super Washing Soda** and **20 Mule Team Borax.** To make your own automatic dishwashing soap, mix equal parts Arm & Hammer Super Washing Soda and 20 Mule Team Borax.

- **Canada Dry Club Soda.** To shine the exterior of a stainless-steel dishwasher, dampen a clean, soft cloth with Canada Dry Club Soda and wipe clean. (For more ways to clean the outside of stainless-steel dishwashers, see page 331.)

- **Country Time Lemonade.** To clean soap scum from the pipes and tubes of your dishwasher, fill the receptacle dish with Country Time Lemonade drink mix and run the dishwasher through its regular cycle without any dishes inside. The citric acid in the Country Time Lemonade cleans soap scum, grime, and rust from the inside of the dishwasher.

- **Heinz White Vinegar.** To eliminate a soapy film on plates and glassware, place a bowl containing two cups Heinz White Vinegar on the bottom rack of your dishwasher and run the machine for five minutes without any detergent. Then add the detergent and run the dishes and glasses through the regular cycle.

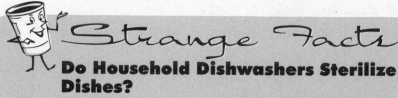

Do Household Dishwashers Sterilize Dishes?

Household dishwasher temperatures are not high enough to sterilize dishes or utensils. To do that, the dishwasher would have to spray the dishes and utensils at 250 degrees Fahrenheit with pressurized wet steam for more than fifteen minutes. Most household dishwashers do not exceed 170 degrees Fahrenheit, sanitizing the dishes (making them clean and hygienic), but not sterilizing the dishes (killing any bacteria and microorganisms). Commercial dishwashers have a special cycle with water heated above 180 degrees Fahrenheit, sanitizing (not sterilizing) the dishes. The Association of Home Appliance Manufacturers estimates that using a dishwasher saves about six hours of manual work per week and uses just over eight gallons of water for one load of dishes. Washing the same load of dishes by hand uses an average of sixteen gallons of water.

- **Kool-Aid.** To clean soap scum from the tubes and pipes of a dishwasher, empty one packet of Kool-Aid drink powder into the detergent dish and run the dishwasher through its regular cycle without any dishes inside. The citric acid in Kool-Aid cleans the soap scum and rust stains.

- **Pam Cooking Spray.** To make the racks in your dishwasher slide in and out easily, spray the rollers with Pam Cooking Spray, an edible, non-toxic vegetable oil.

- **Post-it Notes.** To alert others that the dishes in the dishwasher are clean, stick a Post-it Note on the front of the dishwasher after turning on the machine. After emptying out the dishes, be sure to remove the Post-it Note.

- **ReaLemon.** To eliminate nasty smells from your dishwasher, fill the receptacle dish with one-quarter cup ReaLemon lemon juice and run it through the rinse cycle without any dishes in the machine.

- **Tang.** To clean soap scum from the pipes and tubes of a dishwasher, fill the receptacle dish with Tang powdered drink mix and run the dishwasher through its regular cycle without any dishes inside. The citric acid in Tang cleans the soap scum and mineral and iron stains.

- **20 Mule Team Borax.** To reduce water spots and film from glasses and dishes, add one-quarter cup 20 Mule Team Borax to the floor of the dishwasher. Borax boosts the cleaning power of regular dishwashing detergent by removing hard water minerals and residues from the wash water.

- **20 Mule Team Borax.** To deodorize any stench from a dishwasher, sprinkle 20 Mule Team Borax on the floor of the dishwasher and let sit overnight. Borax neutralizes acidic odors. In the morning, use a damp sponge to wipe the borax on the interior walls of the dishwasher. The next time you run the dishwasher, the regular cycle will wash away the borax.

Eggbeater

- **Johnson's Baby Oil.** To lubricate an eggbeater, apply a few drops of Johnson's Baby Oil. Unlike vegetable oil, baby oil (also known as mineral oil) will not corrode the movable parts, and like vegetable oil, mineral oil is edible.

- **Pam Cooking Spray.** Before beating eggs or any other ingredients, spray the beaters with Pam Cooking Spray so sticky foods wash off with ease.

Electric Skillet

- **Arm & Hammer Baking Soda.** To make cleaning burned-on grease from an electric skillet a simple task, cover the grease with Arm & Hammer Baking Soda and let sit for fifteen minutes, allowing the baking soda to absorb much of the grease. Then scrub with a damp sponge, putting the baking soda's abrasiveness to work. Rinse clean with warm water.

Fire Extinguisher

- **Arm & Hammer Baking Soda.** Keep a box of Arm & Hammer Baking Soda near your stove. Baking soda is a fire extinguisher in a box. The sodium bicarbonate is the same ingredient found in fire extinguishers. Simply pour the baking soda over the flames of a grease fire to extinguish the blaze.

- **Morton Salt.** To extinguish an oil fire in a pan, quench the fire with handfuls of Morton Salt.

Food Processor

- **Canada Dry Club Soda.** Dampen a sponge with Canada Dry Club Soda and wipe down the exterior of the food processor to keep it clean and shiny. Buff dry with a soft cloth.

- **Clorox Bleach.** Clean the exterior of a white food processor by mixing three-quarters cup Clorox Bleach and a gallon of water, apply with a sponge, let sit for ten minutes, and then rinse and dry thoroughly.

- **Dawn Dishwashing Liquid.** To clean a food processor, carefully fill the processor halfway with boiling water, add a few drops of Dawn Dishwashing Liquid, and let sit until the water cools. Add a handful of ice cubes, secure the lid in place, and process for thirty seconds. Rinse clean and dry thoroughly.

- **Forster Toothpicks.** To clean tight crevices on the outside of a food processor, dip a Forster Toothpick in alcohol and work along the tight spaces.

- **Huggies Baby Wipes.** To clean smudge marks, grease, or food stains from the outside of a food processor, simply wipe clean with a Huggies Baby Wipe.

- **Oral-B Toothbrushes.** To clean tight crevices on the outside of a food processor, scrub with a clean, old Oral-B Toothbrush.

- **Q-tips Cotton Swabs.** Dip a Q-tips Cotton Swab in alcohol to clean the crevices between the push buttons on the food processor.

- **Saran Wrap.** After placing the food to be processed in the machine's bowl, cover the bowl with a sheet of Saran Wrap and secure the lid in place. After processing the food, remove the clean lid and toss out the sullied plastic wrap.

- **Uncle Ben's Converted Brand Rice.** To deodorize a food processor bowl, fill the bowl with Uncle Ben's Converted Brand Rice and pulverize it. The rice absorbs the foul odors.

- **Wonder Bread.** Another way to eliminate food odors from a food processor bowl is to place several slices of Wonder Bread in the food bowl and grind them up. The bread absorbs any pungent odors.

Freezer

- **Arm & Hammer Baking Soda.** Aside from placing an open box of Arm & Hammer Baking Soda in the back of the compartment to deodorize the freezer, you can clean and deodorize the freezer by sprinkling Arm & Hammer Baking Soda on a damp sponge, scrubbing, and then rinsing clean.

- **Campbell's Tomato Juice.** If the stench of spoiled meat pervades your freezer, saturate a sponge with Campbell's Tomato Juice and wipe down the entire interior of the freezer compartment. The acids in the tomato juice neutralize the heinous odor. Wash out the tomato juice with soapy water, rinse clean, and dry well.

- **Conair Hair Dryer.** To expedite the defrosting of a freezer, aim the nozzle of a Conair Hair Dryer set on hot at the ice—making sure not to get the blow dryer wet.

- **Conair Hair Dryer.** If your automatic icemaker gets jammed with a frozen mass of ice cubes, hold a Conair Hair Dryer eight inches from the obstruction and blow hot air until the ice cubes melt apart.

- **Dawn Dishwashing Liquid** and **Heinz White Vinegar.** To eliminate the stench of spoiled food from the freezer, wash the interior with a solution made from one tablespoon Dawn Dishwashing Liquid and one gallon of water, and then rinse clean with a solution made from one cup Heinz White Vinegar and one gallon of water.

- **Maxwell House Coffee.** To neutralize the stench of spoiled food in your freezer, empty the freezer, fill a pan with Maxwell House Coffee grounds, place the pan in the freezer, and shut the door. Let sit undisturbed for several days, allowing the coffee grounds to absorb the putrid aroma.

- **Pam Cooking Spray.** To make defrosting a freezer effortless, spray a light coat of Pam Cooking Spray on the clean interior walls before plugging in the freezer. When you defrost the freezer, any ice that has accumulated on the walls will fall off shortly after you unplug the freezer.

- **Pam Cooking Spray.** To clean any ink on the interior walls of the freezer left by packages of frozen food, spray the markings with Pam Cooking Spray and wipe clean.

- **Pam Cooking Spray.** To prevent ice cubes from sticking to the inside of the removable ice bucket in your freezer, spray the inside of the clean, dry tray with a light coat of Pam Cooking Spray, and wipe off any excess oil.

- **Reynolds Cut-Rite Wax Paper.** To prevent food containers or ice cube trays from sticking to the floor of the freezer, place a sheet of Reynolds Cut-Rite Wax Paper under any moist-bottomed container you store in the freezer.

- **Tidy Cats.** To deodorize the smell of spoiled food from the freezer, after cleaning the freezer interior thoroughly, pour unused Tidy Cats in a flat box, place it in the freezer, and shut the door for several days. The cat box filler absorbs odors.

- **20 Mule Team Borax.** To clean and deodorize a freezer, mix one tablespoon 20 Mule Team Borax in one quart of warm water and use a sponge to wash the interior of the freezer with the solution. Rinse with cold water and dry thoroughly with a soft, clean cloth.

- **Vaseline Petroleum Jelly.** To prolong the life of the rubber gaskets on the freezer door and guarantee a tight seal, rub a thin coat of Vaseline Petroleum Jelly on the rubber gaskets.

- **USA Today.** To eliminate foul odors from a freezer, empty the freezer, fill it with crumpled-up pages of *USA Today,* shut the door, and let sit undisturbed for several days, giving the newsprint plenty of time to absorb the stink.

Garbage Disposer

- **Arm & Hammer Baking Soda.** To degrease and deodorize the inner workings of a garbage disposer, take the box of Arm & Hammer Baking Soda sitting in the refrigerator or freezer, pour half of it down the drain, flush with water, and repeat with the rest of the baking soda. Be sure to place a new box of Arm & Hammer Baking Soda in the refrigerator or freezer.

- **Dawn Dishwashing Liquid.** To clean a garbage disposer, plug the drain, fill the sink halfway with hot soapy water made with one teaspoon Dawn Dishwashing Liquid, unplug the drain, and turn on the disposer, allowing the soapy water to run its course. Dawn cuts through grease.

- **Heinz White Vinegar.** To clean a garbage disposer and simultaneously sharpen the blades, fill an ice cube tray with Heinz White Vinegar, freeze (leaving a note on the ice cube tray to prevent anyone from accidentally using the cubes of frozen vinegar), and grind the ice cubes through the disposer, flushing with cold water.

- **Morton Salt.** To deodorize a kitchen garbage disposer, pour one-half cup Morton Salt into the garbage disposer and flush with water for two minutes while running the disposer. The abrasive salt cleans the disposer and absorbs any pungent odors.

- **ReaLemon.** To freshen your garbage disposer, put a handful of ice cubes and two tablespoons of ReaLemon lemon juice in the garbage disposer and grind for two minutes. The ice cubes clean and sharpen the blades while the lemon juice deodorizes the disposer.

- **20 Mule Team Borax.** To deodorize the garbage disposer, sprinkle two to three tablespoons 20 Mule Team Borax down the drain, let sit for fifteen minutes, and then flush with water while running the disposer. Borax neutralizes acidic odors.

Juicer

- **Canada Dry Club Soda.** Dampen a sponge with Canada Dry Club Soda and wipe down the exterior of the juicer to keep it clean and shiny. Buff dry with a soft cloth.

- **Dawn Dishwashing Liquid.** To clean a juicer, place all the detachable parts (excluding the base) in a sink of warm soapy water made with one teaspoon Dawn Dishwashing Liquid. Let soak, rinse clean, and dry thoroughly.

- **Oral-B Toothbrush.** To clean the filter and blade of a juicer, carefully scrub with a clean, used Oral-B Toothbrush, and run water through the outside of the filter to remove any lingering pulp. Rinse and dry thoroughly.

Meat Grinder

- **Cheerios.** To clean a meat grinder quickly, run one-half cup Cheerios through the grinder to push out any remnants and absorb any residual moisture.

- **Nabisco Original Premium Saltine Crackers.** To clean meat scraps and absorb moisture from a meat grinder, simply grind several Nabisco Original Premium Saltine Crackers through the device.

- **Wonder Bread.** Another simple way to clean meat scraps and moisture from a meat grinder is to run a few slices of Wonder Bread through the grinder.

Microwave Oven

- **Arm & Hammer Baking Soda.** Dissolve two tablespoons Arm & Hammer Baking Soda in one cup of water. Boil the mixture in a bowl or coffee mug in the microwave oven for five minutes, allowing the steam to condense on the inside walls of the oven. Wipe clean with a sponge.

- **Bon Ami.** To scrub stubborn stains from the inside of a microwave oven, sprinkle Bon Ami on a damp sponge, scrub gently, and rinse clean.

- **Bounce.** To clean the exterior of a microwave oven, dampen a clean, used sheet of Bounce with water and wipe down the outside of the appliance. The abrasive dryer sheet makes a gentle scrubber, and the pleasant fragrance helps mask odors.

- **Dixie Paper Plates.** To prevent splatters and spills from messing up the inside of a microwave oven, place one Dixie Paper Plate under the cup, bowl, or plate to catch any spills and flip over a second paper plate to use as a lid to shield spatters.

- **Efferdent.** To clean yellowish brown stains from the interior of a microwave oven, dissolve two Efferdent denture cleansing tablets in a glass of water, use a sponge to apply the solution to the inside of the microwave oven, and let soak for five minutes. If necessary, scrub with a nylon brush or non-abrasive scrubbing pad. Rinse thoroughly with a clean sponge and water.

- **Heinz White Vinegar.** To deodorize a foul stench from inside a microwave oven, unplug the microwave, place one cup Heinz White Vinegar inside the oven, leave the door open, and let sit for at least twenty-four hours. Vinegar absorbs and neutralizes odors.

- **Maxwell House Coffee.** To deodorize a microwave oven, mix two tablespoons Maxwell House Coffee in a coffee mug filled halfway with water and heat for two minutes on high.

- **McCormick Pure Vanilla Extract.** To eliminate the smell of burned popcorn from a microwave oven, pour one tablespoon McCormick Pure Vanilla Extract in a coffee mug, heat for thirty seconds to one minute, and let sit in the microwave with the door sealed shut overnight. In the morning, use a damp sponge to wipe down the inside of the microwave oven.

- **Mr. Coffee Filters.** To prevent food spatters in the microwave oven, cover the cup, bowl, or plate of food with a Mr. Coffee Filter.

- **ReaLemon.** To deodorize a microwave oven, mix two tablespoons ReaLemon lemon juice in one cup of water and heat the lemony solution in the microwave oven for one minute. With a sponge, wipe the condensation from the inside walls of the microwave oven.

- **Reynolds Cut-Rite Wax Paper.** For another simple way to prevent food spatters in the microwave oven, cover the cup, bowl, or plate with a sheet of Reynolds Cut-Rite Wax Paper.

Mixer

- **Canada Dry Club Soda.** Dampen a sponge with Canada Dry Club Soda and wipe down the exterior of the mixer to keep it clean and shiny. Buff dry with a soft cloth.

- **Pam Cooking Spray.** To prevent an electric mixer from making a mess, spray the beaters with Pam Cooking Spray before putting them to use. The oil helps keep the batter in the bowl and makes cleanup a snap. (Do not spray beaters with oil before beating egg whites; the oil prevents egg whites from stiffening.)

- **Reynolds Cut-Rite Wax Paper.** To prevent food from spattering when using a mixer, cover the mixing bowl with a piece of Reynolds Cut-Rite Wax Paper, cut two holes for the beater stems to fit through, insert the stems through the holes, and attach the beaters to the mixer. The waxed paper covering catches any spatters.

- **Reynolds Wrap.** For a convenient alternative to using waxed paper to prevent food from spattering when using a mixer, cover the bowl with

WHAT'S COOKING

MIXING THINGS UP

- To prevent a mixing bowl from sliding around on the countertop while you mix ingredients, place the bowl on a folded damp towel.

a sheet of Reynolds Wrap and punch holes in the aluminum foil to insert the stems of the beaters.

Oven

- **Arm & Hammer Baking Soda.** To clean a cool oven, wipe the inside with a wet sponge or cloth, sprinkle Arm & Hammer Baking Soda on the wet surfaces, and let sit overnight, allowing the baking soda to absorb the grease and grime. In the morning, wipe the oven clean.

- **Canada Dry Club Soda.** To clean the exterior of a stainless-steel oven, saturate a soft clean, cloth with Canada Dry Club Soda, and wipe clean. (For more ways to clean the outside of a stainless-steel oven, see page 331.)

- **Heinz White Vinegar.** To eliminate the lingering smell of aerosol oven cleaner from your oven and prevent the oven from smoking, saturate a sponge with Heinz White Vinegar and wipe down the inside of the oven.

- **Kool-Aid.** To clean an oven, combine the contents of one packet of any flavor Kool-Aid and one cup of water and use the drink mix like cleanser. The citric acid in the Kool-Aid cuts through the grease and grime in the oven.

- **Morton Salt.** To clean a wet spill from inside an oven, immediately and carefully cover the spill with Morton Salt. When the oven cools down, scrape up the mess.

- **Pam Cooking Spray.** To avoid having to scour baked-on food and grease from a broiler pan, before cooking, spray the pan with Pam Cooking Spray.

- **Parsons' Ammonia.** Warm the oven at 200 degrees Fahrenheit for twenty minutes, turn it off, set a small bowl of Parsons' Ammonia on the top shelf of the oven, and place a glass bowl filled with two cups of boiling water on the bottom shelf. Close the oven door securely, and let sit undisturbed overnight. In the morning, open all the kitchen windows, and—making sure the room is well ventilated—stand back, open the oven, carefully remove the saucer and bowl, discard the contents, and let the oven air out for one hour.

Wash the oven walls and floor with soap and water, rinse, and wipe clean. Ammonia fumes loosen grease and grime from oven walls.

- **Reynolds Wrap.** To prevent messy oven drips, either spread a large sheet of Reynolds Wrap under the baking pan or place it on a rack under the baking pan to catch any drips and prevent an unwelcome mess.

- **Spray 'n Wash.** Preheat the oven to 150 degrees Fahrenheit, turn off, spray the interior walls with Spray 'n Wash, and let sit for fifteen minutes to cool. Rinse clean with a soft, clean cloth.

- **Tang.** To scrub baked-on food and grease from inside an oven, mix two tablespoons Tang powdered drink mix and one cup of water, apply the orange solution to the inside of the oven, and scrub with a nylon brush or nonabrasive scrubbing pad. The citric acid in the Tang miraculously cuts through the grease and grime.

- **Wonder Bread.** To prevent grease and juices from getting baked onto a broiling pan, before using the oven broiler, place a slice of Wonder Bread in the bottom of the pan to absorb the imminent drips.

Oven Racks

- **Dawn Dishwashing Liquid** and **Heinz White Vinegar.** To clean the oven racks, place an old towel on the floor of the bathtub, fill the tub with enough hot water to cover the racks, add one-third cup Dawn Dishwashing Liquid and one cup Heinz White Vinegar, and let sit for one hour. Wipe the racks clean with a sponge and rinse.

- **Easy-Off Oven Cleaner.** To clean grease, grime, and baked-on food from an oven rack, place the oven rack outside. Wearing rubber gloves and protective eyewear, spray the rack with Easy-Off Oven Cleaner and let sit for several hours. Carefully rinse the oven cleaner off the rack with a garden hose, and then bring it back inside to wash thoroughly with soapy water. Rinse clean and dry.

- **Pam Cooking Spray.** To prevent food from sticking to an oven grill, before cooking, spray the grill with Pam Cooking Spray.

- **Parsons' Ammonia, Bounty Paper Towels,** and **Glad Trash Bags.** To clean an oven rack, take the rack outside, wrap Bounty Paper Towels around it, place the rack inside a Glad Trash Bag, and saturate the paper toweling with one cup Parsons' Ammonia—being careful not to breath the ammonia fumes. Close the bag securely with a twist tie and let sit overnight outside or in a well-ventilated garage. The ammonia fumes loosen the baked-on food and grease from the racks. The next morning, open the bag outdoors (again being careful to avoid breathing the fumes) and remove the rack, leaving the paper towels in the bag. Discard the bag. Rinse the rack with a garden hose, and then bring it back inside the house to wash thoroughly with soapy water, rinse clean, and dry.

- **Reynolds Wrap.** To clean excessive baked-on food and grease from an oven rack, remove the rack from the oven, wrap it with a sheet of Reynolds Wrap Heavy Duty aluminum foil with the shiny-side facing the grids, and slide it back into the oven. Heat at 250 degrees Fahrenheit for fifteen minutes. Let cool completely and remove the aluminum foil. The baked-on food and grease will come off with the aluminum foil. If not, crumple up a sheet of Reynolds Wrap into a ball and use it to scrub the grill.

- **Tide.** To clean an oven rack, place an old towel on the floor of the bathtub, place the rack on top, fill the tub with enough hot water to cover the rack, add one cup liquid Tide laundry detergent, and let sit for one hour. Wipe the rack clean with a sponge and rinse clean.

- **Vaseline Petroleum Jelly.** If your oven racks stick, clean them thoroughly using a wire brush, and then coat the sliding portions lightly with Vaseline Petroleum Jelly.

Pressure Cooker

- **Arm & Hammer Baking Soda** and **Ziploc Storage Bags.** If you use your pressure cooker infrequently, place one teaspoon Arm & Hammer Baking Soda in a Ziploc Storage Bag, add the gasket and weight, seal shut, and store this inside the cooker. Sprinkle one to two tablespoons baking soda inside the pot and close the lid. Store in a cool, dry place. The baking soda will absorb any excess moisture and odors. Before using again, wash the pressure cooker in warm soapy water and rinse clean.

- **Bon Ami.** To clean stubborn spots from a pressure cooker, use nonabrasive Bon Ami on a damp sponge. Rinse clean and dry thoroughly.

- **Dawn Dishwashing Liquid.** To clean burned-on foods from inside a pressure cooker, pour one cup of cold water inside the pressure cooker, heat over a low flame, and use a wooden spoon to loosen the burned food. Add a few drops of Dawn Dishwashing Liquid and scrub with a long-handled nylon scrub brush. Rinse clean and dry thoroughly.

- **McCormick Cream of Tartar** and **Heinz White Vinegar.** To lighten or possibly remove discolorations from the inside of an aluminum pressure cooker, boil two tablespoons McCormick Cream of Tartar, two tablespoons Heinz White Vinegar, and one quart of water for ten minutes in the uncovered pot. Then scrub the pot with a soapy, nonabrasive cleanser on a plastic scouring pad. Repeat if needed.

- **ReaLemon.** To prevent stains in an aluminum pressure cooker, add one tablespoon ReaLemon lemon juice to the water whenever cooking.

- **Wesson Oil.** To prolong the life of the plastic handles on a pressure cooker, rub in a few drops of Wesson Oil.

Range Hood

- **Bon Ami.** To clean grease and spatters from a range hood, sprinkle Bon Ami on the hood, rub with a wet sponge, rinse, and wipe dry with a soft, clean cloth.

- **Cascade.** To clean grease and grime from the filters from the oven fan in the range hood, place the filters in the upper rack of your dishwasher, pour the regular amount of Cascade in the detergent cup, and run through the regular cycle.

- **Shout.** To clean stubborn grease stains from a range hood, spray Shout stain remover on the grease stains, let set for a few minutes, and then wipe clean with a soft cloth.

- **Vaseline Petroleum Jelly.** To clean grease and grime from an oven range hood, rub a dab of Vaseline Petroleum Jelly into the stains, let sit for five minutes, and wipe clean with a soft, clean cloth.

Refrigerator

- **Arm & Hammer Baking Soda.** To clean and deodorize a refrigerator, sprinkle Arm & Hammer Baking Soda on a damp sponge, scrub, and rinse clean.

- **Arm & Hammer Baking Soda.** Everyone seems to know that keeping an open box of Arm & Hammer Baking Soda on a shelf in the refrigerator absorbs foul odors. Church & Dwight, the company that manufactures Arm & Hammer Baking Soda, started advertising this alternative use in 1972, increasing sales of the product by 72 percent within two years.

- **Bon Ami.** To clean stains and spills from inside a refrigerator, sprinkle Bon Ami on a damp sponge, scrub, and rinse clean.

- **Bounty Paper Towels.** Lining the inside of the crisper drawers with a sheet of Bounty Paper Towels not only absorbs moisture, keeping fruit and vegetables fresh longer, but the towels also make the drawers easy to clean.

- **Canada Dry Club Soda.** To clean a stainless-steel refrigerator, dampen a sponge with Canada Dry Club Soda, wipe clean, and dry with a soft cloth. (For more ways to clean a stainless-steel refrigerator, see page 331.)

- **Crisco All-Vegetable Shortening.** To slide your refrigerator forward with ease so you can clean behind it, rub some Crisco All-Vegetable Shortening on the floor in front of the appliance. After rolling the refrigerator back in place, wipe the slippery substance from the floor.

- **Kingsford Charcoal Briquets.** To neutralize smelly odors in the refrigerator, place a cup of untreated Kingsford Charcoal Briquets on a back shelf.

- **L'eggs Sheer Energy Panty Hose.** To clean the dust bunnies from under a refrigerator, use a pair of scissors to snip off one leg from a clean, used pair of L'eggs Sheer Energy Panty Hose. Place the lone leg over the end of a yardstick or a broomstick, slide the nylon-covered stick under the refrigerator, and move the wand back and forth to capture the dust, which clings to the nylon.

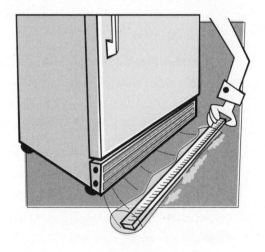

- **Listerine.** To clean and deodorize the inside of the refrigerator and prevent mildew, wipe the interior with a sponge or rag dampened with Listerine antiseptic mouthwash.

- **Maxwell House Coffee.** To absorb musty odors from inside a refrigerator, place a bowl filled with Maxwell House Coffee grounds on the back shelf.

- **McCormick Pure Lemon Extract.** Need another way to freshen the air in the refrigerator? Add a few drops of McCormick Pure Lemon Extract to a cotton ball and place it on a saucer in the refrigerator.

- **McCormick Pure Orange Extract.** If you don't have lemon extract, dampen a cotton ball with a few drops of McCormick Pure Orange Extract and place it on a saucer in the refrigerator to mask objectionable odors.

- **McCormick Pure Vanilla Extract.** To camouflage nasty odors inside a refrigerator, saturate a sponge with McCormick Pure Vanilla Extract and wipe down the inside walls of the refrigerator. Or dampen a cotton ball with McCormick Vanilla Extract and place it on a saucer.

- **Pam Cooking Spray.** If you need to clean behind a heavy refrigerator, spray a small amount of Pam Cooking Spray on the vinyl, linoleum, or tile floor in front of the refrigerator, enabling the weighty appliance to glide easily. Be certain to clean up the slippery oil after moving the refrigerator back in place.

- **ReaLemon.** To determine if that box of baking soda sitting on the back shelf of the refrigerator remains fresh enough to absorb stale odors, add a pinch of the baking soda to one teaspoon ReaLemon lemon juice. If the solution fails to bubble and fizz, replace the box of baking soda.

- **Saran Wrap** and **Scotch Tape.** To avoid having to wipe down the top of your refrigerator to remove the inevitable layer of dust, line the top with a few sheets of Saran Wrap, held in place with a few small strips of Scotch Tape. When dust accumulates, peel off the Saran Wrap, carefully rolling it up to keep the dust contained, and replace the plastic liner with fresh sheets of Saran Wrap and new strips of Scotch Tape.

- **Tidy Cats.** To prevent a clean, empty, unplugged refrigerator from attracting mold or mildew and acquiring a fetid odor, pour unused Tidy Cats in a flat box, place it on the middle shelf, and shut the door. The cat box filler absorbs excess moisture.

- **20 Mule Team Borax.** To clean and deodorize a refrigerator, mix one tablespoon 20 Mule Team Borax in one quart of warm water. Dampen a sponge in the solution and wash. Rinse clean with cold water and dry with a soft cloth.

- **USA Today.** To eliminate rancid odors from inside a clean, empty, unplugged refrigerator, fill the appliance with crumpled up pages of *USA Today*, close the door, and let sit undisturbed for several days. Newsprint absorbs putrid odors.

- **Vaseline Petroleum Jelly.** To prevent the drawers in the refrigerator from getting stuck, rub a dab of Vaseline Petroleum Jelly along the runners so the drawers glide easily.

- **Vaseline Petroleum Jelly.** To prevent the gasket (the white rubber trim around the inside of the refrigerator door) from drying up and cracking, give it a light coat of Vaseline Petroleum Jelly.

- **Wonder Bread.** To remove sour odors from a refrigerator, place a few slices of Wonder Bread on the back of a middle shelf. White bread absorbs odors.

Refrigerator Drip Trays

- **Listerine.** To kill the mold that grows in the refrigerator drip tray, remove the tray from underneath the refrigerator, wash it with soapy water, rinse clean, add one cup Listerine antiseptic mouthwash, and fill the rest with water. Let sit undisturbed for one hour; rinse clean; dry with a soft, clean cloth; and return it to its original spot.

- **20 Mule Team Borax.** For another way to kill mold in a refrigerator drip tray, pull out the tray and fill it with water. Add one tablespoon 20 Mule Team Borax and scrub. Rinse well; dry with a soft, clean cloth; and put the tray back in place.

Rice Cooker

- **Canada Dry Club Soda.** Dampen a sponge with Canada Dry Club Soda and wipe down the exterior of the rice cooker to keep it clean and shiny. Buff dry with a soft cloth.

- **Pam Cooking Spray.** To prevent rice from sticking to the inside of the cooker, spray the bottom and sides with Pam Cooking Spray before adding the rice and water. The oil does not affect the taste of the rice and makes cleanup effortless.

- **3M Sandpaper.** To remove burnt grains of rice or baked-on food from the rice cooker hot plate, rub with a piece of fine 3M Sandpaper.

Slow Cooker

- **Murphy Oil Soap.** If baked-on food has gunked up the inside of a slow cooker, fill the stoneware pot with water, add one tablespoon Murphy Oil Soap, and heat the slow cooker on high for one hour. Let cool, rinse clean, and dry.

- **Pam Cooking Spray.** To prevent food from sticking to the inside of the slow cooker and make cleaning easy, spray the inside of the stoneware pot with Pam Cooking Spray before adding food.

Stove

- **Arm & Hammer Baking Soda.** To clean grease from a stovetop, make a thick paste from Arm & Hammer Baking Soda and water, apply the paste to the surface, and let sit for one hour to give the baking soda sufficient time to absorb the grease. Rinse clean and dry thoroughly.

- **Calgon Water Softener.** To clean grease and food stains from a stovetop, fill a clean, empty sixteen-ounce trigger-spray bottle with water, add one tablespoon Calgon Water Softener, and shake well. Spray the stove and use a sponge to wipe up the mess. Calgon leaves the stove clean, shiny, and smelling fresh.

- **Colgate Regular Flavor Tooth-paste.** To scrub grease stains and

burned-on food spatters from a stovetop, squeeze some Colgate Regular Flavor Toothpaste on a sponge and scrub the spots. Then wipe clean with a damp cloth.

- **Heinz White Vinegar.** To clean a stovetop, dampen a sponge with Heinz White Vinegar, scrub clean, and buff dry to a gleaming finish with a soft, clean cloth. Vinegar shines and deodorizes stovetops.

- **Morton Salt.** To clean a hot grease spill from a stovetop, sprinkle Morton Salt over the liquid, let cool, and scrape clean with a sponge. The salt absorbs the grease and acts as a mild abrasive to help scour up the mess.

- **Nestea Iced Tea Mix.** Dissolve two teaspoons Nestea Iced Tea Mix in one cup of water and dampen a sponge with the strong tea to clean grease from a stovetop. The tannic acid does the trick.

- **Shout.** For an effective yet simple way to clean baked-on grease from a stovetop, spray the affected area with Shout stain remover, let sit five minutes, and wipe clean.

Stove Burner Drip Plates and Burner Grates

- **Arm & Hammer Baking Soda.** Are your stove burner drip plates and burner grates all gunked up with burned-on food and grease? Fill a large pot with two quarts of water, add two tablespoons Arm & Hammer Baking Soda, put in the stove pit rings, and boil for five minutes. Let cool, rinse clean, and dry.

- **Cascade.** To clean stovetop grease and grime from stove burner drip plates, fill the kitchen sink with hot water, add one-half cup Cascade Gel, and let the drip plates soak for one hour in the solution. Rinse clean and dry.

- **Easy-Off Oven Cleaner.** To clean grease and burned-on food from burner drip plates, place the drip plates outside, and, wearing rubber gloves and protective eyewear, spray with Easy-Off Oven Cleaner. Let sit for one hour. Wash clean with the garden hose.

- **Efferdent.** For a simple way to clean stove burner drip plates, fill the kitchen sink with water, drop in four Efferdent denture cleansing tablets, let the plates soak in the blue solution for one hour, and rinse clean.

- **Parsons' Ammonia** and **Glad Trash Bags.** To clean stove burner drip plates, chrome rings, and burner grates, place the items in a Glad Trash Bag and take the bag outside. Pour in two cups Parsons' Ammonia, tie the bag securely shut, and let sit outside (or in a well-ventilated garage) overnight to give the ammonia fumes sufficient time to loosen the grease and grime. Open the bag outdoors, being careful not to inhale the fumes. Rinse the ammonia off the rings with a garden hose, discard the bag, and then bring the items back inside to wash thoroughly with soapy water.

Stove Knobs

- **Tide.** To clean grease and grime from stove knobs, pull off the knobs (making certain the stove remains turned off), mix one teaspoon liquid Tide laundry detergent and two cups of hot water, and soak the knobs in the solution for one hour. Scrub, rinse clean, and dry.

Teakettle

- **Calgon Water Softener.** To clean limescale from inside an electric teakettle, pour two tablespoons Calgon Water Softener into the water tank, fill the rest with water, and let sit overnight. In the morning, rinse clean.

- **Canada Dry Club Soda.** Dampen a sponge with Canada Dry Club Soda and wipe down the exterior of the teakettle to keep it clean and shiny. Buff dry with a soft cloth.

- **Coca-Cola.** Need another way to clean calcium carbonate deposits from inside an electric teakettle? Fill the teakettle with Coca-Cola, let sit overnight, and in the morning, rinse clean. The phosphoric acid and ascorbic acid in the Coke dissolve the mineral buildup.

- **Efferdent.** For a simple method to clean the mineral deposits from the heating element inside a teakettle, fill the kettle with enough water to cover the heating element, drop in four Efferdent denture cleansing tablets, and let sit overnight. In the morning, scrub with a bottle brush and rinse clean with hot water.

- **Heinz White Vinegar.** For yet another easy way to eliminate lime-scale from the inside of a teakettle, pour three cups Heinz White Vinegar into the teakettle, fill the rest with water, shake well, and let sit overnight. In the morning, rinse clean. The acetic acid in the vinegar dissolves the calcium carbonate.

Toaster

- **Arm & Hammer Baking Soda.** If you accidentally melt a plastic bread bag to the outside of a toaster, sprinkle Arm & Hammer Baking Soda on a damp sponge, gently scrub the cool, unplugged toaster, and wipe clean. Buff dry with a soft cloth. The mildly abrasive baking soda works like a polishing compound, rubbing off the melted plastic.

- **Bon Ami.** To clean a chrome or white plastic toaster, sprinkle Bon Ami on a damp sponge and gently scrub the unplugged toaster. Rinse clean and dry thoroughly.

- **Canada Dry Club Soda.** Dampen a sponge with Canada Dry Club Soda and wipe down the exterior of the unplugged toaster to keep it clean and shiny. Buff dry with a soft cloth.

- **Colgate Regular Flavor Toothpaste.** To shine up an unplugged chrome or plastic toaster, squeeze a dollop of Colgate Regular Flavor Toothpaste on a damp sponge and scrub clean. Rinse and dry with a soft cloth.

- **Cutex Nail Polish Remover.** To remove a stubborn piece of melted plastic bread bag from the outside of a toaster, unplug the toaster, let cool, and use a cotton ball to apply Cutex Nail Polish Remover to the plastic. The acetone gently dissolves the melted plastic, allowing you to scrape it away. Test an inconspicuous spot first to make sure the acetone doesn't harm the finish of the toaster.

- **Heinz White Vinegar.** To give an unplugged chrome toaster a brilliant shine, moisten a sponge with Heinz White Vinegar and apply to the appliance. Buff dry with a soft, clean cloth.

- **Jif Peanut Butter.** To clean and shine a chrome toaster, smear Jif Peanut Butter on the toaster, and then wipe it off with a soft, clean cloth. The oils in the peanut butter dissolve any baked-on food and give the chrome a lustrous shine.

- **Murphy Oil Soap.** To clean the exterior of an unplugged chrome or plastic toaster, add a few drops Murphy Oil Soap to a damp sponge and gently scrub the appliance. Rinse and dry with a soft, clean cloth.

- **Reynolds Wrap.** Rather than turning your toaster upside down and shaking out all the crumbs, line the crumb tray with a sheet of Reynolds Wrap aluminum foil to catch all the crumbs. To clean, simply change the foil lining.

- **Reynolds Wrap.** To clean soap scum off a chrome toaster, crumple a sheet of Reynolds Wrap aluminum foil into a ball and use it as a scrubber.

- **Vaseline Petroleum Jelly** and **Bounty Paper Towels.** To clean a melted plastic bread wrapper from the toaster, rub some Vaseline Petroleum Jelly on the spot, reactivate the toaster, and when the plastic mess warms up, use a sheet of Bounty Paper Towels to wipe it up.

Toaster Oven

- **Arm & Hammer Baking Soda.** To clean the inside and outside of an unplugged toaster oven, sprinkle some Arm & Hammer Baking Soda on a damp sponge. Baking soda cuts through grease.

- **Canada Dry Club Soda.** Dampen a sponge with Canada Dry Club Soda and wipe down the exterior of the unplugged toaster oven to keep it clean and shiny. Buff dry with a soft cloth.

- **Reynolds Wrap.** To avoid having to scrub the bottom tray of a toaster oven, cover it with Reynolds Wrap to catch messy crumbs and messy spills.

Waffle Iron

- **Oral-B Toothbrush.** To scrub between the grids of a waffle iron, use a clean, used Oral-B Toothbrush.

- **Pam Cooking Spray** and **Bounty Paper Towels.** To season a new waffle iron before putting it to use for the first time, turn on the heat, and when warm, spray the upper and lower grids with plenty of Pam Cooking Spray. Then unplug the waffle iron and let cool. Wipe off the excess oil with a few sheets of Bounty Paper Towels. Plug in the iron again, let it heat up, and then unplug it once more and let cool. Wipe off the excess oil one last time. Make the first waffle, remove it from the iron, and discard. The waffle iron is now properly seasoned and ready for you to make waffles.

- **Reynolds Cut-Rite Wax Paper.** When you finish baking waffles, place a sheet of Reynolds Cut-Rite Wax Paper across the bottom grid of the waffle iron, close the iron, and let it cool. Store with the sheet of waxed paper in place to keep the grids waxed and moisture-free.

- **Reynolds Cut-Rite Wax Paper.** If the nonstick coating on the grids of your waffle iron loses its effectiveness, temporarily fix the problem by placing two sheets of Reynolds Cut-Rite Wax Paper between the plates of your waffle iron while it heats up for a few minutes. The moment the waxed paper turns brown, remove it from the waffle iron. The wax sticks to the plates, enabling you to make waffles that pop out of the iron.

CHAPTER 4

Food Secrets

Apples

- **Miracle Whip.** When dicing apples to make a large apple salad, mix them with Miracle Whip as you chop to prevent the slices from discoloring before you finish dicing them all.

- **Morton Salt.** To prevent sliced apples from browning, dissolve one-quarter teaspoon Morton Salt in two cups of cold water and immerse the slices in the salt water for ten minutes before using.

- **Mott's Apple Juice.** To impede sliced apples from browning, place the slices in a bowl, cover with Mott's Apple Juice, and refrigerate for thirty minutes. The apple juice revitalizes and flavors dry apple slices.

- **ReaLemon.** To hinder peeled or sliced apples from browning, toss them into a bowl of cold water and one tablespoon ReaLemon lemon juice. If you slice an apple in half, rub a small amount of lemon juice over the open half you intend to save for later.

- **ReaLemon.** To prevent apples from becoming granular while baking, remove a one-half-inch-thick ribbon of peel from around the equator of each apple before baking and sprinkle the bare strip on each apple with ReaLemon lemon juice.

- **SueBee Honey.** Immediately upon removing hot baked apples from the oven, top with SueBee Honey. The apples absorb the honey, giving them a sweet taste.

Food for Thought
HOW ABOUT THEM APPLES?

- To prevent apples from shrinking while baking, remove a one-half-inch-thick ribbon of peel from around the equator of the apple before baking.

- To prevent the skin of an apple from splitting or wrinkling when baking, cut several shallow slits around the skin before baking to let steam escape.

- Add apple slices to tuna or chicken salads for a delicious variation.

Artichokes

- **Campbell's Broth.** Cooking artichokes in Campbell's Broth (any flavor) makes artichokes far tastier than cooking them in water.

- **Gold Medal Flour** and **ReaLemon.** To prevent artichoke hearts and bottoms from discoloring, bring one quart of water to a boil, beat in one-quarter cup Gold Medal Flour and two tablespoons ReaLemon lemon juice, and blanch the artichoke in the solution by immersing and removing it quickly.

- **Heinz White Vinegar.** To prevent artichokes from becoming discolored when cooking and simultaneously make the flesh more succulent, mix one tablespoon Heinz White Vinegar for every quart of cold water in a pot, and soak the artichokes in the solution for one hour prior to cooking.

- **Land O Lakes Butter** and **Morton Salt.** To serve an artichoke elegantly, cut out the choke, melt Land O Lakes Butter, stir in a pinch of Morton Salt, and pour the salted butter into the cup left behind by the choke.

- **Morton Salt.** To remove any insects harbored amidst the artichoke leaves, dissolve one-quarter cup Morton Salt in one quart of water and soak the artichokes in the salty water for thirty minutes. Rinse clean in clear cold water.

- **Playtex Living Gloves.** To avoid pricking your fingers when clipping off the ends of artichoke leaves with a pair of scissors, wear a pair of Playtex Living Gloves.

- **ReaLemon.** For another way to prevent artichokes from discoloring when cooking, prior to cooking, dip the trimmed end of the artichoke in ReaLemon lemon juice.

- **ReaLemon.** To enhance the taste of an artichoke, add one teaspoon ReaLemon lemon juice for each artichoke when cooking in water or broth.

Food for Thought
THE HEART OF THE MATTER

- Never cook artichokes in an aluminum or iron pot. The artichokes turn the cookware gray.

- You need not remove the choke of an artichoke before cooking. However, to do so, pry open the center leaves at the top and use a paring knife to cut out the fine prickly leaves and the choke. If you prefer to wait until after cooking to remove the choke, use a spoon to excise the fine prickly leaves in the center and scoop out the choke.

- An artichoke is finished cooking when a slight pull removes the leaves easily.

Asparagus

- **Bounty Paper Towels.** Before serving asparagus, roll the stalks quickly in a sheet of Bounty Paper Towels to remove all the water from boiling.

- **L'eggs Sheer Energy Panty Hose.** To cook asparagus, tie the spears together in bundles of ten with a strip of nylon cut from the leg of a pair of clean, used L'eggs Sheer Energy Panty Hose, so you will be able to remove the spears easily from the water without breaking off the tips. Stand the bundles of asparagus in a pot of gently boiling water with the tips just above the water level and cover with a lid for twelve minutes, allowing the boiling water to cook the stems while the steam softens the tips to perfection.

- **ReaLemon.** To revitalize wilted asparagus, cut an inch off the bottom of the stalk, mix one teaspoon ReaLemon lemon juice and two quarts of cool water, and soak the asparagus in the solution for thirty minutes to an hour.

Food for Thought
ASPARAGUS TIPS

- To avoid breaking the tips of canned asparagus, open the bottom of the can rather than the top.

- To tenderize the thick ends of asparagus stalks, use a potato or carrot peeler to pare the tougher outer portion of the stalks down to the tender section.

- Asparagus continues to harden after being cut, so cook asparagus soon after buying.

- To cut an asparagus stalk, bend it at the spot where you'd like to cut it in two, and the stalk will snap.

- Before adding asparagus tips to an omelet, boil fresh asparagus tips for six minutes in gently boiling water, pat dry, and sauté lightly in butter.

Avocados

- **ReaLemon.** To prevent a freshly peeled avocado from turning brown, rub any cuts accidentally made into the surface with ReaLemon lemon juice.

- **ReaLemon.** To keep one half of an unused avocado fresh, gently brush the open side with ReaLemon lemon juice, wrap tightly with Saran Wrap, and refrigerate.

- **ReaLemon.** To prevent freshly made guacamole from turning brown, drizzle ReaLemon lemon juice over the surface of the dip, preserving the green color.

Bacon

- **Bounty Paper Towels.** After frying bacon, drain the excess grease from the strips by placing them on a sheet of Bounty Paper Towels (or between two sheets), allowing the quicker-picker-upper to absorb the fat.

- **Forster Toothpicks.** To make bacon curls, fry the bacon strips until halfway cooked and remove the bacon from the skillet. Twirl each individual strip around the tines of a fork and pierce with a Forster Toothpick to hold the curl together. After preparing all the strips of bacon, broil the assembled curls over a low flame until crisp.

- **Gold Medal Flour.** To give bacon more bulk, bring the uncooked bacon to room temperature, slice the strips into halves, and dip them in Gold Medal Flour before frying.

- **Maxwell House Coffee.** Pouring bacon drippings down the drain will eventually clog the drain. Instead, pour bacon drippings into a clean, empty Maxwell House Coffee can, seal with the plastic lid, and place in the freezer to harden the fat. When the can is full, discard it in the garbage.

- **Playtex Living Gloves.** To prevent bacon slices from sticking together in the refrigerator, use a pair of scissors to slice thin strips from the cuff of a clean, used pair of Playtex Living Gloves to make giant rubber bands. Roll the package of bacon into the shape of a tube and secure it in place with one of the jumbo rubber bands.

- **Reynolds Cut-Rite Wax Paper** and **Ziploc Storage Bags.** To store cooked bacon, line a cookie sheet with a piece of Reynolds Cut-Rite Wax Paper, place the bacon strips on the waxed paper, and freeze. Once the bacon strips have frozen, place them in a Ziploc Storage Bag.

- **SPAM.** For an inexpensive and equally tasty substitute for bacon, fry thin slices of SPAM luncheon meat.

- *USA Today.* To reduce the amount of paper towels you use to absorb the fat from bacon strips, place several sections of *USA Today* under a sheet of paper towels. The newsprint will absorb any fat that penetrates the paper towels.

Food for Thought
SAVING YOUR BACON

- Before frying bacon, soak the strips in cold water for a few minutes. The bacon will curl less in the frying pan.

- To prevent bacon from shrinking excessively when frying, place the strips of uncooked bacon in a cold skillet before turning on the stove and, as you fry them, prick them thoroughly with a fork.

Baking Powder

- **McCormick Cream of Tartar, Arm & Hammer Baking Soda,** and **Kingsford's Corn Starch.** To make baking powder, mix two teaspoons McCormick Cream of Tartar, one teaspoon Arm & Hammer Baking Soda, and one teaspoon Kingsford's Corn Starch.

Baking Soda

- **Heinz White Vinegar.** To test whether that open box of baking soda sitting on the shelf is still fresh, pour one-quarter cup Heinz White

Vinegar into a bowl or drinking glass and add one teaspoon of the baking soda in question. If the mixture bubbles and fizzes, the baking soda remains fresh. Otherwise, pour the baking soda down the drain, which helps freshen the drain.

Bananas

- **Hershey's Chocolate Syrup.** To make a frozen chocolate-covered banana, freeze a peeled banana, dip the frozen banana in Hershey's Chocolate Syrup, and refreeze. To make the chocolate-covered banana easier to eat, insert a wooden Popsicle stick into the banana at the start of the process.

- **Jif Peanut Butter** and **Saran Wrap.** To make frozen peanut butter bananas, cut a peeled banana into quarters lengthwise, spread Jif Peanut Butter (either crunchy or creamy) on the cut sides, reassemble the banana, wrap in Saran Wrap, and freeze.

- **Land O Lakes Butter.** To turn bananas into a tasty side dish for any meal, melt two tablespoons Land O Lakes Butter in a saucepan over low heat, use a spoon to skim off the butter fat (the bubbly coagulant) from the surface. Quarter bananas lengthwise and sauté them in the pan of clarified butter.

- **Mott's Apple Juice.** To prevent sliced bananas from burning inside a cake, dip the slices in Mott's Apple Juice before adding them to the cake mix.

- **ReaLemon.** To slow an unpeeled banana from turning brown, brush the banana skin with ReaLemon lemon juice.

- **Reynolds Wrap.** To make a tasty frozen dessert or preserve overripe bananas, cut each peeled, ripe banana into one-inch slices, wrap it in Reynolds Wrap aluminum foil, and place in the freezer. Eat the frozen slices at your leisure, or add them to the blender when mixing up a milk shake.

- To make breakfast more exciting, add banana slices to your morning cereal.

Barbecue Sauce

- **Coca-Cola** and **Heinz Ketchup.** To make an excellent barbecue sauce, simply mix Coca-Cola and Heinz Ketchup.

- **Maxwell House Coffee.** To give store-bought barbecue sauce a Cajun tang, dissolve one tablespoon Maxwell House Instant Coffee in one tablespoon of water and stir into the barbecue sauce.

Beans

- **Arm & Hammer Baking Soda.** To prevent dry beans from cracking and getting mushy, add a pinch of Arm & Hammer Baking Soda to the water when cooking.

Food for Thought
FULL OF BEANS

- One cup of raw, small, dried beans yields roughly 2½ cups when cooked. One cup of raw large beans yields approximately 2 cups when cooked.

- To soften dried beans, cover the beans with boiling water and let sit for one hour before cooking.

- To cook dried beans, simmer the beans over low heat to avoid boiling over, and stir occasionally and gently with a wooden spoon to avoid breaking the skins.

- Dried beans cooked without salt attain tenderness more rapidly than beans cooked with salt.

- **Coca-Cola.** To stop beans from causing flatulence, add one-half can Coca-Cola to the water while cooking the beans.

- **Heinz Apple Cider Vinegar.** To prevent beans from giving you gas, soak the beans overnight in a pot of water and add one-quarter cup Heinz Apple Cider Vinegar. The following morning, wash the beans, refill the pot with fresh water and two tablespoons Heinz Apple Cider Vinegar, and cook as usual.

- **L'eggs Sheer Energy Panty Hose** and **McCormick Fennel Seed.** Another way to prevent beans from causing flatulence: Cut off the toe from a pair of used, clean L'eggs Sheer Energy Panty Hose, place one teaspoon McCormick Fennel Seed in the toe, and tie a knot to secure the open end closed. Soak the beans overnight in a pot of water with the sachet of fennel seed. In the morning, remove the sachet, pour out the water, and cook the beans in fresh water.

✻ Recipe Magic ✻

Bean Croquettes

- 1 can Heinz Baked Beans
- ¼ cup minced onion
- ¼ teaspoon Morton Salt
- ¼ teaspoon McCormick Black Pepper
- Progresso Breadcrumbs
- 1 egg, beaten
- Vegetable oil, for frying

Mash the Heinz Baked Beans with a fork; mix in the onion, Morton Salt, and McCormick Black Pepper; and shape into croquettes. Roll the croquettes in Progresso Breadcrumbs, dip them in the beaten egg, dip in breadcrumbs a second time, and then fry in vegetable oil until brown.

- **McCormick Curry Powder.** To enhance the flavor of canned baked beans, add some McCormick Curry Powder and mix well.

- **Star Olive Oil.** To prevent beans from boiling over the edge of the pot, add one tablespoon Star Olive Oil to the cooking water.

Beets

- **ReaLemon.** To help boiled beets retain their bright color, add one teaspoon ReaLemon lemon juice to the cooking water.

- **Heinz White Vinegar.** To keep beets bright red, add two tablespoons Heinz White Vinegar to the cooking water and boil the beets in their skins, leaving at least two inches of stem.

- **McCormick Cream of Tartar.** Prevent the red color of beets from fading by adding two teaspoons McCormick Cream of Tartar to the cooking water.

Berries

- **Dannon Yogurt.** To make Dannon Plain Yogurt or Dannon Vanilla Yogurt more interesting, drop in some fresh berries and stir well.

Food for Thought
CHILLING OUT

- Chill berries in the refrigerator before washing them to prevent the berries from absorbing too much water and becoming soggy.

Beverages

- **Canada Dry Club Soda.** Make inexpensive soft drinks by adding Canada Dry Club Soda to fruit juice for a delicious and healthy beverage.

- **Kool-Aid** and **Canada Dry Club Soda.** To make bubbly fruit drinks, mix Kool-Aid with Canada Dry Club Soda instead of water.
- **Tabasco Pepper Sauce** and **Coca-Cola.** To make a cola volcano, mix one or two drops Tabasco Pepper Sauce to a glass of Coca-Cola, stir well, add ice, and enjoy.

Biscuits

- **Crisco All-Vegetable Shortening.** The secret to making tender, flaky biscuits is to mix in one-third cup Crisco All-Vegetable Shortening for every two cups flour—and handle the biscuit dough as little as possible to prevent the shortening from melting.
- **McCormick Curry Powder.** To give biscuits a spicy zest, add one teaspoonful McCormick Curry Powder to the biscuit dough.
- **Pam Cooking Spray.** For browner biscuits, lightly spray the tops of the biscuit dough with butter-flavored Pam Cooking Spray before placing in the oven.

Bratwurst

- **Maxwell House Coffee** and **Budweiser.** To grill bratwurst over a barbecue or campfire, use a clean, empty Maxwell House Coffee can as a pot and grill the bratwurst in Budweiser beer.

Bread

Baking

- **Crisco All-Vegetable Shortening** and **Gold Medal Flour.** To make bread easy to remove from the pan after baking, grease the bread pan with a generous amount of Crisco All-Vegetable Shortening (instead of oil), and then dust the greased pan with Gold Medal Flour.

- **Heinz White Vinegar.** To bake a shiny loaf of bread, five minutes before the bread finishes baking, use a pastry brush to paint the top of the loaf with Heinz White Vinegar.

- **Land O Lakes Butter.** To give freshly baked bread a soft crust, spread Land O Lakes Butter on the warm crust.

- **Maxwell House Coffee.** A clean, empty eleven-ounce Maxwell House Coffee can doubles as an excellent pan for baking an eleven-ounce loaf of bread. Using a can opener, remove the bottom of the can. Grease the inside of the can thoroughly and dust with flour. Stand the can upright on a cake pan or cookie sheet, press the dough into the can, and cover the open end of the can with a clean, dry hand towel. Let the dough rise until it reaches or rises above the top of the can. Bake the dough in the can on the cake pan or cookie sheet in the oven just like any other bread. When you remove the finished bread from the oven, use a knife to slice off the protruding ends of the bread and gently shake the can to remove the cylindrical loaf.

- **Nestlé Carnation Nonfat Dry Milk.** To bake a loaf of bread with a shiny crust, mix one beaten egg, one teaspoon Nestlé Carnation Nonfat Dry Milk, and one tablespoon of water. Before putting the bread in the oven, use a pastry brush to paint the mixture on the top of the loaf.

- **Reynolds Wrap.** If a loaf of bread baking in the oven appears to be browning too fast, cover the loaf loosely with a sheet of Reynolds Wrap for the last twenty minutes of baking.

- **Wesson Oil.** To bake bread with a soft crust, use a pastry brush to give the top of the loaf a light coat with Wesson Oil several times while the bread bakes in the oven—or once after removing the finished bread from the oven but while the loaf remains warm.

Food for Thought
LOAFING AROUND

● To brown the sides of a loaf of bread similar to the top, bake the bread in an aluminum pan with a dull finish, a dark metal pan, or a glass pan. To give a shiny new bread pan a dull finish, bake the empty pan in an oven set at 350 degrees Fahrenheit.

● To prevent bread from getting a hard crust when baking, place a small pan of water in the oven along with the bread.

● After baking bread, remove the loaf from the pan and let cool on a rack. Allowing a freshly baked loaf of bread to cool in the pan results in soggy sides and a soggy bottom.

Bread Bags

● **Forster Clothespins.** To seal a bread bag firmly shut, use a Forster Clothespin to clip the bag closed.

Breadbaskets

● **Reynolds Wrap.** To keep bread warm in a breadbasket, line the basket with a sheet of Reynolds Wrap and cover the foil with a napkin. The aluminum foil reflects the heat of the bread.

Corn Bread

● **Crisco All-Vegetable Shortening** and **Quaker Yellow Corn Meal.** To prevent corn bread from sticking to the baking pan, grease the pan with Crisco All-Vegetable Shortening, and then powder it with Quaker Yellow Corn Meal.

Dough

● **Clabber Girl Baking Powder.** When making dough, use one teaspoon Clabber Girl Baking Powder for each cup of flour.

● **Crisco All-Vegetable Shortening.** To prevent dough from forming a crust while rising in the bowl, grease the bowl with Crisco

All-Vegetable Shortening, press the dough into the greased bowl, turn the dough upside down (with the greased side up), and cover.

- **Domino Sugar.** To give the bread a soft brown crust and make the bread dough rise quicker, add a little Domino Sugar to the dough.

- **Fleischmann's Yeast.** To make heavy bread dough (dark pumpernickel or whole wheat) rise quicker, double the amount of yeast used. The additional yeast will not affect the taste of the bread, although it may coarsen the texture slightly.

- **Glad Trash Bags.** To stimulate dough to rise, place the container holding the dough inside a clean, unused Glad Trash Bag and fold the ends of the plastic bag under the container.

- **Gold Medal Flour.** To prevent dough from sticking to your work surface when kneading, occasionally sprinkle a little Gold Medal Flour over the board.

✳ Recipe Magic ✳

Garlic Bread

- 2 large garlic cloves, smashed and minced
- 1 tablespoon McCormick Parsley Flakes
- ½ cup Land O Lakes Butter
- 1 loaf French or Italian bread

To make authentic garlic bread, mix the garlic, McCormick Parsley Flakes, and Land O Lakes Butter into a smooth paste; slice a loaf of French or Italian bread in half the long way (or cut the loaf into thick slices, but not all the way through to the bottom of the loaf, leaving them attached); and spread the mixture on the bread. Press the loaf back together and heat for five minutes in an oven preheated to 350 degrees Fahrenheit.

Food for Thought
WHAT THE WORLD KNEADS NOW

● To prevent a mixing bowl from sliding around on the countertop while you mix ingredients, place the bowl on a folded damp towel.

● To make dough rise in a cool room, place a small pan of hot water on a shelf in the oven, set the pan of dough on top of it, and shut the oven door until the dough rises.

● Force dough to rise in a cool room by placing the pan of dough on a heating pad set on medium.

● **Kingsford's Corn Starch.** To prevent pastry dough from sticking to the cutting board and rolling pin, sprinkle both those items with Kingsford's Corn Starch before rolling out the dough. The corn starch absorbs excess moisture and remains flavorless in the bread.

● **McCormick Curry Powder.** To spice up your bread, add one or more teaspoons McCormick Curry Powder to the dough.

● **Nestlé Carnation Nonfat Dry Milk.** Use milk as the liquid in bread dough if you like a velvety grain and browner crust.

● **Pam Cooking Spray.** To prevent pastry dough from sticking to the cutting board and rolling pin, give those two items a light coat of Pam Cooking Spray.

● **SueBee Honey.** To bake sweeter bread, substitute SueBee Honey for some or all of the sugar in the bread dough recipe. If you substitute honey for half of the sugar, reduce the amount of liquid in the recipe by one-fourth. If you substitute honey for all of the sugar, reduce the amount of liquid by half. Add one-half teaspoon Arm & Hammer Baking Soda for each cup of honey used, and reduce the oven temperature by 25 degrees Fahrenheit to prevent overbrowning.

● **ReaLemon.** To bake fluffy whole-wheat bread, add one tablespoon

ReaLemon lemon juice to the dough to make the bread rise higher. Oddly, you won't be able to taste the lemon in the finished bread.

- **Wesson Oil.** To make kneading heavy dough like pumpernickel, rye, or whole wheat easier, oil your hands first with a few drops of Wesson Oil.

- **Ziploc Storage Bags.** To avoid messy hands, knead the dough inside a large Ziploc Storage Bag, sealed securely shut. The dough will neither stick to the plastic nor dry out.

Reheating

- **Reynolds Wrap.** To rejuvenate a stale loaf of bread, mist the bread with water, wrap it in Reynolds Wrap, and heat it in an oven set at 350 degrees Fahrenheit for approximately eight minutes. To freshen a stale loaf of Italian or French bread, after eight minutes in the oven, carefully open the foil wrapping and continue heating the bread in the oven for another three to five minutes.

Rolls

- **Bounty Paper Towels.** To warm rolls in the microwave oven, wrap each roll in a sheet of Bounty Paper Towels. The paper towel absorbs moisture, preventing the rolls from getting soggy.

- **Domino Sugar.** To give rolls a beautiful glaze, dissolve one tablespoon Domino Sugar in one-quarter cup milk and brush the mixture on the rolls before baking them in the oven.

- **Knorr Beef Bouillon.** To give rolls an amber crust, dissolve two Knorr Beef Bouillon cubes in one-quarter cup of boiling water and use a pastry brush to paint this broth on the rolls before baking them in the oven.

- **Oral-B Dental Floss.** To cut dough for rolls into clean, neat slices, slide a strand of Oral-B Dental Floss under the roll, cross the two ends over the top of the roll, and pull.

- **Reynolds Wrap.** To keep rolls warmer longer in a breadbasket, place a sheet of Reynolds Wrap in the basket, cover with a napkin, and fill with rolls. The aluminum foil reflects the heat.

- **Reynolds Wrap.** To freshen stale rolls, mist them with water, wrap them loosely in Reynolds Wrap, and warm them in the oven (preheated to 350 degrees Fahrenheit) for roughly ten to fifteen minutes.

Yeast

- **Domino Sugar.** To test whether your yeast remains active, dissolve one teaspoon yeast and one-half teaspoon Domino Sugar in a cup of tepid water. If the mixture bubbles and foams lightly in five minutes, the yeast is alive.

Breadcrumbs

- **Kellogg's Corn Flakes.** For an excellent substitute for bread-crumbs, run Kellogg's Corn Flakes through the blender. (Or fill a Ziploc Storage Bag with the cereal and crush it into crumbs by running over it with a rolling pin.)

- **Lay's Potato Chips.** Potato chip crumbs make another wonderful substitute for breadcrumbs. Simply run over a bag of Lay's Potato Chips with a rolling pin, breaking the chips into whatever size crumbs you desire.

- **McCormick Oregano.** Season breadcrumbs with a few shakes of McCormick Oregano for a zesty flavor.

- **Nabisco Original Premium Saltine Crackers.** If you're all out of breadcrumbs, crush Nabisco Original Premium Saltine Crackers into crumbs and substitute three-quarters cup cracker crumbs for every cup of breadcrumbs demanded by a recipe.

- **Wonder Bread.** To make soft, fresh breadcrumbs, cut off the crust from day-old Wonder Bread (toast the bread lightly if desired) and crumble the bread gently. Rub the crumbled bread through a coarse strainer or run it through the blender or food processor.

Broccoli

- **Heinz White Vinegar.** To purge insects from broccoli, mix two tablespoons Heinz White Vinegar and one quart of cold water, soak the broccoli in the solution for fifteen minutes, and rinse clean.

- **Morton Salt.** Another way to purge insects from broccoli: Dissolve two tablespoons Morton Salt in one quart of cold water, soak the broccoli in the solution for fifteen minutes, and rinse clean.

- **Morton Salt.** Before adding broccoli to a casserole or mixed dish, partially cook the broccoli by boiling it for five minutes in water with a pinch of Morton Salt.

Food for Thought
THE WILD BUNCH

- One bunch of broccoli serves four adults.

- To assure that the broccoli stalks finish cooking at the same time as the flowerets, use a knife to cut an X from the top to the bottom of each stalk.

- To hasten the cooking of thick broccoli stalks, cut them in half lengthwise.

- Cooking a stalk of celery with broccoli prevents the broccoli from emitting a strong odor.

- **ReaLemon.** To revitalize wilted broccoli, cut an inch off the bottom of the stalk, mix one teaspoon ReaLemon lemon juice and two quarts of cool water, and soak the broccoli in the solution for thirty minutes to an hour.

- **Wonder Bread.** To minimize the pungent odors produced by cooking broccoli, place a slice or two of stale Wonder Bread in the cooking water. After cooking, discard the bread.

Brown Sugar

- **Arm & Hammer Baking Soda.** When substituting brown sugar for all or some of the white sugar in a cake recipe, add three-quarters teaspoon Arm & Hammer Baking Soda for every one cup brown sugar to counteract the acidity, which might otherwise prevent the cake from rising properly.

- **Grandma's Molasses** and **Domino Sugar.** To make brown sugar, mix one-quarter cup Grandma's Molasses (unsulfured mild) with one cup Domino Sugar.

- **Jet-Puffed Marshmallows.** To unclump hardened brown sugar, empty the brown sugar into a plastic airtight container, place a couple of Jet-Puffed Marshmallows on top of the sugar, seal the lid securely, and let sit for two or three days.

- **Saran Wrap** and **Forster Toothpicks.** To unclump brown sugar, place the brown sugar in a microwave-safe bowl, cover the bowl with Saran Wrap, and use a Forster Toothpick to poke a few holes in the middle of the plastic. Heat in the microwave for thirty seconds. Repeat if necessary.

- **Wonder Bread.** To revive a box of hardened brown sugar, empty the brown sugar into a plastic container, place a slice or two of Wonder Bread on top of the sugar, seal the lid on the container, and let sit for two or three weeks. The bread absorbs the problematic moisture from the brown sugar.

Brownies

- **Coca-Cola.** To bake delicious, moist brownies, substitute Coca-Cola for the water called for in the recipe.

- **Domino Brown Sugar.** To add a butterscotch flavor to brownies, substitute Domino Brown Sugar for the white sugar in the recipe.

- **Mr. Coffee Filters.** To separate brownies, place Mr. Coffee Filters between layers of brownies or cookies when serving on a plate to keep the layers from sticking to each other.

- **Reynolds Wrap.** To keep the tops of brownies moist, the moment you remove the pan from the oven, cover it with a sheet of Reynolds Wrap. The aluminum foil keeps the steam inside, which moistens the brownies.

Brussels Sprouts

- **McCormick Ground Nutmeg.** To give Brussels sprouts a wonderful flavor, add McCormick Ground Nutmeg to the dish.

- **Morton Salt.** To remove any insects hiding in the leaves of Brussels sprouts, dissolve one-quarter cup Morton Salt in one quart of water and soak the Brussels sprouts in the salty water for thirty minutes. Rinse clean in clear cold water.

- **Wonder Bread.** To prevent Brussels sprouts from exuding an unpleasant odor while cooking, place a slice of stale Wonder Bread in the water when cooking the Brussels sprouts to absorb the odor. When finished cooking, discard the bread.

Butter

- **Saran Wrap.** To cut butter smoothly into clean pats, cover the knife blade with Saran Wrap (or heat the blade).

- **Star Olive Oil.** To avoid burning butter when sautéing, add a few drops of Star Olive Oil to the melted butter. Or, if you don't mind the overpowering taste of olive oil, skip the butter and use only olive oil, which consists mostly of monounsaturated fat, unlike butter, which consists mostly of saturated fat.

- **Wesson Oil.** To cut calories and fat grams from your diet, substitute Wesson Oil for any butter called for in a recipe—using one-third less vegetable oil than butter. For instance, if a recipe calls for three tablespoons butter, substitute two tablespoons vegetable oil instead.

- **Ziploc Storage Bags.** To make decorative butter swirls, place a stick of softened butter in a Ziploc Storage Bag, snip off one of the bottom corners of the bag with a pair of scissors, and squeeze individual servings onto a cookie sheet. Refrigerate to harden the butter again.

Cabbage

- **Arm & Hammer Baking Soda.** To reduce the smell of cabbage while it cooks, add one-quarter teaspoon Arm & Hammer Baking Soda to the cooking water.

- **Heinz White Vinegar.** To minimize the odor of cooking cabbage, fill a drinking glass halfway with Heinz White Vinegar and set the glass near the stove. Vinegar absorbs odors.

- **Heinz White Vinegar.** To prevent red cabbage from turning purple while cooking, add one tablespoon Heinz White Vinegar for every two cups of cooking water.

- **Heinz White Vinegar.** To purge insects from cabbage, mix two tablespoons Heinz White Vinegar and one quart of cold water, soak the cabbage in the solution for fifteen minutes, and rinse clean.

- **Morton Salt.** Another way to purge insects from cabbage: Dissolve two tablespoons Morton Salt in one quart of cold water, soak the cabbage in the solution for fifteen minutes, and rinse clean.

- **Planters Walnuts.** To eliminate the odor of cooking cabbage, add a few unshelled Planters Walnuts to the cooking water in the pot.

- **ReaLemon.** To reduce the odor of cooking cabbage and simultaneously enhance the taste, mix two tablespoons ReaLemon lemon juice in the cooking water before adding the cabbage.

- **ReaLemon.** For another way to maintain the color of red cabbage while cooking, add one tablespoon ReaLemon lemon juice for every two cups of cooking water.

- **Wonder Bread.** To prevent cooked cabbage from exuding an odor, place a slice of stale Wonder Bread on top of the cabbage to absorb the odor. When finished cooking, discard the bread.

Food for Thought
TURNING A NEW LEAF

- One pound of cabbage yields five cups of raw, shredded cabbage.

- To remove cabbage leaves easily when preparing stuffed cabbage, bring a pot of water to boil, insert a fork into the base of the cabbage, and carefully dunk the head in the boiling water for one minute. Remove the head, drain, and gently pull off all softened leaves. Repeat the process until you have peeled off all the necessary leaves.

- Rather than boiling cabbage, shred the cabbage and steam it for ten minutes for fresher, quicker results.

- Cooking a stalk of celery with cabbage prevents the cabbage from emitting strong odors.

- To make cabbage leaves easy to peel off, freeze the cabbage head, and then let it thaw.

Cake

Angel Food Cake

- **Jell-O.** To add fruit flavor to angel food cake, substitute one packet of your favorite flavor Jell-O for the same amount of sugar in the recipe.

Baking

- **Bounty Paper Towels.** To prevent a cake from sticking to the pan, when you take the pan out of the oven, place it on a damp sheet of Bounty Paper Towels for several minutes. The dampness cools the pan and the cake, averting a sticky mess.

- **Bounty Paper Towels.** To remove parchment paper from the bottom of a cake, soak a sheet of Bounty Paper Towels with water, set the cake paper-side down on the saturated paper towel, and let sit until the edges of the parchment paper start to curl. At that point, lift up the cake and peel off the parchment paper.

- **Creamettes Spaghetti.** To test if a cake is done, insert an uncooked piece of Creamettes Spaghetti into the middle of the cake. If the piece of spaghetti comes out clean, the cake is ready.

- **Forster Toothpicks.** To test if a cake is finished baking, insert a Forster Toothpick into the center of the cake, and then pull it back out. If the toothpick comes out clean, the cake is done.

- **Maxwell House Coffee.** Use a clean, empty Maxwell House Coffee can as a cake pan. Fill the can with cake batter no higher than you would any other pan to assure that the cake bakes through properly. After the cake cools, store it in the can.

- **Reynolds Wrap.** To prevent cake from developing a hump while baking and remain level, cover the pan with a sheet of Reynolds Wrap before placing it in the oven. Remove the aluminum foil for the last ten to fifteen minutes to allow the top of the cake to brown.

Food for Thought
THAT TAKES THE CAKE

- To avoid getting holes in angel food cake, run a knife in a circular pattern through the batter in the pan, allowing the knife to touch the sides of the pan. This will free the air pockets—trapped in the batter near the walls of the pan, which will otherwise cause the holes during baking.

- If a cake (or cake layers) sticks to the bottom of the pan, reheat the pan in a warm oven for a few minutes. The heat will help separate the cake from the pan.

- To prevent the top of a cake from browning rapidly when baking, place a pan of warm water on the rack above the cake. The water keeps the top of the baking cake moist.

- **Reynolds Wrap.** To keep the top of a cake moist, the moment you remove the pan from the oven, cover it with a sheet of Reynolds Wrap. The aluminum foil contains the steam, moistening the cake.

Bananas

- **Mott's Apple Juice.** To prevent sliced bananas from burning inside a cake during baking, dip the slices in Mott's Apple Juice before adding them to the cake mix.

Batter

- **Arm & Hammer Baking Soda.** Substituting buttermilk for regular milk in a cake recipe yields a much lighter cake. However, when doing so, add one-quarter teaspoon Arm & Hammer Baking Soda to the dry ingredients for each one-half cup buttermilk used.

- **Gold Medal Flour.** To prevent nuts and raisins from sinking in a cake during baking, before adding the nuts and raisins to the batter, warm the nuts and raisins, place them in a Ziploc Storage Bag, add a little Gold Medal Flour, and shake well until the nuts and dried fruit are evenly coated with flour. Add the powdered ingredients to the nearly finished cake batter and mix well.

- **Land O Lakes Butter.** Another simple way to prevent nuts, fruit, and raisins from sinking to the bottom of the cake is to heat them gently in the oven and roll them in butter before adding them to the cake batter.

- **McCormick Anise Seed.** To add a delightful flavor to a sponge cake, mix one teaspoon McCormick Anise Seed into the batter.

- **McCormick Pure Vanilla Extract.** To enhance the taste of any cake whose recipe calls for vanilla extract, double the amount of McCormick Pure Vanilla Extract to give the cake an exquisite vanilla flavor.

- **Mott's Apple Juice** and **Arm & Hammer Baking Soda.** Try substituting Mott's Apple Juice for the milk called for in a recipe for cake batter. To reduce the acidity of the apple juice, add one-half teaspoon Arm & Hammer Baking Soda to the dry ingredients.

- **Mott's Applesauce.** To avoid using fats like butter, margarine, or oil in a cake mix, substitute an equal amount of Mott's Applesauce for the butter, margarine, or oil called for in the recipe. Applesauce works best with cake recipes that call for milk or fruit.

- **Reynolds Cut-Rite Wax Paper.** To prevent cake batters from spattering when using a mixer, cover the bowl with a piece of Reynolds Cut-Rite Wax Paper, cut two holes for the beater stems to fit through, insert the stems through the holes, and attach the beaters to the mixer.

- **SueBee Honey.** To make cake batter more delicious, substitute Sue-Bee Honey for the sugar called for in the recipe. If you substitute honey for half of the sugar, reduce the amount of liquid in the recipe by one-fourth. If

● To avoid making a mess on the kitchen countertop when mixing cake batter, place a damp kitchen towel on the floor of your sink and place the mixing bowl on top of it. The towel prevents the bowl from sliding around in the sink, and splashes and splatters will be confined to the sink.

● When mixing cake mix, put the water in the mixing bowl first, then add the powdered mix, and stir. This way, the water and powder mix evenly, and you won't end up with lumps of dry powder on the bottom of the bowl.

● To prevent a cake from cracking when baking, do not overbeat the cake mix. Overbeating adds excess air to the batter, which causes cracking during baking.

you replace all of the sugar with honey, reduce the amount of liquid by half. Add one-half teaspoon Arm & Hammer Baking Soda for each cup of honey used, and reduce the oven temperature by 25 degrees Fahrenheit to prevent overbrowning.

● **Tang.** Add between one-quarter and one-half cup Tang powdered drink mix to your cake mix for an "orange zest."

● **Wesson Oil.** To keep a cake mix moist and avoid crumbs, add two tablespoons Wesson Oil to the batter. If you wish to substitute Wesson Oil for solid vegetable shortening, use one-third less than the amount of solid shortening recommended.

● **Ziploc Storage Bags.** To mix cake batter, fill a gallon-size Ziploc Storage Bag with cake batter ingredients, and then squeeze the bag to mix.

Berries

● **McCormick Cinnamon Sugar.** Before adding frozen berries to cake batter, sprinkle McCormick Cinnamon Sugar on the berries. The cinnamon sugar enhances the taste of the berries and helps distribute them evenly throughout the batter.

Bundt Cakes

- **Crisco All-Vegetable Shortening** and **Domino Sugar.** To prevent Bundt cakes from sticking to the pan, grease the pan with Crisco All-Vegetable Shortening and then sprinkle the shortening with Domino Sugar. After baking, let the cake cool for ten minutes and remove it from the pan.

Candles

- **Creamettes Spaghetti.** For an easy way to light birthday candles on a cake without burning yourself, light the end of an uncooked stick of Creamettes Spaghetti and use it as a long matchstick.

- **Jet-Puffed Miniature Marshmallows.** To prevent wax from birthday candles from dripping all over the cake, use Jet-Puffed Miniature Marshmallows as candleholders.

Cheesecake

- **Breakstone's** or **Knudsen Sour Cream** and **Domino Sugar.** To cover up the cracked surface of a cheesecake, mix one cup Breakstone's or Knudsen Sour Cream with one tablespoon Domino Sugar and spread the mixture across the surface of the cheesecake to make an attractive and delicious topping. (Breakstone's is available in the eastern, southeastern, and midwestern United States; Knudsen is sold in the western United States.)

- **Hershey's Milk Chocolate Bar.** To cover up cracks in the surface of a cheesecake, slide a vegetable peeler along the side of a Hershey's Milk Chocolate Bar to make chocolate shavings and decorate the cracked surface of the cheesecake with the shaved shards of chocolate.

- **Oral-B Dental Floss.** To cut a cheesecake into neat, clean slices, use the technique embraced by fancy restaurants everywhere. Cut a strand of Oral-B Dental Floss a few inches longer than the diameter of the cake. Hold the ends of the strand in each hand, making the floss taut, and press the string down to cut the cake in half. Slide the floss out from under the bottom of the cake and repeat the process, cutting the cake into clean slices.

Chocolate Cake

- **Gold Medal Flour.** To remove the last bits of melted chocolate remaining in a pan, mix in a little Gold Medal Flour and add the floured remains into the cake batter.

- **Heinz White Vinegar.** To bake a moist and fluffy chocolate cake, add one teaspoon Heinz White Vinegar to the baking soda when mixing the batter. The vinegar helps neutralize the sharpness of the baking soda.

- **Hershey's Cocoa.** If you add Hershey's Cocoa to a cake recipe on your own accord, use two tablespoons less flour for every one–quarter cup cocoa you add.

- **Morton Salt.** To enhance the flavor of the chocolate, add a teaspoon Morton Salt to the batter.

Chocolate Slivers

- **Hershey's Milk Chocolate Bar.** If a recipe calls for chocolate slivers, make them yourself by running a potato peeler along the side of a Hershey's Milk Chocolate Bar.

Cooling

- **Bounty Paper Towels.** Cover the cake rack with a sheet of Bounty Paper Towels and set the cake on it to cool. The paper towel provides a buffer that allows the cake to take in air as it cools, so the cake remains moist.

Covers

- **Pam Cooking Spray.** To prevent Saran Wrap from sticking to a cake's icing, spray the underside of the plastic wrap with a thin coat of Pam Cooking Spray.

Cutting

- **Oral-B Dental Floss.** To cut clean slices of cake, hold a strand of Oral-B Dental Floss as if you were going to floss your teeth, and cut through the cake.

Dates

- **Gold Medal Flour.** To prevent chopped dates from sinking to the bottom of the cake during baking, toss the dates in Gold Medal Flour to give them a powdery coating before adding the dates to the batter.

Dusting

- **Hershey's Cocoa.** Instead of dusting cake pans with flour, dust them with Hershey's Cocoa to give the finished cake an added boost of chocolate.

Egg Substitute

- **Arm & Hammer Baking Soda** and **Heinz White Vinegar.** If you run out of eggs while mixing up batter for a cake, substitute one teaspoon Arm & Hammer Baking Soda and one teaspoon Heinz White Vinegar for each egg.

Flour Substitutes

- **Pillsbury Softasilk Cake Flour.** If you're all out of all-purpose flour, substitute one cup and two tablespoons Pillsbury Softasilk Cake Flour for each cup all-purpose flour needed.
- **Gold Medal Flour.** If you run short of cake flour, use one cup minus two tablespoons Gold Medal All-Purpose Flour for each cup cake flour needed.

- **Gold Medal Flour, Clabber Girl Baking Powder,** and **Morton Salt.** If you need a substitute for self-rising flour, in a measuring cup mix 1½ teaspoons Clabber Girl Baking Powder, one-half teaspoon Morton Salt, and fill the rest of the cup with Gold Medal All-Purpose Flour.

Freezing

- **Reynolds Wrap.** Slice leftover cake into appropriate-sized servings and place them on a plate in the freezer, unwrapped. The next day, use a spatula to remove each individually frozen slice and wrap them one by one in their own piece of Reynolds Wrap. To serve, remove the number of slices you need, unwrap the foil, and let defrost.

Greasing and Flouring

- **Crisco All-Vegetable Shortening.** When greasing a cake pan, use solid Crisco All-Vegetable Shortening rather than vegetable oil, which tends to burn, particularly on exposed surfaces.

- **Crisco All-Vegetable Shortening, Wesson Oil,** and **Gold Medal Flour.** Instead of greasing and flouring the inside of cake pans the traditional way, mix five ounces Crisco All-Vegetable Shortening, one ounce Wesson Oil, and one ounce Gold Medal Flour in a bowl until creamy. Grease the inside of cake pans with the mixture and refrigerate any excess in an airtight container.

- **Gold Medal Flour.** After greasing a cake pan with vegetable shortening, sprinkle a little Gold Medal Flour into the pan, tilt the pan on different angles to give the sides and bottom a light coat of flour, and then empty any excess flour into the sink. Pour the cake batter into the pan and bake. The prepared pan allows the cake to rise more evenly and makes removing the finished cake much easier.

- **Reynolds Cut-Rite Wax Paper.** To avoid greasing a cake pan, place each pan on a sheet of Reynolds Cut-Rite Wax Paper, trace around the bottom of the pan, cut out the waxed paper circle, and place it in the pan. After baking and cooling, loosen the sides of the cake with a knife. Invert the cake onto a cooling rack, remove the pan, and peel off the waxed paper to reveal a smooth surface ready to frost.

- **Ziploc Storage Bags.** Wear a Ziploc Storage Bag as a glove to grease or butter the inside of a cake pan. When you're finished, turn the bag inside out—to avoid getting any left-over shortening or butter on yourself— and discard the bag.

Icing

- **Betty Crocker Devil's Food Cake Mix.** Instead of using cocoa to make icing, use Betty Crocker Devil's Food Cake Mix for a rich, chocolate flavor.

- **Clabber Girl Baking Powder.** When making frosting from powdered sugar, mix in a pinch of Clabber Girl Baking Powder. The sodium bicarbonate prevents the frosting from solidifying and cracking.

- **Conair Hair Dryer.** To set icing on a cake, turn a Conair Hair Dryer on warm and dry the frosting.

- **Dole Crushed Pineapple** and **Jell-O Instant Vanilla Pudding Mix.** For an excellent icing for lemon cake, mix a twenty-ounce can Dole Crushed Pineapple (including the juice) with the contents of a 5.1-ounce box Jell-O Instant Vanilla Pudding Mix.

- **Domino Confectioners Sugar.** To prevent icing from soaking into the cake, sprinkle a light coat of Domino Confectioners Sugar over the cake before spreading the icing.

- **Domino Confectioners Sugar.** To decorate a cake without using frosting, fold a Mr. Coffee Filter in half several times and use a pair of scissors to cut tiny holes

Where Did German Chocolate Cake Originate?

In 1852, an Englishman named Samuel German, a senior chocolate maker at Walter Baker & Company in Dorchester, Massachusetts, developed a bittersweet chocolate baking bar. The company named the product Baker's German's Sweet Chocolate in honor of Samuel German. In 1957, more than a century later, a Texas homemaker sent a recipe for "German's Chocolate Cake" to a Dallas newspaper, which published the recipe. The resulting spike in German's Sweet Chocolate sales prompted General Foods (then owners of Baker's Chocolate) to send copies of the recipe and photos of the cake to newspapers across the nation. Sales of German's Sweet Chocolate jumped 73 percent. In 1958, General Foods renamed the recipe German Sweet Chocolate Cake and began printing it on the wrapper of every bar of German's Sweet Chocolate. Most recipes for the cake drop the apostrophe and the letter *s* from the word *German's*, propagating the fallacy that the cake is German.

along the folds. When opened, the coffee filter will look like a snowflake. Center the paper snowflake on top of the cake and sprinkle a light coat of Domino Confectioners Sugar on it, filling all the openings in the snowflake. Then carefully lift the coffee filter to reveal an elaborate, symmetrical design on the cake.

● **Forster Toothpicks.** Before decorating on cake frosting, use a Forster Toothpick to trace your message or designs on the cake. Use a French's Mustard bottle (see page 114) or Ziploc Storage Bag (see page 115) to pipe the icing.

● **Forster Toothpicks.** If the top layer of a double-layer cake continually slides off the bottom layer as you attempt to ice it, secure the top layer in place by inserting three or four Forster Toothpicks through the layers, spaced far apart from each other. Be sure to remove the toothpicks before serving the cake.

- **French's Mustard.** To decorate a cake with frosting, fill a clean, empty French's Mustard squeeze bottle with icing and use it to decorate or write your message on the cake.

- **Hershey's Cocoa** and **Land O Lakes Butter.** If you don't have any baking chocolate to make chocolate icing, substitute one-third cup Hershey's Cocoa and one tablespoon melted Land O Lakes Butter for every two ounces chocolate called for by the recipe.

- **Jif Peanut Butter.** To make chocolate–peanut butter frosting, simply mix one tablespoon Jif Creamy Peanut Butter into chocolate frosting.

- **Kingsford's Corn Starch.** To make incredibly smooth frosting, add one teaspoon Kingsford's Corn Starch to the mixture.

- **Kool-Aid.** To make virtually any color icing you desire (red for Valentine's Day, green for St. Patrick's Day, orange for Halloween), mix one packet of your choice of any flavor Kool-Aid drink mix with powdered sugar frosting.

- **Morton Salt.** To prevent icing from becoming granular, add a pinch Morton Salt to the sugar.

- **ReaLemon.** To keep icing soft and pliable when beating, add a few drops ReaLemon lemon juice when mixing up the frosting. The lemon juice prevents the icing from hardening and granulating.

Food for Thought
THE ICING ON THE CAKE

- Before adding frosting to a cake, chill the cake in the refrigerator. It's easier to frost a cold cake.

- When icing a cake, put on a thin base coat first, let set, and then apply a second, more luxurious layer.

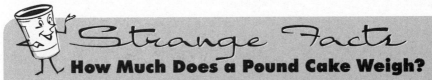

Strange Facts

How Much Does a Pound Cake Weigh?

Originating several centuries ago in England, the pound cake was named for the one pound of butter, one pound of sugar, one pound of eggs, and one pound of flour it contained. Instead of using yeast to leaven the cake, the cook whipped air into the batter. In the twentieth century, chefs added baking powder or baking soda to the recipe and altered the proportions of the original ingredients, to produce a lighter cake. Still, today's typical pound cake weighs considerably more than one pound.

- **ReaLemon.** To thin thick icing and improve its texture, add a few drops ReaLemon lemon juice and mix well.

- **Reynolds Cut-Rite Wax Paper.** To ice a cake without getting any icing on the cake plate, cut triangles from a sheet of Reynolds Cut-Rite Wax Paper and arrange them, overlapping slightly, to form a circle on the cake plate. Place the cake on top of this waxed-paper arrangement. After icing the cake, gently pull the triangles of waxed paper from under the cake.

- **Ziploc Storage Bags.** To pipe icing on a cake, fill a Ziploc Storage Bag with icing, twist the bag to force icing to one corner, seal, and use scissors to snip a small bit off the corner. Squeeze out icing to make polka dots or squiggles or to write names. Use a separate bag for each color.

- **Ziploc Storage Bags** and **Hershey's Semi-Sweet Chocolate Chips.** To decorate cookies and cakes with melted chocolate, fill a Ziploc Storage Bag with Hershey's Semi-Sweet Chocolate Chips, seal the bag shut, and place in a pot of boiling water to melt the chocolate. Use a pair of scissors to snip off one corner and pipe the melted chocolate to decorate the cookies or cake.

Layers

- **Creamettes Spaghetti.** Before icing a layered cake, insert a few uncooked sticks of Creamettes Spaghetti into the cake to secure the layers in place. When you finish decorating the cake, remove the spaghetti.

- **Saran Wrap** and **Oral-B Dental Floss.** Instead of pouring the batter into several cake pans to make different layers, bake one thick layer, let cool, and remove from the pan. Wrap the layer in Saran Wrap and freeze it. Hold a strand of Oral-B Dental Floss as if you were going to floss your teeth and slice the frozen cake neatly into layers.

Moistness

- **Saran Wrap.** To make an exceptionally moist and tender cake, wrap the finished cake tightly in Saran Wrap and let sit for twenty-four hours before serving. The plastic wrap seals in the moistness.

Molds

- **Domino Brown Sugar.** To bake a cake in a Jell-O mold, grease and flour the mold thoroughly, and then sprinkle the bottom of the mold well with brown sugar before pouring in the batter. The detailed design on the bottom of the mold will be transferred to the top of the cake, glazed with brown sugar.

Oil Substitute

- **Miracle Whip.** If you run out of vegetable oil when mixing up cake batter, simply add the same amount of Miracle Whip, which contains oil and doesn't affect the taste of the finished cake. (The Miracle Whip Chocolate Cake, developed by consumers during World War II food rationing, has been the most requested recipe from the Kraft Kitchens.)

Plates

- **Domino Confectioners Sugar.** To prevent a cake from sticking to its serving plate, sprinkle the cake plate with Domino Confectioners Sugar before placing the cake on it.

- **Reynolds Wrap.** To make a disposable cake plate, cover an old vinyl record album with Reynolds Wrap.

Raisins

- **Land O Lakes Butter.** Before adding raisins to cake batter, roll the raisins in Land O Lakes Butter to prevent them from sinking to the bottom.

Sauce

- **Kingsford's Corn Starch.** To make a delicious sauce for cakes, save the liquids drained from canned fruits, thicken to the consistency of cream with a little Kingsford's Corn Starch, and heat.

Sponge Cake

- **McCormick Anise Seed.** To add a delightful flavor to a sponge cake, mix one teaspoon McCormick Anise Seed to the batter.

- **Tang.** To give a sponge cake a zesty flavor, mix two tablespoons Tang powdered drink mix to the water before making the batter.

Sugar

- **SueBee Honey.** To reduce the amount of sugar in a cake recipe, substitute half the sugar with SueBee Honey, add one-half teaspoon Arm & Hammer Baking Soda for each cup of honey used, reduce the amount of liquid in the recipe by one-quarter cup for each cup of honey used, and reduce the oven temperature by 25 degrees Fahrenheit to prevent overbrowning.

Candy

- **Kingsford's Corn Starch.** After placing hard candy in a serving bowl, sift a bit of Kingsford's Corn Starch over the candy to prevent it from sticking together and to the bowl.

- **Land O Lakes Butter.** To prevent liquid from boiling over when boiling homemade candy, before you get started, butter about one inch around the inside of the top edge of the pot.

Colorful Rock Candy

- 2 cups Domino Sugar
- 1 packet Kool-Aid (any flavor)

Fill a clean, empty jar with one-quarter cup boiling water and slowly add the Domino Sugar and the Kool-Aid powder. Stir well. Attach a clean nail to one end of a string and a pencil to the other end of the string. Place the pencil on the mouth of the jar so the nail hangs down into the thick sugar water without touching the bottom of the jar. Place the jar in a warm place and let sit for a few days. As the water evaporates, colorful rocklike sugar crystals form on the string.

- **Mr. Coffee Filters.** To make party favors, place candy in the middle of Mr. Coffee Filters and tie the sides together with ribbons.

Cantaloupe

- **Morton Salt.** Sprinkling cantaloupe with Morton Salt gives the melon an exquisite taste.

- **ReaLemon.** To enhance the taste of cantaloupe, sprinkle the orange flesh of the fruit with a few drops of ReaLemon lemon juice.

- **Saran Wrap.** A sliced cantaloupe readily absorbs odor from other foods. To prevent this, wrap the fruit tightly with Saran Wrap before storing it in the refrigerator.

Carrots

- **Forster Toothpicks.** To make carrot curls, peel a carrot, cut off one-half inch of the thin end of the carrot, and then use the peeler to peel the

Strange Facts

Are All Carrots Orange?

Carrots originated around 3000 b.c.e. in what is present-day Afghanistan, and they were originally white, purple, red, yellow, green, and black—not orange. In the fourteenth century, southern Europeans imported purple, white, and yellow carrots. Flemish refugees introduced carrots to England in the fifteenth century. In the sixteenth century, the Dutch bred orange carrots, containing the pigment carotene, to match the colors of the royal House of Orange as an emblem in the struggle for Dutch independence. By the eighteenth century, Holland had become the leading country in carrot breeding. Dutch breeders crossed pale yellow carrots with red varieties containing anthocyanin to produce orange-colored roots, employing successive hybridization to intensify the orange color. Today's widely distributed orange carrot is a direct descendant of those Dutch-bred carrots, yet white, yellow, red, and purple carrots are still grown throughout the world.

carrot lengthwise into long, thin slivers. Curl the sliver as tightly as possible, insert a Forster Toothpick through the curl to hold it in place, and place the curl in a bowl of ice water. Place the bowl in the refrigerator for eight hours (or overnight). Remove the curls from the ice water, remove the toothpicks, and use the curls as garnish.

Food for Thought
CARROT TOPS

- One pound carrots yields approximately four cups sliced or diced carrots.

- Use a potato or carrot peeler to shave off thin strips as a colorful topping for salads.

- To peel carrots with ease, scrub the carrots clean, boil the carrots in water for five minutes, and then place the carrots in cold water. The skins rub off easily.

- To firm up limp raw carrots, soak them in ice cold water for thirty minutes.

Cauliflower

- **Domino Sugar.** To keep cauliflower white when cooking, add one teaspoon Domino Sugar to the cooking water.

- **Heinz White Vinegar.** Another simple way to keep cauliflower white when cooking is to add one teaspoon Heinz White Vinegar to the cooking water.

- **Heinz White Vinegar.** To purge insects from cauliflower, mix two tablespoons Heinz White Vinegar and one quart of cold water, soak the cauliflower in the solution for fifteen minutes, and rinse clean.

- **Morton Salt.** Another way to remove insects from cauliflower: Dissolve two tablespoons Morton Salt in one quart of cold water, soak the cauliflower in the solution with the florets facing down for fifteen minutes, and rinse clean.

- **Nestlé Carnation Nonfat Dry Milk.** For yet another way to keep cauliflower bright white, add one tablespoon Nestlé Carnation Nonfat Dry Milk to the cooking water.

- **Planters Walnuts.** To eliminate any pungent odors when cooking cauliflower, place a few unshelled Planters Walnuts into the pot of cooking water.

Food for Thought
CAULIFLOWER POWER

- One cauliflower yields three to four vegetable servings for adults.

- Cooking cauliflower in an aluminum pot will darken the cauliflower.

- To add cauliflower to a casserole or other dish that requires baking or cooking, parboil the cauliflower for eight minutes, drain, and cool the cauliflower in a pot of cold water. Otherwise, the cauliflower will dry out when baked or cooked in the casserole.

- **ReaLemon.** Cauliflower will remain white when cooking if you add one teaspoon ReaLemon lemon juice to the cooking water before adding the cauliflower.

- **Wonder Bread.** To prevent odors from pervading the house when cooking cauliflower, place a slice of stale Wonder Bread on top of the cauliflower as you steam the vegetable. The bread absorbs the odors.

Celery

- **Jif Peanut Butter** and **Sun-Maid Raisins.** To make "Ants on a Log," fill celery stalks with Jif Peanut Butter and sprinkle with Sun-Maid Raisins.

- **Philadelphia Cream Cheese.** For a nice appetizer or snack, fill celery stalks with Philadelphia Cream Cheese.

- **ReaLemon.** To prevent celery from turning brown, mix one teaspoon

Food for Thought
GETTING FRESH

- To make celery curls, cut cleaned celery into four-inch lengths. Fringe each piece by cutting narrow six to eight slices lengthwise, leaving an inch uncut at the end to hold the celery piece together. Place the pieces in a bowl of ice water for thirty minutes or more, until the strips of celery curl.

- Rather than discarding celery leaves, chop them up to use in soups and stews and to garnish salads.

- To trim celery strings quickly and efficiently, use a knife with a short blade to scrape the celery stalk from top to bottom.

- To revitalize limp celery, place the stalks in a bowl of ice water, add a few slices of raw potato, and let sit for one hour. Or trim the bottom of the stalks, stand them in a tall drinking glass filled with cold water, and refrigerate for several hours.

ReaLemon lemon juice per one quart of cold water in a pitcher and stand the celery in the solution in the refrigerator. If the celery begins to wilt in the refrigerator, perk it up by following the same instructions.

- **Reynolds Wrap.** To prolong the shelf life of trimmed celery for weeks, wrap the celery stalk in Reynolds Wrap when storing it in the refrigerator.

Cereals

- **Pam Cooking Spray.** When cooking hot cereal such as Cream of Wheat or Quaker Oats with milk, spray the pan with Pam Cooking Spray to prevent the dish from sticking to the inside of the pot.

✳ Recipe Magic ✳

Cheerios Treats

- 1 teaspoon Crisco All-Vegetable Shortening
- 3 tablespoons Blue Bonnet Margarine
- 6 cups Jet-Puffed Miniature Marshmallows
- ½ cup Jif Peanut Butter (creamy or chunky)
- 1 cup M&M's Chocolate Candies
- 5 cups Cheerios

Grease a rectangular pan (13 x 9 x 2 inches) with Crisco All-Vegetable Shortening. Microwave the Blue Bonnet Margarine in a large microwaveable bowl on high for 45 seconds, or until melted. Add the Jet-Puffed Miniature Marshmallows. Toss to coat with margarine. Microwave on high for 45 seconds, stir, and then microwave for another 45 seconds (or until smooth when stirred). Stir in the Jif Peanut Butter and M&M's Chocolate Candies. Immediately add the Cheerios cereal. Mix until well coated. Using a greased spatula, press the mixture into the prepared pan. Cool. Cut into squares. Makes about 24.

● To enhance cottage cheese, top with grated carrot or mix the cottage cheese with slices of banana.

Cheese

Cottage Cheese

● **Dole Pineapple Chunks.** To enhance cottage cheese, top with Dole Pineapple Chunks.

● **McCormick Curry Powder.** To spice up cottage cheese, mix in one teaspoon (or more) McCormick Curry Powder.

Cream Cheese

● **Breakstone's** or **Knudsen Cottage Cheese.** To make a substitute for cream cheese or sour cream in a dip recipe, blend cottage

✳ Recipe Magic ✳

Low-Cal Lunch

- 1 cup Breakstone's or Knudsen Cottage Cheese
- 1 apple, sliced or cubed
- 1 stalk celery, sliced
- ⅛ cup Sun-Maid Raisins
- 1 large leaf lettuce

To make a low-calorie lunch, mix Breakstone's or Knudsen Cottage Cheese and the apple, celery, and Sun-Maid Raisins, and place on a bed of lettuce.

WHAT'S COOKING

GRATE IDEAS

● To clean a cheese grater, rub the grater with a raw potato to push the chunks of cheese from the holes.

● If you don't have a grater, you can grate soft cheese by using a potato masher to force the cheese through a colander.

● Use a potato peeler or carrot peeler to cut cheese into decorative strips to be added to salads or as a garnish to any meal.

● To make soft cheese easier to grate, place it in the freezer for fifteen minutes before grating. Grating cheese is easier when the cheese is cold.

● Freezing Parmesan cheese or Romano cheese makes it easier to grate.

cheese in a blender until it reaches the consistency of sour cream. (Breakstone's is available in the eastern, southeastern, and midwestern United States; Knudsen is sold in the western United States.)

● **Dannon Yogurt.** To thin cream cheese for use in dips, mix the cream cheese with Dannon Plain Nonfat Yogurt.

● **Dannon Yogurt, Mr. Coffee Filters,** and **Saran Wrap.** For a nonfat alternative to cream cheese, place a Mr. Coffee Filter inside a small strainer and sit it inside a bowl. Fill the coffee filter with Dannon Plain Nonfat Yogurt. Cover the strainer and bowl with a sheet of Saran Wrap and refrigerate overnight (or at least eight hours). The moisture drains from the yogurt, leaving a thick paste that spreads like cream cheese.

● **Jell-O.** To enhance the taste of cream cheese, spread the cream cheese on your bagel, English muffin, or toast, and then sprinkle with your favorite flavor of Jell-O powder.

- To harden any firm cheese for grating, simply expose the cheese to air.

- Excellent cheeses for grating and sprinkling on casseroles and vegetable dishes include Cheddar, Gruyère, Parmesan, Swiss, and Romano.

- Grating cheese yourself costs half as much as purchasing grated cheese, and the flavor of freshly grated cheese far surpasses factory-grated cheeses.

- To grate extremely dry cheese into fine grains, slice the cheese into small chunks and use a blender to grate the cheese.

- Toss grated cheese into a hot dish immediately before serving to prevent the heat from the dish from making the grated cheese stringy.

- Four ounces of cheese yields one cup of grated cheese.

- To avoid injuring your fingers when grating cheese, wear a metal thimble on each endangered finger.

- **McCormick Food Coloring.** To color cream cheese for various holidays, add a few drops of McCormick Food Coloring and mix well.

- **Ziploc Storage Bags.** Rather than warming cream cheese in the microwave oven where it might melt, seal the container or block of cream cheese inside a Ziploc Storage Bag and submerge it in warm water for five minutes, allowing the warmth of the water to soften the cream cheese.

Grating

- **Bounty Paper Towels.** To dry a block of cheese for grating, wrap the block tightly in a sheet of Bounty Paper Towels and set on a counter in room temperature. After the paper towel absorbs sufficient oil from the cheese, discard the paper towel and repeat the process with fresh sheets of Bounty Paper Towels as many times as you deem desirable.

Cheese Croutons

- French bread
- Star Olive Oil
- Crumbled Cheddar, chèvre, or any semisoft cheese.

To top soups with cheese croutons, place cubes of French bread on a cookie sheet; sprinkle with a few drops of Star Olive Oil and bits of crumbled Cheddar, chèvre, or any semisoft cheese; and heat under the broiler until the cheese melts. Let cool and add to the soup.

- **Gold Medal Flour.** When grating cheese, you can prevent the grated cheese from sticking to the inside of a bowl by dusting the inside of the bowl with Gold Medal Flour.

- **Pam Cooking Spray.** Before grating cheese, spray the grater with a thin coat of Pam Cooking Spray to make cleaning the grater easier. Reapply as needed.

- **Playtex Living Gloves.** To avoid injuring your fingers when grating cheese, wear thick Playtex Living Gloves.

- **Wesson Oil.** To make cleaning the grater less cumbersome, use a pastry brush to paint a thin coat of Wesson Oil on the grater before grating any cheese.

Grilled Cheese Sandwiches

- **Reynolds Wrap.** To make a grilled cheese sandwich, wrap a cheese sandwich in Reynolds Wrap and iron each side with a clothes iron until golden brown.

Hardening

- **Land O Lakes Butter.** To prevent a sliced block of cheese from drying out and hardening, butter the cut end with a thin coat of Land O Lakes Butter, and then wrap the cheese in a sheet of Saran Wrap or place it inside a Ziploc Storage Bag.

- **Knudsen Buttermilk.** Soaking a block of hardened cheese in Knudsen Buttermilk softens the cheese.

- **Reynolds Wrap.** To prevent cheese from drying out, wrap the block of cheese in Reynolds Wrap. The aluminum foil also keeps the fragrance in the cheese, rather than spreading the odor throughout the refrigerator.

- **Star Wine Vinegar.** To flavor and refresh a block of cheese, saturate a cloth with Star Wine Vinegar, wrap it around the cheese, and store in an airtight container in the refrigerator.

Slicing

- **Oral-B Dental Floss.** To cut cheese into nice, clean slices, wrap a long piece of Oral-B Dental Floss around your opposing forefingers as if you were going to floss your teeth and press it through the block of cheese.

Food for Thought
ANY WAY YOU SLICE IT

- When slicing cheese, a dull knife actually cuts through cheese with greater ease than a sharp knife. Warming the knife enables the utensil to glide through the cheese like butter.

Straining

- **L'eggs Sheer Energy Panty Hose.** To strain homemade cheese, boil a clean, used pair of L'eggs Sheer Energy Panty Hose in water, let cool, and use to strain cheese before pressing.

WHAT'S COOKING

SAY CHEESE!

● To make a crust of cheese that floats on top of the soup, use freshly grated Cheddar, Gruyère, Parmesan, Swiss, or Romano cheese. Store-bought grated cheese, when added to soup, merely turns the soup cloudy.

● When cooking with hard, dry cheeses like Cheddar, Parmesan, or Romano, grate the cheese before attempting to melt it for sauces and recipes, enabling the cheese to melt faster and more uniformly.

● When cooking with processed cheeses, cut the cheese into cubes. Processed cheeses melt faster than natural cheeses.

● When heated, soft cheeses tend to liquefy while hard cheeses remain more malleable, solidifying, when cooled, into a firm topping.

● To melt cheese smoothly in a milk sauce, add the cheese to the cold milk and heat them together slowly, stirring continuously.

● Never cook cheese at a high temperature; otherwise it turns tough and stringy. To avoid high temperatures, cook cheese sauce in a double boiler.

● To melt cheese over a vegetable dish, cook the vegetable first, and then place a slice of cheese over the cooked vegetable, place it in the oven, and heat until the cheese melts.

● When baking casseroles and other dishes, sprinkle the grated cheese over the dish ten minutes prior to completion.

● When cooking with cheese on a stove, use low to medium heat for a short period of time. Cheese separates when cooked over high heat or for a lengthy period of time.

Chicken

Broiling

● **Arm & Hammer Baking Soda.** If the fat from broiling chicken catches fire, throw a handful of Arm & Hammer Baking Soda on the flames

● When cooking cheese dishes in a microwave oven, use a lower power setting to prevent the cheese from separating.

LEFTOVERS

● To make a tasty cheese sauce from leftover cheeses, mix a small amount of skim milk and the cut-up chunks of leftover cheese in a double boiler, warm over a low heat, and stir continuously (to prevent the cheese from separating or becoming stringy). Use the cheese sauce to top noodles or vegetables.

SERVING

● Serve cheese at room temperature. To do so, remove cheese from the refrigerator one hour before serving. (When using a large block of cheese, cut off the amount you anticipate using and keep the remainder refrigerated to avoid unnecessary spoilage.)

● To break Roquefort cheese into crumbly cubes, slice the cheese with a fork.

● To enhance the flavor of any hard cheese, warm the block of cheese in the microwave oven for ten seconds.

● Aged cheeses have a more intense flavor than younger cheeses, which tend to demand additional seasoning.

● To create an alluring cheese tray, serve no more than five different cheeses of different sizes, shapes, flavors, and textures, providing individual knives for each cheese. Avoid placing pungent cheeses next to mild-flavored cheeses.

● Garnish a cheese tray with apple slices, pear slices, grapes, strawberries, fresh figs, and melon slices.

to extinguish the fire. The sodium bicarbonate in baking soda is the same ingredient found in fire extinguishers.

● **Land O Lakes Butter.** To prevent a broiler chicken from drying out in the oven, coat the chicken with Land O Lakes Butter before cooking and baste frequently.

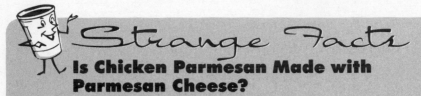

Is Chicken Parmesan Made with Parmesan Cheese?

Chicken Parmesan is made with slices of mozzarella cheese, which are melted over breaded chicken breasts topped with tomato sauce. The famous Italian dish is named after the city of Parma, Italy, where the recipe originated. Parmesan cheese is called Parmigiano-Reggiano in Italian because the cheese originated in the areas outside the cities of Parma and Reggio-Emilia, in Emilia-Romagna, Italy. Parmesan is the French word for Parmigiano.

- **Miracle Whip.** To give broiled chicken a crisp brown crust, rub Miracle Whip over the skin before cooking.

- **Morton Salt** and **Bounty Paper Towels.** To make cleaning the broiler pan easier, immediately after removing chicken from the broiler, sprinkle the pan with Morton Salt, and then cover with wet Bounty Paper Towels. Let sit until you're ready to wash the dishes.

- **Oral-B Dental Floss.** To truss a chicken, tie the ends of the drumsticks together with a strand of Oral-B Dental Floss.

- **Playtex Living Gloves.** To lift a cooked chicken out of a pot or pan, put on a pair of Playtex Living Gloves and use your hands.

- **ReaLemon.** To prevent a broiled chicken from drying out during cooking, use a pastry brush to paint the uncooked chicken with ReaLemon lemon juice. The lemon juice flavors the chicken and keeps it moist in the oven.

- **ReaLemon** and **Morton Salt.** To deodorize uncooked chicken and improve the taste as well, mix two tablespoons ReaLemon lemon juice and one-quarter teaspoon Morton Salt and massage the solution into the skin of the plucked fowl.

- **Reynolds Wrap** and **Forster Toothpicks.** To reduce the mess when broiling chicken, line a cake or pie tin with Reynolds Wrap, and then stretch a second sheet of Reynolds Wrap taut across the top of the tin, crimping the edges over the rim. Using a Forster Toothpick, perforate the stretched sheet of Reynolds Wrap with a few small holes for drainage and broil the chicken on this surface. When finishing cooking, discard the aluminum foil.

- **Wonder Bread.** When broiling chicken, place a few slices of Wonder Bread under the rack in the broiling pan. The bread will absorb fat drippings, reducing smoke and the possibility of the grease catching fire.

Croquettes

- **Gold Medal Flour.** To make chicken croquettes easier to handle, dust your hands with Gold Medal Flour.

- **Kellogg's Corn Flakes.** For an excellent alternative for breadcrumbs for chicken croquettes, run Kellogg's Corn Flakes through the blender. (Or fill a Ziploc Storage Bag with the cereal and crush it into crumbs by running over it with a rolling pin.) Simply roll the chicken croquettes in the corn flake crumbs.

- **Lay's Potato Chips.** For another tasty alternative to breadcrumbs, run a rolling pin over a bag of Lay's Potato Chips to make fine crumbs, and then roll the chicken croquettes in the potato chip crumbs.

- **Nabisco Original Premium Saltine Crackers.** To make chicken croquettes, grind Nabisco Original Premium Saltine Crackers in a blender (or place in a Ziploc Storage Bag and run over with a rolling pin) and combine with the chicken in the croquettes.

Defrosting

- **Morton Salt.** To thaw a frozen chicken in the refrigerator, dissolve one-third cup Morton Salt to one gallon of cold water and immerse the chicken in the salty water. The salt draws out the blood, so the breast meat, when cooked, will be absolutely white.

Deodorizing

- **ReaLemon** and **Morton Salt.** To eliminate fetid odors from chicken, wash the bird with ReaLemon lemon juice and rub it with Morton Salt.

Frying

- **Arm & Hammer Baking Soda.** To give fried chicken a crisper and more delicate coating, add one teaspoon Arm & Hammer Baking Soda to the batter.

- **Bounty Paper Towels.** Before preparing chicken parts for frying, use a few sheets of Bounty Paper Towels to dry the raw chicken thoroughly. Otherwise, the moisture from the chicken, combined with the hot fat, will give the coating a tough crust.

- **Bounty Paper Towels.** To extract excess oil from fried chicken before serving, gently press the fried chicken between sheets of Bounty Paper Towels.

- **Clabber Girl Baking Powder** and **Canada Dry Club Soda.** To make a light and delicate crust on fried chicken, add three-quarters teaspoon Clabber Girl Baking Powder to the batter and substitute Canada Dry Club Soda for any liquid called for in the recipe. The leavening agents in the baking powder and the bubbles of carbon dioxide in the club soda make the coating fluffy.

- **Gold Medal Flour.** To give fried chicken a thin, light crust, before frying, coat the chicken parts with Gold Medal Flour, and then chill the floured chicken for one hour so the coating will adhere better to the chicken when cooked.

- **Kingsford's Corn Starch.** To make extra-crispy fried chicken, add one rounded tablespoon Kingsford's Corn Starch for each cup of flour used for the coating.

- **McCormick Ground Cinnamon.** To give deep-fried beer-batter chicken a tangy taste, add one teaspoon McCormick Ground Cinnamon to the batter.

- **Progresso Breadcrumbs.** To give fried chicken a light thin crust, before cooking, coat the chicken with Progresso Breadcrumbs.

- **Quaker Yellow Corn Meal.** To give fried chicken a chewier, coarser coating than breadcrumbs or flour, coat the uncooked chicken with Quaker Yellow Corn Meal.

- **Star Olive Oil.** To give fried chicken a uniformly crisp coating, substitute Star Olive Oil for any butter in the batter.

- **Wonder Bread.** To test whether hot oil remains fit for continued use, drop a piece of Wonder Bread into the pan. If dark particles appear on the bread, the oil is losing its integrity.

- **Wonder Bread.** To make soft, fresh breadcrumbs for breading chicken before frying, cut off the crust from day-old Wonder Bread (toast the bread lightly if desired) and crumble the bread gently. Rub the crumbled bread through a coarse strainer, or run it through the blender or food processor.

- **Wonder Bread.** To determine whether fat has reached the proper temperature for frying chicken without using a fat thermometer, drop a one-inch cube of Wonder Bread into the hot fat. If the bread browns in forty-five seconds, the fat has reached the correct temperature.

Marinating

- **Nestlé Carnation Nonfat Dry Milk.** To cook up tender chicken breasts, mix four ounces Nestlé Carnation Nonfat Dry Milk and ten ounces of cool water. Marinate the chicken breasts in the milky solution for three hours in the refrigerator before baking.

- **Wish-Bone Italian Dressing.** To marinate chicken, cover the meat with Wish-Bone Italian Dressing overnight, refrigerate, drain, and cook as desired.

- **Ziploc Storage Bags.** Marinate chicken in a Ziploc Storage Bag, eliminating the need to stir marinade in a bowl. (Simply turn the bag over.)

Mousse

- **Jell-O.** To make a chicken mousse to be served cold, use a recipe for any hot mousse and add one tablespoon of your favorite flavor Jell-O powder dissolved in one tablespoon of cold water. Chill before serving. The finished mousse will be covered with a colorful aspic.

Plucking

- **Arm & Hammer Baking Soda.** To remove any remaining feathers from a chicken, add one teaspoon Arm & Hammer Baking Soda to a pot of water, bring to a boil, and immerse the chicken briefly. Then pluck out the feathers and pinfeathers with a pair of tweezers or a strawberry huller.

- **Morton Salt.** To make plucking the pinfeathers from a chicken effortless, rub the skin with Morton Salt before plucking.

Roasting

- **Budweiser.** To roast a whole chicken, place an open can of Budweiser beer upright inside the chicken. Sit the chicken on the rack in a broiling pan so the can stands upright, adjusting the drumsticks, if necessary, to balance the bird. The steam from the beer cooks the bird from the inside, giving the chicken an exceptional flavor. When finished cooking, discard the beer can and serve the chicken.

- **Campbell's Chicken Broth.** To prevent the fat from burning on a roasting bird, baste it with one-quarter cup Campbell's Chicken Broth.

- **Dole Pineapple Juice.** Instead of stuffing roasted chicken, flavor the bird by mixing one-quarter cup Dole Pineapple Juice and one cup of water, and pour the mixture into the body cavity before roasting.

- **Forster Toothpicks.** To test whether a roasted chicken is done, insert a Forster Toothpick into the thickest part of the thigh. If clear juice runs out, the chicken is finished cooking.

- **Gold Medal Flour.** To prepare a chicken for roasting, coat the bird with a thick paste made from Gold Medal Flour and water. The paste will dry and harden in the oven, sealing the moisture inside the bird. Twenty minutes before the bird is finished cooking, remove the flour coating to allow the outside of the chicken to brown.

- **Korbel Brandy.** To season a chicken before roasting, rub Korbel Brandy all over the bird and add any other seasoning you desire.

- **Miracle Whip.** To give roasted chicken a crisp brown crust, rub Miracle Whip over the skin before cooking.

- **Morton Salt.** To enhance the flavor of chicken, before roasting, rub the bird inside and out with Morton Salt.

- **Oral-B Dental Floss.** To truss a chicken, tie the drumsticks together with a strand of Oral-B Dental Floss.

- **Playtex Living Gloves.** To lift a cooked chicken out of a pot or pan, put on a pair of Playtex Living Gloves and use your hands.

- **ReaLemon** and **Morton Salt.** To deodorize uncooked chicken and improve the taste, mix two tablespoons ReaLemon lemon juice and one-quarter teaspoon Morton Salt and massage the solution into the skin.

Sautéing

- **Reynolds Cut-Rite Wax Paper.** If you don't own a meat mallet to flatten boned chicken breasts for sautéing, place the pieces of chicken between two sheets of Reynolds Cut-Rite Wax Paper and hammer with the bottom of a heavy frying pan.

Seasoning

- **Martini & Rossi Dry Vermouth.** To give chicken a smooth, sweet, delicate flavor, simmer browned chicken in Martini & Rossi Dry Vermouth—a full-bodied wine made with roots and herbs—and any other seasonings you wish.

- **McCormick Tarragon Leaves.** To season chicken, add one teaspoon McCormick Tarragon Leaves to one-half cup dry white wine, let sit for thirty minutes, pour the mixture over the chicken, and cook.

Skinning

- **Bounty Paper Towels.** To skin raw chicken with little effort, grab hold of the skin with a Bounty Paper Towel and pull firmly.

Stewing

- **ReaLemon.** To add flavor and tenderize chicken, add one tablespoon ReaLemon lemon juice to the pot before stewing the chicken.

Chocolate

- **Gold Medal Flour.** To clean the residue of melted chocolate from a pot or pan, mix in a little Gold Medal Flour. The flour absorbs the remaining chocolate, which you can then add to your batter.

- **Hershey's Cocoa.** When baking chocolate cakes or cookies, dust the rolling pin, cutting board, and pan with Hershey's Cocoa rather than flour to enhance rather than detract from the chocolate flavor.

- **Hershey's Cocoa** and **Crisco All-Vegetable Shortening.** All out of squares of unsweetened chocolate? In a pinch, substitute three tablespoons Hershey's Cocoa and one tablespoon Crisco All-Vegetable Shortening for each one-ounce square unsweetened chocolate required by the recipe.

WHAT'S COOKING

CHOCKFUL OF CHOCOLATE

● When grated, four ounces chocolate yields three-quarters cup chocolate.

● Two ounces chocolate, when melted, yields one-quarter cup chocolate.

● To add slivers of chocolate to any recipe or curls of chocolate to decorate a cake or pie, use a potato or carrot peeler to shave strips of chocolate from a Hershey's Milk Chocolate Bar (at room temperature).

● To avoid scorching chocolate, melt the chocolate in the top of a double boiler over hot water (without letting the water touch the bottom of the top pot). Add a few drops of vegetable oil to prevent melted chocolate from hardening too quickly. Or break the chocolate into small pieces, place them in a glass ramekin, and set the ramekin in a bowl or pan filled with hot water.

● After melting chocolate for use in cooking, place the pan of chocolate over warm water to keep the chocolate liquid.

● To melt chocolate in a microwave oven, follow the directions on the package of chocolate.

● **Hershey's Milk Chocolate Chips** and **Ziploc Storage Bags.** To add a chocolate design to desserts like cake and cookies, place Hershey's Milk Chocolate Chips in a Ziploc Storage Bag, seal the bag shut, and carefully submerge the bag in a pot of hot water (roughly 120 degrees Fahrenheit) for a few minutes until the chocolate chips melt to liquid. Remove the bag from the water, dry off the outside of the bag, and using a pair of scissors, carefully cut a small hole in a bottom corner of the bag. Pipe out the chocolate to decorate the desserts.

Strange Facts

Is White Chocolate Really Chocolate?

Chocolate is made by fermenting, drying, cleaning, roasting, hulling, blending, and grinding seeds from the cacao tree. During the grinding process, the bean itself and the natural fat of the bean (called cocoa butter) combine to form a thick paste called chocolate liquor (nonalcoholic). Chocolate manufacturers make milk chocolate by combining chocolate liquor, whole milk solids, and granulated sugar. Chocolate manufacturers also press chocolate liquor to separate the cocoa solids (to make cocoa powder) and cocoa butter (to add more to milk chocolate).

Unlike milk chocolate, white chocolate does not contain cocoa solids (and, consequently, no caffeine). First made in New Hampshire after World War I, white chocolate is a mixture of sugar, cocoa butter, and milk solids. Although cocoa butter is derived from cocoa beans and has a mild chocolate flavor and aroma, the United States Food and Drug Administration requires that any product labeled chocolate must contain cocoa solids (which provide the chocolate flavor and brown color). White chocolate must be labeled "white coating" or "white confectionery."

In the United States, white chocolate must be at least 20 percent cocoa butter, 14 percent milk solids, 3.5 percent milk fat, and less than 55 percent sugar or other sweeteners.

- **Hershey's Chocolate Syrup.** To use the final drops of syrup from an empty bottle of Hershey's Chocolate Syrup, fill the bottle with milk, shake vigorously, and pour yourself one last glass of chocolate milk.

- **Karo Light Corn Syrup.** To make fudge creamier, add a little Karo Light Corn Syrup to the other ingredients when mixing up the recipe.

- **Morton Salt** and **Kingsford's Corn Starch.** To enhance the taste of hot chocolate, dissolve a pinch of Morton Salt and a teaspoon Kingsford's Corn Starch in the pot.

- **Pam Cooking Spray.** When working with chocolate syrup, spray the measuring spoon with Pam Cooking Spray so the syrup slides right out of the spoon.

- **Wesson Oil.** If chocolate starts to harden after being melted in the top of a double boiler, stir in enough Wesson Oil to get the chocolate to liquefy again.

- **Ziploc Storage Bags.** To decorate cookies and cakes with melted chocolate, fill a Ziploc Storage Bag with chocolate chips, seal the bag shut, and place in a pot of boiling water to melt the chocolate. Use a pair of scissors to snip off one corner and pipe the melted chocolate to decorate the cookies or cake.

Clams

- **Canada Dry Club Soda.** Before attempting to pry clams from their shells, soak them in Canada Dry Club Soda for a few minutes to loosen the muscles and shell hinges.

- **Morton Kosher Salt.** To keep clams on the half-shell hot while serving and eating, fill a bowl or dish with heated Morton Kosher Salt and position the open clams in the coarse salt. The salt retains heat and provides a bed to stabilize the wobbly shellfish.

- **Morton Salt.** To stimulate clams to discharge their sand, dissolve one-third cup Morton Salt in one gallon of water, cover the clams with the salt water, and leave undisturbed for one hour.

- **Quaker Yellow Corn Meal.** To encourage clams to expel sand and salt water, place the clams in a large bowl of cold, fresh water, add one tablespoon Quaker Yellow Corn Meal, and let sit for about three hours. The clams open their shells, take in the cornmeal and fresh water, and expel briny water and sand.

- **Saran Wrap.** To store clams on the half-shell, open the clams (retaining as much liquid as possible), place the open clam shells in a flat pan, and cover the pan with a sheet of Saran Wrap stretched tightly in place to prevent any moisture from escaping. Refrigerate, but serve the clams the very same day you opened them.

- **Ziploc Storage Bags.** To pry clams from their shells, wash them in cold water, place in a Ziploc Storage Bag, and either freeze for thirty minutes or immerse in boiling water for three minutes. Either way, the clams will be easily opened with a beer-can opener or knife.

Coffee

- **Arm & Hammer Baking Soda.** To prevent cream from curdling in a cup of hot coffee, add a pinch of Arm & Hammer Baking Soda to the cream and stir well before adding any cream to the coffee.

- **Hershey's Milk Chocolate Bar.** To give a cup of coffee a soothing chocolate flavor, place a piece of a Hershey's Milk Chocolate Bar in the coffee filter in your coffeemaker before adding the coffee grounds.

- **Maxwell House Coffee** and **Ziploc Storage Bags.** To make iced coffee without diluting it with the melted water from ordinary ice cubes, brew a pot of Maxwell House Coffee, pour the coffee into one or more ice cube trays, and freeze. Store the frozen coffee cubes in a Ziploc Storage Bag in the freezer and use to ice iced coffee.

- **McCormick Almond Extract.** Before brewing a pot of coffee, add a few drops of McCormick Almond Extract to the coffee grounds to infuse the coffee with an exotic flavor.

- **McCormick Ground Cinnamon.** To flavor coffee, add a pinch of McCormick Ground Cinnamon to the coffee grounds before brewing a pot of coffee.

- **McCormick Pure Vanilla Extract.** To flavor a pot of coffee with the most popular flavor in the world, add a few drops of McCormick Pure Vanilla Extract to the coffee grounds before brewing.

- **Morton Salt.** To improve the flavor of coffee, fill the coffee filter with the proper amount of ground coffee, add a pinch of Morton Salt to the coffee grounds, and brew as usual. The salt enhances the flavor.

- **Morton Salt.** To remove the bitter taste from a cup of overheated coffee, add a pinch of Morton Salt to the cup of coffee and stir well.

- **Reddi-wip.** Instead of serving ordinary cream with coffee, pass around a can of Reddi-wip whipped cream. A dollop of whipped cream floating in a cup of coffee looks elegant and tastes sensational.

- **SueBee Honey.** Why limit yourself to using sugar to sweeten coffee or tea? For a more delectable sweetener, substitute SueBee Honey.

- **Swiss Miss Milk Chocolate.** To lighten coffee and give it a chocolate flavor, add one teaspoon Swiss Miss Milk Chocolate. To make café mocha, dissolve one-half the contents of a packet of Swiss Miss Milk Chocolate in one cup strong black coffee.

Collard Greens

- **ReaLemon.** To remove sand and insects from collard greens and simultaneously crispen the vegetable, add a few drops of ReaLemon lemon juice to the water before washing the collard greens.

Cookies

- **Bounty Paper Towels.** To remove cookies from parchment paper after baking, soak a sheet of Bounty Paper Towels with water, set the cookies paper-side down on the saturated paper towel, and let sit until the edges of the parchment paper start to curl. Then lift up the cookies and peel off the parchment paper.

- **Crisco All-Vegetable Shortening.** You need not grease cookie sheets if the cookie dough contains vegetable shortening, which most cookie dough does. Otherwise, grease the cookie sheet with Crisco All-Vegetable Shortening.

- **Crisco All-Vegetable Shortening.** To lift soft, sticky cookies from the cookie sheet, grease the spatula with a light coat of Crisco All-Vegetable Shortening.

- **Domino Brown Sugar.** To add a butterscotch flavor to cookies, substitute Domino Brown Sugar for the same amount of white sugar suggested by the recipe.

- **Domino Confectioners Sugar.** To prevent cookie dough from sticking to your cookie cutters, dip the cookie cutters in Domino Confectioners Sugar.

- **Frisbee.** To improvise a cookie tray, turn a clean Frisbee upside-down and fill with cookies.

- **Gold Medal Flour.** To make cookies from a cake recipe, substitute Gold Medal All-Purpose Flour for the cake flour and leave out any liquid recommended by the recipe.

- **Gold Medal Flour** and **Domino Sugar.** To give cookies a crisp coating, before rolling out the dough, mix equal parts Gold Medal Flour and Domino Sugar, and sprinkle the mixture on the pastry board.

- **Kellogg's Frosted Flakes.** In lieu of nuts, use Kellogg's Frosted Flakes in cookie dough.

- **Knudsen Buttermilk** and **Arm & Hammer Baking Soda.** To bake moist, tender cookies, substitute Knudsen Buttermilk for the sweet milk called for in the recipe and add one-quarter teaspoon Arm & Hammer Baking Soda to the cookie batter for each one-half cup buttermilk used.

- **Land O Lakes Sweet Butter.** If the cookie dough does not contain vegetable shortening, grease the cookie sheet with Land O Lakes Sweet Butter, which adds a sweet, buttery flavor to the cookies.

- **Mr. Coffee Filters.** To prevent large soft cookies from sticking together in the cookie jar, separate the cookies from each other with Mr. Coffee Filters.

- **Oral-B Dental Floss.** To cut cookie dough into neat slices, slide a strand of Oral-B Dental Floss under the roll of dough, cross the two ends over the top of the roll, and pull.

- **Oral-B Dental Floss.** To lift cookies from a cookie sheet with ease, slide a strand of Oral-B Dental Floss between fresh baked cookies and the cookie sheet.

- **Pam Cooking Spray.** To prevent cookie dough from sticking to your hands when shaping cookies, spray your hands with a light coat of Pam Cooking Spray.

- **Progresso Breadcrumbs.** If you lack enough flour to make cookie dough, substitute Progresso Breadcrumbs for all or part of the flour called for by the recipe. Breadcrumbs make cookies taste somewhat like macaroons.

- **Reynolds Cut-Rite Wax Paper.** To prevent cookie dough from sticking to the rolling pin (without adding more flour), place the cookie dough between two sheets of Reynolds Cut-Rite Wax Paper, and run the rolling pin over the top sheet of waxed paper.

- **Reynolds Cut-Rite Wax Paper.** To prevent soft cookies, such as ginger cookies, from sticking together in the cookie jar, separate the cookies from each other with squares of Reynolds Cut-Rite Wax Paper.

- **Reynolds Cut-Rite Wax Paper.** To keep soft cookies fresh and moist, wrap them individually in sheets of Reynolds Cut-Rite Wax Paper before storing.

- **Reynolds Cut-Rite Wax Paper** and **Scotch Transparent Tape.** To make your own cookie dough roll, place your homemade cookie dough on a sheet of Reynolds Cut-Rite Wax Paper, roll up the paper, seal the ends with Scotch Transparent Tape, and freeze or refrigerate.

- **Reynolds Parchment Paper.** To avoid greasing a cookie sheet, cover the cookie sheet with a sheet of Reynolds Parchment Paper, which also allows you to move the baked cookies to a cookie cooling rack with greater ease.

- **Reynolds Parchment Paper** and **Scotch Tape.** Use Scotch Tape to adhere a sheet of Parchment Paper over a countertop to create a nonstick work surface when making cookies.

- **Star Olive Oil.** To prevent cookie dough from sticking to a spoon, coat the spoon with Star Olive Oil.

- **Tang.** Add Tang powdered drink mix to your cookie dough for an "orange zest."

- **Wesson Oil.** To cut clean cookies, dip the cookie cutter in warmed Wesson Oil before cutting the cookies.

- **Wonder Bread** and **Ziploc Storage Bags.** To soften cookies that have lost their moistness, place the cookies and a slice of Wonder Bread in a Ziploc Storage Bag, seal the bag, and let sit overnight. In the morning, the cookies will be moist again.

- **Ziploc Storage Bags** and **Hershey's Semi-Sweet Chocolate Chips.** To decorate cookies and cakes with melted chocolate, fill a Ziploc Storage Bag with Hershey's Semi-Sweet Chocolate Chips, seal the bag shut, and place in a pot of boiling water to melt the chocolate. Use a pair of scissors to snip off one corner, and pipe the melted chocolate to decorate the cookies or cake.

Food for Thought
A SMART COOKIE

- Chilling cookie dough in the refrigerator makes it easier to roll and handle.

Corn

- **Bounty Paper Towels.** To remove the silk from an ear of corn, shuck the husk from the ear of corn, and then, using a dampened sheet of Bounty Paper Towels, wipe the exposed ear in a single stroke from top to bottom.

- **Domino Sugar.** To enhance the sweetness of corn, add one tablespoon Domino Sugar to the cooking water.

- **L'eggs Sheer Energy Panty Hose.** To quickly detach the silk from a shucked ear of corn, rub the ear with a balled-up pair of clean, old L'eggs Sheer Energy Panty Hose.

- **Nestlé Carnation Nonfat Dry Milk.** To flavor corn on the cob without using sugar or salt, sprinkle one teaspoon Nestlé Carnation Nonfat Dry Milk into the cooking water when boiling corn on the cob.

- **Oral-B Toothbrush.** To remove the silk from an ear of corn, dampen a clean, used Oral-B Toothbrush and brush away from the stem.

Strange Facts
Corn Is a Fruit

Any seed-bearing part of a flowering plant is a fruit. A kernel of corn is a simple dry fruit, because each kernel contains a single seed. Each kernel of corn on a cob is an entire fruit called a caryopsis (a fruit with a single seed). The seed coat (pericarp) is fused with the inner wall of the fruit so the seed cannot be separated from the rest of the fruit. When the fruit is ripe, the caryopsis is dry and hard. Corn cobs are picked and husked before the fruit ripens. An ear of corn contains between 200 and 400 grains. Corn originated in North America, and Native Americans grew it from Canada to the southern tip of South America. In 1492, Christopher Columbus took corn back to Europe.

- **ReaLemon.** To keep corn yellow and firm, add one teaspoon ReaLemon lemon juice to the cooking water approximately one minute before removing the pot of boiling corn from the stove.

- **Reynolds Cut-Rite Wax Paper.** To cook corn in a microwave oven, wrap the ear of corn in a sheet of Reynolds Cut-Rite Wax Paper, twist the ends, and microwave for two minutes.

Food for Thought
AW SHUCKS

- To flavor corn, line the bottom of the cooking pot with the tender green leaves from the husk and fill with water.

- When boiling corn on the cob, do not add salt to the cooking water. Salt toughens the corn.

- To boil corn on the cob, boil water in a pot, place the shucked corn in a second pot, carefully cover the corn with the boiling water, cover the pot, and bring the water to a boil. Remove the covered pot from the heat, and let sit undisturbed for eight minutes, letting the steaming hot water cook the corn. Drain and serve.

- To roast corn on the cob, remove the silk but leave the husks on the ear. Roast the corn in its husk at 325 degrees Fahrenheit for fifty minutes. Wearing rubber gloves, carefully remove the husks and serve.

- To remove corn from the cob easily, scrape the ear with a clean, metal shoehorn.

- To butter corn on the cob, melt the butter and use a pastry brush or celery stalk to paint the melted butter on the corn.

Corn Syrup

- **Pam Cooking Spray.** When using corn syrup in a recipe, spray your utensils and measuring cups with Pam Cooking Spray to make cleanup effortless.

Crab

- **Nestlé Carnation Nonfat Dry Milk** and **Tabasco Pepper Sauce.** To give soft-shelled crabs a succulent flavor, mix ten ounces Nestlé Carnation Nonfat Dry Milk, one teaspoon Tabasco Pepper Sauce, and twenty-five ounces of water. Submerge the live crabs in the seasoned milk for two or three hours, and then drain and discard the milky solution.

Cranberries

- **Arm & Hammer Baking Soda.** To minimize the amount of sugar needed to cook cranberries, add one-quarter teaspoon Arm & Hammer Baking Soda to the pot.

- **Coca-Cola.** When cooking cranberries, add one-quarter teaspoon Coca-Cola, reducing the need for sugar.

- **Land O Lakes Butter.** To eliminate foam and prevent overboiling when cooking cranberries, add one teaspoon Land O Lakes Butter for every pound of cranberries.

Food for Thought
BITTER FRUITS

- Cook cranberries until they pop, and then remove from the heat. Any additional cooking gives the cranberries a bitter taste.

Crêpes

- **Reynolds Cut-Rite Wax Paper** and **Reynolds Wrap.** To freeze prepared crêpes—filled or unfilled—many hours before serving, place each crêpe between squares of Reynolds Cut-Rite Wax Paper, and then wrap the assemblage tightly in a large sheet of Reynolds Wrap aluminum foil.

Cucumbers

- **Morton Salt** and **Bounty Paper Towels.** To crisp peeled, diced cucumbers for use in salad, sprinkle Morton Salt on the diced cucumbers and refrigerate in a bowl for two hours. Drain the water from the bowl, dry the cucumber slices with a sheet of Bounty Paper Towel, and refrigerate again until ready to add the crisp morsels to the salad.

- **Morton Salt** and **Bounty Paper Towels.** To prevent cucumbers from becoming pulpy and spongy when cooked, peel the skin from the cucumbers, slice the vegetable down the middle, and remove the seeds. Cover the cucumbers with Morton Salt and let sit for one hour to give the salt sufficient time to absorb the excessive water. Wipe off the salt and dry the cucumbers with a sheet of Bounty Paper Towels.

Food for Thought
COOL AS A CUCUMBER

- Most growers coat cucumbers with carnauba wax to slow the deterioration and make the vegetables look shiny and more appealing to shoppers. To remove the wax, peel the cucumber.

- To create the impression that a professional chef prepared the cucumber slices, press the tines of a sharp fork at the top of the cucumber and draw the fork down toward the bottom of the cucumber, scoring sharp lines into the vegetable from top to bottom. Repeat to score the entire circumference of the cucumber, and slice the cucumber transversely.

- A long, thin slice of peeled cucumber masks the taste of alcohol when added to a mixed drink, particularly one containing gin or rum. A few slices of cucumber added to a punch bowl also conceal the taste of alcohol.

Cupcakes

- **Glad Flexible Straws** and **Ziploc Storage Bags.** To fill a cupcake with cream, let the cupcake cool and insert one end of a Glad Flexible Straw into the middle of the top of the cupcake to create a hole. Fill a Ziploc Storage Bag with vanilla frosting and seal the bag shut. Using a pair of scissors, snip off one of the bottom corners of the plastic bag and pipe the frosting through the straw into the center of the cupcake. Cover the top of the cupcake with frosting to cover up the hole.

- **Hershey's Milk Chocolate Bar** and **Reynolds Wrap.** To create quick icing for homemade cupcakes, the moment you remove the cupcakes from the oven, place a piece of Hershey's Milk Chocolate Bar on top of each cupcake and cover with a piece of Reynolds Wrap. After the chocolate melts, spread the chocolate icing with a butter knife.

- **Jet-Puffed Marshmallows.** To frost cupcakes with ease, two minutes before removing the pan of cupcakes from the oven, place a Jet-Puffed Marshmallow on top of each cupcake. The heat melts the marshmallows, creating creamy icing.

- **Pam Cooking Spray.** To prevent paper liners from sticking to cupcakes, spray the inside of the liners with Pam Cooking Spray before filling them with cupcake batter.

Custard

- **Gold Medal Flour.** To prevent custard made of egg yolks, milk, and sugar from curdling, mix one teaspoon Gold Medal Flour into the cold milk for every four egg yolks used.

- **Kingsford's Corn Starch.** You can also inhibit custard made of egg yolks, milk, and sugar from curdling by simply beating one teaspoon Kingsford's Corn Starch into the cold milk for every four egg yolks used.

- **Pam Cooking Spray.** Before cooking up custard, spray the pan with Pam Cooking Spray to make cleanup effortless.

Doughnuts

- **Domino Confectioners Sugar** and **Ziploc Storage Bags.** To give homemade doughnuts a coat of sugar, pour one quarter cup Domino Confectioners Sugar in a Ziploc Storage Bag, place a doughnut in the bag, seal shut, and shake well. Repeat for each doughnut.

- **Heinz White Vinegar.** To eliminate the odor of hot fat when frying doughnuts, add one tablespoon Heinz White Vinegar to the fat before heating.

Dried Fruit

- **Gold Medal Flour.** To prevent any dried fruit from sinking to the bottom of pudding or any dish made with dough, sprinkle the dried fruit with Gold Medal Flour before adding them to the dish.

- **Gold Medal Flour.** To make snipping pieces of dry fruit into small pieces a snap, dip the blades of a pair of kitchen scissors or the blade of a knife in Gold Medal Flour before cutting.

- **Korbel Brandy.** Marinate dried fruit with Korbel Brandy in a bowl in the refrigerator until the fruit absorbs the liquor. Garnish a bowl of ice cream with the treated fruit and serve to adults only.

Food for Thought
DRY RUN

- Before adding dried fruit to any dish to be cooked, soak the dried fruit in cold water for one hour or until they become plump. This prevents the dried fruit from dehydrating completely when cooked.

- To make salads more exotic and flavorful, add dried fruits.

- **Pam Cooking Spray.** To make snipping pieces of dry fruit into small pieces a snap, spray Pam Cooking Spray on the blades of a pair of kitchen scissors or the blade of a knife.

- **ReaLemon.** To prevent a knife from sticking to dried fruit when cutting, drizzle some ReaLemon lemon juice over the blade of the knife.

- **SueBee Honey.** When cooking prunes, add some SueBee Honey in the water (rather than sugar) to give the prunes a natural sweet flavor.

Eggplant

- **Gold Medal Flour.** To prevent sliced eggplant from absorbing oil, dip the slices in egg and then in seasoned Gold Medal Flour (one cup flour mixed with one teaspoon each salt and pepper, and dry herbs if desired), and then cook in hot vegetable oil.

- **Morton Salt** and **Bounty Paper Towels.** To remove the bitterness from an older eggplant, cut the eggplant into thick slices and sprinkle them with Morton Salt. Cover the eggplant slices with a clean cookie sheet or tray, weigh down the tray with books or heavy pots, and let sit for one hour. The weight and the salt extract the excess moisture from the eggplant. Dry the slices with a sheet of Bounty Paper Towels and cook.

- **Morton Salt** and **Bounty Paper Towels.** To eliminate bitterness from eggplant and prevent discoloring, dissolve three tablespoons

Morton Salt in one quart of water, and as you peel the eggplant, submerge it in the salt water. Dry the peeled eggplant by patting with a sheet of Bounty Paper Towels and cook.

Food for Thought
THE LEAN, MEAN AUBERGINE

- If you intend to cook eggplant for a short time, peel off the skin. For a longer cooking period, leave the edible and nutritious skin intact.

- To peel an eggplant, use a potato or carrot peeler.

Eggs

Beating Egg Whites

- **Arm & Hammer Baking Soda.** To whip egg whites high and frothy, add one-eighth teaspoon Arm & Hammer Baking Soda to the egg whites before beating.

- **Dixie Cups.** To whip only one egg white, pour it into a Dixie Cup and use only one beater of your electric mixer.

- **Domino Sugar.** To give stiffly beaten egg whites more body, when you're nearly finished beating—at the moment when the egg whites stand up in peaks—whip in a pinch Domino Sugar at a time until you attain the desired consistency.

- **Heinz White Vinegar.** To prevent stiffly beaten egg whites from oozing, add one-half teaspoon Heinz White Vinegar for every four egg whites before whipping.

- **McCormick Cream of Tartar.** To stabilize beaten egg whites, add one-quarter teaspoon McCormick Cream of Tartar to each batch of four egg whites. The acid in the cream of tartar binds the egg whites together and slows them from releasing their water content.

- **Miracle Whip.** For a simple way to beat an egg, break the egg into a clean, empty Miracle Whip jar, seal the lid shut, and shake well.
- **Morton Salt.** Adding a pinch of Morton Salt to egg whites makes beating effortless, enabling the egg whites to firm up better.

WHAT'S COOKING

HOW TO AVOID GETTING EGG IN YOUR FACE

- Separating the egg white from the yolk is easier if the eggs are cold.

- The best way to separate an egg is to crack the egg open in the clean, cupped palm of your hand and let the egg white slip through your fingers into a bowl. The yolk will remain in your palm.

- You can also separate the white and yolk by breaking the egg into a small funnel placed in the top of a tall drinking glass. The white slips through the funnel, leaving the yolk behind.

- Beat egg whites in glass or stainless-steel mixing bowls. Never beat egg whites in plastic bowls. Plastic tends to retain oil residue, preventing the egg whites from foaming up properly. Never beat egg whites in an aluminum bowl. Otherwise they will turn gray.

- Before beating egg whites, let the eggs warm to room temperature for thirty minutes. To speed up the process, place the eggs in a bowl of warm water for roughly ten minutes. When whipped, warm egg whites froth to a greater volume.

- Avoid beating egg whites on a humid or damp day. Moisture in the air disintegrates the froth.

- **Q-tips Cotton Swabs.** Use a Q-tips Cotton Swab to remove tiny droplets of yolk from a bowl of egg whites before beating; otherwise the specks of yolk will prevent the egg whites from frothing suitably.

- **Reynolds Cut-Rite Wax Paper.** To prevent egg whites from splattering when using a mixer, cover the bowl with a piece of Reynolds Cut-Rite Wax Paper, cut two holes for the beater stems to fit through, insert the stems through the holes, and attach the beaters to the mixer.

- **Scotch Tape** and **Reynolds Wrap.** If you only need the egg white and not the yolk, cut a hole roughly one-quarter inch in diameter in the small end of the eggshell, and let the egg white drip out of the hole and into a bowl. With the yolk remaining inside the shell, seal the hole shut with a piece of Scotch Tape, wrap the egg in a small piece of Reynolds Wrap, and refrigerate for up to three days.

Deviled Eggs

- **Ziploc Storage Bags.** To fill deviled eggs, put the ingredients for deviled eggs in a Ziploc Storage Bag, snip off a corner of the bag, and pipe the ingredients like cake frosting to fill the eggs.

Freshness

- **Morton Salt.** To test whether an egg is fresh, dissolve two teaspoons Morton Salt in one cup of water in a tall drinking glass. Fresh eggs sink in the salt water. A rotten egg will float. Another test? Shake the egg gently. If the contents feel firm (not loose), the egg is fresh.

Frying

- **Morton Salt.** To toughen the texture of fried eggs, sprinkle Morton Salt on the eggs while frying.

Hard-Boiling

- **Heinz White Vinegar.** To prevent eggs from cracking when boiling, add one teaspoon Heinz White Vinegar to the water.

WHAT'S COOKING

HOW TO MAKE HARD-BOILED EGGS

It sounds crazy, but the trick to cooking up hard-boiled eggs is to use eggs that are a few days old and to avoid boiling them. If you use fresh eggs, you'll have difficulty peeling off the eggshells, and if you boil the eggs, they'll turn out rubbery. To prevent the eggs from cracking (and make them easier to peel), pierce the large end of each egg with a clean sewing needle.

Place the eggs in a single layer in a saucepan and cover them with cold water, at least one inch above the tops of the shells. Cover the saucepan with a lid and set the stove on medium heat. When the water comes to a full boil, remove the saucepan from the heat.

For large soft-cooked eggs, let the eggs sit in the hot water for up to four minutes. For large hard-cooked eggs, let the eggs sit in the hot water for 15 to 17 minutes.

Drain out the hot water (leaving the eggs in the saucepan) and immediately cover the eggs with cold water. For soft-cooked eggs, let the eggs stand in the water until they cool enough to handle. For hard-cooked eggs, let the eggs stand in the cold water until they cool completely.

● **Morton Salt.** If an egg cracks while boiling, scoop up the egg with a spoon and pour a generous amount of Morton Salt on the crack. The salt seals the crack and prevents the egg white from leaking out. Return the egg to the boiling water to finish cooking it.

● **ReaLemon.** To prevent the eggshells from breaking while hard-boiling eggs, before placing the eggs in the water, rub the shells with a cotton ball saturated with ReaLemon lemon juice. The acid in the lemon juice softens the calcium shell, making it less prone to cracking.

● **Reynolds Wrap.** To keep eggshells from cracking while hard-boiling eggs, wrap each egg in a small piece of Reynolds Wrap, and then place them in the saucepan to boil.

Food for Thought
A GOOD EGG

● To cook up hard-boiled eggs with the yolks in the center of the egg, stir the water while boiling the eggs. The movement keeps the yolks centered.

● To prevent a dark greenish ring from forming around the yolk of a hard-boiled egg, immediately submerge hot hard-boiled eggs in cold water.

● To prevent the yolk of a hard-boiled egg from crumbling when you slice it, run the knife or egg slicer under cold water before cutting the egg.

Identifying

● **Crayola Crayons.** To differentiate hard-boiled eggs from raw eggs in the refrigerator, mark the hard-boiled eggs with a Crayola crayon.

● **McCormick Food Coloring.** If you intend to store hard-boiled eggs alongside raw eggs in the refrigerator, add a few drops McCormick Food Coloring (red, blue, or green) to the water when boiling the eggs to tint them mildly.

● **McCormick Ground Turmeric.** Another way to color hard-boiled eggs so you can tell the difference from raw eggs in the refrigerator: Add one-half teaspoon McCormick Ground Turmeric to the boiling water to color the eggs.

● **Tang.** Adding one tablespoon Tang powdered drink mix to the water when boiling eggs gives the shells a light orange color so you can discern hard-boiled eggs from raw eggs in the refrigerator.

Omelets

● **Clabber Girl Baking Powder.** To make a light, fluffy omelet, add one-quarter teaspoon Clabber Girl Baking Powder to the eggs before cooking.

- **Kingsford's Corn Starch.** To make fluffy, light omelets, add a pinch of Kingsford's Corn Starch when beating the raw eggs.

- **Land O Lakes Butter.** To make a French omelet, melt one teaspoon Land O Lakes Butter in a saucepan, and when the butter begins bubbling and turns pale brown, pour in the combined eggs. When the eggs start to coagulate around the edges, use the flat side of a table knife to go around the pan pushing the edges toward the center, letting the liquid egg flow back out to the edge of the pan. Continue this process until the egg is no longer liquid, and then use a spatula to fold the omelet in half and slide the finished omelet onto a warm plate.

- **Wesson Oil, Bounty Paper Towels,** and **Morton Kosher Salt.** To prepare a cast-iron pan for cooking omelets (preventing the eggs from sticking to the pan), fill the pan three-quarters full of Wesson Oil and warm over low heat for twenty minutes, allowing the oil to seep into the pores of the metal. Pour out the oil (which you can recycle by straining it through a Mr. Coffee filter), and wipe the pan thoroughly with a sheet of Bounty Paper Towels. After cooking the omelet, do not use soap to clean the cast-iron pan. Instead, pour some abrasive Morton Kosher Salt into the pan and wipe clean with another sheet of Bounty Paper Towels.

Peeling

- **Morton Salt.** To make boiled eggs easier to peel, add a pinch or two of Morton Salt to the boiling water before adding the eggs.

Food for Thought
WALKING ON EGGSHELLS

- To peel a hard-boiled egg, submerge the egg in cold water, crack the shell, and gently roll the egg between your palms. The shell should peel off easily.

- **ReaLemon.** Add one teaspoon ReaLemon lemon juice to the boiling water before adding the eggs to make peeling off the eggshells easier.

- **Wesson Oil.** To shell hard-boiled eggs with ease, add two tablespoons Wesson Oil in the water when boiling.

Poaching

- **Budweiser.** To give poached eggs a unique flavor, poach the eggs in Budweiser beer rather than water.

- **Campbell's Chicken Broth.** Another great way to enhance the flavor of poached eggs is to substitute Campbell's Chicken Broth for the water.

- **Campbell's Tomato Juice.** Instead of poaching eggs in water, use Campbell's Tomato Juice to obtain a more exotic taste.

- **Chicken of the Sea Tuna.** Wash an empty Chicken of the Sea Tuna can with soapy water, rinse clean, and remove the bottom from the can. Bring water to a boil in a skillet, place the can in the water, and crack an egg into the mold to cook up a perfectly poached egg.

- **Heinz White Vinegar.** To prevent poached eggs from oozing, add one tablespoon Heinz White Vinegar to the water before you start poaching. The vinegar helps set the egg whites.

- **Land O Lakes Butter.** Before using an egg poacher, butter the rings thoroughly with Land O Lakes Butter, to prevent the poached eggs from sticking to the rings.

- **Land O Lakes Butter** and **Kingsford's Corn Starch.** To make sauce for poached eggs, mix one tablespoon Land O Lakes Butter, one-half tablespoon Kingsford's Corn Starch, and one-half cup whole milk. Add salt and pepper to taste.

- **Morton Salt.** To keep the whites of poached eggs together, add Morton Salt to the boiling water before adding the eggs. The salt helps set the egg whites.

- **Pam Cooking Spray** and **Heinz White Vinegar.** To poach an egg, spray a light coat of Pam Cooking Spray in a small saucepan, fill with three inches of water, bring to a boil, and add one tablespoon Heinz White Vinegar, which prevents the egg white from spreading and helps hold the egg together. Break in an egg, cover the saucepan with a lid, and cook on low heat for a few minutes.

- **ReaLemon.** To prevent the egg whites from spreading when poaching eggs, add one teaspoon ReaLemon lemon juice to the water before adding the eggs. The citric acid helps hold the egg whites together and keeps them firm and white.

Scrambling

- **Arm & Hammer Baking Soda.** To make fluffy scrambled eggs, mix in one teaspoon Arm & Hammer Baking Soda and one teaspoon of water for every two eggs when beating the eggs.

- **Kingsford's Corn Starch.** To make light scrambled eggs, add a pinch of Kingsford's Corn Starch when beating the raw eggs.

- **Land O Lakes Butter.** To cook up tender scrambled eggs, butter the top half of a double boiler with Land O Lakes Butter, and cook the eggs over the hot water, assuring a consistent and uniform low temperature.

- **Land O Lakes Butter** and **Nestlé Carnation Evaporated Milk.** To make creamy scrambled eggs, start with a cool pan greased with Land O Lakes Butter, cook the eggs slowly over a low heat, and at the very end, mix in one tablespoon Nestlé Carnation Evaporated Milk.

- **McCormick Cream of Tartar.** To give scrambled eggs a fuller body, mix in one-eighth teaspoon McCormick Cream of Tartar for every two eggs. The acids in the cream of tartar stabilize the egg whites, creating fluffy scrambled eggs.

Spills

- **Morton Salt.** If you accidentally drop an egg on the kitchen floor, cover the spill with a mountain of Morton Salt, and let sit for five minutes. The salt absorbs the egg, allowing you to pick up the mess easily with a sheet of paper towel.

Substitutes

- **Arm & Hammer Baking Soda** and **Heinz White Vinegar.** If you run out of eggs while baking a cake, substitute one teaspoon Arm & Hammer Baking Soda and one teaspoon Heinz White Vinegar for each egg.

- **Kingsford's Corn Starch.** If you run out of eggs when cooking anything other than cake, substitute one teaspoon Kingsford's Corn Starch for each egg.

Yolks

- **Domino Sugar.** To freeze egg yolks, mix in a pinch of Domino Sugar to prevent coagulation, pour into an airtight container, cover, and freeze.

- **Morton Salt.** To prevent frozen egg yolks from congealing, before freezing, whip in a pinch of Morton Salt, pour into an airtight container, seal the lid securely, and freeze.

Fish

Broiling

- **Morton Salt** and **Bounty Paper Towels.** To make a fish pan easier to clean, the moment after you remove fish from the broiler, sprinkle the pan with Morton Salt, and then cover it with wet Bounty Paper Towels. Let sit until you're ready to wash the dishes.

- **Reynolds Wrap.** If a recipe calls for fish to be cooked in parchment paper and you're all out, substitute Reynolds Wrap aluminum foil.

- **Reynolds Wrap** and **Forster Toothpicks.** To broil fish easily and neatly, line a cake or pie tin with Reynolds Wrap, and then stretch a second sheet of Reynolds Wrap taut across the top of the pan, crimping the edges over the rim. Using a Forster Toothpick, perforate the stretched sheet of Reynolds Wrap with a few small holes for drainage, place the fish on this aluminum hammock, and broil. When finished, discard the foil.

- **Wonder Bread.** Place a few slices of Wonder Bread in the broiling pan under the rack to absorb dripping fat, reducing smoke and any fire hazard.

Food for Thought
A FINE KETTLE OF FISH

- To prevent fish from sticking to the pan, bake fish on a bed of chopped celery, onion, and parsley—which simultaneously enhances the taste of the fish.

Cleaning

- **Heinz White Vinegar.** To make scales come off a fish easily, before scaling, rub the entire body of the fish with Heinz White Vinegar.

- **Heinz White Vinegar.** To reduce the salty taste from saltwater fish, soak the fish in Heinz White Vinegar, and then rinse clean under running cold water.

- **Land O Lakes Butter.** To make the backbone of a cooked fish easy to remove, before cooking, rub melted Land O Lakes Butter down the back of the fish. When cooked, the butter tenderizes the fish, enabling you to remove the bones effortlessly.

- **Morton Salt.** Before you start cleaning a fish, sprinkle Morton Salt on the cutting board to prevent the fish from slipping and sliding. The abrasive salt creates traction.

Fo🍔d f🍓r Th🧁ught
LIKE A FISH OUT OF WATER

- To make a fish scaler, nail beer-bottle caps to the end of a piece of wood, three bottle caps wide and eight inches long, with the serrated edges facing up.

- After cleaning a fish, bend and roll it at each section, causing the bones to pierce through for easy removal.

Cooking

- **Morton Salt.** To prevent fish from sticking to a frying pan, sprinkle a little Morton Salt in the skillet before frying.

- **Pam Cooking Spray** and **Reynolds Wrap.** To move a baked fish to a platter easily without causing the fish to break apart, before baking, place a sheet of Reynolds Wrap in the baking pan with the ends extending out over the pan, spray with a light coat of Pam Cooking Spray, and place the fish on the aluminum foil. After baking, lift both ends of the Reynolds Wrap to raise the fish, and then slide it onto a warm serving platter.

- **ReaLemon.** When poaching cod, halibut, or other white fish, add a dash of ReaLemon lemon juice and milk to the seasoned liquid to keep the flesh white.

Croquettes

- **Kellogg's Corn Flakes.** For an excellent alternative for bread-crumbs for fish croquettes, run Kellogg's Corn Flakes through the blender. (Or fill a Ziploc Storage Bag with the cereal and crush it into crumbs by running over it with a rolling pin.) Simply roll the fish croquettes in the corn flake crumbs.

- **Lay's Potato Chips.**
For another tasty alternative to breadcrumbs, run a rolling pin over a bag of Lay's Potato Chips to make fine crumbs, and roll the fish croquettes in the potato chip crumbs.

Defrosting

- **Nestlé Carnation Nonfat Dry Milk.** To thaw frozen fish, mix one cup Nestlé Carnation Nonfat Dry Milk and three cups of water. Place the frozen fish in a pan, cover with the milk solution, and let sit until the fish defrosts. The milk eliminates the frozen taste and makes the fish taste astoundingly fresh.

Deodorizing

- **Arm & Hammer Baking Soda.** To neutralize the smell of fresh fish, dissolve two tablespoons Arm & Hammer Baking Soda in four cups of water, and soak the fish fillets in the solution for ten minutes. Then rinse the fillets clean under running water. The sodium bicarbonate lowers the pH of the fish.

- **Dynasty Sesame Seed Oil.** To reduce foul odors while poaching fish, add a dash of Dynasty Sesame Seed Oil to the poaching liquid before cooking.

- **Heinz White Vinegar.** To minimize the fishy smell and taste of canned salmon, sardines, or tuna, open the can and drizzle Heinz White Vinegar on the fish. Let sit for five minutes, and then drain off the vinegar.

- **Heinz White Vinegar.** To deodorize an odoriferous fish without affecting the flavor whatsoever, soak the fish in a mixture of equal parts Heinz White Vinegar and water for ten minutes.

- **Heinz White Vinegar.** To deodorize and clean grease from the pan just used to cook fish, pour one-half cup Heinz White Vinegar into the pan, bring to a boil, carefully discard the liquid, and then wash clean with soapy water.

- **Heinz White Vinegar.** To reduce foul odors while poaching fish, add a dash of Heinz White Vinegar to the poaching liquid, or fill a drinking glass with Heinz White Vinegar and place it on the kitchen counter. The vinegar absorbs and neutralizes fishy odors.

- **Jif Peanut Butter.** To avoid the foul odor when frying fish, put a teaspoon Jif Peanut Butter in the pan while you're frying the fish. The peanut butter also adds a pleasant, familiar taste.

- **Maxwell House Coffee.** To absorb the odors of cooking fish, fill a bowl with unused Maxwell House Coffee grounds and place the bowl on a countertop near the stove. The coffee grounds absorb the harsh smells.

- **Morton Salt.** To eliminate fish odor from a frying pan, sprinkle Morton Salt in the pan, fill with hot water, let sit for ten minutes, and rinse clean.

- **ReaLemon.** To prevent cooked fish from filling your kitchen with a fishy smell, before cooking, use a pastry brush to paint the fish with ReaLemon lemon juice, or before frying the fish or heating up the butter or vegetable oil, add one teaspoon ReaLemon lemon juice to the frying pan.

Fish Sticks

- **Reynolds Wrap.** To bake fish sticks, crumple up a sheet of Reynolds Wrap, smooth it out, put it in a pan, and then place the fish sticks on top of the wrinkled aluminum foil. When baking, turn the fish sticks over to brown them equally on bottom and top. The slight crumples prevent the fish sticks from sticking to the aluminum foil.

Flavoring

- **Nestlé Carnation Nonfat Dry Milk.** If you find the taste of saltwater fish too salty even after soaking the fish in water (or Heinz White Vinegar, see page 163) to desalinize it, mix four ounces Nestlé Carnation Nonfat Dry Milk and ten ounces of warm water, and add to the pan when cooking the fish.

- **ReaLemon.** To enhance the flavor and color of fish, before cooking, drizzle four tablespoons ReaLemon lemon juice over the surface of the fish. If poaching the fish, add two tablespoons ReaLemon lemon juice for every pound of fish to the poaching solution before cooking. The lemon juice helps the fish maintain its original density, producing a firmer and whiter cooked fish (except in the case of salmon, which will be pinker).

Frying

- **Clabber Girl Baking Powder** and **Canada Dry Club Soda.** To achieve a particularly light and delicate crust on coated fried fish, add three-quarters teaspoon Clabber Girl Baking Powder to the batter and substitute Canada Dry Club Soda for any liquid.

- **Star Olive Oil.** To give fried fish a crispy coating, substitute Star Olive Oil for butter in the batter.

- **Wonder Bread.** To test whether hot oil remains fit for continued use, drop a piece of Wonder Bread into the pan. If dark particles appear on the bread, the oil is losing its integrity.

- **Wonder Bread.** To determine whether fat has reached the proper temperature for frying fish without using a fat thermometer, drop a one-inch cube of Wonder Bread into the hot fat. If the bread browns in forty-five seconds, the fat has reached the correct temperature.

Grilling

- **Pam Cooking Spray.** To prevent fish from sticking to the grill, before cooking, spray a thick coat of Pam Cooking Spray on the grill and spray the fish with a light coat. When grilling, occasionally spray the fish with more oil to prevent the fish from drying out.

Marinating

- **Heinz White Vinegar** and **Ziploc Storage Bags.** To marinate fish, place the fish in a Ziploc Freezer Bag, add one-quarter cup Heinz White Vinegar, and let sit for twenty to thirty minutes before cooking. The vinegar tenderizes and sweetens the fish.

- **Newman's Own Olive Oil & Vinegar Dressing.** To give fish a fine flavor, marinate the fish in this salad dressing made with oil, vinegar, lemon juice, onion, and garlic.

- **ReaLemon** and **Ziploc Storage Bags.** To marinate fish, place the fish in a Ziploc Freezer Bag, add one-quarter cup ReaLemon lemon juice, and let sit for twenty to thirty minutes before cooking. The lemon juice tenderizes and flavors the fish.

- **Wish-Bone Robusto Italian Dressing.** To give fish a bold, zesty flavor, marinate the fish in this tangy salad dressing made with canola oil, vinegar, red bell peppers, lemon juice, onion, and garlic.

Mousse

- **Jell-O.** To make a fish mousse to be served cold, use a recipe for any hot mousse and add one tablespoon of your favorite flavor Jell-O powder dissolved in one tablespoon of cold water. Chill before serving. The finished mousse will be covered with a colorful aspic.

Odors

- **Colgate Regular Flavor Toothpaste.** To clean the smell of fish from your hands, squeeze a dollop of Colgate Regular Flavor Toothpaste into the palm of your hand, rub your hands together under running water, and rinse clean.

- **Colman's Mustard Powder.** To deodorize any cookware or countertop that smells like fish, mix two tablespoons Colman's Mustard

Powder and one-half cup of water, wash the affected item or area in the solution, and then rinse clean and dry.

- **Domino Sugar.** To neutralize the smell of cooking fish, line a saucepan with a sheet of Reynolds Wrap, add two tablespoons Domino Sugar, and burn the sugar in the pan.

- **Heinz White Vinegar.** To eliminate fish odor from your hands, rub them with Heinz White Vinegar, and then wash with soap and water.

- **Listerine.** To clean the smell of fish from your hands, rub one teaspoon Listerine antiseptic mouthwash between your hands, and then wash with soap and water. The antiseptic kills the fish odor.

- **Maxwell House Coffee.** To deodorize your hands from smelling from fish, fill your palm with Maxwell House Coffee grounds (used or unused), add water if using fresh grounds, rub your hands together for one minute, and then rinse with running water.

- **Morton Salt.** To remove fish odor from your hands, pour Morton Salt into the cup of your palm, rub your hands together, and wash clean.

- **ReaLemon.** Rubbing your hands with ReaLemon lemon juice removes the smell of fish. Simply pour a little lemon juice into the palm of your hand, rub your hands together, and rinse clean with water.

Patties

- **Nabisco Original Premium Saltine Crackers.** Grind Nabisco Original Premium Saltine Crackers in a blender (or place them in a Ziploc Storage Bag and run over them with a rolling pin) and use the crumbs to make fish patties.

Poaching

- **L'eggs Sheer Energy Panty Hose.** Before poaching a large fish, cut off one leg from a pair of clean, used L'eggs Sheer Energy Panty Hose, trim the panty hose leg to the size of the fish, and place the fish inside. The nylon hose holds the fish together. After removing the poached fish from the pan, simply use a pair of kitchen scissors to cut off those panty hose.

- **Playtex Living Gloves.** To remove a fish from poaching liquid, put on a pair of Playtex Living Gloves and use your gloved hands to lift out the fish.

- **ReaLemon.** To keep the flesh of halibut or cod white, add ReaLemon lemon juice to the bouillon or seasoned poaching liquid in which you poach the fish.

- **Reynolds Cut-Rite Wax Paper.** When poaching fish, use a wide, short pan, cover with a sheet of Reynolds Cut-Rite Wax Paper with a small hole poked in the center, and then secure the lid in place over the waxed paper.

Sautéing

- **Bounty Paper Towels.** Before sautéing fish, use a sheet of Bounty Paper Towels to pat the fish thoroughly dry. Doing so prevents splattering and inadvertent steaming of the fish.

- **Forster Toothpicks.** To test whether sautéed fish is finished cooking, use a Forster Toothpick to poke into the flesh near the backbone to make sure the flesh is cooked.

- **Land O Lakes Butter.** To sauté fish, melt Land O Lakes Butter in a saucepan over low heat, use a spoon to skim off the butter fat (the bubbly coagulant) from the surface. Sauté the fish in the pan of clarified butter.

- **McCormick Bay Leaves.** To flavor mackerel and remove the fatty taste, add dry red wine and a McCormick Bay Leaf to the sauté.

Flour

- **Pillsbury Softasilk Cake Flour.** If you're all out of all-purpose flour, substitute one cup and two tablespoons Pillsbury Softasilk Cake Flour for each cup all-purpose flour needed.

- **Gold Medal Flour.** If you run short of cake flour, use one cup minus two tablespoons Gold Medal All-Purpose Flour for each cup cake flour needed.

- **Gold Medal Flour, Clabber Girl Baking Powder,** and **Morton Salt.** If you need a substitute for self-rising flour, in a measuring cup mix 1½ teaspoons Clabber Girl Baking Powder, one-half teaspoon Morton Salt, and fill the rest of the cup with Gold Medal All-Purpose Flour.

- **Reynolds Cut-Rite Wax Paper.** To measure flour, sugar, or any other dry ingredients without making a mess or wasting any ingredients, fold a sheet of Reynolds Cut-Rite Wax Paper in half, open it up, and place the creased sheet on the kitchen countertop. Using the waxed paper as a work surface, spoon the ingredients into a dry measuring cup, leveling it off with a knife or spatula, allowing any excess to fall on the waxed paper. When you're finished, pick up the waxed paper and pour the excess back into its original canister.

Frozen Food

- **Forster Clothespins.** To seal open bags of frozen food, use a Forster Clothespin to clip bags of frozen vegetables closed.

Fruit

Cleaning

- **Arm & Hammer Baking Soda.** To clean pesticides and insects from fruits, wet the fruits, sprinkle them with a little Arm & Hammer Baking Soda, and then rinse well.

- **Bounty Paper Towels.** To keep fruit fresh in the refrigerator, line the bottom of the fruit bin in your refrigerator with Bounty Paper Towels to absorb the excess moisture.

- **Clorox Bleach.** To clean pesticides and insects from fruits, add one-half cup Clorox Bleach in a sink filled with enough water to cover the fruit. Let soak for ten minutes and rinse clean. The chlorine bleach kills lingering bugs.

- **Dawn Dishwashing Liquid.** To remove any insecticides or preservatives from fruit, add one teaspoon Dawn Dishwashing Liquid to a sink full of warm water, and wash the fruit in the soapy water. Rinse clean and dry.

- **Heinz White Vinegar.** To wash sprays and chemicals from store-bought fruits, fill your kitchen sink with cold water and add three-quarters cup Heinz White Vinegar. Soak the fruits in the water for ten minutes, and then wipe them with a clean sponge to loosen any residue. Rinse clean with cold water and dry.

- **Hydrogen Peroxide.** To remove pesticides from fruit, fill a sink with cold water, add one-quarter cup Hydrogen Peroxide, wash the fruits in the solution, rinse clean with water, and then dry.

- **Morton Salt** and **ReaLemon.** Another way to remove pesticides from fruit: Fill the sink with cold water, add four tablespoons Morton Salt and two tablespoons ReaLemon lemon juice, soak the fruit for five to ten minutes or berries for one to two minutes. Rinse with clean water and dry.

Preparing

- **Gold Medal Flour.** Before adding any fruits to cake or pudding batters, heat them in the oven briefly and dust them with Gold Medal Flour to help prevent them from sinking in the mold.

- **Mr. Coffee Filters.** To weigh chopped foods on a kitchen scale without creating a mess, place the chopped ingredients in a Mr. Coffee Filter and weigh that.

- **Pam Cooking Spray.** To prevent fruits and berries from staining your hands, before working with the fruit, spray your hands with a light coat of Pam Cooking Spray.

- **ReaLemon.** To prevent freshly cut slices of fruit from discoloring, use a pastry brush to paint the sliced fruit with ReaLemon lemon juice.

Food for Thought
ANY WAY YOU SLICE IT

- To peel thick-skinned fruit, place the fruit in a bowl, cover with boiling water, and let sit for one minute—allowing the boiling water to soften the skin. Then peel with a paring knife.

Garlic

- **Colgate Regular Flavor Toothpaste.** To clean the smell of garlic from your hands, squeeze a dollop of Colgate Regular Flavor Toothpaste into the palm of your hand, rub your hands together under running water, and rinse clean.

- **Domino Sugar** and **ReaLemon.** To deodorize the smell of garlic from your breath, mix one-quarter teaspoon Domino Sugar and one teaspoon ReaLemon lemon juice, swish the solution around your mouth for a minute or two, and then rinse clean.

- **Forster Toothpicks.** To make a garlic clove easy to handle, insert a Forster Toothpick into a clove of garlic before tossing it into a marinade, so you can remove the clove easily.

- **Heinz Red Wine Vinegar.** To make garlic-flavored vinegar, place several sliced cloves of garlic in a jar and cover with Heinz Red Wine Vinegar, seal with a lid, and let sit for several weeks. Remove the garlic and use the flavored vinegar in dressings.

- **Morton Salt.** To prevent garlic from sticking to a mincing knife, sprinkle Morton Salt on the cutting board and the garlic clove. The abrasiveness of the salt impedes the knife from sticking to the garlic.

- **Morton Salt.** To make fresh garlic salt, sprinkle the cutting board with Morton Salt before mashing garlic cloves. The salt absorbs the garlic oil.

- **Morton Salt** and **Heinz White Vinegar.** To clean the smell of garlic from your hands, wet your hands with Heinz White Vinegar, rub a teaspoon Morton Salt between them, and then wash with soap and water.

- **ReaLemon.** To remove the smell of garlic from your hands, rub your skin with ReaLemon lemon juice, and then rinse your hands clean with water.

- **Reynolds Cut-Rite Wax Paper.** To avoid sullying your hands with garlic oil when mashing a clove, crush the clove between a folded sheet of Reynolds Cut-Rite Wax Paper, and then skim the garlic off the paper into a bowl or dish.

- **Star Olive Oil.** To roast your own garlic, remove the outer layers from the bulb, leaving the individual covering on each clove. Using a knife, slice one-quarter inch from the pointed tops to expose the cloves. Place the heads of garlic in a small baking dish, with the cut tops facing up. Drizzle one tablespoon Star Olive Oil on the cloves. Cover the dish and bake at 400 degrees Fahrenheit for roughly thirty minutes (or until the cloves feel soft to the touch). Let cool and remove the softened garlic from each clove.

Gelatin

- **Dannon Yogurt.** To make a creamy gelatin dessert, dissolve the flavored gelatin powder in the proper amount of hot water according to the directions on the box, and then substitute one cup Dannon Yogurt for every cup of cold water required.

- **Heinz White Vinegar.** To prolong the firmness of gelatin, add one teaspoon Heinz White Vinegar for every four cups of liquid when preparing the powder.

● **Morton Salt.** To expedite the setting time of a gelatin dessert, set the bowl or gelatin mold over a bowl filled with ice cubes and sprinkled with Morton Salt.

Grapefruit

● **Domino Sugar.** To sweeten a grapefruit half, sprinkle with Domino Sugar just before eating.

● **McCormick Cinnamon Sugar.** Cut a grapefruit in half, loosen the fruit from the skin by cutting around the inside perimeter, and then cut the segments apart. Sprinkle with McCormick Cinnamon Sugar and broil in a preheated oven for four minutes (or until the cinnamon sugar caramelizes). Serve warm.

Grapes

- **Domino Confectioners Sugar.** To make a delicious snack even more sensual, sprinkle a light coat of Domino Confectioners Sugar on frozen grapes (see Ziploc Storage Bags below) and serve.

- **Ziploc Storage Bags.** To make a delicious frozen snack, wash and dry a bunch of grapes, place them in a Ziploc Storage Bag, and put them in the freezer. For parties, instead of using ice, add frozen grapes to a bowl full of punch.

Food for Thought
GRAPE IDEAS

- Add sliced grapes to tuna salad or chicken salad to make the dish more elegant.

- To remove seeds from grapes quickly, slice the grapes slightly off-center, exposing the seeds and making them easy to flick away.

Gravy

- **Arm & Hammer Baking Soda.** To tame greasy gravy, add one-quarter teaspoon Arm & Hammer Baking Soda to the sauce.

- **Campbell's Beef Bouillon.** To enhance gravy with a rich flavor, substitute Campbell's Beef Bouillon for any water in the recipe.

- **Cheerios.** To thicken gravy, grind up Cheerios in the blender and stir the powdered oats into the gravy.

- **Crisco All-Vegetable Shortening.** Before adding flour to thicken gravy, melt some Crisco All-Vegetable Shortening in a saucepan and mix in the flour, coating it with shortening and warming it for a few minutes. The flour will mix better with the drippings and have a less floury taste.

- **Dannon Yogurt** and **Kingsford's Corn Starch.** To make delicious gravy for meat or chicken, mix Dannon Plain Yogurt into the pan drippings and add one tablespoon Kingsford's Corn Starch for each cup of yogurt to prevent it from separating.

- **Domino Sugar.** To darken pale gravy, dissolve one tablespoon Domino Sugar in one tablespoon of water, heat the mixture in a heavy saucepan until the sugar starts turning to caramel, and then mix the pale gravy into the sugared pan.

- **Gold Medal Flour.** To make gravy, mix Gold Medal All-Purpose Flour and enough water to make a smooth paste. Add the mixture gradually to a pan of meat or chicken drippings, stirring the opaque gravy continuously while bringing it to a boil. To achieve a richer flavor, use unbleached flour.

- **Hunt's Tomato Paste.** To enhance the taste of meat gravy, add one or two tablespoons Hunt's Tomato Paste (and one-half cup red wine, if desired) and cook gently for twenty minutes, stirring frequently.

- **Jif Peanut Butter.** To rescue burnt gravy, remove any burnt particles from the gravy in the saucepan, add one tablespoon Jif Peanut Butter (creamy), and stir over a low heat. The peanut butter eliminates the burnt taste.

- **Kingsford's Corn Starch.** To make clear gravy, mix Kingsford's Corn Starch and enough water to make a smooth paste. Add the mixture gradually to a pan of meat or chicken drippings, stirring the gravy continuously while bringing it to a boil.

- **Lipton Recipe Secrets Onion Soup Mix** and **Wesson Oil.** To make a dark, rich gravy, mix the contents from a packet of Lipton Recipe Secrets Onion Soup Mix with enough water to make a watery paste, add one teaspoon Wesson Oil, and brown the meat in this solution. Use the resultant mixture as the base for your gravy.

- **Manischewitz Potato Starch.** To thicken clear gravy and keep it translucent, add Manischewitz Potato Starch.

- **Maxwell House Coffee.** To make red-eye gravy, fry ham, add water to the drippings, and add one teaspoon Maxwell House Instant Coffee.

- **Maxwell House Coffee.** To darken pale gravy without altering the taste, add percolated Maxwell House Coffee. Or add one-half teaspoon Maxwell House Instant Coffee granules to the gravy to attain a rich brown color and enhance the flavor.

- **McCormick Powdered Arrowroot.** To thicken clear gravy without turning it opaque, add McCormick Powdered Arrowroot.

- **ReaLemon.** To prevent meat blood from causing gravy to curdle, add a little ReaLemon lemon juice and mix thoroughly.

- **Wonder Bread.** Use a slice of Wonder Bread to blot up any fat floating on top of gravy.

Food for Thought
RIDING THE GRAVY TRAIN

- To make greaseless gravy, pour the pan drippings into a tall glass, and let sit for ten minutes. The grease will rise to the surface, where you can spoon it out.

- To remove lumps from gravy, pour the gravy into a blender and give it a whirl.

Ham

- **Bounty Paper Towels.** To avoid making a mess when slicing a freshly baked ham, place a few layers of Bounty Paper Towels under the cutting board before cutting the ham. The paper towels will absorb the excess juices.

- **Canada Dry Ginger Ale.** If a partially baked ham tastes too salty, drain all the juices from the pan, pour two cups Canada Dry Ginger Ale over the ham, and bake until finished. The ginger ale will neutralize the salty taste.

- **Coca-Cola.** To bake a moist ham wrapped in aluminum foil in a pan, baste the ham with one can of Coca-Cola. For the last half hour of cooking, remove the aluminum foil and allow the ham to bake directly in the cola. The cola and juices from the ham make delicious gravy.

- **Dole Pineapple Slices.** To enhance a baked ham, arrange six Dole Pineapple Slices on top of the ham for the last thirty minutes of baking.

- **Domino Sugar.** To glaze an unbaked ham, remove the rind (leaving roughly one-half inch of fat over the ham), sprinkle Domino Sugar (or Domino Brown Sugar) amply and evenly over the surface, and then bake the sugar-coated ham at 450 degrees Fahrenheit. The heat will caramelize the sugar over the fat, giving the ham a luscious dark brown glaze.

- **Maxwell House Coffee.** To make red-eye gravy, fry ham, add water to the drippings, and add one teaspoon Maxwell House Instant Coffee.

- **Saran Wrap** and **Reynolds Wrap.** To freeze leftover ham, wrap the slices tightly in Saran Wrap, cover securely with Reynolds Wrap aluminum foil, and freeze for up to six weeks.

Hamburgers

- **Angostura Aromatic Bitters.** To give hamburgers a magnificent flavor, add one teaspoon Angostura Aromatic Bitters for every 1½ pounds ground beef before making the hamburger patties.

- **Breakstone's** or **Knudsen Cottage Cheese.** To make moist hamburgers, place one tablespoon Breakstone's or Knudsen Cottage Cheese inside each patty. (Breakstone's is available in the eastern, southeastern, and mid-western United States; Knudsen is sold in the western United States.)

- **Gold Medal Flour.** To cook up a crusty hamburger, dip the ground beef patty in Gold Medal Flour before frying it in hot fat.

- **Kellogg's Rice Krispies.** To stretch ground beef further and simultaneously enhance the taste, grind up Kellogg's Rice Krispies in a blender (or run a rolling pin over a Ziploc Storage Bag filled with the cereal) and mix the crumbs into the ground beef before making hamburger patties.

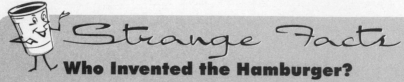

Who Invented the Hamburger?

No one knows for certain where the hamburger originated, but contrary to popular belief, the ground beef patty served on a bun did not get its start in Hamburg, Germany. Germans in Hamburg did cook patties of ground beef that became known as "Hamburg steak," but it was not eaten on a bun.

In his book *The Origin of Hamburgers and Ketchup*, professor Giovanni Ballarini contends that in the late 1800s, European emigrants traveling to America on the ships of the Hamburg Lines were served cooked meat patties placed between two pieces of bread.

However, several Americans claim to have invented the hamburger.

● In 1885, fifteen-year-old Charlie Nagreen sold meatballs from his ox-drawn food stand at the first Outagamie County Fair in Seymour, Wisconsin. To improve business, he purportedly flattened a meatball between two slices of bread and called his new creation a hamburger. Nicknamed "Hamburger Charlie," he returned to the fair every year to sell his hamburgers. In 2007, the Wisconsin Legislature declared the town of Seymour, Wisconsin, to be the "Original Home of the Hamburger," and the town is home to a Hamburger Hall of Fame and hosts an annual Hamburger Festival in August.

● The Menches brothers—Frank and Charles—of Akron, Ohio, insisted that they invented the hamburger in 1885 while working with a traveling

● **Maxwell House Coffee.** To make perfectly round hamburger patties, press down on the flat patties with the bottom of a Maxwell House Coffee can, and then trim the excess meat from around the patty.

● **Morton Salt.** To lessen the calories in a hamburger, fry the ground beef patty in a skillet salted with Morton Salt, without adding any fat whatsoever. The salt absorbs the juices from the beef, allowing the hamburger to cook in its own fat.

circus at the Erie County Fair in Hamburg, New York. The brothers purportedly ran out of pork for their hot sausage patty sandwiches, so instead they cooked up ground beef, served it between two slices of bread, and named the sandwich the "hamburger" after the city where the fair was being held.

● Oscar Weber Bilby claimed that he served the first-known hamburger on a bun on his farm just west of Tulsa, Oklahoma, on July 4, 1891. Bilby cooked ground Angus beef patties on a hand-made grill and put them on his wife Fanny's homemade yeast buns. In 1933, Oscar and his son, Leo, opened a hamburger stand in Tulsa, Oklahoma, called Weber's Superior Root Beer Stand. On April 13, 1995, Oklahoma Governor Frank Keating proclaimed Tulsa, Oklahoma, as the genuine birthplace of the hamburger on the bun.

● Louis Lassen, the proprietor of a small lunch wagon named Louis' Lunch on Meadow Street in New Haven, Connecticut, said he invented the hamburger in 1900. Lassen, who sold steak sandwiches to local factory workers, ground up the excess beef from his daily lunch rush, broiled it in patties, and served it between two slices of toast. Louis' Lunch, now a storefront luncheonette on Crown Street in New Haven, is owned and operated by Lassen's grandson, Ken; his wife, Lee; and their son, Kenneth. Hamburgers remain the house specialty, and the Lassens grind fresh steak daily and hand mold it into patties that are broiled and served between two slices of toast. Patrons have included Bing Crosby, Rudy Vallee, Charles Lindbergh, William F. Buckley, and George W. Bush.

● **Nabisco Original Premium Saltine Crackers.** Grind Nabisco Original Premium Saltine Crackers in a blender (or seal them inside a Ziploc Storage Bag and run a rolling pin over them) and mix the cracker crumbs with the ground beef to stretch the hamburger meat further.

● **Playtex Living Gloves.** When shaping hamburger patties, wear a pair of Playtex Living Gloves. The rubber gloves give you neat, even patties, and the gloves wash clean with hot soapy water.

Food for Thought
GETTING GRILLED

- Before freezing hamburger patties, punch a doughnut hole roughly the diameter of a nickel through the center of each patty. This way, you can cook the frozen hamburger patties without thawing them first. As the burger cooks, the center no longer remains raw and the hole closes back up.

- To cook up a moist hamburger, put a few drops of water on the top of the beef patty as you grill each side.

- To avoid overcooking hamburgers, form the patties around chunks of crushed ice, which melt during grilling, keeping the burger moist.

- To make moist hamburgers, add one stiffly beaten egg white or one grated medium onion to each pound of ground beef.

- **Quaker Oats.** To make delicious hamburger and stretch the ground beef further, combine one pound lean ground beef, one-half cup uncooked Quaker Oats (Quick or Old-Fashioned), and one lightly beaten egg in a mixing bowl. Form hamburger patties and grill or broil.

- **Reynolds Wrap.** To cook hamburgers for a large crowd, line the bottom of a baking pan with a sheet of Reynolds Wrap and cover with neat rows of single hamburger patties. Cover the patties with a second sheet of Reynolds Wrap and arrange the second tier of hamburgers on the aluminum foil. Repeat to create a third and fourth stack. Bake in an oven set at 350 degrees Fahrenheit for roughly thirty-five minutes. Or cook the beef for twenty minutes and finish cooking on an outdoor barbecue grill.

- **Saran Wrap.** Before stacking raw hamburger patties on a platter, cover the plate with a sheet of Saran Wrap. After placing all the patties on the grill, remove the Saran Wrap from the plate, discard the tainted plastic wrap, and place the finished hamburgers on the clean platter.

Herbs and Spices

Bay Leaves

- **Forster Toothpicks.** To make a bay leaf easy to find when cooking a stew or sauce, skewer the herb with a Forster Toothpick.

- **L'eggs Sheer Energy Panty Hose.** To make removing bay leaves from your sauce, soup, or stew effortless, use a pair of scissors to clip off the toe section from a pair of clean, used L'eggs Sheer Energy Panty Hose. Place the bay leaves inside the toe section, tie a knot in the open end, and place the sachet in the pot with your sauce, soup, or stew.

Bouquet Garni

- **L'eggs Sheer Energy Panty Hose.** To make a *bouquet garni* that can be removed easily from the cooking pot, use a pair of scissors to clip off the toe section from a pair of clean, used L'eggs Sheer Energy Panty Hose. Place some marjoram, parsley, thyme, and a bay leaf inside the toe section, tie a knot in the open end, and place the sachet in your cooking pot.

Decorating

- **Blue Bonnet Margarine.** To decorate dinner plates with an herbal border, spread a light, even coat of Blue Bonnet Margarine along the rim of each dinner plate, and sprinkle a finely chopped herb that will complement the entrée on the margarine edging. Add the entrée and side dishes.

Flavored Vinegar

- **Star Wine Vinegar.** To make flavored vinegar, pour a bottle of Star Wine Vinegar into a saucepan, add the herbs of your choice—perhaps celery, dill seeds, rosemary, or tarragon—and bring to a simmer. Let cool, pour back into the bottle, and store.

Garlic

See page 171.

Ginger

- **Smirnoff Vodka.** To preserve diced, fresh ginger in your refrigerator, peel and chop fresh ginger, place in a jar, top off with Smirnoff Vodka, and seal the lid securely. The ginger will last up to one year in the refrigerator.

Onion Salt

- **Morton Salt.** To make fresh onion salt, cut off the top of an onion, sprinkle Morton Salt over the open slice, let sit for a few minutes to give the salt time to absorb the onion juice, and scrape off.

Peppers

- **McCormick Black Peppercorns.** To prevent the holes in your pepper shaker from getting clogged, add a few whole black peppercorns into the shaker. The peppercorns absorb excess moisture and give the crushed pepper a fresher flavor.

Pouring

- **Reynolds Cut-Rite Wax Paper.** To avoid messy spills when pouring spices into a shaker or a measuring spoon, pour the spices over a sheet of Reynolds Cut-Rite Wax Paper. Should the spices spill, fold the sheet of waxed paper in half and pour the spice back into its proper canister.

Honey

- **Pam Cooking Spray.** Before working with honey, spray your utensils and measuring cups with Pam Cooking Spray to make cleaning up the mess afterward much simpler.

● To prevent the lid from sticking shut on a honey jar, wipe the rim of the honey jar clean with a damp cloth before replacing the lid.

● If you substitute honey for half of the sugar in baking, reduce the liquid in the recipe by one-fourth. If you substitute honey for all of the sugar in a recipe, reduce the liquid by half. For baked goods, add one-half teaspoon Arm & Hammer Baking Soda for each cup of honey used, and reduce the oven temperature by 25 degrees Fahrenheit to prevent overbrowning.

● Honey never spoils, and crystallization does not affect the taste or purity of honey. If honey crystallizes, just pop it in warm water or in the microwave oven in a microwave-safe container on high for one to three minutes, stirring every thirty seconds.

Honeydew Melon

● **Morton Salt.** Sprinkling honeydew melon with Morton Salt gives the fruit a zesty taste.

● **ReaLemon.** To enhance the taste of honeydew melon, sprinkle with a few drops of ReaLemon lemon juice.

Hot Chocolate

● **Jif Peanut Butter.** To sweeten hot chocolate, add one tablespoon Jif Peanut Butter and stir well.

● **Morton Salt** and **Kingsford's Corn Starch.** To enhance the taste of hot chocolate, dissolve a pinch Morton Salt and a teaspoon Kingsford's Corn Starch in the pot.

● To prevent a skin from coagulating on the top of a pot of hot chocolate, immediately after heating, use a whisk to beat the heated concoction until it froths.

❄ Recipe Magic ❄

Homemade Ice Cream

- 1 box Jell-O Instant Pudding
- 3 cups milk
- 1 Maxwell House Coffee can (11 ounces)
- 1 Maxwell House Coffee canister (33 ounces)
- 1 box Morton Rock Salt

Empty the contents of the Jell-O Instant Pudding mix into a large mixing bowl. Add the milk (according to the directions on the back of the box) and mix well, using a whisk. Pour the pudding solution into a small, clean Maxwell House Coffee can (11 ounces). Secure the plastic lid in place and use electrical tape to make the lid watertight. Place the small coffee can into a large Maxwell House Coffee canister (33 ounces). Fill the rest of the can with ice up to the top of the small can. Fill the rest of the space with Morton Rock Salt. Secure the plastic lid in place and use electrical tape to make the lid watertight.

Take the can outside and roll it back and forth across the lawn or patio for fifteen minutes. Bring the can back inside, peel the tape from the lid of the large can, pour out the melted ice and salt, and refill with fresh ice and fresh salt. Secure the lid in place again and roll the can outside for another fifteen minutes. Bring the can back inside, peel off the tape from the large can, pour out the melted ice and salt, and wash off the small can with tap water from the sink. Dry the can. Store in the freezer for twelve hours. Peel off the tape from the small can, remove the lid, and scoop the contents into bowls.

Ice Cream

- **Conair Hair Dryer.** To soften ice cream that is frozen solid, set a Conair Hair Dryer on cool and blow the container.

- **Jet-Puffed Marshmallows.** To prevent ice cream cone drips, stuff a Jet-Puffed Marshmallow in the bottom of a sugar cone before adding the scoops of ice cream.

- **Jif Peanut Butter.** To stop a leak from an ice cream cone, put a teaspoon of Jif Peanut Butter in the bottom of the cone before adding the ice cream. You not only stop the leaks, but you get a treat at the bottom of the cone.

- **Reynolds Cut-Rite Wax Paper.** To prevent a waxy film from forming on the top of an opened carton of ice cream in the freezer, press a piece of Reynolds Cut-Rite Wax Paper against the surface of the ice cream before resealing the carton and freezing.

Jam and Jellies

- **Land O Lakes Butter.** To prevent a skin from forming over jellies and to eliminate any foam, spread a thin layer of melted Land O Lakes Butter over the jelly immediately after cooking and stir well.

- **Mr. Coffee Filter.** Strain homemade jelly through a Mr. Coffee Filter to eliminate any impurities.

- **Oral-B Dental Floss.** Before sealing a jelly jar with melted paraffin wax, place a strand of Oral-B Dental Floss across the mouth of the jar, letting it rest on the jelly with the ends hanging over rim. Pour the paraffin over the strand of dental floss. When you're ready to open the jar, you'll be able to lift out the layer of paraffin by pulling up on the string.

- **ReaLemon.** To preserve a jam or jelly's original fruit color and to expedite the jelling process, add four tablespoons ReaLemon lemon juice to a jam or jelly while cooking.

Juices

- **Hunt's Tomato Paste** and **Morton Salt.** To make tomato juice, combine the contents of a six-ounce can of Hunt's Tomato Paste, three cans of cold water, and one teaspoon Morton Salt.

- **McCormick Black Pepper, McCormick Garlic Powder, Domino Sugar,** and **ReaLemon.** To make a tomato juice cocktail, add McCormick Black Pepper, McCormick Garlic Powder, Domino Sugar, and ReaLemon lemon juice to taste.

Ketchup

- **Glad Flexible Straws.** To unclog a freshly opened ketchup bottle, insert a Glad Flexible Straw all the way into the bottle to add air so the ketchup will flow out of the bottle.

Kiwi

- **Ziploc Storage Bags.** To ripen kiwifruit quickly, place the kiwi in a Ziploc Storage Bag with an apple and store at room temperature. The ethylene gas from the apple will ripen the kiwi.

Food for Thought
STRANGE FRUIT

- Store ripe kiwifruit in the refrigerator separated in the fruit bin from other fruits to prevent the flavors from mixing.

- The enzymes bromic and actinic in kiwifruit tenderize meat.

- When topping ice cream with kiwifruit, serve the dish immediately—before the enzymes bromic and actinic in the kiwifruit curdle the cream.

Lamb

- **Canada Dry Ginger Ale.** To reduce (and possibly even eliminate) the taste of mutton from lamb, roast and baste the lamb in Canada Dry Ginger Ale.

- **Forster Toothpicks.** To flavor lamb with garlic butter, use Forster Toothpicks to fasten a piece of garlic bread, butter side down, to the lamb. Sprinkle with water and roast.

- **Maxwell House Coffee.** To give lamb a zesty flavor, baste the roasting lamb with a cup of hot Maxwell House Coffee.

- **McCormick Caraway Seed.** Spice up lamb stew by stirring a tablespoon of McCormick Caraway Seed into the pot.

- **McCormick Ground Rosemary.** To give lamb chops an exquisite taste, combine two teaspoons McCormick Ground Rosemary and four garlic cloves in a blender and grate into a paste. Rub the tangy paste into oiled lamp chops before broiling.

- **ReaLemon.** To tenderize and flavor a leg of lamb, drizzle four tablespoons ReaLemon lemon juice over the meat and rub it in well before placing the leg in the oven.

Lemons and Limes

- **Forster Toothpicks.** To get more juice from a lemon or lime, use a Forster Toothpick to poke several holes through the peel. Heat the punctured lemon or lime in a microwave oven for fifteen seconds, and then juice as usual.

- **Forster Toothpicks** and **Saran Wrap.** To use a few drops of juice from a lemon or lime, use a Forster Toothpick to poke a hole through the lemon peel, squeeze out the juice you need, wrap the lemon or lime tightly in Saran Wrap, and refrigerate.

- **Saran Wrap.** Before grating lemon or lime zest, wrap two layers of Saran Wrap around the grater. This way, when you grate the lemon or lime, the zest will stick to the plastic wrap, rather than the grater. When you finish grating, carefully remove the Saran Wrap from the grater, lay it on the countertop, and use a spatula to scrap off the zest.

Food for Thought
GOING SOUR

- The average lemon yields four tablespoons lemon juice.

- Lemons and limes with the smoothest skin and the smallest points at each end contain more juice and provide the best flavor.

- To get more juice from a lemon or lime, submerge the fruit in boiling hot water for fifteen minutes before squeezing it.

- To get more juice out of a lemon, roll the lemon on a hard surface, pressing firmly with your palm, breaking up the pulp inside the lemon. Make sure the lemon is at room temperature.

- Use a nutcracker to squeeze the juice from a lemon.

- To enhance a glass of water or a salad, garnish with thin slivers of lemon.

- To make lemon zest, use a potato peeler or grater to shave off only the yellow portion of the lemon skin.

Lettuce

- **Morton Salt.** To rid curled leaf lettuce of any insects that might be hiding amongst the leaves, dissolve one-half cup Morton Salt in a sink full of cool water and soak the lettuce in the salty water for thirty minutes. Rinse clean in clear cold water.

- **ReaLemon.** To revitalize wilted lettuce, mix one teaspoon ReaLemon lemon juice in a bowl of ice-cold water, and soak the lettuce in the lemony solution for thirty minutes to an hour in the refrigerator.

- **ReaLemon** and **Heinz Apple Cider Vinegar.** To revitalize soggy lettuce, place the lettuce in a bowl filled with cold water and two tablespoons ReaLemon lemon juice, and refrigerate for one hour. Afterward, douse the lettuce quickly in hot water, and then add one tablespoon Heinz Apple Cider Vinegar to a large bowl of ice water and immerse the lettuce.

Food for Thought
LETTUCE REFRESH

- To revive wilted lettuce, place the lettuce in a pan of cold water, add a few slices of raw potato, and place in the refrigerator for thirty minutes.

Lima Beans

- **Arm & Hammer Baking Soda.** When soaking dry lima beans, add a pinch of Arm & Hammer Baking Soda to the water to shorten the soaking time. Discard the soaking water before cooking.
- **Campbell's Chicken Broth.** To give lima beans a wonderful flavor, steam them in Campbell's Chicken Broth.

Food for Thought
A HILL OF BEANS

- One pound of fresh lima beans yields 1¼ cups shelled lima beans, which, in turn, yields two servings.

- To shell fresh lima beans, use a pair of scissors to cut a thin slice along the inner edge of the pod and remove the beans.

- To add a zesty flavor to fresh lima beans, place a whole onion in the pan while cooking, and when finished, add salt and butter.

Liver

- **Campbell's Tomato Juice.** To sweeten the taste of liver, marinate the liver in Campbell's Tomato Juice for two to three hours before cooking.

- **Nestlé Carnation Condensed Milk.** For another way to sweeten liver, soak the liver in Nestlé Carnation Condensed Milk for twenty minutes in the refrigerator. The milk diminishes the otherwise overpowering flavor. Before cooking, dry the liver thoroughly.

Mangoes

- **Domino Sugar** and **Tropicana Orange Juice.** To make a delicious sauce to be served hot or cold with ice cream or fruit salad, chop a peeled mango and cook with one tablespoon of water, two tablespoons Domino Sugar, and two teaspoons Tropicana Orange Juice until creamy.

Mayonnaise

- **Betty Crocker Potato Buds.** To prevent homemade mayonnaise from separating, add one teaspoon Betty Crocker Potato Buds for each cup of mayonnaise.

- **Dannon Yogurt.** To thin mayonnaise for use in recipes, add Dannon Plain Lowfat Yogurt.

- **French's Mustard.** To use homemade mayonnaise that has started to curdle, place one teaspoon French's Mustard in a hot, dry bowl, add one tablespoon of the curdled mayonnaise at a time, beating with a whisk to achieve a thick, smooth mixture.

- **Knox Gelatin** and **Campbell's Chicken Broth.** To make mayonnaise chaud-froid (a stiff mayonnaise that retains its shape and acts like glue), mix one tablespoon Knox Unflavored Gelatin and one-third cup Campbell's Chicken Broth, heat until the gelatin dissolves, and let cool to room temperature. Stir the mixture gradually into 1½ cups mayonnaise (warmed to room temperature) and refrigerate until the gelatin sets. (You can also garnish a dish by piping the chaud-froid through a Ziploc Storage Bag.)

- **Nestlé Coffee-mate Creamer Italian Sweet Crème** and **Domino Sugar.** To revive curdled mayonnaise, beat the mayonnaise briskly with mixer or blender and add a small amount of Nestlé Coffee-mate Creamer Italian Sweet Crème and a pinch of Domino Sugar.

- **Progresso Breadcrumbs.** If you accidentally mix too much mayonnaise into tuna salad, add Progresso Breadcrumbs to absorb the excess.

Meatloaf

- **Betty Crocker Potato Buds.** To stretch meatloaf further, mix in roughly one-half cup Betty Crocker Potato Buds. The potato flakes also help the meatloaf bind more firmly.

- **Betty Crocker Potato Buds.** To top meatloaf with a frosting of lightly browned mashed potatoes, mix up one cup Betty Crocker Potato Buds according to the directions on the box. Fifteen minutes before the meatloaf is finished, spread the mashed potatoes over the meatloaf like icing on a cake, and then finish cooking it in the oven.

- **Campbell's Tomato Juice.** To make meatloaf tender and juicy, mix some Campbell's Tomato Juice into the meatloaf before baking.

- **Hunt's Tomato Sauce.** To bake a meatloaf with a crisp, shiny crust, cover the meatloaf with a light coat of Hunt's Tomato Sauce before baking.

- **Kellogg's Corn Flakes.**
  To stretch ground beef further to make meatloaf, grind Kellogg's Corn Flakes in the blender (or place the cereal in a Ziploc Storage Bag and run over it with a rolling pin) and mix one cup crumbs into every one pound ground beef.

- **Lipton Recipe Secrets Onion Soup Mix.** To spice up meatloaf, mix in the contents (or half the contents) of a packet of Lipton Recipe Secrets Onion Soup Mix.

- **Nabisco Original Premium Saltine Crackers.** Grind Nabisco Original Premium Saltine Crackers in a blender (or place in a Ziploc Storage Bag and run over with a rolling pin) and mix three-quarters cup cracker crumbs for every one pound ground beef to make meatloaf.

- **Nestlé Carnation Evaporated Milk.** To make meatloaf juicy and tender, mix one ounce Nestlé Carnation Evaporated Milk for every one pound ground beef before baking.

- **Reddi-wip.** To make meatloaf more tender and juicy, mix a dollop of Reddi-wip whipped cream into every one pound ground beef before baking the meatloaf.

Food for Thought
A FLASH IN THE PAN

- To prevent meatloaf from cracking in the oven, mist some cold water over the top of the meatloaf before placing the pan in the oven.

- To reduce cooking time down to nearly half, bake individual servings of meatloaf in a muffin tin rather than one large loaf in a loaf pan.

Classic Meatloaf

- 1½ pounds lean ground beef
- ¾ cup Quaker Oats
- ¾ cup onion, finely chopped
- ½ cup Heinz Ketchup
- 1 egg, lightly beaten
- 1 tablespoon Lea & Perrins Worcestershire Sauce
- 2 cloves garlic, minced
- ½ teaspoon Morton Salt
- ½ teaspoon McCormick Black Pepper

To make a fluffy classic meatloaf, preheat the oven to 350 degrees Fahrenheit. In a large bowl combine the ground beef, uncooked Quaker Oats, onion, Heinz Ketchup, egg, Lea & Perrins Worcestershire Sauce, garlic, Morton Salt, and McCormick Black Pepper. Mix lightly but thoroughly. Shape the meatloaf mixture into 10- x 6-inch loaf in a pan. Bake the meatloaf for 50 to 55 minutes, or until the temperature of the meatloaf is 160 degrees Fahrenheit. Let sit for five minutes before slicing. Makes six to eight servings.

- **Ziploc Freezer Bags.** To mix up meatloaf without making a mess of a bowl and your hands, place all the ingredients in a Ziploc Freezer Bag, seal the bag closed, and squeeze the bag to blend. Shape the contents into a loaf, open the bag, and slide the loaf into a pan.

Meats

Bacteria

- **Heinz White Vinegar.** To kill any bacteria in raw meats and tenderize the meat at the same time, marinate a two- to three-pound roast in one-quarter cup Heinz White Vinegar overnight (adding herbs to the vinegar if desired), and then cook the roast without draining or rinsing off the vinegar.

Broiling

- **Arm & Hammer Baking Soda.** If the fat from broiling meat catches fire, throw a handful of Arm & Hammer Baking Soda on the flames to extinguish the fire. The sodium bicarbonate in baking soda is the same ingredient found in fire extinguishers.

- **Morton Salt** and **Bounty Paper Towels.** To make a broiling pan easier to clean, immediately upon removing the cooked meat from the broiler, sprinkle the pan with Morton Salt, and then cover with wet Bounty Paper Towels. Let sit for fifteen minutes before washing with soapy water.

- **Reynolds Wrap** and **Forster Toothpicks.** To reduce the mess when broiling meat, line a cake or pie tin with Reynolds Wrap, and then

✳ Recipe Magic ✳

Delicious Brisket

- 2½ to 3 pounds brisket
- 1 can Coca-Cola
- 1 bottle Heinz Chili Sauce
- 1 package Lipton Recipe Secrets Onion Soup Mix

Brown the brisket in a Dutch oven on medium heat. Mix the Coca-Cola, Heinz Chili Sauce, and Lipton Recipe Secrets Onion Soup Mix in a bowl. Add the sauce to the browned brisket, cover, and simmer for 2½ hours, or until the meat is tender. Slice and serve.

stretch a second sheet of Reynolds Wrap taut across the top of the tin, crimping the edges over the rim. Using a Forster Toothpick, perforate the stretched sheet of Reynolds Wrap with a few small holes for drainage, and broil the meat on this surface. When finished cooking, discard the aluminum foil.

- **Wesson Oil.** To prevent meats from losing moisture when cooking, before broiling, rub or brush the outsides of the meat with Wesson Oil (seasoned, if you wish) and repeat several times during cooking. The oil seals the meat, keeping the juices from escaping.

- **Wonder Bread.** To lessen the chance of dripping fats from boiling meat catching fire or creating smoke, place a few slices of Wonder Bread in the broiling pan under the rack to absorb the dripping juices.

Browning

- **Wesson Oil, Domino Sugar,** and **Bounty Paper Towels.** To brown meat in a heavy frying pan, warm one teaspoon Wesson Oil in the pan, add one teaspoon Domino Sugar, and stir until the sugar darkens. After using a sheet of Bounty Paper Towels to dry pieces of meat, sear the meat in the sugary oil until the meat turns the color of mahogany, and then cook the meat on both sides until uniformly dark. Remarkably, the sugar adds no sweetness to the meat, only color.

Corned Beef

- **Heinz White Vinegar.** To prevent corned beef from shrinking when boiling, add two tablespoons Heinz White Vinegar to the water in the pot.

Defrosting

- **Bounty Paper Towels.** To speed up the time it takes to defrost frozen meat in the refrigerator, place a few sheets of Bounty Paper Towels in a pan, place a trivet (or a grill from one of the stove burners) on top of the paper towels, and place the frozen package of meat on top of that. The trivet (or grill) allows the air to circulate under the meat, speeding up the defrosting process.

- **Morton Salt.** To defrost meat quickly, place the wrapped meat in a bowl of cool water, and pour Morton Salt on the wrapper. Cover the bowl with a lid and let sit for one hour in the refrigerator.

Ground Beef

- **Bounty Paper Towels.** Before cooking ground beef, use Bounty Paper Towels to blot the excess grease and fat from the beef.

- **Morton Salt.** To defrost frozen ground beef more rapidly, sprinkle the beef with the same amount of Morton Salt called for in whatever recipe you intend to use. Salt speeds up the thawing process.

Hot Dogs

- **Eggo Waffles** and **Log Cabin Maple Syrup.** In a pinch, substitute Eggo Waffles, folded in half, for hot dog buns. Add some Log Cabin Maple Syrup as a condiment to bring the two tastes together.

Marinating

- **Newman's Own Olive Oil & Vinegar Dressing.** To give meat a wonderful flavor, marinate the meat in this salad dressing made with oil, vinegar, lemon juice, onion, and garlic.

- **ReaLemon** and **Ziploc Storage Bags.** To marinate meat, place the meat in a Ziploc Freezer Bag, add one-quarter cup ReaLemon lemon juice per pound of meat, and let sit for several hours in the refrigerator before cooking. The lemon juice tenderizes the meat.

- **Wish-Bone Italian Dressing.** To marinate venison or rabbit, cover the meat with Wish-Bone Italian Dressing overnight, refrigerate, drain, and cook as desired.

- **Ziploc Storage Bags.** Marinate meat in a Ziploc Storage Bag. The bag allows the marinade to cover the meat, and you only have to turn over the bag (rather than stirring the marinade in a bowl).

Meat Grinders

- **Nabisco Original Premium Saltine Crackers.** To prevent meat from sticking to a meat grinder, before grinding meat, grind a few Nabisco Original Premium Saltine Crackers first to absorb any residual moisture.

Meatballs

- **Nabisco Original Premium Saltine Crackers.** To stretch ground beef and make meatballs fluffier, grind Nabisco Original Premium Saltine Crackers in a blender (or place them in a Ziploc Storage Bag and run over them with a rolling pin) and use the crumbs in the meatballs.

Food for Thought
GET THE BALL ROLLING

- To prevent meatballs from crumbling apart when frying, chill the uncooked meatballs in the refrigerator for twenty minutes before cooking.

Mousse

- **Jell-O.** To make a meat mousse to be served cold, use a recipe for any hot mousse and add one tablespoon of your favorite flavor Jell-O powder dissolved in one tablespoon of cold water. Chill before serving. The finished mousse will be covered with a colorful aspic.

Roasting

- **Budweiser.** If the recipe calls for adding water to the roast, substitute the same amount of Budweiser beer, which gives the meat a great flavor.

- **Budweiser** and **Hunt's Tomato Paste.** Instead of adding water to a pot roast, combine six ounces Budweiser beer and two tablespoons Hunt's Tomato Paste and add the mixture to the pot to create wonderful gravy.

- **Campbell's Beef Broth.** Instead of adding water to meat as called for by the recipe, substitute the same amount of Campbell's Beef Broth to give the meat a hearty flavor.

- **Campbell's Tomato Juice.** Another great substitute for water in a pot roast is Campbell's Tomato Juice, which flavors the beef and keeps it moist and juicy on the inside.

- **Heinz Ketchup.** Dropping a few tomatoes in the pan will help tenderize a pot roast. Acid from the tomatoes helps break down the roast's stringy fibers.

- **Playtex Living Gloves.** Wear a pair of Playtex Living Gloves to pick up and turn a hot roast without burning your hands.

- **Reynolds Wrap.** To reheat a roast without drying it out, wash some large lettuce leaves, wrap the clean leaves around the roast, and wrap the entire lettuce-covered roast with Reynolds Wrap aluminum foil, crimping it closed. Preheat the oven to somewhere between 425 and 475 degrees Fahrenheit, and, depending on the size of the roast, heat in the oven for two to ten minutes.

- **USA Today.** To thaw a frozen roast in the refrigerator, place the roast on a cake cooling rack (exposing all sides of the roast to air to expedite the process), and place a copy of *USA Today* on a plate positioned under the rack to catch the drippings.

- **Wesson Oil.** To prevent meats from losing all their moisture when broiling or roasting, before cooking, rub or brush the outside of the meat with Wesson Oil (seasoned, if desired) and repeat several times during cooking. The oil seals the meat, preventing excess juices from escaping.

Fo⚬d f⚬r Th⚬ught

GETTING TO THE MEAT OF THE MATTER

● Cook a roast in a shallow pan rather than a deep one to allow the heat to better circulate around the roast.

● Instead of placing a roast on a metal roasting rack, make a grid of carrot and celery sticks and place the meat on it to flavor the pan drippings and avoid having to clean grease from a roasting rack.

● When cooking a roast, do not add salt until the meat is nearly cooked. Salt extracts the juices from the meat, making it moist and tasty. However, if you salt the roast too early, the heat from the oven will dry out those juices.

● To prevent a roast from scorching in the oven, place a pan of cold water in the oven to add humidity to the air.

● To make a roast easier to slice, let the roast stand for ten to fifteen minutes after removing it from the oven.

Sautéing

- **Bounty Paper Towels.** Before sautéing meat, blot the cuts of meat with a sheet of Bounty Paper Towels to absorb any moisture. Otherwise, when sautéing, moisture on the meat impedes proper browning and searing.

Splatters

- **Morton Salt.** To prevent hot fat from splattering when sautéing meat, sprinkle a little Morton Salt in the frying pan before cooking.

Steak

- **Bounty Paper Towels.** Before pan-broiling a steak, blot the beef dry with a sheet of Bounty Paper Towels so the moisture does not prevent the meat from browning properly.

- **Coca-Cola** and **Ziploc Storage Bags.** To grill a steak that melts in your mouth, place the steak in a Ziploc Storage Bag, pour one can of Coca-Cola into the bag, and marinate in the refrigerator for two or three hours. Grill the steak as usual over an open fire or grill.

- **Pam Cooking Spray.** To make cleaning up the broiler a snap, before broiling a steak, give the broiler rack a light coat of Pam Cooking Spray and pour a cup of water into the drip pan. The water absorbs smoke and grease.

- **Reynolds Wrap.** If you like your steak cooked brown on the outside but rare in the middle, wrap the steak in Reynolds Wrap and freeze it. Cook the steak without thawing it, and the center will defrost but remain rare.

Food for Thought
RAISING THE STEAKS

- When broiling a steak, pour one cup of water into the bottom of the broiling pan before placing it in the oven. The water absorbs the grease, preventing smoke.

Stewing

- **Budweiser** and **Lipton Recipe Secrets Onion Soup Mix.** Instead of using water or stock to make beef stew, substitute the contents of a can of Budweiser beer and a packet of Lipton Recipe Secrets Onion Soup Mix for a superb flavor. The Belgians call beef stew made with beer and onions a *carbonnade*.

- **Cheerios.** To thicken a beef stew, grind Cheerios in a blender and add the powdered oat cereal to the stew.

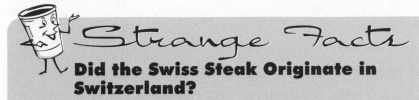

Strange Facts

Did the Swiss Steak Originate in Switzerland?

The name *Swiss steak* refers to the process of swissing—pounding tough, inexpensive cuts of beef with a tenderizing hammer or running the meat through a set of bladed rollers. The Swiss steak originated in the United States and has nothing to do with the nation of Switzerland.

- **Gold Medal Flour.** To thicken a stew, add one tablespoon Gold Medal Flour at a time, stirring continually, until you reach the desired consistency.

- **Lipton Tea Bags.** Add a strongly brewed cup of Lipton Tea to a stew made with tough cuts of meat. The tannic acid in the tea will tenderize the meat.

Swiss Steak

- **Campbell's Soup.** To pound flour into meat to make Swiss steak (see next tip), wash an unopened can of Campbell's Soup and hammer the meat with the bottom of the can. The ridge around the bottom scores the meat.

- **Gold Medal Flour.** To cook up an excellent Swiss steak, pound as much Gold Medal Flour (well-seasoned to your taste) into the strips of steak as they will absorb. Wait twenty minutes and repeat.

Tenderizing

- **Arm & Hammer Baking Soda.** To tenderize an exceptionally tough cut of meat, rub Arm & Hammer Baking Soda into the meat thoroughly. Let the powdered meat stand for several hours, and then wash the baking soda off the meat before cooking.

- **Campbell's Tomato Juice.** To tenderize meat, soak the meat in Campbell's Tomato Juice. The acids in tomatoes tenderize meat.

- **Coca-Cola.** To tenderize beef or pork, soak the meat in Coca-Cola for two to three hours.

- **Gold Medal Flour.** When pounding meat with a meat hammer, sprinkle Gold Medal Flour on the meat and hammer it into the meat. The flour seals in the juices and stops them from being squeezed out.

- **Heinz White Vinegar.** A marinade made from Heinz White Vinegar destroys bacteria and simultaneously tenderizes meat. Use one-half cup vinegar on a four- to six-pound roast, add whatever herbs you desire, and let sit overnight on a shelf in the refrigerator. Prepare the meat without draining or rinsing the vinegar.

- **Lakewood Papaya Juice.** Marinate meat in Lakewood Papaya Juice in the refrigerator for three to four hours, blot dry, and prepare as usual. Papain, an enzyme in papaya, tenderizes meat.

- **Lipton Tea Bags** and **Campbell's Condensed Beef Broth.** Add equal parts strong brewed Lipton Tea and Campbell's Condensed Beef Broth to a tough pot roast. The tannic acid in tea is a natural meat tenderizer. Or remove the strings and paper tabs from two Lipton Tea Bags, add the tea bags to the pot roast pot, and cook as usual. When the roast is done, remove the tea bags from the pot.

- **Nestea Iced Tea Mix** and **Campbell's Beef Broth.** To tenderize a tough pot roast or stew, dissolve one teaspoon Nestea Iced Tea Mix in one can Campbell's Beef Broth, and use the mixture as the liquid in a pot roast or stew.

- **Saran Wrap.** To avoid making a mess when tenderizing meat with a meat mallet, cover the meat with a piece of Saran Wrap before pounding. The plastic wrap prevents the juice from splattering everywhere.

- **7-Up.** To tenderize meat, marinate the beef in 7-Up and let sit in the refrigerator for three to four hours.

- **Star Olive Oil** and **Heinz White Vinegar.** To tenderize tough meat, mix equal parts Star Olive Oil and Heinz White Vinegar, rub the mixture into both sides of the meat, and let sit for two hours in the refrigerator.

- **Ziploc Storage Bags.** Use Ziploc Storage Bags to marinate meat. The bags allow the marinade to cover the meat, and you only have to turn over the bag (rather than stirring the marinade in a bowl).

Food for Thought
IF YOU CAN'T BEAT 'EM

- Rather than beating a piece of tough meat with a meat mallet, roll a pizza cutter over each side of the meat.

Veal

- **Gold Medal Flour** and **Land O Lakes Butter.** To give broiled veal chops a wonderful flavor and golden color, pound Gold Medal Flour into the veal chops, and then use a pastry brush to give them a thin coat of melted Land O Lakes Butter before broiling.

- **Wesson Oil** and **Land O Lakes Butter.** To give sautéed veal chops a lovely butter flavor without burning the butter, sauté the veal chops in Wesson Oil and, just before completion, add a small pat of Land O Lakes Butter to the pan and turn the chops once to get the butter flavor on both sides.

Meringues

- **Arm & Hammer Baking Soda.** To get egg whites to whip higher and firmer, add a pinch of Arm & Hammer Baking Soda to the egg whites before whipping them.

- **Crisco All-Vegetable Shortening.** To make baked meringues easy to remove from a cookie sheet, grease the cookie sheet with Crisco All-Vegetable Shortening—not butter or oil—regardless of what the recipe instructs. Let the meringues cool before removing.

- **Domino Sugar.** To make a thicker meringue, use two-thirds cup Domino Sugar to every three egg whites.

- **Land O Lakes Butter.** To avoid tearing the meringue topping when slicing a pie, butter the knife with Land O Lakes Butter before cutting into the meringue.

- **ReaLemon.** To whip a higher, firmer meringue, add one teaspoon ReaLemon lemon juice for every three egg whites.

Milk and Cream

- **Arm & Hammer Baking Soda.** When using buttermilk, sour cream, or sour milk (or substituting any of them for cream or sweet milk) in a recipe, for each cup of liquid, sift one-half teaspoon Arm & Hammer Baking Soda into the dry ingredients—unless the recipe calls for baking powder, in which case, add one-half teaspoon Arm & Hammer Baking Soda for the third cup of liquid and beyond (not the first two cups).

- **Forster Clothespins.** To prevent milk from absorbing odors in the refrigerator, clip the milk carton shut with a Forster Clothespin.

Buttermilk

- **Dannon Yogurt.** If you do not have any buttermilk called for by a recipe, substitute the same amount of Dannon Plain Nonfat Yogurt.

- **ReaLemon.** Another alternative for buttermilk: Mix one tablespoon ReaLemon lemon juice into one cup milk, let sit for ten minutes, and then substitute for one cup buttermilk.

Cream

- **Arm & Hammer Baking Soda.** If you believe your cream may no longer be fresh, mix in a pinch of Arm & Hammer Baking Soda to prevent the cream from curdling when you add it to hot coffee.

- **Carnation Fat-Free Evaporated Skim Milk.** For a low-calorie substitute for cream in cooking and sauces, use Carnation Fat-Free Evaporated Skim Milk.

- **Morton Salt.** To whip cream with better results, add a pinch of Morton Salt before whipping.

- **Reddi-wip.** A great substitute for cream is Reddi-wip, which is merely whipped cream in an aerosol can.

Sour Cream

See page 254.

Sour Milk

- **Heinz White Vinegar.** To make good sour milk, mix two teaspoons Heinz White Vinegar and one cup milk at room temperature and let the mixture sit for thirty minutes.

- **Nestlé Carnation Evaporated Milk** and **Heinz White Vinegar.** To make sour milk for cooking or baking, mix one-half cup Nestlé Carnation Evaporated Milk, one-half cup of lukewarm water, and one tablespoon Heinz White Vinegar. Let the mixture sit for thirty minutes at room temperature.

- **ReaLemon.** To make sour milk, mix two teaspoons ReaLemon lemon juice and one cup milk at room temperature and let the mixture stand for thirty minutes.

Substitutes

- **Nestlé Carnation Evaporated Milk.** If you need a milk substitute for cooking or baking, use one-half cup Nestlé Carnation Evaporated Milk and one-half cup of water for every one cup whole milk needed.

- **Nestlé Carnation Nonfat Dry Milk.** Another great milk substitute for cooking or baking is one-fourth cup Nestlé Carnation Nonfat

Dry Milk mixed with seven-eighths cup of water for every one cup whole milk called for by the recipe.

Whipped Cream

- **Dixie Cups.** To whip a small amount of cream, put the cream in a Dixie Cup and use only one blade of the mixer.

- **Domino Confectioners Sugar.** To whip fluffier whipped cream more likely to remain solid longer, sweeten the whipping cream with Domino Confectioners Sugar (which is fine) rather than granulated sugar (which is coarse).

- **Karo Light Corn Syrup.** To make whipped cream that will retain its fullness and freshness for a day or more in the refrigerator (without altering the taste), add one teaspoon Karo Light Corn Syrup to each cup cream before whipping.

- **Knox Gelatin.** To prevent homemade whipped cream from separating, add one-quarter teaspoon Knox Unflavored Gelatin for every one cup cream.

- **Nestlé Carnation Evaporated Milk** and **ReaLemon.** In a pinch, substitute a can of Nestlé Carnation Evaporated Milk for whipping cream. Simply place the can in the freezer until almost frozen, pour the evaporated milk into a chilled bowl, add one tablespoon ReaLemon lemon juice, two-thirds cup milk, and whip.

- **Nestlé Carnation Evaporated Milk, Knox Gelatin,** and **Domino Sugar.** For yet another way to make whipped topping, pour one twelve-ounce can Nestlé Carnation Evaporated Milk into a saucepan and heat to the scalding point. Mix three-quarters teaspoon Knox Unflavored Gelatin in three teaspoons of cold water and add to the hot milk, stirring until the gelatin dissolves. Pour into a bowl and chill. Beat with a mixer until stiff, and then sweeten to taste with Domino Sugar.

- **Nestlé Carnation Nonfat Dry Milk, McCormick Pure Vanilla Extract,** and **Domino Sugar.** To make a whipped topping from powdered milk, add equal parts Nestlé Carnation Nonfat Dry Milk and ice water to a bowl and whip with an electric mixer at the highest speed. After three or four minutes, the creamy topping should stand up in peaks. Add a few drops McCormick Pure Vanilla Extract and beat again. Add Domino Sugar to taste and beat well again.

- **ReaLemon.** To expedite the process of making whipped cream by hand, add three or four drops ReaLemon lemon juice to every cup heavy cream.

- **Reynolds Cut-Rite Wax Paper.** To reduce the splatter when whipping cream with an electric mixer, cut a sheet of Reynolds Cut-Rite Wax Paper to cover the bowl, cut two holes in the waxed paper for the stems of the beaters, and insert the stems through the holes. Attach the stems to the mixer, and whip the cream under the waxed paper covering.

- **Reynolds Cut-Rite Wax Paper** and **Ziploc Storage Bags.** To freeze leftover whipped cream, spoon dollops of the whipped cream on a sheet of Reynolds Cut-Rite Wax Paper and freeze. Once the dollops are frozen, put them in a Ziploc Storage Bag and keep in the freezer to use for dessert toppings, allowing ten to fifteen minutes for thawing.

Molasses

- **Arm & Hammer Baking Soda.** When using molasses in batter, add three-quarters teaspoon Arm & Hammer Baking Soda to the dry ingredients for each cup molasses. The baking soda neutralizes the acidity of the molasses and facilitates leavening.

- **Hershey's Semi-Sweet Chocolate Chips** and **Ziploc Storage Bags.** To give a molasses cake or cookies a rich brown color and a slight chocolate flavor, fill a Ziploc Storage Bag with Hershey's Semi-Sweet Chocolate Chips, seal the bag shut, and place in a pot of boiling water to melt the chocolate. Use a pair of scissors to snip off one corner, and pipe the melted chocolate into the cake or cookie batter.

- **Pam Cooking Spray.** Before working with molasses, spray your utensils and measuring cups with Pam Cooking Spray to make cleaning up the mess afterward much simpler.

Food for Thought
A STICKY SITUATION

- To prevent the lid from sticking shut on a molasses jar, wipe the rim of the molasses jar clean with a damp cloth before replacing the lid.

Muffins

- **Dannon Yogurt** and **Arm & Hammer Baking Soda.** To bake light, fluffy muffins, replace the milk called for in a muffin recipe with the same amount of Dannon Plain Nonfat Yogurt and add one-half teaspoon Arm & Hammer Baking Soda for each cup yogurt used.

Food for Thought
DO YOU KNOW THE MUFFIN MAN?

- Fill any empty compartments in the muffin pan halfway with water to prevent the pan from smoking or warping when exposed to heat in the oven.

- To avoid soggy-bottomed muffins, when you remove the muffin pan from the oven, let it cool on a wire rack for ten minutes, and then remove the muffins from the pan and let them cool on the rack.

- Remove warm muffins from the muffin pan with a shoehorn.

Mushrooms

- **Bounty Paper Towels.** To prevent mushrooms from steaming rather than browning when cooking, dry the mushrooms thoroughly before cooking by placing them between two sheets of Bounty Paper Towels to absorb the excess moisture. When cooking, stir the mushrooms with a fork, shake the pan occasionally, and keep the butter hot.

- **Land O Lakes Butter.** Steaming mushrooms in Land O Lakes Butter in a double boiler helps the mushrooms retain their color.

- **Newman's Own Olive Oil & Vinegar Dressing.** To give mushrooms a wonderful flavor, marinate the mushrooms in this salad dressing made with oil, vinegar, lemon juice, onion, and garlic.

- **Oral-B Dental Floss.** To dry mushrooms, wash them quickly, cut them in half lengthwise, and using a large needle and Oral-B Dental Floss, string them together leaving an inch between each mushroom half, and hang them outdoors for two days or until completely dry. Store in an airtight container on the pantry shelf. Rehydrate dried mushrooms by soaking them in water, chicken stock, or beef stock for one hour.

- **ReaLemon.** To prevent mushrooms from shriveling and turning

Food for Thought
MAKE ROOM FOR MUSHROOMS

- Never soak or immerse mushrooms in water. Instead, wash them quickly and pat them dry immediately thereafter with a towel. Otherwise, these absorbent fungi become quickly waterlogged and tasteless. Cook cleaned mushrooms immediately; otherwise the water will cause deterioration.

- To quickly slice fresh mushrooms uniformly, use an egg slicer.

brown while sautéing, add one teaspoon ReaLemon lemon juice for each quarter pound of butter. The lemon juice will help keep the mushrooms white and firm.

- **Wish-Bone Robusto Italian Dressing** and **Ziploc Storage Bags.** To make marinated mushrooms, drain one or two cans button mushrooms, place in a Ziploc Storage Bag, and add Wish-Bone Robusto Italian Dressing—a tangy mixture of canola oil, vinegar, red bell peppers, lemon juice, onion, and garlic. Let sit in the refrigerator for three or four hours.

Mussels

- **Bounty Paper Towels.** After scrubbing each mussel clean, use a sheet of Bounty Paper Towels to grasp the beard, and gently pull toward the hinged side of the mussel to remove it.

- **Colman's Mustard Powder.** To clean any slime from mussel shells, scrub the shells with a little dry Colman's Mustard Powder.

- **Playtex Living Gloves.** To avoid cutting your fingers or hand on sharp mussel shells, wear a pair of Playtex Living Gloves when scrubbing mussels clean.

Mutton

- **ReaLemon.** To subdue the strong flavor of mutton and tenderize the meat, either cut off the outside fat or rub the meat and fat thoroughly with ReaLemon lemon juice before cooking. When boiling mutton, add four tablespoons ReaLemon lemon juice to the cooking water.

Nuts

Almonds

- **McCormick Pure Almond Extract.** When using almonds in

Glazed Walnuts

- 1 teaspoon Land O Lakes Butter
- 1 teaspoon Domino Sugar
- 1 cup Planters Walnuts

Melt the Land O Lakes Butter to coat a frying pan. Add the Domino Sugar. Heat on high until the sugar turns bubbly brown. Pour the shelled, halved Planters Walnuts into the pan. Toss quickly with a spatula, remove the pan from the heat, and pour the glazed walnuts into a bowl. Let cool. Add as a garnish to salads.

cooking, add one-quarter teaspoon McCormick Pure Almond Extract as well to achieve a richer almond flavoring.

Chestnuts

- **Nestlé Carnation Nonfat Dry Milk.** To make mashed boiled chestnuts taste extra-light, mix four ounces Nestlé Carnation Nonfat Dry Milk and ten ounces of water, and simmer the shelled chestnuts in the milky solution for five minutes. Remove the chestnuts and mash.

- **Wesson Oil.** To roast chestnuts in a pan, use a knife to cut a slit down the round and flat sides of each chestnut to prevent them from exploding from the heat. Warm three to four teaspoons Wesson Oil in a skillet over medium heat, lay each chestnut flat in the pan, cover with the lid, and shake the pan frequently for roughly ten minutes. Drain the oil, and let the nuts cool to the touch.

Chopping

- **Ziploc Storage Bags.** To chop walnuts, hazelnuts, almonds, or pecans without making a huge mess, place the nuts in a Ziploc Storage Bag, roll up the bag to let the excess air escape, seal the bag, and hit with a meat hammer or a rolling pin.

Pecans

- **Morton Salt.** To remove the shell from pecans easily, dissolve two tablespoons Morton Salt per cup of water and soak the pecans in the salty solution for several hours. The salt water makes the meat of the nut easier to remove.

Oil

- **Heinz White Vinegar.** To reduce the amount of cooking oil absorbed by fried food, add one tablespoon Heinz White Vinegar to the frying pan before heating the oil.

- **Land O Lakes Butter.** To brown and flavor fried or sautéed foods, add a little Land O Lakes Butter to the cooking oil.

- **Mott's Applesauce.** To reduce the amount of calories and fat grams in home-baked goods, substitute the same amount of Mott's Applesauce for the amount of oil called for by the recipe when mixing up the dough or batter.

- **Mr. Coffee Filters.** To recycle frying oil, line a sieve with a Mr. Coffee Filter to strain oil after deep-fat frying.

- **Wonder Bread.** If you do not own a deep fat thermometer, determine whether hot fat has reached the right temperature for cooking by dropping

Food for Thought
BURNING THE MIDNIGHT OIL

- To eliminate odors and any unpleasant tastes from used frying oil, simmer a dozen sprigs of parsley or a few slices of raw potato in the oil for approximately fifteen minutes before reusing the oil.

a one-inch cube of Wonder Bread into the hot fat. If the piece of bread browns in roughly forty-five seconds, the fat is ready.

Onions

- **Arm & Hammer Baking Soda.** To remove the smell of onions from your hands, wet your hands, pour some Arm & Hammer Baking Soda into one palm, rub your hands together well, and rinse clean.

- **Aunt Jemima Original Pancake and Waffle Mix** and **Bounty Paper Towels.** To make French-fried onion rings, prepare the batter for Aunt Jemima Original Pancake Mix, dry the onion rings on a sheet of Bounty Paper Towel, dip them in the batter, and fry quickly in a buttered pan.

- **Colgate Regular Flavor Toothpaste.** To clean the smell of onions from your hands, squeeze a dollop of Colgate Regular Flavor Toothpaste into the palm of your hand, rub your hands together under running water, and rinse clean.

- **Domino Sugar.** If you want onions well browned when sautéing, add a small touch of Domino Sugar into the fat as you sauté.

- **Domino Sugar.** To remove onion odor from your hands, rub a teaspoon Domino Sugar and a few drops of water between your hands, and then rinse clean.

- **Gold Medal Flour** and **Bounty Paper Towels.** To make crisp onion rings, dip raw onion rings in a bowl of water, dip again in a bowl of Gold Medal Flour, let dry on a sheet of Bounty Paper Towel, and fry in hot fat.

- **Heinz White Vinegar.** To sweeten a strong-tasting onion, slice and separate the onion into rings, mix one teaspoon Heinz White Vinegar in a bowl of cold water, and soak the onion rings in the solution for thirty minutes.

WHAT'S COOKING

NO NEED TO CRY

When you cut into an onion, the onion produces the chemical irritant syn-propanethial-S-oxide as a vapor, which, when it comes into contact with your eyes, irritates the lachrymal glands, which respond by producing the tears. To avoid this scenario . . .

● Refrigerate the onions for at least one hour (or freeze them for thirty minutes) before cutting into them. The cold slows down the enzymes that create the chemical irritant.

● Wear a swimming mask or goggles to prevent the vapor from getting in your eyes.

● Peel the onions under cold, running water, or submerge the onion in a basin of cold water and carefully cut it underwater.

● Keep a lit candle nearby. The flame attracts the vapor and burns up some of the chemical. Or turn on the burner of a gas stove (but be certain to turn it off again).

● Run an exhaust fan to remove the tear-inducing fumes from the room.

● **Heinz White Vinegar.** To rid the smell of onion from your hands, rub Heinz White Vinegar between them, and then wash with soap and water.

● **Land O Lakes Butter.** If you intend to use only half of an onion, after cutting the onion in half, rub the open face of the leftover half with Land O Lakes butter to preserve it longer.

● **Lipton Recipe Secrets Onion Soup Mix.** If a recipe calls for onions, you can substitute Lipton Recipe Secrets Onion Soup Mix, which adds a tangy flavor.

- **Listerine.** To remove the pungent smell of onion from your hands, cover the affected area with Listerine antiseptic mouthwash, rub well, and rinse clean with water.

- **Maxwell House Coffee.** To deodorize your hands from smelling from onions, fill your palm with Maxwell House Coffee grounds (used or unused), add water if using fresh grounds, rub your hands together for one minute, and then rinse with running water.

- **Morton Salt.** To clean the smell of onion from your hands, wet your hands, rub one teaspoon Morton Salt between them, and then wash with soap and water.

- **Playtex Living Gloves.** To keep onion odor off your hands when cutting onions, simply wear a pair of Playtex Living Gloves while performing the task.

- **ReaLemon.** Rubbing your hands with ReaLemon lemon juice removes the smell of onions. Simply pour a little lemon juice into the palm of your hand and rub your hands together. Then rinse clean with water.

Food for Thought
CHEERS AND TEARS

- To make an onion easier to peel, hold it under warm or hot running water for two minutes. Or submerge the onion in boiling water followed by cold water.

- Slicing off the top and bottom of an onion makes the vegetable easier to peel.

- To subdue the strong taste of any onion, slice and separate the onion into rings and then soak the onion rings in cold water for one hour.

- To grate an onion, leave the onion top in place so you have a natural handle to hold.

- To cook a whole onion, cut an X roughly one-quarter inch deep in the stem end to reduce the possibility of the onion bursting.

- **Reynolds Wrap.** To prolong the life of green onions, wrap each one separately in Reynolds Wrap aluminum foil.

- **SueBee Honey.** Before sautéing onions in butter, add a little SueBee Honey to the butter and allow the honey and butter to sizzle. The honey greatly enhances the onions.

- **Wesson Oil.** Before adding sliced onion to a stew or casserole, sauté the onions lightly in Wesson Oil. Doing so vastly improves the taste of the finished dish.

- **Ziploc Storage Bags.** To store chopped onions for months, freeze them in a Ziploc Storage Bag. When you're ready to use the chopped onions, simply cook them without defrosting.

Oranges

- **Forster Toothpicks.** To get more juice from an orange, use a Forster Toothpick to poke several holes through the orange peel, and heat the punctured orange in a microwave oven for fifteen seconds. Then juice as usual.

Food for Thought
ORANGE ALERT

● If you cover an unpeeled orange with boiling hot water for five minutes, when you peel the orange, no white fibers from the peel will adhere to the pulp.

● To use an orange skin as a bowl for a flavored gelatin, pudding, or fruit cup, cut the orange in half through the equator, scoop out the pulp, and soak the skins in ice cold water until you're ready to serve.

● To make orange zest, use a potato peeler or grater to shave off only the orange portion of the fruit's skin.

- **Saran Wrap.** Before grating orange zest, wrap two layers of Saran Wrap around the grater. This way, when you grate the orange, the zest will stick to the plastic wrap, rather than the grater. When you finish grating, carefully remove the Saran Wrap from the grater, lay it on the countertop, and use a spatula to scrap off the zest.

Oysters

- **Canada Dry Club Soda.** Before attempting to pry oysters from their shells, soak them in Canada Dry Club Soda for five minutes to loosen the muscles and shell hinges.

- **Morton Kosher Salt.** To keep oysters on the half-shell hot while serving and eating, fill a bowl or dish with heated Morton Kosher Salt and position the open oysters in the coarse salt. The salt retains heat and provides a bed to stabilize the wobbly shellfish.

- **Ziploc Storage Bags.** To pry oysters from their shells, wash them in cold water, place in a Ziploc Storage Bag, and either freeze for thirty minutes or immerse in boiling water for three minutes. Either way, the oysters will be easily opened with a beer-can opener or short screwdriver.

Pancakes

- **Arm & Hammer Baking Soda.** To cook up delicate pancakes, substitute buttermilk or sour milk for the sweet milk called for in the recipe, and add a pinch of Arm & Hammer Baking Soda to the batter. The acids in the milk trigger the baking soda to emit carbon dioxide, causing the pancake to leaven.

- **Canada Dry Club Soda.** To make pancakes light and fluffy, substitute whatever amount of liquid called for by the recipe with the same amount of Canada Dry Club Soda. The carbonation in the club soda causes the pancakes to rise higher, provided you use the batter immediately.

Candied Fruit Peels

- 2 cups Domino Sugar
- 1 cup water
- ¼ cup Karo Light Corn Syrup
- Fruit peels from approximately twelve citrus fruits (any assortment of grapefruits, lemons, and oranges), washed and diced

Mix the Domino Sugar, water, and Karo Light Corn Syrup in a pot, and boil the mixture over low heat for thirty minutes. Add the fruit peels, and simmer for forty-five minutes or until the peels absorb all the syrup. Sprinkle a light coat of Domino Sugar on a sheet of Reynolds Cut-Rite Wax Paper, place all the candy-coated peels on the paper, and sprinkle with more sugar. Let air-dry for several days. Refrigerate to store.

- **Domino Confectioners Sugar.** To make dessert pancakes, add three to four tablespoons Domino Confectioners Sugar to the dry ingredients of your regular pancake batter.

- **Grandma's Molasses.** To sweeten and brown pancakes, add one teaspoon Grandma's Molasses to the batter.

- **Heinz Ketchup.** To form pancakes easily, pour the prepared batter into a clean, empty Heinz Ketchup squeeze bottle.

- **L'eggs Sheer Energy Panty Hose** and **Morton Salt.** If the pancake griddle gets sticky between batches of pancakes, cut off the foot from a pair of clean, used L'eggs Sheer Energy Panty Hose, fill the foot with Morton Salt, and tie a knot in the end. Rub the hot griddle with the sachet of salt.

- **Morton Salt.** To prevent pancakes from sticking to the griddle, sprinkle Morton Salt on the griddle before pouring the pancake batter.

- **Reynolds Cut-Rite Wax Paper** and **Ziploc Storage Bags.** To freeze pancakes, let the pancakes cool, stack them, separated by squares of Reynolds Cut-Rite Wax Paper, and place the stack in a Ziploc Freezer Bag. To reheat, place the frozen pancakes on a plate, cover with a sheet of paper towel, and reheat in the microwave oven for thirty seconds to two minutes.

- **Tropicana Orange Juice.** To make delicious dessert pancakes from regular pancake batter, substitute Tropicana Orange Juice for the milk called for by the directions on the box, and, if desired, add grated orange rind to the batter.

Pasta

Boiling

- **Crisco All-Vegetable Shortening.** To prevent pasta from boiling over in the pot, before heating up the pot, rub a dab of Crisco All-Vegetable Shortening around the inner rim of the pot.

- **Land O Lakes Butter.** Adding a teaspoon of Land O Lakes Butter to the water before heating also prevents pasta from boiling over and keeps the cooked pasta from sticking together.

- **McCormick Food Coloring.** To make noodles look more festive, add ten drops of your favorite color of McCormick Food Coloring to the water used to cook noodles.

- **Morton Salt.** Dissolve one teaspoon Morton Salt for every three quarts of water in the pot before turning on the heat. The salt helps bring the water to a boil more rapidly and gives the pasta a faint salty taste.

- **Star Olive Oil.** Another great way to prevent pasta from boiling over is to add one tablespoon Star Olive Oil (or any vegetable oil) to the water

WHAT'S COOKING

NOODLING AROUND

- Eight ounces of pasta yields enough spaghetti or noodles to serve three or four adults.

- Raw pasta doubles in volume when cooked, by absorbing water.

- When cooking pasta, use six quarts of water for every one pound pasta.

- To prevent pasta from boiling over in the pot, place a wooden spoon or spatula across the top of the pot.

- To cook pasta to perfection, bring salted water (see Morton Salt on page 219) to a rolling boil, stir in the pasta gradually (to avoid lowering the water temperature), cover the pot, turn off the heat, and let sit undisturbed for twenty minutes. Resist the temptation to lift the lid during that time; otherwise you lose all the steam. Pour the pasta into a colander, run under hot sink water, and then drain.

- Never add the pasta before the water starts boiling. Doing so slows the water from boiling, causing the pasta to stick together.

- When preparing pasta for use in a dish that requires additional cooking time, cook the pasta for two-thirds the regular time.

- If you do not intend to serve the cooked pasta immediately, drain the cooked pasta and rinse with cool water. Cover the pasta with cold water and store in the refrigerator. When ready to serve, reheat the pasta by pouring it in into the colander and running it under hot tap water, shaking well.

- Do not overcook pasta. Instead, cook pasta so it feels firm to the teeth, known in Italian as *al dente*.

- If you place steaming pasta on a plate, the steam condenses, creating a puddle of water on the plate. To avoid this scenario, wait for the pasta to stop steaming before serving.

- To twirl spaghetti or any long pasta onto a fork easily, twirl the fork against the bowl of a tablespoon, or, if need be, use a knife to cut long pasta before twirling onto a fork.

before turning on the heat. The oil also helps stop the cooked pasta from sticking together or to the sides of the pot.

Draining

- **Land O Lakes Butter** or **Wesson Oil.** If you intend to let cooked pasta stand for a while before serving, drain the pasta and mix in some melted Land O Lakes Butter or Wesson Oil to prevent the pasta from sticking together.

- **Pam Cooking Spray.** To prevent pasta from sticking to the inside of a colander, spray the colander with a thin coat of Pam Cooking Spray before draining the pasta.

Food for Thought
DOWN THE DRAIN

- If you don't own a pot with an inset pasta colander, place a large strainer inside the pot when cooking pasta. When the pasta finishes cooking, lift out the strainer and rinse the pasta under tap water.

- If drained pasta sticks together, place it back in the pot of water and boil for another minute or two.

Lasagna

- **Breakstone's** or **Knudsen Cottage Cheese.** If you're all out of ricotta cheese when cooking up lasagna, substitute Breakstone's or Knudsen Cottage Cheese, after first draining out the excess liquid. (Breakstone's is available in the eastern, southeastern, and midwestern United States; Knudsen is sold in the western United States.)

- **Pam Cooking Spray.** To prevent lasagna from sticking to the sheet of aluminum foil used to cover it during baking, spray the foil with a thin coat of Pam Cooking Spray before covering the lasagna.

● Rather than cooking lasagna noodles before assembling the lasagna, layer the uncooked lasagna noodles according to your recipe but add a little more sauce and cheese to furnish more liquid for the noodles to absorb.

Pastry

● **Nestlé Carnation Nonfat Dry Milk** and **ReaLemon.** To create a crisp, flaky pastry, add one tablespoon Nestlé Carnation Nonfat Dry Milk to the flour, use ice-cold water, and add one-half tablespoon ReaLemon lemon juice.

● **ReaLemon.** To create pastries with a crisp, flaky finish, substitute one tablespoon very cold ReaLemon lemon juice for one tablespoon of ice water, or add one tablespoon lemon juice to the batter.

● **Ziploc Storage Bags.** To fill a cream puff or an éclair, use a small knife to cut a small hole in the side of the cream puff or éclair. Place the cream inside a Ziploc Storage Bag, use a pair of scissors to snip off one of the bottom corners of the bag, and pipe the cream into the hole in the cream puff or éclair.

Peaches

● *USA Today.* To make peaches ripen quicker, place the peaches in a box, cover the fruit with sheets of *USA Today,* and seal the box closed. The newsprint keeps the ethylene gas emitted by the peaches close to the fruit, causing the peaches to ripen.

Food for Thought
PEACHY KEEN

● For another way to ripen peaches quickly, place the peaches and one ripe apple together in a brown paper bag, use the tines of a fork to punch a few holes in the bag, and place the bag in a cool, dark place. The ripe apple emits ethylene gas, which ripens the peaches.

● Peel firm peaches with a potato or carrot peeler.

● To peel peaches with ease, bring a pot of water to a boil, turn off the flame, soak the peaches in the water for three minutes, drain, and peel.

Pears

● **Morton Salt.** To prevent sliced pears from browning, toss the slices into a bowl of cold water lightly salted with Morton Salt.

● **ReaLemon.** To prevent peeled pears from discoloring, keep them in a bowl of cold water containing one tablespoon ReaLemon lemon juice.

● **USA Today.** To make pears ripen quicker, place the pears in a box, cover the fruit with sheets of *USA Today,* and seal the box closed. The newsprint keeps the ethylene gas emitted by the pears close to the fruit, causing the pears to ripen.

Food for Thought
A FINE PEAR

● For another way to speed up the ripening of pears, place the pears and one ripe apple together in a brown paper bag, use the tines of a fork to punch a few holes into the bag, and place the bag in a cool, dark place. The ripe apple emits ethylene gas, which ripens the pears.

Peppers

- **Crisco All-Vegetable Shortening.** Baked stuffed peppers retain their shape when baked in a greased cupcake or muffin tin. Fill any empty compartments in the cupcake or muffin tin with water before cooking the peppers to prevent smoking.

- **Playtex Living Gloves.** When working with hot peppers, wear Playtex Living Gloves to protect your skin from the heat.

Pies

- **Breakstone's** or **Knudsen Sour Cream.** To make a flakier piecrust, substitute Breakstone's or Knudsen Sour Cream for the liquid called for in the recipe. (Breakstone's is available in the eastern, southeastern, and mid-western United States; Knudsen is sold in the western United States.)

- **Clabber Girl Baking Powder.** To create a delicate, light pastry, add one pinch Clabber Girl Baking Powder to the flour when mixing pie dough. The baking powder causes the dough to leaven.

- **Crisco All-Vegetable Shortening.** To give a pie a tender crust, substitute Crisco All-Vegetable Shortening for any butter or margarine called for by the recipe. If you want the piecrust to have a buttery flavor, use one-third butter and two-thirds Crisco All-Vegetable Shortening.

- **Dannon Yogurt.** To make a piecrust lighter and flakier, substitute Dannon Plain Yogurt for the liquid suggested in the recipe.

- **Domino Sugar.** When making tart shells, add some Domino Sugar to the pastry dough to create a more delicate crust when baked—even though sugar will make the pastry dough more difficult to roll and shape.

- **Glad Flexible Straws.** To bake a pie without having it boil over, cut a Glad Flexible Straw into three-inch lengths and insert vertically into the piecrust, leaving one end exposed. Bake the pie as directed. The straws allow the steam to escape, preventing the pie from boiling over and making a mess.

- **Gold Medal Flour** and **Domino Sugar.** To prevent the fruit filling from making the bottom of the piecrust soggy, combine one-quarter cup Gold Medal Flour and one-half cup Domino Sugar and dust the powdery mixture over the bottom of the piecrust before adding the filling.

- **Heinz White Vinegar.** When a pie recipe calls for ice water, make a crispier piecrust by substituting one tablespoon Heinz White Vinegar for one tablespoon of ice water.

- **Honey Maid Graham Crackers.** To make graham cracker crust for a pie, crush Honey Maid Graham Crackers. One pound graham crackers yields roughly 4½ cups crumbs.

- **Jell-O.** To add a wonderful flavor and color to apple pie filling, before putting the top crust on a two-crust apple pie, sprinkle one-quarter cup of your favorite flavor Jell-O powder over the apples. Cover with crust and bake.

- **Jell-O Tapioca Pudding.** When preparing a pie filling with particularly juicy fruits, add one teaspoon Jell-O Tapioca Pudding mix to the filling to absorb the excess juice and keep the filling inside the pie.

- **Land O Lakes Butter.** To prevent a frozen pie from drying out when baked, use a pastry brush to paint the frozen pie with melted Land O Lakes Butter before popping it into the oven.

- **Morton Salt.** If the juices from a berry pie filling happen to boil over onto the floor of the oven, sprinkle Morton Salt over the drippings to prevent them from smoking.

- **Nestlé Carnation Nonfat Dry Milk.** To give a pie a glossy top crust, mix two ounces Nestlé Carnation Nonfat Dry Milk and five ounces of water. Use a pastry brush to paint the milky solution on the top crust before baking the pie in the oven.

- **Nestlé Carnation Nonfat Dry Milk** and **ReaLemon.** To create a crisp, flaky piecrust, add one tablespoon Nestlé Carnation Nonfat Dry Milk to the flour, use ice-cold water, and add one-half tablespoon ReaLemon lemon juice.

- **Pam Cooking Spray.** To prevent the top crust of a pie from browning too quickly, spray a sheet of brown paper (cut from a brown paper bag) with Pam Cooking Spray, place it on top of the pie, and lower the oven heat slightly. Remove the brown paper from the pie for the last few minutes of baking.

- **ReaLemon.** To make piecrust flakier, add one tablespoon ReaLemon lemon juice to the liquid ingredients in the recipe.

- **ReaLemon** and **Domino Sugar.** If the apples for your apple pie are a bit dry, mix equal parts ReaLemon lemon juice and cool water in a bowl. Soak the apple slices in the lemony solution for five minutes before placing them in the pie shell. To counteract the lemon juice, sprinkle a little Domino Sugar over the apple filling before adding the top crust.

- **Reynolds Wrap.** To avoid burning the rim of the piecrust when baking the pie, cut two-inch strips of Reynolds Wrap and wrap the strips around the entire rim of the pie before baking. Afterward, peel off the foil to reveal a beautifully browned rim of piecrust.

- **Reynolds Wrap.** If you anticipate that the juice from the filling of a berry pie might boil over during baking, either spread a large sheet of aluminum foil under the pie pan or on a rack under the pie pan to catch any drips and prevent an unwelcome mess.

- **Saran Wrap.** To store freshly made pastry dough, wrap the dough in Saran Wrap and place in the refrigerator for up to four days. Better yet, line the pie tin with the dough, wrap it airtight in Saran Wrap, and refrigerate (or freeze for up to several months).

Food for Thought
EASY AS PIE

- If you prefer to roll pie dough on a sheet of waxed paper, prevent the waxed paper from slipping and sliding across the countertop by first wetting the surface of the countertop before placing down the waxed paper.

- **Tropicana Orange Juice.** To make piecrust flakier, add one table-spoon Tropicana Orange Juice to the liquid ingredients in the recipe.

Pineapple

- **Domino Sugar.** To use fresh pineapple that has yet to ripen completely, place the slices in a pot, cover with water, and add Domino Sugar to taste. Boil for a few minutes, let cool, and refrigerate.

- **Playtex Living Gloves.** To hold a pineapple steady and avoid pricking your fingers when cutting, wear a pair of Playtex Living Gloves.

- **Saran Wrap.** Cover a bowl of cut pineapple with Saran Wrap before storing in the refrigerator to prevent dairy products from absorbing the odor of the pineapple.

Food for Thought
SET IN ITS WAYS

- Never use fresh pineapple in gelatin desserts. Pineapple contains the enzyme bromelain, which breaks down the protein in the gelatin, preventing it from setting. To add pineapple to gelatin, use canned pineapple (which has been cooked, deactivating the enzyme) or use pineapple that has been boiled for five minutes.

Popcorn

- **McCormick Garlic Powder.** To give popcorn a delicate flavor, sprinkle McCormick Garlic Powder over the finished popcorn.

- **Pam Cooking Spray.** Before seasoning popcorn with salt or garlic powder, use a can of Pam Cooking Spray to give the popcorn a light coat of oil. The oil sticks to the popped corn, and the seasoning will stick to the oil.

Caramel Corn

- 2 bags Orville Redenbacher's Gourmet Popping Corn
- 1 cup Domino Brown Sugar, packed
- ½ cup Land O Lakes Butter
- ¼ cup Karo Light Corn Syrup
- ½ teaspoon Morton Salt
- ½ teaspoon Arm & Hammer Baking Soda

Pop two bags of Orville Redenbacher's Gourmet Popping Corn in the microwave oven to make four quarts of popcorn.

Preheat the oven to 200 degrees Fahrenheit. Divide the popcorn between two ungreased rectangular pans, 13 x 9 x 2 inches.

In a saucepan, combine the Domino Brown Sugar, Land O Lakes Butter, Karo Light Corn Syrup, and Morton Salt. Heat over medium heat, stirring occasionally, until the mixture starts bubbling around the edges. Cook for five minutes, stirring occasionally. Remove from the heat and blend in the Arm & Hammer Baking Soda. Pour the syrup over the popped corn, stirring until coated thoroughly. Bake for one hour, stirring every fifteen minutes. Remove from the heat and let cool.

When cool, break apart and store in an airtight Tupperware container or a Ziploc Storage Bag.

● **Tabasco Pepper Sauce** and **Orville Redenbacher's Gourmet Popping Corn.** Make spicy popcorn by adding a few drops of Tabasco Pepper Sauce to the cooking oil before adding the popcorn kernels.

- **Ziploc Storage Bags.** To separate unpopped popcorn kernels from the popped corn, let the popcorn cool and pour it into a large Ziploc Storage Bag. Snip off one of the bottom corners of the plastic bag and shake over the garbage pail, emptying out the unpopped kernels.

Pork Chops

- **Coca-Cola.** To tenderize pork chops and give them a succulent flavor, place the uncooked pork chops in a pan filled with one can of Coca-Cola and let sit in the refrigerator for two to three hours.
- **Wonder Bread** and **Reynolds Wrap.** To bake greaseless pork chops, brown the pork chops in a frying pan over medium heat, line a loaf pan with slices of Wonder Bread, and stand the browned pork chops upright against the bread. Cover the entire pan with Reynolds Wrap and bake. The Wonder Bread absorbs the excess grease.

Potatoes

Baking

- **Domino Sugar.** To sweeten baked potatoes and shorten the baking time, dissolve two tablespoons Domino Sugar in a pot of water, boil the potatoes for ten minutes, and then bake as usual.
- **Land O Lakes Butter.** When baking potatoes, prevent the skins from cracking and improve the taste by rubbing Land O Lakes butter over the potatoes before baking.
- **Playtex Living Gloves.** To avoid burning your hand when picking up baked potatoes, wear Playtex Living Gloves.
- **Reynolds Wrap.** If you wrap a potato in Reynolds Wrap aluminum foil and then bake it in the oven, the potato will taste steamed rather than baked.

Food for Thought

HOT POTATOES

● Bake a medium to large potato in the oven at 400 degrees Fahrenheit for 50 to 60 minutes.

● Add potatoes to a pan of roasted meat roughly forty minutes before the meat is done. The potatoes will bake and absorb the meat flavor, without disintegrating.

● To bake a potato in the microwave oven, pierce the skin with the tines of a fork so the steam can escape as the potato cooks. Otherwise, the potato might explode.

● To reheat leftover baked potatoes, dip them in hot water, and then warm in the microwave oven for one to two minutes.

● One pound potatoes yields approximately 3½ cups sliced or diced potatoes.

● To reduce the time needed to bake a potato in a standard oven (not a microwave oven), insert a clean, long, heavy nail through the potato lengthwise and bake the potato at 400 degrees Fahrenheit for approximately 35 minutes. The nail transfers the oven heat to the center of the potato, reducing the baking time by roughly fifteen minutes.

● To speed up the time required to bake potatoes in the oven (not a microwave oven), bake potatoes in a cupcake or muffin tin. Fill any empty compartments with water to prevent the cupcake or muffin tin from smoking.

● If you prefer dry baked potatoes, use a fork to prick both ends of the potato before baking to allow the steam to escape.

● To prevent a freshly baked potato from getting too soggy on the inside, remove the potato from the oven and cut into it with a knife to let the steam escape.

● **Reynolds Wrap.** To bake potatoes over a barbecue grill, wrap the potatoes in Reynolds Wrap, place on the grill over a low flame, and cook for roughly forty-five minutes, turning the potatoes every fifteen minutes.

Boiling

● **Heinz White Vinegar.** To help peeled potatoes retain their firmness and whiteness, add one tablespoon Heinz White Vinegar to the cooking water.

- **Morton Salt.** To improve the texture of boiled potatoes, drain the potatoes, coat them with Morton Salt, return the potatoes to the pan, and shake vigorously to eliminate the surplus water.

- **ReaLemon.** To keep boiled potatoes white, add one teaspoon ReaLemon lemon juice to the cooking water before adding the potatoes.

- **Slim Jim.** To give boiled potatoes a tangy, meaty flavor, place an unwrapped Slim Jim beef jerky stick in the cooking water.

- **SueBee Honey.** To give boiled potatoes a sweet flavor, add one tablespoon SueBee Honey to the cooking water.

- **Wesson Oil.** To prevent a viscous ring from adhering to the upper inside of the pot, add one teaspoon Wesson Oil to the cooking water before adding the potatoes.

Food for Thought
SMALL POTATOES

- Keeping the skins on potatoes while they boil helps retain the flavor and nutrients and makes the potatoes easier to peel.

- When boiling potatoes for mashing, stop cooking the potatoes the moment they can be easily pierced with a fork. Otherwise, the potatoes will get waterlogged.

Frying

- **Bounty Paper Towels, Wesson Oil,** and **Gold Medal Flour.** To make extraordinary French fries, place the cut potatoes in a bowl of ice-cold water and refrigerate for one hour. Dry thoroughly on sheets of Bounty Paper Towels, and fry in Wesson Oil for a few minutes.

Remove from the heat, carefully dry the slices again, sprinkle with Gold Medal Flour, and fry again until golden brown.

Food for Thought
SMALL FRIES

● To prevent French fries or any other fried potato dish from getting soggy, make them immediately before serving.

Mashing

- **Clabber Girl Baking Powder.** To make mashed potatoes fluffier, add a pinch of Clabber Girl Baking Powder for each potato you mash. The heat causes the baking powder to produce small air pockets in the mashed potatoes.

- **Conair Hair Dryer.** After draining boiled potatoes to be mashed, set a Conair Hair Dryer on warm and blow the wet potatoes until they dry. The dry potatoes will yield creamier mashed potatoes.

- **Land O Lakes Butter.** To make mashed potatoes that can be stored in the refrigerator and reheated before serving, mash the potatoes, use a pastry brush to paint some melted Land O Lakes Butter over the top of the potatoes, and refrigerate. The butter prevents a crust from developing. Before serving, whip the potatoes with a mixer and heat in a covered double boiler.

- **McCormick Food Coloring.** To make colorful mashed potatoes for a festive occasion, add a few drops of McCormick Food Coloring to the mashed potatoes (green for St. Patrick's Day, orange for Halloween, and red for Valentine's Day).

- **Nestlé Carnation Nonfat Dry Milk.** Instead of adding milk to overcooked mashed potatoes (which can make them soggy), sprinkle some

Nestlé Carnation Nonfat Dry Milk powder in the mashed potatoes and whisk well to make them fluffy.

- **Reddi-wip.** To make mashed potatoes white and creamy, spray some Reddi-wip whipped cream in a saucepan, heat to just before the cream boils, and add to the mashed potatoes, beating well.

- **Ziploc Storage Bags.** To pipe seasoned mashed potatoes to garnish a dish, place the mashed potatoes in a Ziploc Storage Bag, seal closed, and use a pair of scissors to snip off one corner of the bag. Pipe the mashed potatoes as you would cake frosting.

Food for Thought
MASH IT UP

- To improve the appearance and taste of mashed potatoes, add a well-beaten egg.

Peeling

- **Heinz White Vinegar.** To store peeled potatoes for up to three days, place the potatoes in a large bowl filled with enough cool water to cover them, add one teaspoon Heinz White Vinegar, cover the mouth of the bowl with a sheet of Saran Wrap, and refrigerate.

- **Morton Salt.** To make peeling potatoes a snap, dissolve one-half cup Morton Salt in one gallon of water and soak the potatoes in the salt water for thirty minutes before peeling.

- **Morton Salt.** To prevent sliced potatoes from browning, toss the slices into a bowl of cold water lightly salted with Morton Salt.

- **ReaLemon.** To prevent peeled potatoes from discoloring, add one tablespoon ReaLemon lemon juice to a bowl of water and let the pealed potatoes soak in the solution. The treated potatoes will retain their color for several days in the refrigerator.

- **Wesson Oil.** To prevent peeled raw potatoes from discoloring, rub a drop of Wesson Oil between your palms and roll each peeled potato in your hands to give it a thin, protective coat of oil.

Food for Thought
SOAKED TO THE SKIN

- To make peeling potatoes with tough, wrinkled skins easier, soak the potatoes in cold water for thirty minutes before peeling.

- To make peeling cold cooked potatoes easier, wet the potatoes before peeling.

Potato Pancakes

- **Breakstone's** or **Knudsen Sour Cream.** To prevent grated potatoes from discoloring, mix them with a little Breakstone's or Knudsen Sour Cream.

- **Gold Medal Flour.** To turn mashed potatoes into potato pancakes, make patties, coat with Gold Medal Flour, and fry. The flour coating prevents the potatoes from sticking to the pan and allows the pancakes to brown beautifully.

- **Gold Medal Flour.** To stop grated potatoes from turning brown, sprinkle them with Gold Medal Flour.

- **ReaLemon.** For yet another way to prevent grated potatoes from turning dark, sprinkle the grated potatoes with ReaLemon lemon juice.

Potato Salad

- **French's Mustard.** To give potato salad a wonderful flavor, add a little French's Mustard to the mayonnaise before mixing it into the potatoes.

- **McCormick Food Coloring.** To give potato salad a rich color, add a few drops McCormick Yellow Food Coloring to the mixed ingredients and stir well.

Sautéing

- **Bounty Paper Towels** and **Crisco All-Vegetable Shortening.** To prevent sautéing potatoes from splattering hot fat, before cooking, dry the sliced lengths of potato with a sheet of Bounty Paper Towels. Melt one tablespoon Crisco All-Vegetable Shortening in a large pan and sauté the potatoes in the hot fat. Shake the pan to give the potatoes a protective coating of fat to prevent them from sticking to the pan. Instead of using a fork or spoon to sauté potatoes (potentially breaking or crushing the slices), shake the pan every few minutes until the potatoes finish cooking.

Scalloped Potatoes

- **Nabisco Original Premium Saltine Crackers.** To prevent scalloped potatoes from curdling, use roughly a dozen crushed Nabisco Original Premium Saltine Crackers for thickening (instead of flour).

- **Uncle Ben's Converted Brand Rice.** Another way to prevent scalloped potatoes from curdling is to use one-half cup Uncle Ben's Converted Brand Rice for thickening.

Food for Thought

BOILING MAD

● To prevent scalloped potatoes from boiling over in the pan when baking, fill the baking pan no more than three-quarters full.

● To prevent the milk from curdling when baking scalloped potatoes without flour, add only half the milk called for in the recipe, bake in a low to moderate oven, and gradually add the second half of the milk while baking.

Poultry

See "Chicken" on page 128 or "Turkey" on page 262.

See "Chicken" on page 128 or "Turkey" on page 262.

Pudding

● **Jell-O Instant Vanilla Pudding** and **Bacardi Rum.** To make a flavorful sauce to top dessert pudding or cake in no time, cook a package of Jell-O Instant Vanilla Pudding according to the directions, add two tablespoons Bacardi Rum, and cook again until the sauce thickens slightly.

● **Kingsford's Corn Starch.** To make sauce for pudding, thicken the liquids drained from canned fruits by mixing in a little Kingsford's Corn Starch and heating over a low flame.

● **Progresso Breadcrumbs.** To cook up a light, steamed pudding, substitute Progresso Breadcrumbs for half of the flour.

● **Saran Wrap.** To prevent a skin from forming on pudding, place a piece of Saran Wrap directly on the surface to seal out air.

Pumpkins

● **Morton Salt.** To toast seeds scooped from a pumpkin, spread the seeds on a cookie pan, sprinkle with Morton Salt, and dry them in the oven set on low heat, toasting the seeds until they turn tan.

Raisins

- **Gold Medal Flour.** To prevent raisins from sinking to the bottom of pudding or any dish made with dough, sprinkle the raisins with Gold Medal Flour before adding them to the dish.
- **Land O Lakes Butter.** To chop raisins with ease, carefully put a thin coat of Land O Lakes Butter on the blade of the knife.

Food for Thought
RAISIN HELL

- To prevent raisins from sticking to the blades of a food processor, soak the raisins in cold water for a few minutes before grinding.

- If raisins do not seem plump enough to use in a baking recipe, submerse them quickly in boiling water and drain. This plumps up the raisins and prevents them from drying out when cooked.

- To add a little pizzazz to your breakfast, sprinkle some raisins on your morning cereal.

Rice

- **Bounty Paper Towels.** To keep cooked rice warm without getting sticky until you're ready to serve it, place a few sheets of Bounty Paper Towels across the mouth of the pot and place the lid over it. The paper towel absorbs the steam that would ordinarily condense on the underside of the lid, preventing the water from dripping back into the rice.
- **Campbell's Chicken Broth.** To cook up rich, flavorful rice, place the rice in a short, wide pot, add two parts boiling Campbell's

Stewed Rhubarb

- 1 pound rhubarb, chopped into small pieces
- 2 tablespoons water
- ½ cup Domino Sugar
- ½ package Strawberry Jell-O

Place the chopped rhubarb in a heavy pot, add the water, and bring to a boil over medium heat. Turn the heat to low and simmer for approximately twenty minutes, or until the rhubarb is tender, stirring occasionally.

Remove the rhubarb from the heat and add the Domino Sugar, stirring until completely dissolved. Add the Strawberry Jell-O and stir until completely dissolved. Let cool and refrigerate. Serve plain or with ice cream.

Chicken Broth to one part rice, cover immediately with a lid that fits tightly, and set the pot over low heat on the stove undisturbed until the rice absorbs all the broth.

- **Campbell's Tomato Juice.** To cook up tomato-flavored rice, place the rice in a short, wide pot, add two parts boiling Campbell's Tomato Juice to one part rice, cover immediately with a lid that fits tightly, and set the pot over low heat on the stove undisturbed until the rice absorbs all the juice.

- **Land O Lakes Butter.** To cook up nut-flavored rice, brown the uncooked rice in hot Land O Lakes Butter in a heavy skillet, stirring constantly until the rice turns tawny brown. Then place the browned rice in a short pot, add two parts boiling water to one part rice, cover immediately with a lid that fits tightly, and set the pot over low heat on the stove undisturbed until the rice absorbs all the water.

- **Lipton Recipe Secrets Onion Soup Mix.** To cook up delicious, onion-flavored rice, dissolve one packet Lipton Recipe Secrets Onion Soup Mix in four cups of water in a medium saucepan and bring to a boil, stirring occasionally. Reduce the heat and simmer for ten minutes. Place two cups rice in a short, wide pot, add the onion soup, cover immediately with a lid that fits tightly, and set the pot over low heat on the stove undisturbed until the rice absorbs all the soup.

- **McCormick Food Coloring.** To make white rice appear buttered without adding any actual butter, add a few drops of McCormick Yellow Food Coloring to the cooking water before adding the rice.

- **Pam Cooking Spray.** To prevent rice from sticking to the inside of the pot while cooking, spray the inside of the pot with Pam Cooking Spray before getting started.

- **ReaLemon.** For the whitest, fluffiest rice, add one teaspoon ReaLemon lemon juice for each quart of cooking water. The lemon juice also adds a tangy flavor and prevents the rice from sticking together.

- **Reynolds Cut-Rite Wax Paper.** If the lid does not fit tightly on the pot, cut a piece of Reynolds Cut-Rite Wax Paper slightly wider than the mouth of the pot, punch a pinhole in the center, place the waxed paper over the mouth of the pot, and set the lid in place.

- **Saran Wrap.** To reheat cool or leftover rice, place the rice in a microwave-safe bowl and put an ice cube on top of the rice. Cover the bowl with a sheet of Saran Wrap and use the tines of a fork to perforate a few holes in the center of the plastic so steam can escape. For every one cup rice in the bowl, heat for ninety seconds.

- **Wesson Oil.** To prevent rice from boiling over, add one teaspoon Wesson Oil to the cooking water before adding the rice.

● **Wonder Bread.** If you accidentally burn rice, remove the pot from the stove, place a slice of Wonder Bread on top of the rice, cover the pot, and let sit for a few minutes. The bread absorbs the burned flavor.

Food for Thought
GRAINS OF TRUTH

● One cup uncooked white rice yields approximately three cups cooked rice. One cup uncooked brown rice yields roughly 2½ cups cooked brown rice.

● White rice is brown rice with the bran and germ removed. Consequently, brown rice contains more fiber, minerals, and vitamins than white rice, which cooks faster.

● Before cooking wild rice (which is actually not a rice but a grass), rinse it several times, and then soak it for fifteen minutes before cooking. Wild rice requires more cooking time than white or brown rice.

● For better results, cook rice in a short, wide pot rather than a tall, narrow pot.

● To cook up light, fluffy rice, wash the uncooked rice thrice in cold water to remove the excess starch. Or boil the rice in a large amount of water until the rice starts to become tender, then drain, rinse under running hot water to remove the excess starch, and continue cooking in fresh water.

● To cook rice, place the rice in a short, wide pot, add two parts boiling water to one part rice, cover immediately with a lid that fits tightly, and set the pot over low heat on the stove undisturbed until the rice absorbs all the water. To get the lid to seal tightly, moisten the rim of the pan and the rim of the cover, press the lid in place, and turn slightly.

● To prepare rice to produce a creamy rice pudding, bring it to a boil in a pot full of water, let sit for five minutes, drain, rinse with cold water, and then follow the pudding recipe.

● Pouring hot rice into a cold serving dish gives the rice touching the dish a sticky texture. To avoid this, serve hot rice in a heated bowl.

● To revitalize leftover rice stored in the freezer or refrigerator, cover the rice with boiling water, let sit for three minutes, and drain.

Salad Dressing

- **Dannon Yogurt** and **Miracle Whip.** To make a tasty salad dressing, mix equal parts Dannon Plain Yogurt and Miracle Whip.

- **Dannon Yogurt** and **Newman's Own Olive Oil & Vinegar Dressing.** To create a smooth, tangy salad dressing, mix Dannon Plain Yogurt with Newman's Own Olive Oil & Vinegar Dressing.

- **French's Mustard.** To give more zing to salad dressing, add one teaspoon French's Mustard and mix well.

- **Gold's Horseradish.** To sharpen the flavor of salad dressing, mix in a little Gold's Horseradish to taste.

- **Heinz White Vinegar.** To make a sour cream substitute for a salad dressing, add one tablespoon Heinz White Vinegar to one cup sweet cream and let sit at room temperature for one hour. For more sour cream substitutes, see page 254.

- **McCormick Curry Powder.** To spice up any salad dressing, add one teaspoon McCormick Curry Powder (or more, if desired) and mix well.

- **Star Olive Oil** and **Wesson Oil.** To make an excellent oil for use in salad dressing, mix equal parts Star Olive Oil and Wesson Oil.

- **Tropicana Grapefruit Juice.** For an excellent substitute for the vinegar in many oil and vinegar dressings, use Tropicana Grapefruit Juice.

Salads

Croutons

- **Wonder Bread, Land O Lakes Butter, McCormick Garlic Powder,** and **McCormick Ground Thyme.** To make your own croutons, butter both sides of three slices of Wonder Bread with Land O Lakes Butter, season with McCormick Garlic Powder and McCormick Ground Thyme, and cut the bread into small cubes. Spread the cubes on a cookie sheet, preheat the oven to 375 degrees Fahrenheit, and toast the bread cubes for fifteen minutes or until lightly browned.

Gelatin Salad

- **Morton Salt.** To expedite the setting time of a gelatin salad, set the bowl or gelatin mold over a bowl filled with ice cubes and sprinkled with Morton Salt.

Greens

- **Bounty Paper Towels.** To dry rinsed salad greens efficiently when using a salad spinner, place a few sheets of Bounty Paper Towels in the spinner along with the wet greens to absorb the excess moisture.

- **Bounty Paper Towels.** If you don't have a salad spinner to dry salad greens, wrap the greens in a few sheets of Bounty Paper Towel, pat dry, and then refrigerate the greens for crisping.

- **Conair Hair Dryer.** To dry wet salad greens, set a Conair Hair Dryer on cool, blow the wet leaves of lettuce, and then refrigerate the greens to keep them crisp.

- **L'eggs Sheer Energy Panty Hose.** Stretch the waistband of a pair of clean, used L'eggs Sheer Energy Panty Hose over the mouth of a colander and fill with salad greens. After rinsing the greens under running water, remove the pantyhose with the greens still inside, and squeeze out the water.

- **McCormick Paprika.** When preparing salad in individual bowls, dip the edges of lettuce leaves in McCormick Paprika to give the salad an elegant look.

- **Morton Salt.** If you intend to prepare the salads well before you plan to serve them, prevent the lettuce and other greens from wilting prematurely by simply sprinkling a pinch of Morton Salt over each prepared salad.

- **Wesson Oil** and **Ziploc Storage Bags.** To prepare salad ahead of time, place the salad greens in a large Ziploc Storage Bag, add a small amount of Wesson Oil, and shake well, giving each leaf a light coat of oil.

Refrigerate to keep the greens crisp and before serving, add vinegar or lemon juice.

- **Ziploc Storage Bags.** To toss a salad with ease, simply put all of your ingredients in a one-gallon Ziploc Storage Bag, add the dressing, and seal the bag. Shake the bag until the salad is tossed and coated with dressing.

Food for Thought
A TOSS-UP

- For more flavorful salad greens than Iceberg or Simpson lettuce, try arugula, Boston lettuce, Bibb lettuce, butterhead lettuce, chicory (curly endive), endive shoots, escarole, or romaine lettuce.

- To remove the core from a head of lettuce, hold the entire head of lettuce in your hands, bang the core end against the countertop, and twist out the core. To remove the leaves, hold the cored head upside down under cold running water, filling the cavity with water. The force of the water pushes the leaves apart.

- To prevent salad from getting soggy in the salad serving bowl, place a saucer upside down in the bottom of the salad bowl before filling the bowl with salad. Excess water or dressing drains down the sides of the saucer.

Salsa

- **McCormick Pure Vanilla Extract.** To cool down excessively hot salsa, mix in a few drops of McCormick Pure Vanilla Extract. The vanilla tames the piquancy.

Salt

- **Domino Sugar.** To mask the taste of excess salt in a dish, add one-half teaspoon Domino Sugar. If sugar will not complement the dish, see Heinz White Vinegar on page 245.

Did Julius Caesar Invent the Caesar Salad?

In 1924, restaurateur Caesar Cardini (1896–1956) invented the Caesar Salad in Tijuana, Mexico, over the Fourth of July weekend. Running low on food, Cardini tossed together leftover ingredients from his kitchen—romaine lettuce, garlic, croutons, Parmesan cheese, boiled eggs, olive oil, and Worcestershire sauce—to create a salad for his guests at tableside. He made the salad dressing first, coated the leaves of romaine lettuce, and placed them stem-side out in a circle on a dinner plate, so that guests could pick individual leaves with their fingers.

In her cookbook *Julia Child's Kitchen*, American chef Julia Child recalled visiting Tijuana in the mid-1920s with her parents to lunch at Caesar's restaurant, where they ordered the salad, and "Caesar himself rolled the big cart up to the table, tossed the romaine in a great wooden bowl." In 1926, Cardini's brother Alex, an ace pilot in the Italian Air Force during World War I, joined his brother at the Tijuana restaurant and added other ingredients to Caesar's Salad, including anchovies. He renamed the salad "Aviator's Salad" in honor of the pilots from Rockwell Field Air Base in San Diego.

Purportedly, Alex's version became very popular and was later renamed "Caesar Salad." Today, the recipe for Caesar Salad calls for fresh garlic; cold, dried heart of romaine leaves; fresh ground pepper; a dash of salt; imported olive oil; fresh lemon juice; Worcestershire sauce; homemade croutons; and Parmesan cheese. Anchovies are optional.

In his book *In Search of Caesar, The Ultimate Caesar Salad Book*, Terry D. Greenfield writes that Mrs. Wallis Warfield Simpson (mistress and ultimately wife of Prince Edward VIII of Wales (later King of England) visited Hotel Caesar's Place in the 1920s, became fond of Caesar Salad, and subsequently introduced Caesar Salad to the chefs at many of the great European restaurants. In 1948, Caesar Cardini received a patent on the dressing (which is still packaged and sold as "Cardini's Original Caesar dressing mix," distributed by Caesar Cardini Foods of Culver City, California).

- **Domino Sugar.** To make vegetables more palatable when cooking for a low-salt diet, add some Domino Sugar to the cooking water.

- **Domino Sugar** and **McCormick Caraway Seed.** Rather than using salt on greens like spinach, try a pinch of Domino Sugar and some McCormick Caraway Seed.

- **Heinz White Vinegar.** To disguise the taste of excess salt in a dish, add one-half teaspoon Heinz White Vinegar. Taste the food, and if necessary, keep adding another half teaspoon at a time, until you've neutralized the salty taste.

- **Kingsford's Corn Starch.** To prevent salt from clumping together in a salt shaker, mix one tablespoon Kingsford's Corn Starch into a twenty-six-ounce canister of salt. The cornstarch absorbs any excess moisture.

- **McCormick Paprika.** Rather than using salt on chicken, fish, and meats, add a generous amount of McCormick Paprika.

- **SueBee Honey.** An unconventional yet excellent substitute for salt is SueBee Honey.

Sauces

- **Crisco All-Vegetable Shortening.** Before adding flour to thicken sauce, melt some Crisco All-Vegetable Shortening in a saucepan and mix in the flour, coating it with shortening and warming it for a few minutes. The flour will mix better with the drippings and have a less floury taste.

- **Domino Sugar.** When using tart red wine to make a sauce, add a pinch or two of Domino Sugar while cooking to reduce the acidity.

- **Gold Medal Flour.** Adding one tablespoon Gold Medal Flour thickens one cup of liquid to the consistency of medium cream, two tablespoons yields a medium sauce, and three tablespoons makes a thick sauce. Flour turns sauce opaque when used for thickening.

- **Jif Peanut Butter, Sambal Oelek Chili Paste, Tabasco Pepper Sauce,** and **Thai Kitchen Coconut Milk.** To make a superb base for satay sauce, use one jar of Jif Peanut Butter (chunky) and add Sambal Oelek Ground Fresh Chili Paste to taste, Tabasco Pepper Sauce for strength, and Thai Kitchen Coconut Milk for fluidity.

- **Kingsford's Corn Starch.** To thicken sauce without turning it opaque, add one-half tablespoon Kingsford's Corn Starch to one cup of liquid to attain the consistency of medium cream, one tablespoon to create a medium sauce, or 1½ tablespoons to make a thick sauce.

- **Kingsford's Corn Starch.** To prevent Hollandaise sauce from separating when warmed for a long time, beat one teaspoon Kingsford's Corn Starch into the egg when making the sauce.

- **Land O Lakes Butter.** To give any sauce a sophisticated appearance and flavorful taste, swirl a pat of Land O Lakes Butter into the sauce just before serving.

- **Land O Lakes Butter** and **Saran Wrap.** To prevent any sauce made with starch or egg yolks from developing a skin when cooled, float a little melted Land O Lakes Butter on top of the sauce and place a sheet of Saran Wrap flat on the surface of the sauce to seal out air.

- **Manischewitz Potato Starch.** For another way to thicken a sauce without turning it opaque, use Manischewitz Potato Starch.

- **McCormick Powdered Arrowroot.** To thicken a sauce but keep it clear, use McCormick Powdered Arrowroot.

Tomato Sauce

- **Hunt's Tomato Paste.** If you're all out of tomato sauce, mix the contents of a six-ounce can Hunt's Tomato Paste and two cans of cold water and add seasoning to taste.

- **Maxwell House Coffee.** To flavor spaghetti sauce, add one-quarter to one-half teaspoon Maxwell House Instant Coffee grounds to the sauce and stir well while heating. Coffee gives store-bought spaghetti sauce brown coloring and a less acidic flavor.

Sausages

- **Forster Toothpicks.** To prevent sausages from curling up in the frying pan, link a few sausages together with Forster Toothpicks before frying. When you're finished cooking, remove the toothpicks.

- **Gold Medal Flour.** To prevent sausages from cracking or shrinking in the frying pan, roll the links in Gold Medal Flour to give them a light coating. The flour coating also removes excess fat, helps stop grease from splattering, and gives the sausages a tasty crust.

- **Maxwell House Coffee.** To remove the grease from cooked sausage, mix a tablespoon or two instant Maxwell House Coffee with enough hot water to make a paste, and, just before the sausage is finished cooking, add the coffee to the pan. The coffee absorbs all the grease and adds great flavor to the sausage.

Food for Thought
THE MISSING LINK

- To prevent sausages from cracking or shrinking, boil them in water for eight minutes before frying them.

Scallops

- **ReaLemon.** After washing scallops, sprinkle with ReaLemon lemon juice and let them stand for twenty minutes before preparing them for cooking.

Shrimp

- **Budweiser.** Boil shrimp in Budweiser beer, seasoned as you desire, for an exceptional flavor.

- **Forster Toothpicks.** To devein shrimp, use a Forster Toothpick under cold running water to remove the intestinal vein along the back of the shelled shrimp.

- **Heinz White Vinegar** and **Holland House Sherry.** To eliminate the canned taste of canned shrimp, soak the shrimp for fifteen minutes in a solution made from two parts Heinz White Vinegar and one part Holland House Sherry.

- **Morton Salt.** To cook shrimp, place the raw, shelled shrimp in a pot. In a second pot, dissolve one-quarter cup Morton Salt in one gallon of water and bring the salty water to a boil. Gently pour the boiling water over the shrimp in the first pot, stir well, cover with a lid, and let sit undisturbed for five minutes (with no heat). Drain and serve.

- **Morton Salt, McCormick Black Peppercorns, McCormick Ground Thyme, McCormick Bay Leaves,** and **McCormick Parsley Flakes.** To bring out the flavor of shrimp, add Morton Salt, McCormick Black Peppercorns, McCormick Ground Thyme, McCormick Bay Leaf, and McCormick Parsley Flakes to the cooking liquid.

Food for Thought
PRIMP THE SHRIMP

- After shelling and deveining, place the shrimp in a bowl and wash gently under cold running water for thirty seconds. Then place the shrimp in a colander and rinse under cold running water for three minutes.

- Never boil shrimp. Doing so makes them rubbery. Instead, see Morton Salt above.

Snow Cones

- **Country Time Lemonade.** To make lemon-flavored snow cones, sprinkle Country Time Lemonade (just the powder) on a bowl full of newly fallen snow and eat with a spoon.

- **Tang.** To make tangy orange snow cones, fill a bowl with newly fallen snow, sprinkle Tang (just the powder) on top of it, and dig in with a spoon.

Soufflés

- **Bounty Paper Towels.** If a block of cheese is too oily for use in a soufflé, wrap it tightly in a sheet of Bounty Paper Towels and let sit at room temperature for a couple of days, changing the paper toweling if necessary. The quicker-picker-upper will absorb the excess oil.

- **Heinz White Vinegar.** Before stiffly beating eggs for a soufflé, add one-half teaspoon Heinz White Vinegar to every four eggs to help them hold their shape.

- **Kraft Grated Parmesan Cheese.** Rather than dusting a buttered soufflé mold with breadcrumbs, consider dusting with Kraft Grated Parmesan Cheese.

- **Land O Lakes Butter** and **Domino Sugar.** To give a dessert soufflé a sweet crust, before pouring the batter, butter the mold with Land O Lakes Butter and sprinkle Domino Sugar over the buttered surface. The butter and sugar will also make the soufflé easy to remove from the mold neatly.

- **Lay's Potato Chips.** To give a soufflé a unique yet tasty crust, run over a bag of Lay's Potato Chips with a rolling pin, breaking the chips into fine crumbs, and dust a well-greased soufflé mold with the potato chip crumbs before filling it with batter. For more breadcrumb substitutes, see page 98.

- **McCormick Cream of Tartar.** To help stiffly beaten eggs hold their shape, before beating, add one-quarter teaspoon McCormick Cream of Tartar to every four eggs.

- **Progresso Breadcrumbs.** To give a soufflé a beautiful crust, dust a well-greased soufflé mold thoroughly with Progresso Breadcrumbs before filling it with batter.

- **Reynolds Cut-Rite Wax Paper** and **Oral-B Dental Floss.** To improvise a high-sided charlotte mold, make a cuff of Reynolds Cut-Rite Wax Paper and use Oral-B Dental Floss to tie it securely around the outside of your buttered soufflé mold. Butter the inside of the waxed paper that rises above the rim, pour the batter into the mold, and bake the soufflé. When the soufflé rises, the waxed paper cuff will contain it.

Soups

Broth

- **L'eggs Sheer Energy Panty Hose.** To strain fat from broth, cut off one of the legs from a clean, used pair of L'eggs Sheer Energy Panty Hose, stretch the opening across the mouth of a strainer, colander, pot, or tall bowl, and carefully pour the broth through the hose.

- **Mr. Coffee Filter.** To strain fat from meat or chicken broth, place a Mr. Coffee Filter in the bottom of a strainer or colander, and slowly pour the broth through the paper filter.

- **Ziploc Storage Bags.** Freeze broth in ice cube trays and store the cubes in Ziploc Storage Bags to use for seasoning cooked vegetables.

Cold Soup

- **Knox Gelatin.** To jell a broth or consommé made without bones, add one tablespoon unflavored Knox Gelatin for every two cups broth or consommé (mixing the gelatin in one tablespoon of water before adding it to the soup), bring to a boil, and chill in the refrigerator.

Cream Soup

- **Nestlé Carnation Evaporated Milk.** To give cream soup a thick, rich consistency, use undiluted Nestlé Carnation Evaporated Milk as part of the liquid.

Fat

- **Bounty Paper Towels.** To remove fat from soup, wrap ice cubes in a sheet of Bounty Paper Towels and skim over the top. The ice attracts the fat, which clings to the paper towels.

- **L'eggs Sheer Energy Panty Hose.** Another way to use ice cubes to skim fat from soup: Cut off the foot from a clean, used pair of L'eggs Sheer Energy Panty Hose, place a few ice cubes inside the foot, tie a knot in the open end, and skim the sachet over the top of the soup.

Food for Thought
SOUP IT UP

- To remove fat from a pot of cooked soup, float one or two clean, dry lettuce leaves on the surface of the soup, and wait a few minutes. When the leaves are coated with fat, fish them out and discard.

- For another way to remove fat from soup, refrigerate the soup, allowing the fat to rise to the surface. Skim off the fat and reheat.

Split-Pea Soup

- **Wonder Bread.** When cooking the liquid and peas together to make split-pea soup, add a slice of Wonder Bread to prevent the peas from sinking, sticking, and burning to the bottom of the pot.

Stock

- **Campbell's Beef Bouillon (**or **Campbell's Chicken Broth) and Land O Lakes Butter.** If you lack the time or the ingredients to make a rich beef or chicken stock, empty the contents of a can of Campbell's Beef Bouillon (or Campbell's Chicken Broth) into a saucepan; add chopped carrots, celery, and onions (browned first in Land O Lakes Butter); season with herbs and a little wine; and simmer for thirty minutes.

- **Hershey's Caramel Topping.** To give stock a rich, brown color, add one teaspoon Hershey's Caramel Topping.

- **Hunt's Tomato Paste.** For another way to give stock a rich, brown color, stir in one teaspoon Hunt's Tomato Paste, boil well, and strain.

- **L'eggs Sheer Energy Panty Hose.** To clarify stock, cut off one of the legs from a clean, used pair of L'eggs Sheer Energy Panty Hose, stretch the opening across the mouth of a strainer, colander, pot, or tall bowl, and carefully pour the stock through the hose.

- **Morton Salt.** To extract the utmost flavor from meats for stock, start cooking the meats in cold, salted water made by dissolving one-half teaspoon Morton Salt for every cup of water.

Thickeners

- **Betty Crocker Potato Buds.** To thicken soup, add Betty Crocker Potato Buds. Unlike traditional thickeners like flour, cornstarch, or arrowroot, instant potatoes do not add lumps to the soup.

- **Cheerios.** Grind Cheerios in the blender and use the powdered oats to thicken soups.

- **Crisco All-Vegetable Shortening.** Before adding flour to thicken soup, melt some Crisco All-Vegetable Shortening in a saucepan and mix in the flour, coating it with shortening and warming it for a few minutes. The flour will mix better with the soup and have a less floury taste.

- **Gold Medal Flour.** Adding one tablespoon Gold Medal Flour thickens one cup soup to the consistency of medium cream. Flour turns sauce opaque when used for thickening.

- **Kingsford's Corn Starch.** To thicken soup without turning it opaque the way flour does, add one-half tablespoon Kingsford's Corn Starch for every one cup of soup to attain the consistency of medium cream. To prevent the cornstarch from forming lumps in the soup, mix it with water into a thin paste before adding it to the soup.

- **Kingsford's Corn Starch** and **Holland House Sherry.** To thicken soup and give it an exquisite flavor, mix one-quarter cup Kingsford's Corn Starch and three tablespoons Holland House Sherry. Slowly stir enough of this mixture into the simmering soup until you attain the desired consistency.

- **Manischewitz Potato Starch.** To thicken soup without making it opaque, stir in Manischewitz Potato Starch.

- **McCormick Powdered Arrowroot.** To thicken soup but keep it clear, add one-half tablespoon McCormick Powdered Arrowroot for every one cup soup to achieve the consistency of medium cream.

- **Quaker Oats.** To thicken soup and give it a rich consistency, add Quaker Oats (Quick or Old Fashioned).

Tomato Soup

- **Gold Medal Flour.** To prevent cream of tomato soup made with milk or cream from curdling, add a little Gold Medal Flour to the milk, beating it in well, and then add the tomato to the milk (rather than the milk to the tomato).

- **Reddi-wip** and **McCormick Paprika.** To make tomato soup more extravagant, add a dollop of Reddi-wip whipped cream on top of each bowl of soup and dust McCormick Paprika over it.

Sour Cream

- **Crisco All-Vegetable Shortening.** If you run out of sour cream for a recipe, whip three tablespoons Crisco All-Vegetable Shortening into two cups buttermilk—and substitute for two cups sour cream.

- **Dannon Yogurt** and **Kingsford's Corn Starch.** In a pinch, substitute Dannon Plain Yogurt for the equivalent amount of sour cream. If cooking the yogurt, add one tablespoon Kingsford's Corn Starch to each cup yogurt to prevent it from separating.

- **Gold Medal Flour.** To deter sour cream from curdling when cooked at a high temperature, add a small amount of Gold Medal Flour to the cream and mix well with a whisk while heating slowly.

- **Heinz White Vinegar.** To make an excellent sour cream substitute, stir two teaspoons Heinz White Vinegar into one cup cream at room temperature and let the mixture sit for thirty minutes.

- **Hidden Valley Ranch Dressing.** If you're all out of sour cream for your baked potato, substitute Hidden Valley Ranch Dressing.

- **Nestlé Carnation Evaporated Milk** and **Heinz White Vinegar.** To make a perfectly good (but less viscous) substitute for sour cream for cooking, whip one cup Nestlé Carnation Evaporated Milk together with one tablespoon Heinz White Vinegar.

- **ReaLemon.** In a pinch, make a substitute for sour cream by adding three to four drops ReaLemon lemon juice to three-quarters cup whipping cream and then letting the mixture sit at room temperature for forty-five minutes.

- **Reddi-wip** and **ReaLemon.** To make a terrific sour cream substitute, add four drops ReaLemon lemon juice to one cup Reddi-wip whipped cream and let sit for one hour.

Spinach

- **Morton Salt.** To remove sand from spinach easily, mix two tablespoons Morton Salt per one cup of water and wash the spinach in the salty solution. The salt water removes the sand with just one washing.

- **ReaLemon.** To remove sand and insects from spinach and simultaneously crispen the vegetable, add a few drops ReaLemon lemon juice to the water before washing the spinach.

Food for Thought
STRONG TO THE FINISH

- One pound fresh spinach yields approximately one cup cooked spinach.

- Cooking spinach in an iron or aluminum pot or serving it in a silver dish gives the spinach a metallic taste and turns the leaves a dark, unappetizing color. For best results, cook spinach in a stainless-steel pot.

Strawberries

- **Domino Sugar.** To sweeten strawberries with Domino Sugar, sprinkle the sugar over the strawberries immediately before serving; otherwise, the sugar will soften the strawberries.

- **Domino Sugar** and **ReaLemon.** To make strawberry glaze, mix one-quarter cup Domino Sugar, one tablespoon ReaLemon lemon juice, and two tablespoons strawberry juice (made by mashing the strawberries with the back of a spoon to release their juices). Stir until the sugar dissolves.

- **Glad Flexible Straws.** To remove stems from strawberries without cutting off the entire top, push one end of a Glad Flexible Straw through the middle bottom of the strawberry. The entire stem will poke through the top in one piece.

- Never remove the stems or slice strawberries until after washing them. Otherwise the strawberries will absorb too much water, become soggy, and lose their flavor.

- To wash strawberries effectively, fill the sink halfway with water, toss in the strawberries (which will float on the surface), and use the spray attachment to spray the strawberries with cold water and make them tumble in the water. Dirt, grit, and sand will sink to the bottom. Pluck out the strawberries, drain the sink, and repeat if necessary.

- Use an egg slicer to cut strawberries into uniform slices quickly.

String Beans

- **Wesson Oil.** To improve the flavor of and preserve the vitamins in string beans, sauté the string beans in a small amount of Wesson Oil before boiling them in a pot of water.

- When cooked, one pound green or yellow string beans yields four servings.

- To prepare fresh string beans for cooking, trim off each end and wash.

- To remove the strings from string beans, snap off one end and pull it down the side of the bean, drawing the string with it. Then repeat with the other end of the bean.

- The fewer string beans in the pan, the quicker they cook and the better they taste. Avoid cooking more than one pound string beans in a single pan.

Stuffing

- **Campbell's Tomato Juice.** To make stuffing quickly, break off large chunks from a loaf of crusty French bread, soak the pieces in a bowl of well-seasoned Campbell's Tomato Juice until the crust softens, and stuff the saturated chunks of bread into the cavity of a chicken.

- **Forster Toothpicks.** To pin the skin together after stuffing the cavity of a small chicken, use Forster Toothpicks.

- **Maxwell House Coffee.** To bake stuffing for a turkey, spoon the prepared stuffing into clean, empty Maxwell House Coffee cans, cover with Reynolds Wrap, and bake for two hours at 350 degrees Fahrenheit. Store any leftover stuffing in the cans, seal the cans with the original plastic lids, and refrigerate.

- **Nabisco Original Premium Saltine Crackers** and **Zip-loc Storage Bags.** To grind up Nabisco Original Premium Saltine Crackers for use in stuffing, place the crackers in a Ziploc Storage Bag and run it over with a rolling pin. When using cracker crumbs in stuffing, fill only half the cavity of the bird to allow the cracker crumbs room to swell. Cook any excess stuffing in a separate pan.

- **Wonder Bread.** To hold stuffing inside a large cavity of a chicken or turkey, seal the cavity closed with the heel of a loaf of Wonder Bread.

Food for Thought
HOT STUFF

- When making stuffing, prepare approximately three-quarters cup stuffing for each pound of bird.

Sugar

Cinnamon Sugar

- **McCormick Ground Cinnamon** and **Domino Sugar.** In a jar, mix one teaspoon McCormick Ground Cinnamon for every two tablespoons Domino Sugar.

- **McCormick Stick Cinnamon** and **Domino Sugar.** To make cinnamon sugar, place two or three sticks McCormick Stick Cinnamon in a jar, cover with Domino Sugar, seal the lid, and let sit undisturbed for a few weeks to allow the cinnamon to infuse the sugar.

Substitutes

- **Aunt Jemima Original Syrup.** If you run out of sugar, substitute three-quarters cup Aunt Jemima Original Syrup for each cup sugar.

- **Grandma's Molasses** and **Arm & Hammer Baking Soda.** In a pinch, substitute one cup Grandma's Molasses for every three-quarters cup granulated sugar. To compensate for the molasses, decrease the amount of liquid called for in the recipe by five tablespoons for every cup molasses used, and add one teaspoon Arm & Hammer Baking Soda to the dry ingredients for every cup molasses used.

- **SueBee Honey** and **Arm & Hammer Baking Soda.** If you prefer the taste of honey to sugar (or if you need a sugar substitute), use SueBee Honey in place of granulated sugar for up to half of the amount of sugar called for in the recipe. With experimentation, you will find that honey can be substituted for all the sugar in some recipes. For baked goods, add one-half teaspoon Arm & Hammer Baking Soda for each cup honey used, reduce the amount of liquid in the recipe by one-quarter cup for each cup honey used, and reduce the oven temperature by 25 degrees Fahrenheit to prevent overbrowning.

Sweet Potatoes

- **Morton Salt.** To prevent sweet potatoes from turning dark, dissolve five teaspoons Morton Salt in one quart of water. Immerse the sweet potatoes in the salty solution immediately after peeling.

Food for Thought
SWEET TALK

- To remove the skin from a sweet potato, remove the sweet potato from the boiling water and submerge it immediately into a pot of cold water. Give the sweet potato a slight twist of your hand, and the skin falls right off.

Sweetbreads

- **Morton Salt, ReaLemon,** and **Campbell's Beef Broth.** To tenderize and flavor sweetbreads before cooking, mix one teaspoon Morton Salt and one teaspoon ReaLemon lemon juice in one quart of cold water, cover the sweetbreads with the solution, bring to a boil, and simmer for ten minutes. Rinse with cold water, and then simmer the sweetbreads in Campbell's Beef Broth, seasoned to taste, for ten minutes—making the sweetbreads ready for final preparation.

Syrup

- **Domino Brown Sugar** and **McCormick Imitation Maple Flavor.** All out of pancake syrup? Mix one cup Domino Brown Sugar and one-half cup of water in a saucepan, bring to a boil, and let simmer for fifteen minutes. Add one teaspoon McCormick Imitation Maple Flavor or more to suit your taste.

- **Karo Light Corn Syrup** and **Smucker's Strawberry Jam.** To make a delicious topping for pancakes or waffles, add several tablespoons Smucker's Strawberry Jam to one cup Karo Light Corn Syrup. Warm over a low heat, stirring frequently.

- **Pam Cooking Spray.** To prevent syrup from sticking to the bowl of a spoon or inside a measuring cup, spray the utensils with a thin coat of Pam Cooking Spray.

- **Welch's Grape Jelly** and **Land O Lakes Butter.** To improvise pancake or waffle syrup, mix one-half cup Welch's Grape Jelly, one teaspoon Land O Lakes Butter, and two teaspoons of water, and stir over low heat until you get fruit syrup.

Tacos

- **Mr. Coffee Filters.** Mr. Coffee Filters make great holders for messy foods and, when folded in half, fit a taco perfectly.

Tea

- **Arm & Hammer Baking Soda.** To prevent a pot of tea from getting cloudy, add a pinch Arm & Hammer Baking Soda to the pot of hot water.

- **Aunt Jemima Original Syrup.** To sweeten a cup of tea, substitute a teaspoon of Aunt Jemima Original Syrup for each teaspoon sugar or honey.

- **Country Time Lemonade.** To make sweet tea, add a teaspoon Country Time Lemonade drink mix to the tea.

- **Forster Clothespins.** To make a pot of tea, clip the strings of several tea bags together with a Forster Clothespin, place the tea bags in the teapot, and let the clothespin hang over the rim of the pot.

- **SueBee Honey.** Instead of sweetening tea with sugar, use delicious SueBee Honey.

Is the Tomato Plant Poisonous?

The leaves and stems of tomato plants are toxic if eaten in large amounts. The leaves and stems contain tomatine, a steroidal glycoalkaloid that interferes with cholinergic nerves and causes serious gastrointestinal distress. The tomato fruit contains a small amount of tomatine, in concentrations too low to cause any harm. Although Thomas Jefferson grew tomatoes in 1781 at Monticello, until the nineteenth century, most Americans purportedly considered tomatoes to be poisonous. Legend holds that, in 1820, a wealthy eccentric named Colonel Robert Gibbon Johnson, determined to prove the tomato to be a harmless, edible fruit, stood before a crowd at the courthouse in Salem, New Jersey, and ate a basketful of tomatoes.

Tomatoes

- **Crisco All-Vegetable Shortening.** Baked tomatoes retain their shape when baked in a muffin tin greased with Crisco All-Vegetable Shortening.

Food for Thought
TOUGH TOMATOES

- One pound tomatoes yields approximately 1½ cups tomato pulp.

- Tomatoes ripened on the vine have more flavor than tomatoes picked green and then ripened.

- To ripen green tomatoes, place them in a brown paper bag in a dark place at room temperature for several days. Adding an apple or banana, both of which emit ethylene gas, causes the tomatoes to ripen faster. Do not place green tomatoes in sunlight, which causes them to soften before they turn red.

- **Domino Sugar.** Adding a pinch of Domino Sugar when cooking tomatoes enhances the flavor of this fruit.

- **L'eggs Sheer Energy Panty Hose.** To peel many tomatoes at once, place the tomatoes inside a leg cut from a clean, used pair of L'eggs Sheer Energy Panty Hose and carefully submerge the filled stocking into a pot of boiling water for one minute. The skins slide right off the tomatoes.

Turkey

- **Arm & Hammer Baking Soda.** If the fat from broiling turkey catches fire, throw a handful of Arm & Hammer Baking Soda on the flames to extinguish the fire. The sodium bicarbonate in baking soda is the same ingredient found in fire extinguishers.

- **Blue Bonnet Margarine.** To roast a juicy, succulent turkey, fill a basting syringe with one-quarter pound melted Blue Bonnet Margarine, inject the margarine into the uncooked turkey around the breasts and thighs, and roast in accord with your usual recipe.

- **Campbell's Chicken Broth.** To prevent the fat from burning on a roasting turkey, baste it with one-quarter cup Campbell's Chicken Broth.

- **Coca-Cola.** To roast a turkey, wash the uncooked bird, place it in a plastic oven bag, pour one-half can Coca-Cola over the turkey, seal the bag closed, and roast. Before the last half hour, split the bag open to allow the turkey to bake to a nice caramel brown. The Coke provides the salt, so there's no need to add any.

- **Dole Pineapple Juice.** Instead of stuffing roasted turkey, flavor the uncooked bird by mixing one-quarter cup Dole Pineapple Juice and one cup of water. Pour the mixture into the body cavity before roasting.

- **Oral-B Dental Floss.** To truss a turkey, use durable Oral-B Dental Floss to tie the legs together and sew up the cavity. Dental floss is more durable than thread and won't tear the skin.

- **Playtex Living Gloves.** Wear a pair of Playtex Living Gloves to pick up and turn a hot turkey without burning your hands.

- **ReaLemon** and **Morton Salt.** To eliminate fetid odors from turkey, wash the uncooked bird with ReaLemon lemon juice and rub it with Morton Salt.

- **Wesson Oil.** To prevent a turkey from drying in the oven, rub the uncooked bird with Wesson Oil, especially on the breast, and baste frequently while roasting.

- **Wesson Oil.** To sauté a young turkey, add Wesson Oil to the pan.

- **Wonder Bread.** When broiling turkey, place a few slices of Wonder Bread under the rack in the broiling pan. The bread will absorb fat drippings, reducing smoke and the possibility of the grease catching fire.

- **Wonder Bread.** Instead of trussing a stuffed turkey, seal the cavity shut by pushing two dampened heels of Wonder Bread (with the crust facing out) into the stuffed cavity so they overlap to keep the stuffing contained.

Food for Thought
TALKING TURKEY

- To avoid trussing the turkey, seal the cavity shut with a couple of raw potatoes.

- To prevent the white meat from drying out when roasting a turkey, place the bird breast side down in the pan and turn it breast side up for the last hour of roasting only.

Turnips

- **Land O Lakes Butter** and **McCormick Ground Nutmeg.** For a flavorful dish, mash boiled turnips with Land O Lakes Butter and McCormick Ground Nutmeg.

Vegetables

- **Arm & Hammer Baking Soda.** To keep vegetables bright and colorful when boiling, add a pinch of Arm & Hammer Baking Soda to the cooking water.

- **Bounty Paper Towels.** To revive wilted or blemished fresh vegetables, remove any discolored bits, sprinkle the vegetables with cool water, wrap in a sheet of Bounty Paper Towel, and refrigerate for at least an hour.

- **Campbell's Beef Bouillon.** To enhance the flavor of vegetables, simmer them in Campbell's Beef Bouillon rather than boiling them in water. The vegetables also enrich the bouillon, creating a rich stock.

- **Forster Toothpicks.** To prevent vegetables from boiling over and making a mess, before turning on the stove, insert a Forster Toothpick between the lid and the pot to let excess steam escape.

- **Heinz White Vinegar.** To revitalize vegetables, add three tablespoons Heinz White Vinegar to a sink full of cold water. Soak the vegetables for one hour.

- **Morton Salt.** To remove any insects harbored amidst the leaves of vegetables like artichokes, broccoli, Brussels sprouts, and curled leaf lettuce, dissolve one-quarter cup Morton Salt in one quart of water. Soak the vegetables in the salty water for thirty minutes. Rinse clean in clear cold water.

- **Nestlé Carnation Evaporated Milk.** To give creamed vegetables a rich flavor and consistency, use Nestlé Carnation Evaporated Milk instead of fresh milk.

- **ReaLemon.** To refresh vegetables, add four tablespoons ReaLemon lemon juice to a sink full of cold water and immerse the vegetables for one hour.

- **ReaLemon.** To help vegetables retain their vitamin content and make green vegetables stay green, add a little ReaLemon lemon juice to the cooking liquid to make the solution slightly acidic.

- **Reynolds Wrap.** To boil two different vegetables at the same time in one pot, wrap each batch of vegetables in a separate sheet of Reynolds Wrap.

Food for Thought
BREAKING THE ICE

- To make frozen vegetables taste fresh, before cooking, pour boiling water over the frozen vegetables to wash away any trace of stale, frozen water.

Waffles

- **Arm & Hammer Baking Soda.** To make soft, delicate waffles, substitute buttermilk for regular milk in the batter and add a pinch of Arm & Hammer Baking Soda.

- **Canada Dry Club Soda.** To make light and fluffy waffles, substitute whatever amount of liquid called for by the recipe with the same amount of Canada Dry Club Soda. The carbonation in the club soda causes the pancakes to rise higher, provided you use the batter immediately.

- **Crisco All-Vegetable Shortening.** When using a new waffle iron for the first time, add a little Crisco All-Vegetable Shortening to the batter to help temper the metal in the waffle iron.

- **Domino Sugar.** To make waffles soft, add a little Domino Sugar to the waffle batter.

- **Pam Cooking Spray.** To prevent waffles from sticking to a waffle iron, spray a light coat of Pam Cooking Spray on the grids.

- **Reynolds Cut-Rite Wax Paper** and **Ziploc Storage Bags.** To freeze waffles, let cool and stack the waffles, separating them from each other with a square of Reynolds Cut-Rite Wax Paper, and place in a Ziploc Freezer Bag. To reheat the frozen waffles without thawing, simply heat them in the toaster.

- **Star Olive Oil.** To give waffles a crisp crust, substitute Star Olive Oil for melted butter in the batter.

Watermelon

- **Morton Salt.** Sprinkling watermelon with Morton Salt gives the fruit a unique taste.

- **Saran Wrap.** To keep a cut watermelon fresh in the refrigerator and prevent it from absorbing odors from other foods, wrap it tightly with Saran Wrap.

Strange Facts
The Watermelon Is a Berry

A berry is a fruit with many seeds embedded in the flesh of a single, juicy, enlarged ovary. That description clearly fits the watermelon (*citrullus lanatus*). Berries do not necessarily have a soft outer skin, such as blueberries or cranberries. Berries may also have a tough rind like the watermelon and other members of the gourd family. Scientists believe the watermelon originated in the Kalahari Desert in southern Africa. The fruit was cultivated as early as the second millennium b.c.e. in Egypt.

Wine

- **Domino Sugar.** When adding tart red wine to a sauce, add a pinch or two of Domino Sugar while cooking to balance the acidity.

- **Heinz White Vinegar.** Add leftover wine to a bottle of Heinz White Vinegar to make wine vinegar.

- **Star Olive Oil.** To keep an open bottle of dry cooking wine fresh, add a few drops Star Olive Oil. The oil creates a fine film on the surface of the wine, protecting the wine from bacteria in the air.

- **Ziploc Storage Bags.** To chill wine more quickly than putting the bottle on ice, pour the wine into a one-gallon Ziploc bag and swirl it around in a sink filled with ice water.

Food for Thought
WINING AND DINING

- Wine connoisseurs tend to recommend dry white wines with fish, seafood, poultry, and light meats; pink rosé wine with all types of food; and robust red wines with red meat and game. However, drink whichever wine tastes best to you.

- Chefs often cook chicken with red wine and beef with white wine.

- There is no correlation between the price of a bottle of wine and its taste. Enjoy whatever wine appeals to your taste. Oftentimes, an inexpensive bottle of wine will taste better than an expensive bottle of wine.

Yogurt

● **Dannon Yogurt.** To make homemade yogurt, pour one quart half-and-half into a glass mixing bowl. Using a cooking thermometer, heat the half-and-half in a microwave oven at fifty percent power for one minute at a time until the temperature of the half-and-half reaches 180 degrees Fahrenheit. (Use the spoon to stir the liquid between time breaks to prevent scalding and skim off any film from the surface.) Remove from the microwave and let cool to about 115 degrees Fahrenheit. Add three tablespoons Dannon Plain Yogurt, mix well, pour into a clean, empty glass jar, and seal the lid tightly. Place the warm jar inside an insulated picnic cooler, close the lid, and let sit undisturbed for eight hours. Refrigerate when ready. If desired, add vanilla extract, strawberries, peaches, or raspberries to taste. Three tablespoons yogurt from this batch can be used to start a new batch, ideally within five days.

CHAPTER 5

Astonishing Kitchen Remedies

Arthritis

- **Heinz Apple Cider Vinegar.** Add one teaspoon Heinz Apple Cider Vinegar to one cup of water. Drink the solution two to three times a day. Purportedly, apple cider vinegar puts the acid crystals that harden in the joints and tissues in solution so they can be flushed from the body.

- **Jell-O.** To reduce arthritis pain, eat one serving Jell-O brand gelatin every day. The amino acids purportedly stimulate production of collagen and provide nutritional support for cartilage structure, lessening pain. You should start noticing a significant improvement after three months.

- **Quaker Oats.** Mix two cups Quaker Oats and one cup of water in a bowl, and then heat in the microwave oven for one minute. Apply the warm mixture to your hands to soothe arthritis pain.

Athlete's Foot

- **Listerine.** Soaking your lesions in Listerine antiseptic mouthwash will sting and burn fiercely, but the antiseptic will also kill the bacteria and stop your feet from smelling.

- **Morton Salt.** To eliminate athlete's foot, dissolve a handful of Morton Salt in a footbath filled with warm water. Soak each foot in the salty solution for five to ten minutes. The salt helps kill the foot fungus and softens the skin, enabling antifungal medication to better penetrate the skin.

- **ReaLemon.** To help cure athlete's foot, wash and dry your feet, and then rub liberal amounts of ReaLemon lemon juice over the affected areas. Note that the acids in the lemon juice may sting cracked skin.

Backache

- **Tabasco Pepper Sauce.** Massage the hot sauce into your back and sore muscles. The alkaloid capsaicin in Tabasco Pepper Sauce deadens pain when applied topically. Capsaicin enters nerves and temporarily depletes them of the neurotransmitter that sends pain signals to the brain. If you feel any burning, apply some Colgate Toothpaste over the dried Tabasco Pepper Sauce. The glycerin in the toothpaste minimizes the sting and may also boost the capsaicin's analgesic properties. Do not apply Tabasco Pepper Sauce to an open wound.

- **Uncle Ben's Converted Brand Rice.** Fill a sock with Uncle Ben's Converted Brand Rice, tie a knot in the open end, and heat in a microwave oven for ninety seconds. Place the rice-filled sock on your back as a heating pad. Reheat when desired. The reusable heating pad conforms wherever applied.

- **Wilson Tennis Balls.** Put several Wilson Tennis Balls inside a sock and tie a knot at the end. Have a friend roll this over your back. Labor coaches frequently use this technique to massage the backs of women in labor.

Bad Breath

- **Alka-Seltzer.** Dissolve two Alka-Seltzer tablets in a glass of warm water, and swish the fizzy solution through your mouth as a refreshing mouthwash (unless you are allergic to aspirin, a key ingredient in Alka-Seltzer). The sodium bicarbonate in the Alka-Seltzer lowers the pH level in your mouth, killing odor-producing bacteria.

- **Arm & Hammer Baking Soda** and **Morton Salt.** To make an all-natural mouthwash, dissolve one teaspoon Arm & Hammer Baking Soda and one teaspoon Morton Salt in one-half cup of water. Rinse your mouth or gargle with the solution.

- **McCormick Fennel Seed.** Chewing a few fennel seeds destroys the bacteria in your mouth that cause bad breath.

- **ReaLemon.** To freshen your breath, dissolve one teaspoon ReaLemon lemon juice in one cup of water. Swirl the lemony solution around in your mouth and rinse clean.

Blisters

- **Fruit of the Earth Aloe Vera Gel.** To heal a blister, rub Fruit of the Earth Aloe Vera Gel over the blister. Aloe is an analgesic that will soothe the burning sensation.

- **Kingsford's Corn Starch.** To prevent blisters on your feet, gently powder your feet with Kingsford's Corn Starch before putting on your socks, so the socks better glide over your feet.

- **Nestlé Carnation Nonfat Dry Milk.** To soothe intact blisters on your feet, mix three ounces Nestlé Carnation Nonfat Dry Milk and one cup of water. Soak your foot in the milky solution to reduce the pain.

Body Odor

- **Arm & Hammer Baking Soda.** To minimize underarm odor, dust Arm & Hammer Baking Soda into your armpits. Baking soda absorbs moisture, neutralizes odors, and kills odor-causing bacteria.

- **Dial.** Frequently scrubbing your entire body—particularly your armpits and groin—with an antibacterial soap like Dial eliminates body odor by killing the bacteria that thrive in the moist areas of your body.

- **Purell Instant Hand Sanitizer.** To prevent underarm odor, rub a dollop of Purell Instant Hand Sanitizer into your underarms. Purell kills the existing bacteria and prevents new bacteria from populating your armpits, where they die, decompose, and emit foul smells.

Bruises

- **Heinz Apple Cider Vinegar.** To reduce swelling and decrease discoloration from a bruise, dampen a washcloth in equal parts Heinz Apple Cider Vinegar and water. Apply the cloth to the bruise for several hours.

- **Orajel.** To prevent a bruise from appearing or reduce the discoloration, rub a dollop of Orajel into the skin on and around the bruise. The numbing ointment stops the blood vessels from constricting, preventing discoloration.

- **ReaLemon.** Saturate a gauze pad or a washcloth with ReaLemon lemon juice and press it against the bruise to relieve the discoloration.

Burns

- **Clabber Girl Baking Powder.** To treat a minor burn quickly, mix enough Clabber Girl Baking Powder with water to make a paste, apply to the burn, and cover with clean gauze.

- **Colgate Toothpaste.** To prevent blistering from a mild burn and speed up the healing process, spread a dollop of Colgate Toothpaste on the skin immediately after burning, let dry, and leave on for several hours. The toothpaste protects the skin from exposure to oxygen (lessening the burning pain almost immediately) and dries the skin (preventing liquid from building up under the skin).

- **French's Mustard.** Here's a trick embraced by short-order cooks to prevent blistering or pain from a mild burn. Immediately rub French's Yellow Mustard into the burn. The mustard stings momentarily, but then the burn stops stinging completely. Let the mustard dry and cake up, and then wash it off.

- **Lipton Tea Bags.** To soothe a minor burn, apply wet Lipton Tea Bags directly to the affected area, or secure them in place with gauze. The tannic acid in the tea relieves the burning pain.

- **Vaseline Petroleum Jelly.** When rubbed on a minor burn, Vaseline Petroleum Jelly expedites healing.

Chapped Lips

- **Alberto VO5 Conditioning Hairdressing.** To soothe chapped lips, rub in a dab of Alberto VO5 Hairdressing.

- **Crisco All-Vegetable Shortening.** Moisturize chapped lips with a dab of Crisco All-Vegetable Shortening.

- **SueBee Honey.** Mix one tablespoon SueBee Honey and one teaspoon of water and melt the mixture in a microwave oven for approximately twenty seconds. Let cool, and then apply to chapped lips.

- **Vaseline Petroleum Jelly.** Applying a dab of Vaseline Petroleum Jelly to your lips moisturizes and protects your lips just like ChapStick.

Colds and Flu

- **Campbell's Chicken Noodle Soup.** According to research conducted by the Mount Sinai Medical Center in Miami Beach, Florida, sipping a bowl of hot chicken soup helps decongest nasal passages while simultaneously rehydrating and reenergizing the body with essential salts.

- **Campbell's Tomato Juice** and **Tabasco Pepper Sauce.** To decongest the nose, sinuses, and lungs, mix ten to twenty drops Tabasco Pepper Sauce in one cup Campbell's Tomato Juice. Drink several glasses of this spicy tonic daily. Or gargle with ten to twenty drops Tabasco Pepper Sauce mixed in a glass of water to clear out the respiratory tract.

- **Morton Salt** and **Glad Flexible Straws.** To make nose drops to relieve congestion from a stuffy nose, dissolve one-quarter teaspoon Morton Salt in one cup of warm water. Insert a Glad Flexible Straw into the liquid, cover the open end of the straw with your finger, insert the straw in your nostril, release your finger from the straw, and inhale the liquid. Repeat several times, and then blow your nose thoroughly.

- **ReaLemon** and **McCormick Ground Ginger.** To relieve a cough or any chest congestion, mix two teaspoons ReaLemon lemon juice, one-half teaspoon McCormick Ground Ginger, and one cup of hot water, and drink the mixture slowly. The lemon and ginger alleviate a scratchy throat and work as an expectorant.

✳ Recipe Magic ✳

Homemade Cough Syrup

- 4 tablespoons ReaLemon lemon juice
- 1 cup SueBee Honey
- ½ cup Star Olive Oil

Mix the ReaLemon lemon juice, SueBee Honey, and Star Olive Oil in a saucepan and warm over low heat for five minutes. Stir vigorously for several minutes until the mixture attains the consistency of syrup. To relieve a cough, take one teaspoon of the formula every two hours. Store in an airtight container.

Constipation

- **Coca-Cola.** For many people, drinking a can of Coca-Cola has a laxative effect. Caffeine triggers muscular contractions in the intestines.

- **Quaker Oats.** Eating one cup Quaker Oats adds eight grams of fiber to your diet. Thirty grams of fiber daily puts an end to constipation, helping your body produce soft bowel movements.

- **ReaLemon.** To alleviate constipation, mix two tablespoons ReaLemon lemon juice and one cup of warm water, and drink the lemony solution before breakfast. Drinking water on an empty stomach stimulates the intestines, and lemon juice stimulates the intestines further.

- **Star Olive Oil.** Taking one to three tablespoons Star Olive Oil works as a natural, mild laxative.

Cuts and Scrapes

- **Gold Medal Flour.** In an emergency, apply flour to a laceration to stop excessive bleeding. The flour helps the blood clot until you can get to a doctor.

- **Lipton Tea.** To stop minor bleeding from a cut, dampen a Lipton Tea Bag with warm water and press the tea bag over the wound. The tannic acid stops the bleeding.

- **Listerine.** To disinfect cuts and scrapes, pour Listerine antiseptic mouthwash over the laceration or abrasion. Listerine is an astringent, reducing bleeding.

- **ReaLemon.** To hasten the healing of a minor bleeding cut, put a few drops of ReaLemon lemon juice on the cut followed by a bandage. Lemon juice, which does sting, disinfects wounds and helps the body heal itself.

- **Stayfree Maxi Pads.** In a pinch, use a Stayfree Maxi Pad as a compress to stop a wound from bleeding.

- **SueBee Honey.** Applying SueBee Honey to a laceration or abrasion as an ointment disinfects the wound, kills bacteria, and hastens healing. Honey is hygroscopic and absorbs water, creating an environment in which disease-producing microorganisms, deprived of their moisture, cannot live.

Dandruff

- **Listerine.** After shampooing your hair, rinse with Listerine antiseptic mouthwash. Thymol, one of the active ingredients in Listerine, is a mild antiseptic that helps reduce dandruff.

- **McCormick Ground Thyme.** Bring one cup of water to a boil, add two tablespoons McCormick Ground Thyme, and let simmer for ten minutes. Let cool, strain out the thyme, and, after shampooing and rinsing your hair clean, massage the thyme solution into your scalp. Let dry and do not rinse out.

- **Purell Instant Hand Sanitizer.** Rub Purell Instant Hand Sanitizer into your scalp, wait five minutes, and then rinse clean. The ethyl alcohol in Purell kills the bacteria responsible for your dry scalp.

- **ReaLemon.** To eliminate dandruff, apply two tablespoons ReaLemon lemon juice to your scalp, shampoo your hair, and then rinse with a mixture of two tablespoons ReaLemon lemon juice and two cups of water. Repeat every two days until the dandruff vanishes.

Diarrhea

- **Domino Sugar** and **Morton Salt.** To replace lost fluids and electrolytes in the body after a bout with diarrhea, dissolve two teaspoons Domino Sugar and one-half teaspoon Morton Salt in two cups of water and drink the solution. Repeat every hour.

- **Gatorade.** After a bout of diarrhea, drink Gatorade to replace the electrolytes and prevent dehydration.

- **Heinz Apple Cider Vinegar.** To reduce the intensity of diarrhea while allowing nature to take its course, mix one teaspoon Heinz Apple Cider Vinegar in one cup of water. Drink six cups of this solution a day (every three hours). The acetic acid in vinegar kills some of the bacteria that cause diarrhea, and the pectin helps stiffen the stool.

Eyes

- **Arm & Hammer Baking Soda, Morton Salt,** and **Mr. Coffee Filters.** In a pinch, you can make storage fluid for hard contact lenses by dissolving one-quarter teaspoon Arm & Hammer Baking Soda, one-quarter teaspoon Morton Salt, and one cup of sterile water in a sterile container. Strain the solution through a Mr. Coffee Filter to remove any undissolved particles, and store the liquid in a sterile dropper bottle.

- **Chicken of the Sea Tuna.** To reduce the risk of dry eye syndrome, eat five servings Chicken of the Sea Tuna during the week. Doing so reduces the chances of getting dry eye syndrome by 68 percent, according to a study conducted in 2005 at Brigham & Women's Hospital and Schepens Eye Research Institute in Boston.

- **Glad Flexible Straws.** If you don't have an eyedropper, improvise one with a Glad Flexible Straw. Submerge the bottom of the straw into the saline solution, place the tip of your finger over the opening at the top of the straw, lift the straw from the solution, position it over your open eye, and remove your fingertip from the top of the straw.

- **Lipton Tea Bags.** Soothe tired eyes by immersing two Lipton Tea Bags in warm water, squeezing out the excess moisture, and placing them over your closed eyes for twenty minutes. The tannin in the tea reduces the puffiness and revitalizes tired eyes. Chamomile tea bags also help relieve tired eyes.

- **Morton Salt.** To revitalize dry eyes with a soothing saline solution, dissolve one-quarter teaspoon Morton Salt in one cup of water, and using an eyedropper, bathe your eyes with the solution.

- **Morton Salt** and **Stayfree Maxi Pads.** To reduce puffy eyes caused by excessive crying or sleep deprivation, dissolve one teaspoon Morton Salt in two cups of hot water, saturate a Stayfree Maxi Pad in the solution, and apply the pad to your puffy eyes.

Facials

- **Colgate Toothpaste.** Squeeze a dollop of Colgate Regular Flavor Toothpaste into the cupped palm your hand, add a few drops of water, and rub your hands together to create a lather. Coat your face with the toothpaste lather, and then rinse thoroughly. Toothpaste is a mild abrasive that cleanses the skin and leaves your face feeling minty fresh.

- **Cool Whip.** For an invigorating and moisturizing facial, cover your face with Cool Whip, wait twenty minutes, and then wash clean with warm water followed by cold water. The coconut and palm kernel oils in Cool Whip moisturize and soothe the skin.

- **Hunt's Tomato Paste.** Spread Hunt's Tomato Paste over your face, wait ten minutes, then rinse clean and pat dry with a towel. The acids from the tomatoes balance the pH level of the skin, exfoliate dead skin, and tighten pores.

- **Morton Salt** and **Star Olive Oil.** To give yourself a revitalizing facial, mix equal parts Morton Salt and Star Olive Oil; wash your face; apply warm, wet washcloths to your face to open the pores; and then apply the pasty solution, massaging the face with long upward and inward strokes for five minutes. Remove the concoction, and then rinse your face clean with warm water, followed by cool water.

- **Mott's Applesauce.** Rub Mott's Applesauce over your face, wait thirty minutes, and wash with lukewarm water. The applesauce cleans dry skin, and the pectin in the applesauce absorbs excess oil.

- **Nestlé Carnation Nonfat Dry Milk.** Mix one-quarter cup Carnation Nonfat Dry Milk with enough water to make a thick paste. Apply the milky paste to your face, let dry, and then wash off. The lactic acids remove grime and exfoliate dead skin, and the proteins in the milk leave the skin feeling silky smooth.

- **Quaker Oats** and **SueBee Honey.** Mix up a cup of warm Quaker Oats, add enough SueBee Honey to thicken, let cool to the touch, and then apply to your dry face. Wait ten minutes, and then rinse with warm water. The warmth and the honey draw the oil from your skin, and the oatmeal absorbs it.

Feet

- **Cool Whip.** Soothe hot, tired feet by giving them a coat of Cool Whip. Wait fifteen minutes, and then rinse clean. The coconut and palm kernel oils cool achy feet, moisturizing and softening the skin.

- **Listerine.** Cure toenail fungus by soaking your toes in Listerine antiseptic mouthwash four times daily for a couple of weeks. Listerine is an antiseptic that kills foot fungus.

- **Morton Salt.** To relieve sore feet, dissolve a handful of Morton Salt in a small basin of warm water and soak your feet in the revitalizing solution.

- **ReaLemon.** After soaking your feet in a salt bath (see Morton Salt, page 279), rub a generous amount of ReaLemon lemon juice into your feet for several minutes, rinse with cool water, and dry thoroughly. The lemon juice improves the skin condition and deodorizes your feet as well.

- **Vicks VapoRub.** Cure toenail fungus by applying a thick coat of Vicks VapoRub over the affected nail several times a day.

Food Poisoning

- **Coca-Cola.** Open a can or bottle of Coca-Cola, let sit until it goes flat (roughly thirty minutes), and then drink the flat soda. Pharmacies sell cola syrup as a cure for upset stomachs. Letting the bubbles out of the soda prevents the carbonation from further aggravating your stomach.

- **Domino Sugar, ReaLemon,** and **Morton Salt.** To replace the glucose, minerals, and vitamin C being flushed out of your body during a bout of diarrhea and vomiting, drink a rehydrating solution made from three teaspoons Domino Sugar, two teaspoons ReaLemon lemon juice, and one teaspoon Morton Salt in a tall glass of water.

- **Nabisco Original Premium Saltine Crackers.** When you're feeling ready for food again, start with bland foods like Nabisco Original Premium Saltine Crackers, which you can easily digest.

Gum in Hair

- **Jif Peanut Butter.** To remove chewing gum from hair, rub a dollop of Jif Peanut Butter into the gum, let sit for five minutes, and comb out. The oils in the peanut butter dissolve the adhesives in the chewing gum.

- **Pam Cooking Spray.** Spray some Pam Cooking Spray on the wad of chewing gum and massage with your fingers. The oil dissolves the gum, making it easy to comb out of hair.

Hands

- **McCormick Pure Vanilla Extract** and **Crisco All-Vegetable Shortening.** Mix one-half tablespoon McCormick Pure Vanilla Extract and one tablespoon Crisco All-Vegetable Shortening and massage the mixture into your hands. The vanilla provides aromatherapy, and the shortening moisturizes the skin.

- **Playtex Living Gloves** and **Lubriderm.** Before washing the dishes, apply Lubriderm skin cream to your hands, and then put on a pair of Playtex Living Gloves. The heat from the warm water helps the skin cream penetrate your skin, deeply moisturizing your hands.

- **Quaker Oats.** Blend a cup Quaker Oats into a fine powder, and then rub the powdered oats over your hands to exfoliate the dry skin. Wash your hands with cool water, dry well, and then apply a moisturizing cream.

Headache

- **Gatorade.** Headaches are frequently a symptom of dehydration. Drinking two glasses of Gatorade replaces electrolytes (the potassium and salt lost through perspiration) and relieves headache pain almost immediately.

- **Lipton Peppermint Herbal Tea.** To relieve headache pain, drink a strongly brewed cup of Lipton Peppermint Herbal Tea. Peppermint has a calming and numbing effect.

- **Maxwell House Coffee.** Drinking a couple of cups of Maxwell House Coffee can reduce a headache. Coffee is a vasoconstrictor, reducing the swelling of blood vessels that cause headache pain.

Heartburn

- **Heinz Apple Cider Vinegar.** To relieve heartburn, mix two teaspoons Heinz Apple Cider Vinegar in one cup of water and sip the solution during your meal. Heartburn is often caused by low stomach acid, and the acetic acid in the vinegar corrects this deficiency.

- **ReaLemon** and **Morton Salt.** To alleviate heartburn, mix two tablespoons ReaLemon lemon juice, one-half teaspoon Morton Salt, and one cup of warm water. Drink the mixture slowly.

- **Uncle Ben's Converted Brand Rice.** Eating Uncle Ben's Converted Brand Rice, a food high in complex carbohydrates, absorbs acid in the stomach, relieving heartburn.

Hiccups

- **Domino Sugar.** To cure the hiccups, swallow one heaping teaspoon dry Domino Sugar, without water. The coarse texture of the sugar apparently reprograms the nerve receptors that control the diaphragm.

- **Jif Peanut Butter.** Eating one heaping spoonful Jif Peanut Butter frequently works to cure the hiccups.

- **ReaLemon.** To end the hiccups, briskly swallow a jigger of ReaLemon lemon juice. The sour taste of the lemon juice may shock the diaphragm's nerves out of spasm.

Ice Packs

- **Birds Eye Baby Peas.** Use a plastic bag of frozen Birds Eye Baby Peas as an ice pack. The sack of peas conforms to the contours of your body, and you can refreeze the peas for future ice-pack use. Be sure to label the bag for ice-pack use only. If you want to eat the peas, cook them after they thaw the first time, never after refreezing.

- **Jell-O** and **Ziploc Freezer Bags.** Prepare Jell-O according to the directions and let cool enough to pour into a Ziploc Freezer Bag until three-quarters full. Seal the bag shut securely and freeze, creating a homemade, flexible ice pack that conforms to the shape of your body. When the Jell-O melts, simply refreeze.

- **Pampers.** To make an ice pack, saturate a Pampers disposable diaper with water and freeze. The superabsorbent polymer flakes in the diaper absorb 300 times their weight in liquid.

Indigestion

- **Altoids Mints.** To soothe indigestion, chew an Altoids Peppermint Mint. Peppermint soothes stomach upset.

- **Arm & Hammer Baking Soda.** According to the instructions on the side of the box of Arm & Hammer Baking Soda, drinking one-half teaspoon baking soda dissolved in one-half glass of water relieves indigestion by neutralizing an acid stomach. Read the instructions on the side of the box carefully before using this remedy.

- **SueBee Honey.** Taking two teaspoons honey tends to relieve indigestion, perhaps because this sweet antibacterial inhibits the growth of *Salmonella, Shigella, E. coli*, and *V. cholerae* in the intestinal track. Do not feed honey to infants under one year of age. Honey often carries a benign strain of *C. botulinum*, and an infant's immune system requires twelve months to develop to fight off disease and infection.

Insect Bites

- **Adolph's Meat Tenderizer.** Make a paste of Adolph's Meat Tenderizer and water and immediately apply to the sting. The enzymes in meat tenderizer break down the proteins in insect venom.

- **French's Mustard.** To relieve an insect sting, apply French's Mustard to the affected area.

- **Heinz White Vinegar.** Using a cotton ball to apply a dab of Heinz White Vinegar on insect bites relieves the itch almost instantly.

- **ReaLemon.** To relieve the itching and swelling from an insect bite, use a cotton ball to rub ReaLemon lemon juice on the bug bite. Although it may sting at first, lemon juice soothes the pain, alleviates the itch, and works as both an antiseptic and anti-inflammatory.

Insomnia

- **SueBee Honey.** Take one teaspoon SueBee Honey before bedtime, and you should be asleep within one hour. Honey acts as a sedative to the nervous system. Do not feed honey to an infant under one year of age.

Itchy Skin

- **Fruit of the Earth Aloe Vera Gel.** To soothe itchy skin, smooth Fruit of the Earth Aloe Vera Gel over the affected area. The analgesic soothes itching.

- **Quaker Oats** and **L'eggs Sheer Energy Panty Hose.**
  Using a blender, grind one cup Quaker Oats into a fine powder. Cut off the foot from a clean, used pair of L'eggs Sheer Energy Panty Hose, fill with the powdered oats, and tie a knot in the nylon. Tie the oatmeal sachet to the spigot, letting it dangle in the flow of water as the tub fills with warm water. Soak for thirty minutes in this inexpensive and soothing oatmeal bath.

Nausea

- **Altoids Mints.** To quell nausea, chew an Altoids Peppermint Mint. Peppermint settles stomach upset.

- **Coca-Cola.** Open a can or bottle of Coca-Cola, let sit until it goes flat (roughly thirty minutes), and then drink the flat soda. Pharmacies sell cola syrup as a cure for upset stomachs. Letting the bubbles out of the soda prevents the carbonation from further aggravating your stomach.

- **Gatorade.** Drink a glass of Gatorade. This sports drink helps maintain the body's balance of electrolytes, which regulate the body's electrochemical balance, alleviating the queasiness of nausea.

Shaving

- **Clairol Herbal Essences Conditioner.** Instead of using shaving cream on your legs, use Clairol Herbal Essences Conditioner. The lavish emollients in conditioner moisturize the skin, preventing rashes and bumps.

- **Cool Whip.** Apply Cool Whip to wet skin as shaving cream. The coconut and palm kernel oils in Cool Whip moisturize the skin for a close shave, leaving your skin feeling soft and smooth.

- **Land O Lakes Butter.** In a pinch, you can slather Land O Lakes Butter on wet skin for a silky, smooth shave that simultaneously moisturizes your skin.

- **Miracle Whip.** To avoid razor burn in your bikini area, shave with Miracle Whip, which hydrates the skin and also doubles as shaving cream on your legs.

Skin

- **Crisco All-Vegetable Shortening.** To relieve dry skin, rub in a dab of Crisco All-Vegetable Shortening, which doubles as a moisturizing cream.

- **Morton Salt.** To soothe dry skin or relieve itchy skin, dissolve one-half cup Morton Salt in a bathtub full of warm water and soak in the salty water, which also helps alleviate muscle aches.

- **Morton Salt, Epsom Salt,** and **Wesson Oil.** To soften and exfoliate rough skin from your elbows, knees, and feet, mix one-quarter cup Morton Salt, one-quarter cup Epsom Salt, and one-quarter cup Wesson Oil. Massage the paste into the dry skin for a few minutes, and then wash with soapy water and rinse clean.

- **Pam Cooking Spray.** Spray your hands with a light coat of Pam Cooking Spray and rub into the skin. The oils moisturize dry skin.

Smoking

- **McCormick Cream of Tartar** and **Tropicana Orange Juice.** To quit smoking cigarettes and minimize your cravings for nicotine, mix one-half teaspoon McCormick Cream of Tartar in a medium glass of Tropicana Orange Juice, and drink the solution every night before bedtime for thirty days. The cream of tartar (potassium hydrogen tartrate) helps ease nicotine cravings by replacing the potassium that smoking robs from the cardiovascular system. The orange juice replenishes the vitamin C that smoking cigarettes robs from your body. Each cigarette you smoke depletes roughly 25 milligrams of vitamin C.

Sore Throat

- **McCormick Ground (Cayenne) Red Pepper, McCormick Ground Ginger,** and **SueBee Honey.** In a mug, combine one-quarter teaspoon McCormick Ground (Cayenne) Red Pepper, one-half teaspoon McCormick Ground Ginger, two teaspoons SueBee Honey, and one cup of boiling water. Stir well and swish each mouthful of the solution around your mouth and throat before swallowing.

- **Morton Salt.** To temporarily relieve a sore throat immediately, dissolve one teaspoon Morton Salt in one cup of warm water and gargle with the salty solution. Repeat four times a day.

Tongue Burn

- **Dannon Yogurt.** If eating spicy food seems to ignite your tongue on fire, swish Dannon Yogurt (any flavor) around your mouth to quickly soothe your taste buds.

- **Hershey's Milk Chocolate Bar.** If you burn your tongue on chili peppers or cayenne pepper, take a bite of a Hershey's Milk Chocolate Bar. The casein in the chocolate apparently absorbs the capsaicin from the nerve receptors of your tongue.

- **Reddi-wip.** To soothe tongue burn or a burn on the roof of your mouth, grab a can of Reddi-wip whipped cream, fill your mouth with the dessert topping, and use your tongue to press the Reddi-wip against the roof of your mouth.

Ulcers

- **Dannon Yogurt.** To prevent ulcer-causing bacteria from thriving in the stomach, eat between one and four cups Dannon Yogurt with active cultures daily. The *Lactobacillus aci-dophilus* in yogurt act like antibiotics in the stomach, and the lactose in yogurt breaks down into lactic acid in the stomach, aiding digestion.

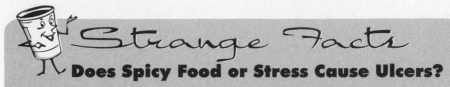

Strange Facts

Does Spicy Food or Stress Cause Ulcers?

Virtually all ulcers in the stomach or upper intestine are caused either by infection with a bacterium called *Helicobacter pylori*; by use of pain medications such as aspirin, ibuprofen, or naproxen; or by cancer. Most *Helicobacter pylori*–related ulcers can be cured with antibiotics. Ulcers caused by the use of aspirin, ibuprofen, or naproxen can be cured with time, stomach-protective medications, antacids, and by refraining from using those pain killers. While spicy food and stress may aggravate ulcer symptoms in some people, they do not cause ulcers.

- **Phillips' Milk of Magnesia.** To soothe the symptoms of an ulcer, take one teaspoon Phillips' Milk of Magnesia. The antacid helps relieve the pain.

- **Tabasco Pepper Sauce.** Dousing your meals with Tabasco Pepper Sauce can actually soothe ulcers. Tabasco Pepper Sauce is made from a variety of pepper called *Capsicum frutescens* that contains the alkaloid capsaicin. Ingesting this spicy compound prompts your digestive system to produce more mucous to coat the walls of the stomach and intestines, protecting the ulcers.

CHAPTER 6
Cleaning Up the Mess

Aluminum Cookware

- **McCormick Cream of Tartar.** To clean stains from a blackened aluminum pot, dissolve one teaspoon McCormick Cream of Tartar for every two cups of water in the pot and boil the solution for roughly five minutes. Wash the pot as usual and rinse clean.

- **ReaLemon.** To remove discoloration from the inside of aluminum cookware, dissolve one tablespoon ReaLemon lemon juice in one quart of water, fill the cookware with the lemony solution, and simmer until the discoloration vanishes. Wash with soapy water and rinse clean.

Bottles

- **Clorox Bleach.** To deodorize an empty glass bottle, wash it with a solution made from three-quarters cup Clorox Bleach and one gallon of water.

- **Efferdent.** To clean the inside of a glass bottle, fill the bottle with water, drop in two Efferdent denture cleansing tablets, wait ten minutes, and then rinse clean. The nontoxic denture cleanser leaves the bottle sparkling clean.

- **French's Mustard.** To deodorize the inside of a glass or plastic bottle, fill the bottle with water, add two teaspoons French's Mustard, shake vigorously, and rinse well.

- **Heinz White Vinegar.** To clean and deodorize the inside of a glass bottle, fill the bottle with equal parts Heinz White Vinegar and water, shake well, let sit thirty minutes, and rinse clean.

- **Nestea Iced Tea Mix.** To clean the inside of an empty bottle, fill the bottle with water, add three tablespoons Nestea Iced Tea Mix, shake well, and let sit overnight. In the morning, wash with soapy water and rinse clean. The tannic acid in the tea dissolves the residue in the bottle.

- **Uncle Ben's Converted Brand Rice** and **Heinz White Vinegar.** To clean the inside of a glass bottle, pour two tablespoons uncooked Uncle Ben's Converted Brand Rice into the bottle and add one-half cup Heinz White Vinegar. Shake vigorously, and then rinse clean. Repeat if necessary.

Broiler Pan

- **Parsons' Ammonia, Bounty Paper Towels,** and **Glad Trash Bags.** To clean a broiler pan, place the pan inside a Glad Trash Bag, place several Bounty Paper Towels in the pan, and saturate the paper toweling with one cup Parsons' Ammonia—being careful not to breath the ammonia. Close the bag securely with a twist tie and let sit overnight outside or in a well-ventilated garage. The ammonia fumes loosen the baked-on food and grease from the broiler pan. The next morning, open the bag outdoors (again being careful to avoid breathing the fumes), and remove the pan, leaving the paper towels in the bag. Discard the bag. Rinse the pan with a garden hose, and then bring it back inside the house to wash thoroughly with soapy water, rinse clean, and dry.

- **Tide** and **Bounty Paper Towels.** To clean grease and grime from a broiler pan, sprinkle Tide powdered detergent on the broiler pan and cover with dampened sheets of Bounty Paper Towels. Let sit for several hours. Rinse clean and dry.

Broken Glass

- **Bounty Paper Towels.** To pick up small pieces of broken glass from the floor, carefully use a sheet of Bounty Paper Towels dampened with water.

- **Playtex Living Gloves.** Before picking up shards of broken glass, put on a pair of Platex Living Gloves to protect your fingers from injury.

- **Wonder Bread.** To clean broken glass from the floor, use a few slices of Wonder Bread to pick up the pieces. The small shards of glass stick to the soft bread.

Brooms

- **Aunt Jemima Corn Meal.** To avoid making huge dust clouds when sweeping the floor, toss a handful of Aunt Jemima Corn Meal on the floor and sweep that around the room. The dust and dirt stick to the corn meal, making sweeping a breeze.

- **Bubble Wrap** and **Scotch Packaging Tape.** If you have difficulty gripping a broom, cut a strip of Bubble Wrap, wrap it around the broomstick several times to make a thicker handle, and secure in place with a piece of Scotch Packaging Tape.

- **Playtex Living Gloves.** To prevent the wooden end of a broom handle from scratching or marking walls, cut off one of the fingers from a clean, used pair of Playtex Living Gloves and slip the rubber finger over the end of the broom handle as a protective sheath.

Butcher Block

- **Arm & Hammer Baking Soda.** To deodorize and clean butcher block, sprinkle Arm & Hammer Baking Soda on the surface, scrub with a damp sponge, let sit for fifteen minutes (to give the sodium bicarbonate time to absorb any odors), and rinse clean.

- **Crisco All-Vegetable Shortening** and **Bounty Paper Towels.** To oil butcher block, put a dollop of Crisco All-Vegetable Shortening on a sheet of Bounty Paper Towel, rub it into the wood, and let sit overnight. In the morning, use another sheet of paper towel to wipe up the excess shortening.

- **Heinz White Vinegar.** To clean butcher block, mix equal parts Heinz White Vinegar and water. Scrub the surface with a sponge saturated with the mixture.

- **MasterCard.** Scrape any food from the butcher block with a clean, used MasterCard.

- **Pam Cooking Spray** and **Bounty Paper Towels.** If you don't have any Crisco All-Vegetable Shortening (see above), preserve butcher block by spraying the entire surface with Pam Original Cooking Spray, use a sheet of Bounty Paper Towels to rub the oil into the wood, and then wipe clean.

- **ReaLemon** and **Morton Salt.** To clean stains from butcher block, pour equal parts ReaLemon lemon juice and Morton Salt over the stains and rub with a damp sponge until clean. Rinse well and dry with a soft, clean cloth.

- **Wesson Oil** and **Bounty Paper Towels.** For another way to preserve butcher block, put a few drops Wesson Oil on a sheet of Bounty Paper Towel, rub it into the wood, and then wipe clean.

Cabinets

- **Huggies Baby Wipes.** For a simple way to clean a sticky mess from cabinets, use a Huggies Baby Wipe.

- **Kiwi Shoe Polish.** To touch up faded spots on wooden cabinet doors, rub a matching color of Kiwi Shoe Polish into the wood and buff to a shine.

- **Murphy Oil Soap.** To clean fingerprints and grime from kitchen cabinet doors, pour a few drops Murphy Oil Soap on a wet soft, clean cloth and rub the woodwork. Buff dry with another soft, clean cloth.

- **Nestea Iced Tea Mix.** Dissolve two teaspoons Nestea Iced Tea Mix in one cup of water; dampen a soft, clean cloth with the solution; and wipe down the wood cabinets. Tea cleans woodwork with excellent results.

Candle Wax

- **Bounty Paper Towels.** To remove candle wax from carpeting or a table cloth, place a sheet of Bounty Paper Towels over the wax stain and press gently and carefully with a warm iron. The heat from the iron melts the wax, and the paper towel absorbs it.

- **Conair Hair Dryer.** To remove candle wax from a table, countertop, or candle holder, aim the nozzle of a Conair Hair Dryer at the dried wax, and blow warm air an inch above the wax. Wipe away the softened wax with a soft cloth or a paper towel.

- **Jif Peanut Butter.** To remove candle wax from a countertop, rub a dollop of Jif Peanut Butter into the wax and wipe clean. The oils from the peanut butter lubricate the wax, making it slide off the surface.

- **MasterCard.** Before using any of the above methods to remove candle wax from a carpet, tablecloth, floor, or countertop, use an old MasterCard to scrape off as much wax as possible.

Carpet Stains

- **Canada Dry Club Soda.** To clean beverage stains (coffee, tea, juice, Kool-Aid, red wine, and soda) from carpet, blot up as much of the stain as possible, pour a small amount of Canada Dry Club Soda onto the stain, and blot with towels. Repeat until the color disappears. The effervescent action of the club soda lifts the stain from the carpet.

- **Gillette Foamy.** To remove stubborn food stains from carpet, spray a small amount of Gillette Foamy over the spot, rub into the affected area with your fingers, and blot clean with a damp, clean cloth.

- **Heinz White Vinegar** and **Kingsford's Corn Starch.** To clean a food stain from carpet, mix equal parts Heinz White Vinegar and Kingsford Corn Starch, work the paste into the stain with a soft, clean cloth, let sit for two days, and vacuum clean. The vinegar dissolves the stain, and the cornstarch absorbs it.

- **Huggies Baby Wipes.** To blot minor food or coffee stains from carpet, gently rub the stain with a Huggies Baby Wipe.

- **Kingsford's Corn Starch.** To clean a wet stain from carpet, sprinkle Kingsford's Corn Starch over the spot, let sit for thirty minutes, and then vacuum clean. Repeat if necessary.

- **Morton Salt.** To clean food or beverage stains from carpeting, dampen the spot with a little water, pour a mountain of Morton Salt to cover the stain, rub the salt into the stain, and let sit for ten minutes. Brush and vacuum. Repeat if necessary.

- **Murphy Oil Soap.** Blot food stains with a clean white cloth to absorb as much of the stain as possible. Mix one teaspoon Murphy Oil

Soap to one cup of water. Using a clean sponge, dampen the spot with the solution, and then blot with a clean cloth. Rinse with clear water on a damp towel. Dry.

- **Pampers.** To blot up spills from carpet, place a Pampers disposable diaper face-down over the stain, and either stand on the diaper or place a few heavy books on top of it to hold it in place for fifteen minutes or longer. The superabsorbent polymer flakes in Pampers absorb three hundred times their weight in liquid.

- **Shout.** To clean stubborn food stains from carpet, spray Shout stain remover on the stain, let sit for five minutes, and then blot clean with a clean, wet cloth.

- **Tide.** Whip one teaspoon liquid Tide and two cups of water with a whisk in a bowl to make a head of foam. Apply the resulting foam to the food stain, rub the foam into the stain, and blot well. Rinse with cool water, blot, and let dry.

- **20 Mule Team Borax.** To clean a food stain from carpeting, blot up as much of the stain as possible, mix one-half cup 20 Mule Team Borax and two cups of warm water, and use a soft cloth to blot the solution onto the carpet stain. Let sit for thirty minutes, rinse with cold water on a sponge, and blot dry. (Before treating, test an inconspicuous spot on the carpeting with a paste made from 20 Mule Team Borax and water to make sure the borax does not remove any color from the carpet.)

- **Windex.** To clean food or juice stains from carpet, blot up as much of the stain as possible, spray the affected area with Windex, and then blot with a towel.

- **Wonder Bread.** To blot cooking oil or grease from carpet, pat a slice of Wonder Bread over the spot to absorb the oil or grease, and then vacuum up the crumbs.

Casserole Dishes

- **Alka-Seltzer.** To clean baked-on food from a casserole dish, fill the cookware with water, drop in six Alka-Seltzer tablets, and let sit for one hour. Wash with soapy water, rinse, and dry.

- **Arm & Hammer Baking Soda.** To remove burned-on food from inside a casserole dish, fill the dish with warm water, dissolve one tablespoon Arm & Hammer Baking Soda in the water, and let sit overnight. In the morning, wash clean.

- **Bounce.** To clean burned-on food from inside a casserole dish, fill the casserole dish with hot water, float a sheet of Bounce in the water, and let sit overnight. In the morning, use the wet dryer sheet to wipe the dish clean. The antistatic elements in the dryer sheet stop the baked-on food from clinging to the dish.

- **Dawn Dishwashing Liquid** and **Morton Salt.** To clean baked-on food from inside a casserole dish, fill the dish with water, add one teaspoon Dawn Dishwashing Liquid and one teaspoon Morton Salt, and stir well. Microwave for three minutes on high, let cool to the touch, and scrub clean with a scouring sponge.

- **Downy Fabric Softener.** Fill a dirty casserole dish with water, add a capful of Downy Fabric Softener, mix well, and let sit overnight. In the morning, wash with soapy water, rinse clean, and dry. The surfactants in Downy loosen the baked-on food from the sides of the cookware.

- **Easy-Off Oven Cleaner.** To clean baked-on food and grease from a casserole dish, place the dish outside, and wearing rubber gloves and protective eyewear, spray the dish with Easy-Off Oven Cleaner and let sit for one hour. Carefully rinse the oven cleaner off the casserole dish with a garden hose, and then bring it back inside to wash thoroughly with soapy water. Rinse clean and dry.

- **Efferdent.** Fill the stained casserole dish with water, drop in two or three Efferdent denture cleansing tablets, and let sit overnight. In the morning, wipe clean with a sponge and rinse.

- **Heinz Ketchup.** To clean baked-on food from inside a casserole dish, squeeze enough Heinz Ketchup to cover the baked-on food and let sit for one hour. The acids in the ketchup soften the baked-on gunk, making it easy to wash clean with soapy water.

- **Heinz White Vinegar.** To clean baked-on food from casserole dishes, fill the dish with equal parts Heinz White Vinegar and water, let sit for thirty minutes, and then scrub with a sponge in hot, soapy water. Rinse clean and dry.

- **Mr. Clean Magic Eraser.** To remove stubborn baked-on stains from a casserole dish, gently rub the stains with a damp Mr. Clean Magic Eraser, wash the item thoroughly with soapy water, rinse clean, and dry.

- **20 Mule Team Borax.** To clean baked-on food from a casserole dish, sprinkle 20 Mule Team Borax on the cookware, rub with a damp sponge, and rinse thoroughly.

Cast-Iron Cookware

- **Canada Dry Club Soda.** For a simple way to clean a cast-iron skillet, pour Canada Dry Club Soda over the hot skillet. The sodium bicarbonate in the club soda cleans the baked-on food from the pan.

- **Dawn Dishwashing Liquid.** Fill a dirty cast-iron pan with water, add one or two tablespoons Dawn Dishwashing Liquid, and bring the pot of soapy water to a simmer on the stove. Turn off the heat, let the water cool to room temperature, and rinse clean. Baked-on food will come right out. Reseason the pan (see page 33).

- **Easy-Off Oven Cleaner.** To clean baked-on grease and grime from the outside (not the inside) of cast-iron cookware, place the cookware outside. Wearing rubber gloves and protective eyewear, spray only the exterior with Easy-Off Oven Cleaner and let sit for one hour. Carefully rinse the oven cleaner off the cookware with a garden hose, and then bring it back inside to wash the outside only with soapy water. Rinse clean and dry. Reseason with Crisco All-Vegetable Shortening (see page 33).

- **Heinz White Vinegar.** For another simple way to clean the inside of a cast-iron pan, fill the pan with warm water, add two or three tablespoons Heinz White Vinegar, and boil. Reseason with Crisco All-Vegetable Shortening (see page 33).

- **Morton Salt.** To clean grease and grime from inside a cast-iron pan, carefully heat the pan on a stove burner set on high. When the pan starts smoking, pour one cup Morton Salt into the pan, and use a wooden spoon to push the salt around the pan to better absorb any grease and grime. When the salt starts turning gray, discard it. If the surface of the pan does not appear dull, repeat the salt treatment. Wash the pan clean with hot water, dry thoroughly with a towel, let air-dry for thirty minutes, and then reseason with Crisco All-Vegetable Shortening (see page 33).

- **Pam Cooking Spray.** To clean rust spots from a cast-iron pot or pan, spray the affected areas with Pam Cooking Spray and rub vigorously with a soft, clean cloth.

- **S.O.S Steel Wool Soap Pads.** To clean stubborn rust stains from a cast-iron pan, scrub with a wet S.O.S Steel Wool Soap Pad, rinse, and wipe clean with a soft cloth. Reseason with Crisco All-Vegetable Shortening (see page 33).

China

- **Bon Ami.** To clean coffee or tea stains from fine china, or gray marks caused by cutlery, sprinkle Bon Ami on a damp cloth or sponge and gently rub the stains or marks until they vanish.

- **Colgate Regular Flavor Toothpaste.** To clean stains or marks of any sort from china, squeeze a dab of Colgate Regular Flavor Toothpaste on a soft, clean cloth and gently rub the offending spots.

- **Efferdent.** To clean stains from a china teacup, fill the cup with water, drop in one Efferdent denture cleansing tablet, and let sit overnight. In the morning, wash the cup clean, rinse, and dry.

- **McCormick Cream of Tartar.** Sprinkle McCormick Cream of Tartar on a damp sponge and rub the inside of the stained china. Rinse and dry.

- **Morton Salt.** To clean tea stains from china, sprinkle Morton Salt on a damp sponge and rub gently.

- **20 Mule Team Borax.** To give china an impeccable shine after washing it with soapy water, fill a sink with water, add one-half cup 20 Mule Team Borax, carefully rinse your fine china in the solution, and then rinse again in clean water.

Cleanser Cans

- **Blue Bonnet Margarine.** To prevent cans of cleansers from leaving rust rings on the kitchen counter, use clean, used lids from empty canisters of Blue Bonnet Margarine as coasters for the cans.

- **Revlon Clear Nail Enamel.** For a more elaborate way to prevent the metal rims on the bottom of cleanser cans from leaving rust stains, paint a protective coat of Revlon Clear Nail Enamel over the metal rim.

- **Scotch Packaging Tape.** To prevent the metal rims on the bottom of cleanser cans from leaving rust stains on sink ledges and countertops, wrap Scotch Packaging Tape around the bottom of the can, covering the metal rim.

Coffee and Tea Cups

- **Arm & Hammer Baking Soda.** To clean unsightly coffee or tea stains from coffee mugs or tea cups, sprinkle Arm & Hammer Baking Soda on a damp sponge, rub off the stains, and rinse clean.

- **Colgate Regular Flavor Toothpaste.** To clean stains from coffee mugs or tea cups, rub some Colgate Regular Flavor Toothpaste into the stain, rinse, and dry.

- **Efferdent.** Fill a stained coffee mug or tea cup with water, drop in one Efferdent denture cleansing tablet, and let sit overnight. In the morning, rinse clean.

- **McCormick Cream of Tartar.** Sprinkle McCormick Cream of Tartar on a damp sponge and rub the inside of the stained cup clean. Rinse and dry.

- **Mr. Clean Magic Eraser.** Rub stubborn stains from inside a mug or teacup with a damp Mr. Clean Magic Eraser, wash with soapy water, and rinse clean.

Coffeepots

- **Arm & Hammer Baking Soda** and **ReaLemon.** To clean the brown residue from inside a glass coffeepot, pour one tablespoon Arm & Hammer Baking Soda and one tablespoon ReaLemon lemon juice into the pot, and scrub with a sponge.

- **Coca-Cola.** Fill a stained glass coffeepot with Coca-Cola, let sit overnight, and rinse clean. The phosphoric acid and ascorbic acid in the Real Thing cleans the coffee residue from the pot.

- **Efferdent.** To clean the gunk from the inside of a glass coffeepot without having to scrub, fill the coffeepot with water, drop in two Efferdent denture cleansing tablets, let sit for twenty minutes, and rinse clean.

- **Heinz White Vinegar.** Pour equal parts Heinz White Vinegar and water into the stained coffeepot, swirl around, and let sit for one hour, and swish again. The acetic acid in the vinegar dissolves coffee stains on glass. Rinse clean and dry with a soft, clean cloth.

- **Morton Salt.** To clean the brown gunk from the inside of a glass coffeepot, drop in a handful of ice cubes, sprinkle with Morton Salt, and swirl around the pot, allowing the salt-covered ice cubes to scrub the pot for you. Rinse clean.

- **Morton Salt** and **ReaLemon.** To clean burned coffee residue from the bottom of a glass coffeepot, fill the coffeepot with two tablespoons Morton Salt, one tablespoon ReaLemon lemon juice, and enough ice cubes to cover the bottom of the pot. Swirl the coffeepot in a circular motion, causing the abrasive salt and acidic lemon juice to scrub the bottom of the pot clean. Wash with soapy water and rinse clean.

- **Mr. Clean Magic Eraser.** To clean stubborn stains from inside a coffeepot, gently rub the stains with a damp Mr. Clean Magic Eraser, wash thoroughly with soapy water, and rinse clean.

Cooktops

- **Arm & Hammer Baking Soda.** To clean a glass or smooth ceramic cooktop, let the cooktop cool, sprinkle Arm & Hammer Baking Soda over the surface, and rub with a damp, soft cloth. Rinse well and dry.

- **Bon Ami.** Sprinkle Bon Ami on a clean, soft, damp cloth and gently wipe burned-on food from a glass or smooth ceramic cooktop (once it has cooled). Rinse clean and dry.

- **Canada Dry Club Soda.** After cleaning a glass or smooth ceramic cooktop with any of the tips listed here, rinse the cooktop with Canada Dry

Club Soda (carbonated or flat) and dry well. The sodium bicarbonate in the club soda gives the cooktop a sensational shine.

- **Colgate Regular Flavor Toothpaste.** To clean stubborn burned-on food from a glass or smooth ceramic cooktop (after allowing it to cool), rub a dollop of Colgate Regular Flavor Toothpaste into the stain. Let sit for five minutes, and then rub clean with a damp, soft cloth. Rinse well and dry.

- **Dawn Dishwashing Liquid.** For a simple way to clean a glass or smooth ceramic cooktop, let the cooktop cool and wipe it clean with a soft cloth dampened with soapy water made with a few drops of Dawn Dishwashing Liquid. Rinse well and dry.

- **MasterCard.** To clean baked-on food from a glass cooktop, let the cooktop cool to the touch, and then use the edge of an old MasterCard to gently scrape off the gunk without scratching the surface.

- **Reynolds Cut-Rite Wax Paper.** To clean a melted plastic bag from a glass cooktop, let the cooktop cool to the touch, cover the melted plastic with a sheet of Reynolds Cut-Rite Wax Paper, and press the waxed paper gently with a warm clothes iron. When the plastic softens from the heat of the iron, use a single-edge razor blade to carefully scrape off the plastic.

Coolers

- **Clorox Bleach.** To clean, disinfect, and deodorize a picnic cooler, mix three-quarters cup Clorox Bleach and one gallon of hot water, wash the cooler with the solution, rinse clean, and let air-dry with the cooler lid open.

- **McCormick Pure Vanilla Extract.** To freshen the air inside a cooler, wash out the cooler with Clorox Bleach (see above tip), put a few drops of McCormick Pure Vanilla Extract on a sponge, wipe down the inside of the cooler, and seal closed.

Copper

- **Colgate Toothpaste.** To remove tarnish from copper pots, rub Colgate Regular Flavor Toothpaste into the stain, let sit for ten minutes, rinse clean, and dry.

- **Gold Medal Flour, Morton Salt,** and **Heinz White Vinegar.** To clean stubborn stains from copper pots, mix equal parts Gold Medal Flour and Morton Salt and add enough Heinz White Vinegar to make a paste. Spread a thick coat of this paste on the copper and let dry, and then rinse and wipe clean.

- **Heinz Ketchup.** Cover the tarnish on the copper pot with Heinz Ketchup, let sit for fifteen minutes, and rinse clean under running water. The acids from the tomatoes and vinegar in the ketchup dissolve the tarnish.

BEFORE | AFTER

- **Heinz White Vinegar** and **Morton Salt.** To clean copper bottoms of pots, mix four parts Heinz White Vinegar and one part Morton Salt in a bowl, dampen a sponge with the solution, and gently rub the copper. Wash, rinse, and dry.

- **Lea & Perrins Worcestershire Sauce.** Rub Lea & Perrins Worcestershire Sauce into the tarnish on the bottom of a copper pot, let sit for fifteen minutes, and rinse clean. The various acids in the sauce clean tarnish from copper.

- **ReaLemon** and **Morton Salt.** Mix two tablespoons ReaLemon lemon juice and one tablespoon Morton Salt and rub the mixture into the tarnished copper. The chemical reaction cleans the copper instantly. Rinse clean and dry.

Countertops

- **Arm & Hammer Baking Soda.** To clean food stains from a countertop, make a paste from Arm & Hammer Baking Soda and water, cover the stains with the paste, let sit for fifteen minutes, and wipe off the stain with a damp cloth.

- **Bon Ami.** Sprinkle Bon Ami on the stained countertop; rub with a damp, soft cloth; and wipe dry.

- **Calgon Water Softener.** To clean a countertop, fill a sixteen-ounce trigger-spray bottle with water, add one tablespoon Calgon Water Softener, and shake well. Spray the surface with this cleanser and sponge clean.

- **Canada Dry Club Soda.** Pour Canada Dry Club Soda directly on the counter, wipe with a sponge, rinse with warm water, and dry with a soft cloth.

- **Colgate Regular Flavor Toothpaste.** To clean dried grease stains from a countertop, rub in a dab of Colgate Regular Flavor Tooth-paste, let sit for ten minutes, and wipe clean with a damp sponge.

- **Gillette Foamy.** Spray some Gillette Foamy shaving cream on a dirty countertop, let your kids or grandchildren have fun rubbing it around on the countertop (doing the work for you), and then rinse clean and wipe with a soft cloth. The condensed soap cleans grease and grime.

- **Heinz White Vinegar.** Fill a sixteen-ounce trigger-spray bottle with Heinz White Vinegar, spray the countertop (except marble), and wipe with a soft, clean cloth.

- **Huggies Baby Wipes.** For a simple way to clean a sticky mess from a countertop, use a Huggies Baby Wipe.

- **Listerine.** To disinfect a countertop, saturate a sponge with Listerine antiseptic mouthwash and wipe down the surface, let sit for ten minutes, rinse clean, and dry.

- **Morton Salt.** To clean stubborn stains from a countertop, mix one-half cup Morton Salt in a bowl with enough water to make a thick paste. Use a damp sponge to rub the abrasive cleanser on the countertop. Rinse clean and dry with a soft, clean cloth.

- **Purell Instant Hand Sanitizer.** To clean a countertop, squirt Purell Instant Hand Sanitizer on the stains and rub with a clean, soft cloth. The antibacterial gel cleans grease and grime while simultaneously disinfecting the surface.

- **ReaLemon** and **Arm & Hammer Baking Soda.** To clean food or ink stains from countertops, apply ReaLemon lemon juice to the entire countertop and let sit for thirty minutes. Sprinkle Arm & Hammer Baking Soda onto a soft, clean cloth and scrub the countertops. Rinse clean.

- **ReaLemon** and **McCormick Cream of Tartar.** To give ReaLemon lemon juice more oomph as a stain remover on countertops, make a paste from ReaLemon lemon juice and McCormick Cream of Tartar, rub the paste into the stain, let sit for ten minutes, rinse clean, and dry.

- **Shout.** To clean stubborn stains from a countertop, spray Shout stain remover on the affected area, let sit for thirty minutes, and then rub with an abrasive sponge. Wash thoroughly with soapy water, rinse, and dry.

- **Wonder Bread.** For a quick way to clean grease and grime from a countertop, wipe the surface with a slice of Wonder Bread. The doughy bread doubles as a kneaded eraser.

Crystal Glassware

- **Colgate Regular Flavor Toothpaste.** To clean superficial scratches from crystal glassware, rub the marks with a dab of Colgate Regular Flavor Toothpaste. Rinse clean and dry well.

- **Heinz White Vinegar.** After washing crystal in soapy water with your regular dishwashing liquid, fill half of the sink with warm water, add one cup Heinz White Vinegar, and rinse the crystal in the solution. The vinegar cuts away any remaining soap film.

- **Oral-B Toothbrush.** To clean decorative etched lines in crystal, rub the ornate lines gently with a soft, clean, used Oral-B Toothbrush.

- **Parsons' Ammonia.** To get crystal glassware shiny clean, place a towel on the bottom of your kitchen sink, fill the sink with warm water, and add one-quarter cup Parsons' Ammonia. Soak the crystal in the sink for thirty minutes, and then rinse clean with water.

- **Saran Wrap.** If you store your crystal glassware in a cabinet or on a shelf for long periods of time without using it, cover each piece with a sheet of Saran Wrap to protect it from collecting dust.

Crystal Vases

- **Alka-Seltzer.** To clean the caked-on residue from the bottom of a glass vase, fill the vase with water, drop in two Alka-Seltzer tablets, wait ten minutes, and then rinse clean. The citric acid and the effervescent action of the sodium bicarbonate scour the vase. Rinse clean and dry.

- **Cascade.** To clean caked-on crud from the inside of a vase, fill the vase with warm water, add one tablespoon Cascade Gel for every cup of water, and let sit overnight. In the morning, rinse clean. The phosphates in Cascade loosen the residue.

- **Clorox Bleach.** To deodorize and sanitize a dirty vase, fill the vase three-quarters full with water, add two tablespoons Clorox for every cup of water, let sit for one hour, and rinse clean.

- **Coca-Cola.** To clean mineral stains and any residual gunk from inside a vase, fill the vase with Coca-Cola, let sit overnight, and rinse clean. The phosphoric acid and ascorbic acid clean the buildup from the crystal.

- **Conair Hair Dryer.** To prevent water spots from forming on a recently cleaned crystal vase, aim the nozzle of a Conair Hair Dryer into the mouth of the vase and blow warm air inside until the remaining water droplets dry.

- **Efferdent.** To clean gunk and mineral film from inside a vase, fill with water, drop in two Efferdent denture cleansing tablets, let sit for several hours, and rinse thoroughly.

- **Heinz White Vinegar.** To clean mineral deposits from inside a crystal vase, fill the vase with Heinz White Vinegar, let sit for three hours, and rinse clean. The acetic acid in vinegar dissolves limescale.

- **Morton Salt.** Drop a handful of ice cubes into the vase, sprinkle with Morton Salt, and then swirl the vase for several minutes so the ice cubes and salt whirl around the bottom of the vase, scouring off the encrusted buildup.

- **Nestea Iced Tea Mix.** Fill a dirty vase with water, add three tablespoons Nestea Iced Tea Mix, cup your hand over the opening, shake well, and let sit overnight. In the morning, rinse clean. The tannic acid in the tea loosens the stains from inside the vase.

- **Parsons' Ammonia.** To clean the dirt and grime from inside a vase, pour two tablespoons Parsons' Ammonia inside the vase, fill the rest with water, and let sit overnight. In the morning, rinse thoroughly.

- **Uncle Ben's Converted Brand Rice** and **Heinz White Vinegar.** To clean the dirty residue from inside a vase, pour two tablespoons uncooked Uncle Ben's Converted Brand Rice into the vase and add one-half cup Heinz White Vinegar. Cup your hand over the opening, shake vigorously, and then rinse clean. The grains of rice work like miniature scrub brushes. Repeat if necessary.

Cutting Boards

- **Arm & Hammer Baking Soda.** For a simple way to clean and deodorize a plastic or wooden cutting board, sprinkle Arm & Hammer Baking Soda on a damp sponge, scour the cutting board, rinse clean, and dry.

- **Clorox Bleach.** To disinfect a cutting board, mix two teaspoons Clorox Bleach and two cups of water, saturate the cutting board with the solution, rinse well, and dry thoroughly. The bleach conveniently kills any disease-causing microorganisms, including *E. coli, Listeria, Salmonella,* and *Staphylococcus.*

- **Colman's Mustard Powder.** Wet a smelly cutting board with water, sprinkle with Colman's Mustard Powder, and scour with a damp sponge. Rinse clean and dry. The mustard miraculously deodorizes the cutting board.

- **Heinz White Vinegar.** To disinfect a plastic or wooden cutting board, apply Heinz White Vinegar to the surface, let sit for ten minutes, rinse clean, and dry well. Vinegar kills bacteria.

- **Listerine.** To sanitize a plastic or wooden cutting board, apply Listerine antiseptic mouthwash to the board, let sit for ten minutes, rinse clean, and dry thoroughly. Listerine disinfects and deodorizes.

- **Morton Salt.** To deodorize pungent odors from a cutting board, cover the cutting board with a liberal amount of Morton Salt and rub with a damp cloth. Wash in warm, soapy water, rinse clean, and dry. The abrasive salt scours the cutting board clean and absorbs odors.

- **ReaLemon.** To remove stains and odors from a cutting board, rub ReaLemon lemon juice into the cutting board until the stains vanish. The lemon juice also leaves the cutting board smelling lemon fresh.

Dishes

- **Arm & Hammer Baking Soda.** To clean stains from plastic dishes, sprinkle Arm & Hammer Baking Soda on a damp sponge and scrub the plasticware. Rinse clean and dry.

- **Heinz White Vinegar.** When washing dishes in the sink, fill the sink with water, add a few drops of your regular dishwashing liquid, and add one-half cup Heinz White Vinegar to help cut through grease and get those dishes sparkling clean.

- **Johnson's Baby Shampoo.** If you run out of dishwashing liquid, wash your dishes in the kitchen sink with Johnson's Baby Shampoo.

- **L'eggs Sheer Energy Panty Hose.** To prolong the usefulness of a sponge, use a pair of scissors to snip off the foot from a pair of L'eggs Sheer Energy Panty Hose, insert a brand new sponge into the foot, and tie a knot in the open end. The nylon sachet keeps the sponge together, even if it starts crumbling apart. You can also cut a section from a leg of the panty hose, tie one end closed, insert the sponge, and then tie the open end shut.

- **MasterCard.** A clean, old MasterCard makes an excellent food scraper for cleaning the dishes.

- **Tide.** To remove stubborn baked-on food from dishes, fill the sink with warm water, add one tablespoon liquid Tide, and soak your dishes in the solution for thirty minutes. Scrub with an abrasive sponge, rinse well, and dry thoroughly.

- **20 Mule Team Borax.** Add one teaspoon 20 Mule Team Borax to the rinse water to prevent spotting on dishes and glassware when washing dishes by hand.

Drain Boards

- **Heinz White Vinegar.** To clean mineral stains from a rubber drain board, lay the drain board in the bottom of the sink and fill the sink with enough Heinz White Vinegar to cover the drain board. Let sit overnight. In the morning, rub with a sponge and rinse clean with water. The acetic acid in vinegar dissolves mineral deposits.

- **Pledge.** To prevent mineral stains on a drain board, give the rubber drain board a light coat of Pledge furniture polish.

Drains

- **Arm & Hammer Baking Soda** and **Heinz White Vinegar.** To unclog a drain, pour one cup Arm & Hammer Baking Soda down the drain. Heat one cup Heinz White Vinegar in the microwave oven for two minutes and pour it down the drain, causing a reaction with the baking soda. Let sit for ten minutes. The bubbling action can unclog your drain by breaking down grease and allowing the clog to wash down the pipe. Then pour a kettle of boiling water down the drain to flush it. Do not put baking soda or vinegar down the drain if you have poured any commercial drain cleaner down the drain or into any standing water.

- **Cascade.** After draining all the water from the clogged sink, pour one-half cup Cascade Gel dishwasher detergent into the drain, and then carefully and slowly pour a kettle of boiling water down the drain. The boiling hot water softens the clog while the phosphates in the Cascade Gel eat away the debris lodged in the drain.

- **Clorox Bleach.** Unless you have a septic tank, pour two cups Clorox Bleach down the drain of the kitchen sink once a month and let sit overnight.

The bleach sitting in the trap saturates and softens any coagulated grease or debris in the trap. The next morning, run the water for three minutes to flush the debris through the pipes. (To avoid permanent bleach stains on a stainless-steel sink, do not let bleach drip or puddle on the stainless steel.)

- **Coca-Cola.** Once a week, pour a can of Coca-Cola down the kitchen drain. Let sit overnight to allow the carbonation and phosphoric acid to dissolve grease buildup and prevent clogs.

- **Conair Hair Dryer.** The blockage causing the clogged drain tends to be located in the bottom of the trap under the sink. Aim the nozzle of a Conair Hair Dryer set on high at the trap, allowing the heat from the blow dryer to warm the pipe and melt the coagulated grease. Then pour a kettle of boiling water down the drain to flush the melted grease through the pipe.

- **Dawn Dishwashing Liquid.** To clear a clogged drain in the kitchen sink, dissolve four tablespoons Dawn Dishwashing Liquid in one quart of boiling water, carefully pour the hot soapy mixture down the drain, and let sit overnight. Dawn cuts through grease and can dissolve most kitchen sink clogs.

- **Efferdent.** Dissolve four Efferdent denture cleansing tablets in two cups of water, pour the blue solution into the clogged drain, and let sit overnight. The denture cleansing tablets loosen the sludge in the trap.

- **Jell-O** and **Heinz White Vinegar.** The acetic acid in vinegar can dissolve a clogged drain; however, if you pour vinegar down a clogged drain, the vinegar will seep down the pipe before it has enough time to eat away the wad of grease and debris. To get the vinegar to saturate the clog long enough to do its magic, dissolve one three-ounce package of Jell-O in one cup of boiling water, add one cup Heinz White Vinegar, and let gel in the refrigerator. Slowly pour the vinegar Jell-O down the drain and let sit overnight. The Jell-O gets stuck behind the clog, giving the acetic acid plenty of time to dissolve the clog. In the morning, flush the drain with water to wash away the Jell-O.

- **Maxwell House Coffee.** To prevent a drain from clogging, pour a tablespoon of used Maxwell House Coffee grounds down the drain and run the hot water for one minute.

- **Morton Salt.** To deodorize the drain in your kitchen sink, pour one-quarter cup Morton Salt down the drain and let sit overnight.

- **Morton Salt.** Prevent a clogged drain by dissolving one-half cup Morton Salt in one quart of hot water and pouring the salty water down the drain once every two weeks.

Eggs

- **Morton Salt.** If you accidentally drop an egg on the kitchen floor, cover the spill with a mountain of Morton Salt. Let sit for five minutes so the salt can absorb the egg, and then pick up the mess with a sheet of paper towel.

Enamel Pots and Pans

- **Arm & Hammer Baking Soda.** To clean baked-on food from the bottom of an enamel pot, fill the pot with two cups of water, add three tablespoons Arm & Hammer Baking Soda, boil for ten minutes, and let cool. Scrub with an abrasive sponge, rinse, and dry.

- **Clorox Bleach.** To clean brown stains from an enamel pot, fill the pot with two cups of water, add two tablespoons Clorox Bleach, and boil until the stain vanishes.

- **Morton Salt.** To clean burned-on food from the bottom of an enamel pot, fill the bottom of the pot with two inches of water, add five tablespoons Morton Salt, and let sit overnight. In the morning, boil the solution. Wash, rinse, and dry.

Flatware

- **Bon Ami.** To clean stubborn stains from flatware, sprinkle Bon Ami on a damp sponge or cloth, rub the affected area, rinse clean, and dry.

- **Canada Dry Club Soda.** To give dull stainless-steel flatware a lustrous shine, place the flatware in a pan and pour in enough Canada Dry Club Soda to cover the flatware. Let sit until the carbonation bubbles stop. Rinse clean and dry thoroughly.

- **Colgate Regular Flavor Toothpaste.** To clean stubborn stains from stainless-steel flatware, massage a dab of Colgate Regular Flavor Toothpaste into the stain and buff with a soft, clean cloth. Rinse clean and dry.

- **Morton Salt** and **ReaLemon.** To clean unsightly stains from stainless-steel flatware, mix together enough Morton Salt and ReaLemon lemon juice to make a gritty paste. Using a soft, clean cloth, rub the paste on the cutlery, rinse clean with warm water, and buff dry with another soft, clean cloth.

- **20 Mule Team Borax.** To clean and disinfect stainless-steel flatware, make a paste from 20 Mule Team Borax and water; use a soft, clean cloth to rub the paste on stainless-steel flatware; rinse clean with warm water; and buff dry with another soft, clean cloth.

Floors

- **Arm & Hammer Baking Soda.** To clean scuffmarks from floors, sprinkle Arm & Hammer Baking Soda on a damp sponge and gently rub the spot.

- **Canada Dry Club Soda.** To get tile or vinyl floors sparkling clean, mop the floor with Canada Dry Club Soda and buff dry with a soft, clean cloth.

- **ChapStick.** To clean a scuffmark from the floor, rub the mark with Chap-Stick lip balm and rub with a soft, clean cloth.

- **Colgate Regular Flavor Toothpaste.** To erase scuffmarks from linoleum, tile, or vinyl floors, squeeze a dab of Colgate Regular Flavor Toothpaste on a damp, clean, soft cloth, and rub. Rinse with a wet cloth.

- **Downy Fabric Softener.** To rejuvenate a dull waxed floor, mix one-half cup Downy Fabric Softener and one gallon of hot water in a bucket and mop the floor with the solution.

- **Heinz White Vinegar.** To give vinyl floors a terrific shine, mop with one-half cup Heinz White Vinegar mixed in one gallon of warm water.

- **Murphy Oil Soap** and **Heinz White Vinegar.** To mop a linoleum, tile, or vinyl floor, mix one ounce Murphy Oil Soap and one-half cup Heinz White Vinegar in a bucket, and then add two gallons of warm water. Mix well. Wash the floor with a mop dampened in a soapy solution.

- **Parsons' Ammonia** and **20 Mule Team Borax.** To mop a tile floor clean, mix two tablespoons Parsons' Ammonia, one tablespoon 20 Mule Team Borax, and one gallon of warm water in a bucket.

- **ReaLemon.** To give a freshly washed linoleum floor a brilliant shine and a fresh lemon scent, mix three tablespoons ReaLemon lemon juice and one quart of water. Mop the floor with the lemony rinse.

- **Vaseline Petroleum Jelly.** To clean scuffmarks from the floor, cover the blemish with a dab of Vaseline Petroleum Jelly, and then rub with a soft, clean cloth. Wash the spot with soapy water, rinse, and dry.

- **Wilson Tennis Balls.** To clean scuffmarks from floors, simply rub the scuffmark with a Wilson Tennis Ball. The tennis ball works like an eraser. To avoid having to get down on your hands and knees, use a knife to carefully cut an X in the tennis ball, unscrew the broomstick from a broom, and insert the end of the broomstick into the X in the tennis ball. Use the tennis ball on the end of the broomstick like a giant pencil eraser on the scuffmarks.

Garbage Pails

- **Clorox Bleach.** To disinfect, deodorize, and clean a garbage pail, wash the inside of the pail with a solution made from three-quarters cup Clorox Bleach to one gallon of water. Let sit for five minutes, and then rinse clean.

- **Heinz White Vinegar** and **Dawn Dishwashing Liquid.** To clean and deodorize a garbage pail, mix one cup Heinz White Vinegar, one tablespoon Dawn Dishwashing Liquid, and two cups of hot water. Use the solution to scrub the inside of the pail. Rinse clean and dry thoroughly.

- **Listerine.** To disinfect the bottom of a kitchen garbage pail, mix one cup Listerine antiseptic mouthwash and one gallon of water. Wash the inside of the pail with the astringent solution. Let sit for five minutes, and then rinse clean.

- **20 Mule Team Borax.** To deodorize and clean a kitchen garbage pail, mix one tablespoon 20 Mule Team Borax and one gallon of warm water. Scrub the inside of the pail with the solution. Rinse clean and dry.

Glassware

- **Colgate Regular Flavor Toothpaste.** To remove scratch marks from glassware, polish the marks with a dab of Colgate Regular Flavor Toothpaste.

- **Efferdent.** To clean mineral deposits from inside glassware, fill the glass with water, drop in one Efferdent denture cleansing tablet, and let sit overnight. In the morning, rinse clean.

- **Heinz Vinegar.** To clean white film from glassware and leave the glassware sparkling, fill the sink with one part Heinz White Vinegar and three parts water and soak the glasses in the solution. Rinse clean. Or fill a glass bowl with two cups Heinz White Vinegar, set the bowl upright in the bottom rack of your dishwasher, and run the glasses through a two-cycle wash.

Graters

- **Oral-B Toothbrush.** To clean a grater, scrub it with a clean, used Oral-B Toothbrush.

Hands

- **Colgate Regular Flavor Toothpaste.** To clean the smell of fish, garlic, or onions from your hands, squeeze a dollop of Colgate Regular Flavor Toothpaste into the palm of your hand, rub your hands together under running water, and rinse clean.

- **Morton Salt** and **Heinz White Vinegar.** To clean the smell of fish, garlic, or onions from your hands, wet your hands with Heinz White Vinegar, rub a teaspoon Morton Salt between them, and then wash with soap and water.

- **ReaLemon.** Clean berry and fruit stains from hands by rubbing a teaspoon ReaLemon lemon juice into the stained skin. Wash with soapy water and rinse clean.

Highchairs

- **Arm & Hammer Baking Soda.** To clean food splatters from a highchair tray and seat, sprinkle some Arm & Hammer Baking Soda on a damp sponge and rub the affected surface. Rinse clean and dry.
- **Huggies Wipes.** Gentle enough for a baby's bottom, Huggies Wipes do a sensational job cleaning the mess from a highchair tray and seat.
- **Listerine.** To disinfect a highchair tray and seat, wipe it down with Listerine antiseptic mouthwash, rinse clean, and dry.

Kitchen Magnets

- **L'eggs Sheer Energy Panty Hose.** To wash kitchen magnets in the dishwasher, cut off one foot from a pair of clean, used L'eggs Sheer Energy Panty Hose, place the kitchen magnets in the foot, knot the open end, and run the magnet-filled sachet through the dishwasher (in the silverware bin or tied to one of the racks).

Lunch Boxes

- **Wonder Bread** and **Heinz White Vinegar.** To deodorize a stinky metal or plastic lunchbox, place a slice of Wonder Bread in the lunch box, dampen the bread with Heinz White Vinegar, seal the lunchbox shut, and let sit overnight. In the morning, discard the soggy bread, wash the lunchbox with soapy water, rinse clean, and dry.

Mops

- **Bounce.** For an inexpensive substitute for Swiffer sheets, attach a clean, used sheet of Bounce to the Swiffer mop. The antistatic elements in the Bounce sheet will attract dust and dirt just as effectively.

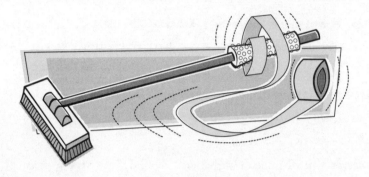

- **Bubble Wrap** and **Scotch Packaging Tape.** If you have difficulty gripping a mop, cut a strip of Bubble Wrap, wrap it around the handle several times to make it thicker, and secure in place with a piece of Scotch Packaging Tape.

- **Downy Fabric Softener.** To soften a cotton deck mop, mix one capful of Downy Fabric Softener in a bucket of water. Soak the mop in the solution for ten minutes, rinse clean, and wring dry.

- **Playtex Living Gloves.** To prevent the end of a mop handle from scratching or marking walls, cut off one of the fingers from a clean, used pair of Playtex Living Gloves and slip the rubber finger over the end of the handle as a protective sheath.

- **Ziploc Storage Bags.** To shake the dirt out of a dry mop indoors without making a big cloud of dust, place a large Ziploc Freezer Bag over the mop head, seal the bag shut up to the mop stick, and shake vigorously. The dirt and dust will shake off into the bag, which you can then discard.

Nonstick Cookware

- **Ajax Oxygen Bleach Cleanser.** To clean stubborn stains or burned-on food from nonstick cookware, fill the cookware with a solution made from three tablespoons Ajax Oxygen Bleach Cleanser for every cup of water and simmer for twenty minutes. Wash with soapy water, rinse clean, and dry.

- **Arm & Hammer Baking Soda** and **ReaLemon.** To clean stubborn stains from nonstick cookware, fill the pot or pan with water and stir in two to three tablespoons Arm & Hammer Baking Soda and one tablespoon ReaLemon lemon juice. Simmer over low heat until the stains disappear.

- **Clorox Bleach** and **Clabber Girl Baking Powder.** To clean stains from a nonstick pot or pan, mix one-half cup Clorox Bleach, two tablespoons Clabber Girl Baking Powder, and one cup of water in the affected pot or pan. Boil for ten minutes without letting the solution bubble over the top. Wash with soapy water, rinse well, and dry.

- **Heinz White Vinegar.** To clean burned-on food from the nonstick surface of cookware, mix three parts water and one part Heinz White Vinegar in the pan, bring to a boil over medium heat for five to ten minutes, remove from the heat, and let cool. Wash the pan with warm, soapy water and a soft nylon brush, rinse clean, and dry.

- **ReaLemon.** To clean lingering odors—like garlic or onions—from a nonstick pan, mix one tablespoon ReaLemon lemon juice into a full pan of water. Let sit for thirty minutes, wash with soapy water, rinse, and dry.

Odors

- **Heinz White Vinegar.** To eliminate the smell of fish, broccoli, cabbage, and other pungent foods from the kitchen, fill a drinking glass halfway with Heinz White Vinegar and set it on the kitchen counter. In five minutes, the vinegar neutralizes the feisty odors.

- **Maxwell House Coffee.** To deodorize cooking smells, fill a bowl with unused Maxwell House Coffee and place it on the counter. The coffee grounds absorb foul odors.

- **McCormick Ground Cinnamon.** To cover up the smell of burned food from the kitchen, sprinkle one teaspoon McCormick Ground Cinnamon in a saucepan and warm it up on the stove.

- **Nestea Iced Tea Mix** and **McCormick Ground Cinnamon.** In a microwave-safe bowl, dissolve one teaspoon Nestea Iced Tea Mix in one cup of water, add two teaspoons McCormick Ground Cinnamon, and heat in the microwave for two minutes. Carefully place the bowl on a countertop and let the enchanting fragrance waft through the kitchen.

- **Pine-Sol.** If your kitchen reeks from burned foods or strong-smelling foods (like fish, garlic, or onions), the steamy food particles have likely adhered to the walls. To eliminate the cooking odors, clean the walls, ceiling, and floor with one-quarter cup Pine-Sol diluted in one gallon of warm water.

- **ReaLemon.** Boil one tablespoon ReaLemon lemon juice in a saucepan for three minutes to mask the smell of burned foods from the kitchen.

- **ReaLemon** and **McCormick Stick Cinnamon.** Mix two tablespoons ReaLemon lemon juice and one cup of water in a small saucepan and add two or three sticks McCormick Stick Cinnamon. Simmer over a low heat for fifteen minutes to fill your kitchen with a pleasant, homey scent.

Oil

- **Gold Medal Flour** and **Bounty Paper Towels.** To clean cooking oil spills from the floor, pour Gold Medal Flour on the spill, let sit a few minutes to give the flour time to absorb the oil, and then wipe up with a few sheets of Bounty Paper Towels.

Pewter

- **Arm & Hammer Baking Soda** and **Star Olive Oil.** To clean liquid stains from a pewter mug, sprinkle Arm & Hammer Baking Soda on the stain; dampen a clean, soft cloth with Star Olive Oil; and rub until the stain disappears. Wash with soapy water, rinse clean, and dry.

- **Johnson's Baby Oil.** To remove tarnish from pewter, dip an extra fine (0000) steel wool pad (available at the hardware store) in Johnson's Baby Oil and rub. Wash with soapy water, rinse clean, and buff dry with a soft, clean cloth.

Plastic Containers

- **Arm & Hammer Baking Soda.** To clean tomato sauce stains from inside plastic Rubbermaid or Tupperware containers, sprinkle Arm & Hammer Baking Soda on a damp sponge and scrub the stains. Rinse clean and dry.

- **Arm & Hammer Baking Soda.** To deodorize a plastic container, make a paste from Arm & Hammer Baking Soda and water and rub the paste on the inside of the container. Or dissolve one-half cup Arm & Hammer Baking Soda in a sink full of water and soak the plastic containers in the solution. Let sit overnight, rinse clean, and dry.

- **Clorox.** To clean tomato sauce stains from plastic containers, fill the stained plastic with warm water and add one tablespoon Clorox for every cup of water. Let sit for thirty minutes, rinse clean, and dry.

- **Colman's Mustard Powder.** To deodorize a plastic Rubbermaid or Tupperware container, fill the container with one quart of warm water, dissolve one-quarter teaspoon Colman's Mustard Powder, and let sit for one hour. Wash with soapy water, rinse clean, and dry.

- **Efferdent.** To clean tomato sauce stains from the insides of Tupperware and Rubbermaid containers, fill the plastic containers with hot water, drop in two Efferdent denture cleansing tablets, and let sit overnight. In the morning, wash with soapy water, rinse clean, and dry.

- **Jif Peanut Butter.** To remove any adhesive residue from a label or price sticker from plastic containers, rub a dab of Jif Peanut Butter into the adhesive and let sit five minutes. The oils in the peanut butter soften and loosen the adhesive. Wipe clean.

- **ReaLemon.** To bleach stains from plastic containers, apply ReaLemon lemon juice to the stain and place the open container in the sun for a few hours. Rinse clean and dry.

- **USA Today.** To deodorize a plastic food container, stuff the container with crumpled pages from *USA Today*, replace the lid securely, and let sit overnight or for several days. Newsprint absorbs odors. When finished, rinse the container with soapy water, rinse clean, and dry.

Pot Scrubber

- **L'eggs Sheer Energy Panty Hose.** To make a scratchless pot scrubber, use a pair of scissors to clip off the two legs from a clean, used pair of L'eggs Sheer Energy Panty Hose, and then snip off the foot from one of those legs. Tie knots along each leg as close together as possible—until each nylon leg is a mass of knots. Stuff the two legs into the empty foot and tie a knot in the open end, completing your new pot scrubber.

- **Reynolds Wrap.** To improvise a great pot scrubber, crumple a sheet of Reynolds Wrap aluminum foil into a ball and use it to clean baked-on food from pots or pans. The soft foil works like a steel wool pad, without scratching the cookware.

Pots and Pans

- **Alka-Seltzer.** To clean baked-on food from pots and pans, fill the cookware with water, drop in six Alka-Seltzer tablets, and let soak for one hour. Scrub with soapy water, rinse clean, and dry.

- **Arm & Hammer Baking Soda.** To clean baked-on food or scorch marks from pots and pans, fill the cookware with enough water to cover the affected area, mix in four tablespoons Arm & Hammer Baking Soda, and bring to a boil for five minutes. Let cool and then scrub with a sponge, rinse, and dry.

- **Bon Ami.** Fill dirty pots and pans with warm water, let sit for thirty minutes, and then wipe with a sponge sprinkled with Bon Ami to remove any caked-on food. Rinse clean and dry.

- **Bounce.** Fill the pot or pan with water, float a sheet of Bounce on the water, and let sit overnight. In the morning, use the sheet of Bounce to wipe the burned-on food out of the pot or pan.

- **Calgon Water Softener.** Fill the dirty pots or pans with water, add one table-spoon Calgon Water Softener, and let sit overnight. In the morning, rinse clean. The zeolites in Calgon remove the ions that cause hardness in the water, loosening the baked-on food.

- **Cascade.** To remove stubborn baked-on food from a pot or pan, pour two tablespoons Cascade Gel in the cookware, fill with hot water, and let sit overnight. In the morning, rinse clean and dry. The phosphates in Cascade loosen all the baked-on food.

- **Coca-Cola.** To clean a moderately scorched pot, boil one cup Coca-Cola in the pot, let cool, and then scrub the pot clean. The phosphoric acid and ascorbic acid in the Coke helps clean the pot.

- **Dawn Dishwashing Liquid.** Fill a dirty pot or pan with water, add one or two tablespoons Dawn Dishwashing Liquid, and bring the pot of soapy water to a boil on the stove. Turn off the heat, let the water cool to room temperature, and rinse clean. Baked-on food will come right out.

- **Downy Fabric Softener.** Fill dirty pots or pans with water, add a capful of Downy Fabric Softener, mix well, and let sit overnight. In the morning, wash with soapy water, rinse clean, and dry. The surfactants in Downy loosen the baked-on food from the sides of the cookware.

- **Easy-Off Oven Cleaner.** To clean burn marks or baked-on grease from a pot or pan (except for aluminum or nonstick cookware), place the cookware outside and, wearing rubber gloves and protective eyewear, spray it with Easy-Off Oven Cleaner. Let it sit for one hour, rinse clean with a garden hose, and then bring the pot or pan back inside to wash thoroughly.

- **Efferdent.** To clean scorch marks from inside a pot or pan, fill the cookware with water, drop in two or three Efferdent denture cleansing tablets, and let sit overnight. In the morning, wash with soapy water, rinse, and dry.

- **Heinz White Vinegar.** To clean baked-on food from pots or pans, fill the cookware with equal parts Heinz White Vinegar and water, let it sit for thirty minutes, and then scrub with a sponge in hot, soapy water. Rinse clean and dry.

- **Maxwell House Coffee.** Use a handful of used Maxwell House Coffee grounds as an abrasive cleanser to scrub baked-on food from pots and pans.

- **Morton Salt** and **Bounty Paper Towels.** Immediately after removing cooked meat from a broiling pan or roaster, sprinkle the pan with Morton Salt and cover with wet Bounty Paper Towels. The salt absorbs the juices and prevents them from adhering to the pan, making the cookware easier to clean later.

- **Mr. Clean Magic Eraser.** Gently rub baked-on food from a pot or pan with a damp Mr. Clean Magic Eraser. Wash with soapy water, rinse clean, and dry. Do not use a Mr. Clean Magic Eraser on nonstick cookware.

- **Pam Cooking Spray.** To clean baked-on food from a cookie pan, spray Pam Cooking Spray on the pan and wipe clean. Then wash thoroughly with soap and water.

- **Parsons' Ammonia** and **Glad Trash Bags.** To remove black burn marks from a pot or pan, place the cookware inside a Glad Trash Bag, place several Bounty Paper Towels in the pan, and saturate the paper toweling with one cup Parsons' Ammonia—being careful not to breathe the ammonia. Close the bag securely with a twist tie and let sit overnight outside or in a well-ventilated garage. The ammonia fumes loosen the baked-on food and grease from the pot or pan. The next morning, open the bag outdoors (again being careful to avoid breathing the fumes), and remove the pot or pan, leaving the paper towels in the bag. Discard the bag. Rinse the pot or pan with a garden hose, and then bring it back inside the house to wash thoroughly with soapy water, rinse clean, and dry.

- **ReaLemon.** To remove white film (left by mineral deposits) from cookware, rub the white spots with a sponge or brush damped with ReaLemon lemon juice. The citric acid washes off the minerals. Wash, rinse, and towel dry.

- **Star Olive Oil.** To eliminate rainbows on stainless-steel pots, rub them with a drop of Star Olive Oil.

- **20 Mule Team Borax.** To clean baked-on food from a pot or pan, sprinkle 20 Mule Team Borax on the cookware and scrub with a damp sponge. Rinse clean and dry.

Scouring Powder

- **Arm & Hammer Baking Soda, 20 Mule Team Borax, and Morton Salt.** To make homemade scouring powder, mix one cup Arm & Hammer Baking Soda, one cup 20 Mule Team Borax, and one cup Morton Salt, and store the mixture in an airtight Rubbermaid container or a large salt shaker, labeled appropriately. Keep out of reach of children and pets.

Silverware

- **Arm & Hammer Baking Soda and Reynolds Wrap.** To remove tarnish from silver quickly and effortlessly, line a metal cake pan with Reynolds Wrap. In a bowl, dissolve four tablespoons Arm & Hammer Baking Soda in two quarts of water. Pour just enough of the solution into the pan to cover the silverware, and heat above 150 degrees Fahrenheit—but do not let the water boil. Place the tarnished silverware in the pan so it touches the aluminum foil. The hydrogen produced from heating the baking soda combines with the sulfur in the tarnish, removing the stains. (Note that this technique removes the patina from silverware.)

- **Colgate Regular Flavor Toothpaste.** To clean tarnish from silverware, squeeze a dollop of Colgate Regular Flavor Toothpaste on a soft, clean cloth and rub the utensils. The mild abrasives in the toothpaste clean the silver. Rinse clean and dry thoroughly.

- **Kingsford's Corn Starch and L'eggs Sheer Energy Panty Hose.** To polish silverware, make a paste with Kingsford's Corn Starch and water. Apply with a damp cloth, let dry, and then rub off with a balled-up pair of used, clean L'eggs Sheer Energy Panty Hose.

- **McCormick Cream of Tartar.** Make a paste with McCormick Cream of Tartar and water, apply to the tarnished silverware with a damp cloth, and let dry. Rub off with a soft, clean cloth, rinse clean, and dry thoroughly.

- **Nestlé Carnation Nonfat Dry Milk** and **Heinz White Vinegar.** To clean tarnish from silverware, mix one-half cup Nestlé Carnation Nonfat Dry Milk, two cups Heinz White Vinegar, and two cups of water. Place the silverware in a pan, cover the cutlery with the milky solution, and let sit overnight. In the morning, wash the silverware with soapy water, rinse clean, and polish dry.

- **Purell Instant Hand Sanitizer.** To remove tarnish from silver, squirt a few drops of Purell Instant Hand Sanitizer on a clean cloth and rub the silver.

- **ReaLemon** and **Morton Salt.** Mix one tablespoon ReaLemon lemon juice and two tablespoons Morton Salt into a gritty paste. Gently rub the paste on the tarnished silver, wipe clean with a dry cloth, and rinse clean. Repeat if necessary. Dry thoroughly.

- **Windex.** To clean minor tarnish from silver, spray some Windex on the silver and wipe clean with a soft cloth. Wash thoroughly with soapy water, rinse, and dry.

Sink Mats

- **Clorox Bleach.** To clean and sanitize a rubber sink mat, fill the sink with water, add one-quarter cup Clorox Bleach, and let the mat soak in the solution for five to ten minutes. Rinse clean.

Sinks

- **Alberto VO5 Conditioning Hairdressing.** To shine a stainless-steel sink, squeeze a dab of Alberto VO5 Conditioning Hairdressing on a soft cloth and rub.

- **Arm & Hammer Baking Soda.** To clean a porcelain or stainless-steel sink, sprinkle Arm & Hammer Baking Soda on a damp sponge, scrub, and rinse clean. Rinse well and dry with a clean, soft cloth.

- **Bon Ami.** To clean a porcelain or stainless-steel sink, sprinkle Bon Ami in the sink, rub with a wet sponge, and rinse.

- **Canada Dry Club Soda.** To clean a porcelain or stainless-steel sink, pour Canada Dry Club Soda over the sink, wipe clean, and dry.

- **Cascade.** To clean stains from a porcelain or stainless-steel sink, fill the sink with hot water, add one tablespoon Cascade Gel, and let sit for about ten minutes. Use an abrasive sponge to scrub the stains, and then rinse clean with water. Repeat if necessary.

- **Clorox Bleach.** To whiten a porcelain sink, fill the sink with a solution of three-quarters cup Clorox Bleach per gallon of water. Let sit for fifteen minutes, and then rinse clean.

- **Coca-Cola.** To clean rust stains from a porcelain sink, cover the stains with Coca-Cola, let sit for one hour, and rinse clean. The phosphoric acid in the Coke removes the rust.

- **Colgate Regular Flavor Toothpaste.** To clean stubborn stains from a porcelain or stainless-steel sink, squeeze a dollop of Colgate Regular Flavor Toothpaste on a damp sponge and scrub. Rinse clean and dry.

- **Easy-Off Oven Cleaner.** To clean persistent stains from a stainless-steel sink, put on protective gloves and eyewear, make sure the room is well ventilated, and spray Easy-Off Oven Cleaner on the affected areas. Let sit for ten minutes, rinse well, and dry.

- **Efferdent.** To clean stains from a porcelain or stainless-steel sink, fill the sink with water, drop in four Efferdent denture cleansing tablets, and let sit for one hour. Rinse clean and dry.

- **Gold Medal Flour.** To polish a stainless-steel sink, dry the sink with a soft, clean cloth; sprinkle one tablespoon Gold Medal Flour in the sink; and rub with a dry, soft, clean cloth. Rinse clean and dry well.

- **Heinz White Vinegar.** To remove rust marks or water spots from a stainless-steel sink, wipe down the sink with a soft, clean cloth saturated with Heinz White Vinegar. Rinse clean with water and dry with a soft, clean cloth.

- **Johnson's Baby Oil.** To give a stainless-steel sink a beautiful shine, rub a few drops of Johnson's Baby Oil into the sink and buff with a soft, clean cloth.

- **Listerine.** To clean hard water stains from a sink, sponge down the sink with Listerine antiseptic mouthwash. The alcohol in the mouthwash dissolves the mineral deposits, and the astringent disinfects the sink.

- **McCormick Cream of Tartar** and **Hydrogen Peroxide.** To clean stains from a porcelain or stainless-steel sink, make a paste from McCormick Cream of Tartar and Hydrogen Peroxide; use a clean, dry washcloth to rub the paste into the sink; and let dry. Wipe clean with a wet sponge and rinse thoroughly.

- **Morton Salt.** To clean grease and soap scum from a porcelain or stainless-steel sink, sprinkle Morton Salt in the sink and scrub with a damp sponge. The abrasive salt scours off the grimy film.

- **Pam Cooking Spray.** To give a stainless-steel sink a lustrous shine, give the sink a very light coat of Pam Original Cooking Spray and buff with a soft, clean cloth.

- **ReaLemon** and **Morton Salt.** To clean a porcelain or stainless-steel sink, make a paste from ReaLemon lemon juice and Morton Salt in a bowl, dip a sponge in the paste, and scrub the sink. Rinse clean and dry thoroughly.

- **Star Olive Oil.** To polish a stainless-steel sink, put a few drops Star Olive Oil on a soft, clean cloth and buff to a glimmering shine.

- **20 Mule Team Borax** and **ReaLemon.** To clean rust stains or yellow stains from a porcelain or stainless-steel sink, scrub with a paste made from 20 Mule Team Borax and ReaLemon lemon juice.

- **Wesson Oil.** Rubbing a stainless-steel sink with a few drops Wesson Oil on a soft, clean cloth produces a beautiful shine.

Spilled Milk

- **20 Mule Team Borax.** To deodorize the sour smell of spilled milk, blot up the milk, dampen the spot with water, rub in 20 Mule Team Borax, and let dry. Vacuum or brush clean.

Sponges

- **Heinz White Vinegar** and **Morton Salt.** To disinfect a sponge, mix one-half cup Heinz White Vinegar, three tablespoons Morton Salt, and one cup of hot water in a bowl. Soak the sponge overnight in the solution and in the morning, rinse it clean.

- **Listerine.** To kill all the germs breeding in your kitchen sponge, fill a bowl with Listerine antiseptic mouthwash, soak the sponge in the medicine-y mouthwash for one hour, and rinse clean.

Food for Thought
SOAK IT UP

- You can also disinfect a sponge by heating it in the microwave oven for one minute or running it through the dishwasher with your regular load of dishes.

Sports Bottles

- **Clorox Bleach.** To deodorize and sanitize a plastic sports bottle, wash it with a solution made from three-quarters cup Clorox Bleach and one gallon of water.

- **Efferdent.** To clean the inside of a plastic sports bottle, fill the bottle with water, drop in two Efferdent denture cleansing tablets, wait ten minutes, and then rinse clean. The nontoxic denture cleanser leaves the bottle sparkling clean.

- **French's Mustard.** To deodorize the inside of a plastic sports bottle, fill the bottle with water, add two teaspoons French's Mustard, shake vigorously, and rinse well.

- **Heinz White Vinegar.** To clean and deodorize the inside of a plastic sports bottle, fill the bottle with equal parts Heinz White Vinegar and water, shake well, let sit thirty minutes, and rinse clean.

- **Nestea Iced Tea Mix.** To clean the inside of an empty sports bottle, fill the bottle with water, add three tablespoons Nestea Iced Tea Mix, shake well, and let sit overnight. In the morning, wash with soapy water and rinse clean. The tannic acid in the tea dissolves the residue in the bottle.

- **Uncle Ben's Converted Brand Rice** and **Heinz White Vinegar.** To clean the inside of a plastic sports bottle, pour two tablespoons uncooked Uncle Ben's Converted Brand Rice into the bottle and add one-half cup Heinz White Vinegar. Shake vigorously, and then rinse clean. Repeat if necessary.

Stainless-Steel Appliances

- **Canada Dry Club Soda.** To clean fingerprints and streaks from the outside of a stainless-steel refrigerator, dishwasher, or oven, fill a sixteen-ounce trigger-spray bottle with Canada Dry Club Soda, spray the outside of the appliance, and wipe clean with a soft cloth.

- **Johnson's Baby Oil.** To give the outside of a stainless-steel refrigerator, dishwasher, or oven an impeccable shine, put a drop of Johnson's Baby Oil on a soft, clean cloth, and then buff.

- **Murphy Oil Soap.** To clean the exterior of a large, stainless-steel appliance, pour a few drops of Murphy Oil Soap on a wet, soft, clean cloth and rub. Rinse clean with a damp cloth and buff dry with another soft, clean cloth.

- **Vaseline Petroleum Jelly.** To give the outside of a stainless-steel appliance a remarkable shine, polish the stainless-steel with a dab of Vaseline Petroleum Jelly, and then buff dry with a soft, clean cloth.

- **Windex.** To clean and shine a stainless-steel appliance, spray Windex on a soft, clean cloth and wipe clean.

Tablecloths and Napkins

- **Arm & Hammer Baking Soda.** To clean grease stains from tablecloths or napkins, sprinkle Arm & Hammer Baking Soda over the stain and scrub gently with a wet brush.

- **Canada Dry Club Soda.** To clean food stains from tablecloths or napkins, blot up the spill, sponge with Canada Dry Club Soda, and launder as usual.

- **Cascade.** To clean stains from a linen tablecloth or napkin, pour liquid Cascade dishwasher detergent over the stains and launder as usual.

- **Coca-Cola.** To clean a grease stain from tablecloths or napkins, pour a can of Coke on the grease stain, let sit for five minutes, and then launder as usual with your regular detergent. The acids in the Real Thing loosen grease stains.

- **Comet.** Wet the grease stain, sprinkle Comet cleanser over the spot, rub in to form a paste, and let sit overnight. In the morning, rinse clean with warm water.

- **Crisco All-Vegetable Shortening.** To clean lipstick stains from napkins, rub a dab of Crisco All-Vegetable Shortening into the stain, and then launder as usual. The shortening breaks down the grease in the lipstick.

- **Dawn Dishwashing Liquid.** Rub a few drops of Dawn Dishwashing Liquid into the grease stain on a tablecloth or napkin, and then launder as usual. Dawn cuts through grease.

- **Formula 409.** To clean tomato sauce stains, fruit stains, or coffee stains from tablecloths or napkins, spray Formula 409 on the trouble area, let set for two minutes, and launder as usual.

- **Huggies Baby Wipes.** To clean a spill from a tablecloth to prevent staining, immediately wipe the spot with a Huggies Baby Wipe.

- **Johnson's Baby Powder.** To absorb a grease stain from tablecloths or napkins, sprinkle Johnson's Baby Powder over the stain, rub into the fabric, and launder in cold water.

- **Kingsford's Corn Starch.** Pour Kingsford's Corn Starch over the grease spot, let sit overnight so the cornstarch can absorb the grease, brush off, and then launder as usual.

- **Murphy Oil Soap.** To clean stains from tablecloths or napkins, dampen the stain, apply a few drops Murphy Oil Soap full strength, and launder as usual.

- **Nestlé Carnation Nonfat Dry Milk.** To whiten a white tablecloth and napkins, mix one cup Nestlé Carnation Nonfat Dry Milk in a bucket of hot water and soak the clothes in the milky solution overnight. In the morning, discard the liquid and launder the clothes as usual.

- **Parsons' Ammonia.** To clean chocolate stains from tablecloths or cloth napkins, mix one teaspoon Parsons' Ammonia and one cup of water and saturate the stain with the solution. Let sit for five minutes, and then launder as usual.

- **Pine-Sol.** To clean food and grease stains from tablecloths or napkins, rub Pine-Sol into the stain, and then launder the garment as usual.

- **Resolve Carpet Cleaner.** To clean juice stains from tablecloths or napkins, spray the spot with Resolve Carpet Cleaner, blot, and rinse thoroughly. Launder as usual with your regular detergent.

- **Spic and Span.** To clean dirt stains from tablecloths or napkins, mix a teaspoon Spic and Span with enough water to make a paste, apply to the stain, and launder as usual.

- **20 Mule Team Borax.** To clean chocolate from tablecloths or napkins, make a thick paste with borax and water, work the paste into the stain, let sit for one hour, rinse with warm water, and launder as usual.

- **Windex.** To clean food stains from tablecloths or napkins, immediately spray the spot with Windex, let sit for three minutes, blot, and rinse clean.

Teapots

- **Arm & Hammer Baking Soda.** To clean a teapot, dissolve one-quarter cup Arm & Hammer Baking Soda in one quart of warm water and wash the teapot in the solution. Rinse clean and dry.

- **Efferdent.** To clean tea stains from inside a china teapot, fill the teapot with water and drop in two Efferdent denture cleansing tablets. Let sit for thirty minutes, rinse thoroughly, and let dry.

- **Mr. Clean Magic Eraser.** To remove tea stains from a teapot, gently rub the stains with a damp Mr. Clean Magic Eraser. Wash the teapot thoroughly with soapy water, rinse clean, and dry.

Thermos Bottles

- **Alka-Seltzer.** To clean residue from inside a Thermos bottle, fill the bottle with water, drop in four Alka-Seltzer tablets, and let sit for one hour. Rinse clean and dry.

- **Arm & Hammer Baking Soda.** To clean and deodorize a Thermos bottle, fill the bottle with warm water, add two tablespoons Arm & Hammer Baking Soda, shake well, and let sit for ten minutes. Rinse well and dry.

- **Arm & Hammer Baking Soda, McCormick Cream of Tartar,** and **ReaLemon.** To clean the inside of a filthy Thermos bottle, mix two teaspoons Arm & Hammer Baking Soda, two teaspoons McCormick Cream of Tartar, and two teaspoons ReaLemon lemon juice in the bottle. Seal the lid shut securely, shake vigorously, rinse clean, and dry.

- **Cascade.** To clean caked-on gunk from inside a Thermos bottle, pour one teaspoon Cascade Gel into the Thermos bottle, add boiling water, screw the lid on the bottle tightly, shake well, and let sit for one hour. Rinse thoroughly and dry.

- **Clorox.** To clean a Thermos bottle, fill the bottle with warm water, add one teaspoon Clorox bleach, let sit for one hour, and rinse well.

- **Domino Sugar.** To prevent a stored Thermos bottle from acquiring a sour smell, place one teaspoon Domino Sugar inside the clean, dry bottle before sealing it shut. The sugar will absorb stale odors.

- **Efferdent.** To clean caked-on stains from the inside of a Thermos bottle, fill the bottle with water, drop in two Efferdent denture cleansing tablets, and let sit overnight. In the morning, rinse clean and dry.

- **Morton Salt.** To deodorize a Thermos bottle, fill the bottle with warm water, add one tablespoon Morton Salt, seal the lid, shake well to dissolve the salt, and let sit for one hour (or overnight). Wash with soap and water and rinse clean.

- **Parsons' Ammonia.** To deodorize a musty Thermos bottle, pour in one teaspoon Parsons' Ammonia, fill the rest of the bottle with water, shake well, let sit for ten minutes, and rinse clean.

- **Uncle Ben's Original Converted Brand Rice** and **Heinz White Vinegar.** To clean residue from inside a Thermos bottle, pour in one-half cup Uncle Ben's Original Converted Brand Rice and one-half cup Heinz White Vinegar. Screw the lid on the bottle and shake vigorously, allowing the grains of rice to work like tiny scrub brushes against the inside walls of the bottle. Wash and rinse clean.

Waffle Iron

- **Wesson Oil.** To clean burned-on batter from a cast-iron waffle iron, let the waffle iron cool, scoop out as much batter as possible, use a pastry brush to apply Wesson Oil to the grids, and scrub with a wire brush.

Walls and Wallpaper

- **Arm & Hammer Baking Soda.** To clean grease stains and food splatters from a tile wall or wallpaper, sprinkle Arm & Hammer Baking Soda on a damp sponge, scrub gently, and wipe clean.

- **Con-Tact Paper.** To prevent stains on the wallpaper behind your stove, clean the wallpaper thoroughly, let dry, and adhere a sheet of clear, washable Con-Tact Paper over the trouble spot.

- **Huggies Baby Wipes.** To clean food splatters from walls, use a Huggies Baby Wipe.

- **Kingsford's Corn Starch.** To clean grease splatters from walls, sprinkle Kingsford's Corn Starch on a soft cloth and rub the spot until the grease disappears. Cornstarch absorbs grease.

- **Nestlé Carnation Nonfat Dry Milk, Clorox Bleach,** and **Bounty Paper Towels.** To clean grease splatters from the wall behind a stovetop, mix one teaspoon Nestlé Carnation Nonfat Dry Milk, one-quarter cup Clorox Bleach, and one-quarter cup of water in a glass bowl. Saturate a sheet or two of Bounty Paper Towels with the solution and drape the wet paper towel so it clings to the wall, covering the grease stains. Let sit for one minute, remove, and rinse clean. Repeat if necessary.

- **Play-Doh.** To clean grease stains and food splatters from wallpaper, roll a ball of Play-Doh along the wallpaper. The modeling dough—originally invented as a wallpaper cleaner—lifts grease and grime.

- **Wonder Bread.** To clean wallpaper, cut off the crust from two day-old slices of Wonder Bread and use the slices of doughy bread as a kneaded eraser to gently rub down the wallpaper.

Wine Stains

- **Arm & Hammer Baking Soda.** After blotting up as much of the wine stain as possible with towels, cover the remaining stain with a mountain of Arm & Hammer Baking Soda, let sit until the baking soda has absorbed the liquid, and vacuum clean.

- **Canada Dry Club Soda.** To clean a wine stain from a tablecloth, upholstered furniture, or carpet, pour Canada Dry Club Soda over the stain, let sit for a few minutes, and blot it up thoroughly with a soft, clean cloth. Repeat if necessary.

- **Gillette Foamy.** To clean spilled wine from carpet, blot the stain, and then rub a dab of Gillette Foamy shaving cream into the remaining color. Sponge with cold water and blot.

- **Morton Salt.** After blotting up as much of the wine stain as possible with towels, pour a mountain of Morton Salt over the wine stain, let sit for fifteen minutes to give the salt ample time to absorb the wine from the carpet, and then sweep up the salt. Repeat if necessary.

- **20 Mule Team Borax.** Use towels to blot up the wine spill, dissolve one cup 20 Mule Team Borax in one quart of water, and sponge the solution into the stain. Let sit thirty minutes, shampoo the spotted area, let dry, and vacuum. (Before treating, test an inconspicuous spot on the carpeting with a paste made from 20 Mule Team Borax and water to make sure the borax does not remove any color from the carpet.)

Wooden Spoons

- **ReaLemon.** To deodorize the pungent odor of garlic and onions from wooden spoons, rub the spoon with ReaLemon lemon juice and let dry. Then wash with soapy water, rinse, and dry.

Acknowledgments

At Rodale, I am grateful to my editor, Karen Bolesta, for her passion, enthusiasm, and excitement for this book. I am also deeply indebted to my agent, Stephanie Tade; researcher Debbie Green, expert copy editor Jennifer Bright Reich, senior project editor Hope Clarke, designer Chris Rhoads, and ace illustrator Scott Burroughs. A very special thank-you for my manager, Barb North, and the hundreds of people who visit my Web site and take the time to send me e-mails sharing their ingenious tips for brand-name products we all know and love.

Above all, all my love to Debbie, Ashley, and Julia.

The Fine Print

- *All-New Hints from Heloise* by Heloise (New York: Perigee, 1989)
- *Another Use For* by Vicki Lansky (Deephaven, Minnesota: Book Peddlers, 1991)
- *Ask Anne & Nan* by Anne Adams and Nancy Walker (Brattleboro, Vermont: Whetstone, 1989)
- *The Bag Book* by Vicki Lansky (Deephaven, Minnesota: Book Peddlers, 2000)
- *Baking Soda Bonanza* by Peter A. Ciullo (New York: HarperPerennial, 1995)
- "Baking Soda's Star Rises: Out of the Fridge, Into…Everything" by Bruce Horovitz, *Los Angeles Times,* August 16, 1994
- "Birthplace of the Burger" by Jim Shelton, *New Haven Register*, January 13, 2002
- *Bottom Line's Best-Ever Kitchen Hints* by Joan Wilen and Lydia Wilen (Stamford, Connecticut: Bottom Line, 2008)
- *The Bread Bible: 300 Favorite Recipes* by Beth Hensperger (San Francisco: Chronicle Books, 1999)
- *Clean & Green: The Complete Guide to Nontoxic and Environmentally Safe Housekeeping* by Annie Berthold–Bond (Woodstock, New York: Ceres Press, 1990)
- *Clean It Fast, Clean It Right: The Ultimate Guide to Making Absolutely Everything You Own Sparkle & Shine* edited by Jeff Bredenberg (Emmaus, Pennsylvania: Rodale, 1998)
- *The Cleaning Encyclopedia* by Don Aslett (New York: Dell, 1993)
- *A Dash of Mustard* by Katy Holder and Jane Newdick (London: Chartwell Books, 1995)
- *The Doctor's Book of Home Remedies* by the Editors of *Prevention* magazine (Emmaus, Pennsylvania: Rodale, 1990)
- *Earl Proulx's Yankee Home Hints* by Earl Proulx and the editors of *Yankee* magazine (Dublin, New Hampshire: Yankee, 1993)

- *Emilie's Creative Home Organizer* by Emilie Barnes (Eugene, Oregon: Harvest House, 1995)

- *Favorite Helpful Household Hints* by the Editors of *Consumer Guide* (Skokie, Illinois: Publications International, 1986)

- *Haley's Hints* by Graham and Rosemary Haley (New York: New American Library, 1995)

- *Hints from Heloise* by Heloise (New York: Arbor House, 1980)

- *Household Hints & Formulas* by Erik Bruun (New York: Black Dog and Leventhal, 1994)

- *Household Hints & Handy Tips* by *Reader's Digest* (Pleasantville, New York: Reader's Digest Association, 1988)

- *Household Hints for Upstairs, Downstairs, and All Around the House* by Carol Reese (New York: Henry Holt and Company, 1982)

- *Joy of Cooking* by Irma von Starkloff Rombauer and Marion Rombauer Becker (New York: Scribner, 1975)

- *Kitchen Hints from Heloise* by Heloise (Emmaus, Pennsylvania: Rodale, 2005)

- *Kitchen Wisdom* by Frieda Arkin (New York: Consumers Union, 1977)

- *Lemon Magic* by Patty Moosbrugger (New York: Three Rivers Press, 1999)

- *Make It Yourself* by Dolores Riccio and Joan Bingham (Radnor, Pennsylvania: Chilton, 1978)

- *Mary Ellen's Best of Helpful Hints* by Mary Ellen Pinkham (New York: Warner/B. Lansky, 1979)

- *Mary Ellen's Best of Helpful Kitchen Hints* by Mary Ellen Pinkham (New York: Warner Books, 1980)

- *Mary Ellen's Greatest Hints* by Mary Ellen Pinkham (New York: Fawcett Crest, 1990)

- *1,628 Country Shortcuts from 1,628 Country People* by the editors of *Country* and *Country Woman* magazines (Greendale, Wisconsin: Reiman Publications, 1996)

- *Panati's Extraordinary Origins of Everyday Things* by Charles Panati (New York: Perennial, 1987)

- *Persuasion: Reception and Responsibility* by Charles U. Larson (Boston: Wadsworth, 2010)

- *Practical Problem Solver* by *Reader's Digest* (Pleasantville, New York: Reader's Digest, 1991)

- *Professional Cooking for Canadian Chefs, Sixth Edition* by Wayne Gisslen (Hoboken, New Jersey: John Wiley & Sons, 2007)

- "Relation Between Dietary n–3 and n–6 Fatty Acids and Clinically Diagnosed Dry Eye Syndrome in Women" by Biljana Miljanovic, Komal A. Trivedi, M. Reza Dana, Jeffery P. Gilbard, Julie E. Buring, and Debra A. Schaumberg, *American Journal of Clinical Nutrition*, October 2005, Vol. 82, No. 4, pages 887–893

- *Rodale's Book of Hints, Tips & Everyday Wisdom* by Carol Hupping, Cheryl Winters Tetreau, and Roger B. Yepsen, Jr. (Emmaus, Pennsylvania: Rodale Press, 1985)

- *Shameless Shortcuts* by Fern Marshall Bradley and the editors of *Yankee* magazine (Dublin, New Hampshire: Yankee, 2004)

- *Shoes in the Freezer, Beer in the Flower Bed* by Joan Wilen and Lydia Wilen (New York: Fireside, 1997)

- *Solve It With Salt* by Patty Moosbrugger (New York: Three Rivers Press, 1998)

- *Talking Dirty with the Queen of Clean* by Linda Cobb (New York: Pocket Books, 1999)

- *Whole Food Facts* by Evelyn Roehl (Rochester, Vermont: Healing Arts Press, 1996)

- *The Woman's Day Help Book* by Geraldine Rhoads and Edna Paradis (New York: Viking, 1988)

- *Yankee Magazine's Practical Problem Solver* by Earl Proulx and the editors of *Yankee* magazine (Dublin, New Hampshire: Yankee, 1998)

- *Yankee Magazine's Vinegar, Duct Tape, Milk Jugs & More* by Earl Proulx and the editors of *Yankee* magazine (Dublin, New Hampshire: Yankee, 1999)

Trademark Information

"Adolph's" is a registered trademark of Unilever.

"Ajax" is a registered trademark of Colgate-Palmolive.

"Alberto VO5" is a registered trademark of Alberto-Culver USA, Inc.

"Alka-Seltzer" is a registered trademark of Miles, Inc.

"Altoids" is a registered trademark of Callard & Bowser.

"Angostura" is a registered trademark of Angostura Bitters Limited.

"Aqua Net" is a registered trademark of Lornamead, Inc.

"Arm & Hammer" and "Clean Shower" are registered trademarks of Church & Dwight Co, Inc.

"Aunt Jemima" is a registered trademark of the Quaker Oats Company.

"Bacardi" is a registered trademark of Bacardi & Company, Limited.

"Betty Crocker" is a registered trademark of General Mills.

"Birds Eye" is a registered trademark of Pinnacle Foods Group LLC.

"Band-Aid" is a registered trademark of Johnson & Johnson.

"Blue Bonnet" is a registered trademark of Con Agra Foods, Inc.

"Bon Ami" is a registered trademark of the Bon Ami Company.

"Bounce" is a registered trademark of Procter & Gamble.

"Bounty" is a registered trademark of Procter & Gamble.

"Breakstone's" and "Knudsen" are registered trademarks of Kraft Foods.

"Bubble Wrap" is a registered trademark of the Sealed Air Corporation.

"Budweiser" is a registered trademark of Anheuser-Busch, Inc.

"Calgon" is a registered trademark of Reckitt Benckiser Inc.

"Campbell" is a registered trademark of the Campbell Soup Company.

"Canada Dry" is a registered trademark of Cadbury Beverages Inc.

"Carnation" and "Nestlé" are registered trademarks of Société des Produits Nestlé S.A., Vevey, Switzerland.

"Cascade" is a registered trademark of Procter & Gamble.

"ChapStick" is a registered trademark of A. H. Robbins Company.

"Cheerios" is a registered trademark of General Mills.

"Chicken of the Sea" is a registered trademark of Chicken of the Sea International.

"Clabber Girl" is a registered trademark of the Clabber Girl Corporation.

"Clairol" and "Herbal Essences" are registered trademarks of Clairol.

"Clorox" is a registered trademark of the Clorox Company.

"Coca-Cola" and "Coke" are registered trademarks of the Coca-Cola Company.

"Coffee-mate" and "Nestlé" are registered trademarks of Société des Produits Nestlé S.A., Vevey, Switzerland.

"Colgate" is a registered trademark of Colgate-Palmolive.

"Colman's" is a registered trademark of World Finer Foods, Inc.

"Con-Tact" is a registered trademark of Rubbermaid, Incorporated.

"Comet" is a registered trademark of Procter & Gamble.

"Conair" is a registered trademark of the Conair Corporation.

"Cool Whip" is a registered trademark of Kraft Foods.

"Country Time" and "Country Time Lemonade" are registered trademarks of Kraft Foods.

"Crayola" is a registered trademark of Binney & Smith Inc.

"Creamettes" is a registered trademark of New World Pasta, Inc.

"Crisco" is a registered trademark of the J. M. Smucker Co.

"Cutex" is a registered trademark of MedTech.

"Dannon" is a registered trademark of the Dannon Company.

"Dawn" is a registered trademark of Procter & Gamble.

"Dial" is a registered trademark of Dial Corp.

"Dixie" is a registered trademark of James River Corporation.

"Dole" is a registered trademark of the Dole Food Company, Inc.

"Domino" is a registered trademark of Domino Foods, Inc.

"Downy" is a registered trademark of Procter & Gamble.

"Dynasty" is a registered trademark of JFC International, Inc.

"Easy-Off" is a registered trademark of Reckitt Benckiser Inc.

"Efferdent" is a registered trademark of Warner-Lambert.

"Eggo" is a registered trademark of the Kellogg Company.

"Elmer's Glue-All" and Elmer the Bull are registered trademarks of Borden.

"Fleischmann's" is a registered trademark of ACH Foods.

"Formula 409" is a registered trademark of the Clorox Company.

"Forster" is a registered trademark of Diamond Brands, Inc.

"French's" is a registered trademark of Reckitt Benckiser Inc.

"Frisbee" is a registered trademark of Mattel, Inc.

"Fruit of the Earth" is a registered trademark of Fruit of the Earth, Inc.

"Gatorade" is a registered trademark of the Gatorade Company.

"Gillette" and "Foamy" are registered trademarks of Procter & Gamble.

"Glad" is a registered trademark of First Brands Corporation.

"Gold Medal" is a registered trademark of General Mills, Inc.

"Gold's" is a registered trademark of Gold Pure Food Products Co., Inc.

"Grandma's Molasses" is a registered trademark of B&G Foods, Inc.

"Heinz" is a registered trademark of the H.J. Heinz Company.

"Hershey's" is a registered trademark of the Hershey Foods Corporation.

"Hidden Valley" is a registered trademark of the HV Foods Products Company.

"Holland House" is a registered trademark of Mizkan Americas, Inc.

"Honey Maid" is a registered trademark of Kraft Foods.

"Huggies" is a registered trademark of the Kimberly-Clark Corporation.

"Hunt's" is a registered trademark of Hunt-Wesson, Inc.

"Jell-O" is a registered trademark of Kraft Foods.

"Jet-Dry" is a registered trademark of Reckitt Benckiser, Inc.

"Jet-Puffed" is a registered trademark of Kraft Foods.

"Jif" is a registered trademark of the J. M. Smucker Co.

"Johnson's" and "Johnson & Johnson" are registered trademarks of Johnson & Johnson.

"Karo" is a registered trademark of CPC International Inc.

"Kellogg's" is a registered trademark of the Kellogg Company.

"Kingsford" is a registered trademark of Kingsford's Products Company.

"Kingsford's" is a registered trademark of ACH Food Companies.

"Kiwi" is a registered trademark of the Sara Lee Corporation.

"Kleenex" is a registered trademark of Kimberly-Clark Corporation.

"Knorr" is a registered trademark of Unilever.

"Knox" is a registered trademark of Kraft Foods.

"Kool-Aid" is a registered trademark of Kraft Foods.

"Korbel" is a registered trademark of F. Korbel & Bros.

"Kraft" is a registered trademark of Kraft Foods.

"L'eggs" and "Sheer Energy" are registered trademarks of Sara Lee Corporation.

"Lakewood" is a registered trademark of a Florida Family Trust.

"Land O Lakes" is a registered trademark of Land O Lakes, Inc.

"Lay's" is a registered trademark of Frito-Lay.

"Lea & Perrins" is a registered trademark of H. J. Heinz Company.

"Lipton," "The 'Brisk' Tea," "Flo-Thru," and "Recipe Secrets" are registered trademarks of Unilever.

"Listerine" is a registered trademark of Warner-Lambert.

"Log Cabin" is a registered trademark of Pinnacle Foods Group LLC.

"Lubriderm" is a registered trademark of Warner-Lambert.

"M&M's" is a registered trademark of Mars, Incorporated.

"Manischewitz" is a registered trademark of the Manischewitz Company.

"Martini & Rossi" is a registered trademark of the Martini & Rossi Wine Company.

"MasterCard" is a registered trademark of MasterCard International Incorporated.

"Maxwell House" and "Good to the Last Drop" are registered trademarks of the Maxwell House Coffee Company.

"McCormick" is a registered trademark of McCormick & Company, Incorporated.

"Miracle Whip" is a registered trademark of Kraft Foods.

"Morton" is a registered trademark of Morton International, Inc.

"Mott's" is a registered trademark of Mott's Inc.

"Mr. Clean" is a registered trademark of Procter & Gamble.

"Mr. Coffee" is a registered trademark of Mr. Coffee, Inc.

"Murphy" is a registered trademark of the Colgate-Palmolive Company.

"Nestea" and "Nestlé" are registered trademarks of Société des Produits Nestlé S.A., Vevey, Switzerland.

"Newman's Own" is a registered trademark of Newman's Own Inc.

"Niagara" is a registered trademark of Phoenix Brands LLC.

"Orajel" is a registered trademark of Church & Dwight Co., Inc.

"Oral-B" is a registered trademark of Oral-B Laboratories.

"Orville Redenbacher's" and "Gourmet" are registered trademarks of Con Agra Foods.

"Pam" is a registered trademark of American Home Foods.

"Pampers" is a registered trademark of Procter & Gamble.

"Parsons'" is a registered trademark of Church & Dwight Co., Inc.

"Philadelphia" is a registered trademark of Kraft Foods.

"Phillips" is a registered trademark of Bayer HealthCare LLC.

"Pillsbury" and "Softasilk" are registered trademarks of General Mills.

"Pine-Sol" is a registered trademark of the Clorox Company.

"Planters" is a registered trademark of Kraft Foods.

"Play-Doh" is a registered trademark of Hasbro, Inc.

"Playtex" and "Living" are registered trademarks of Playtex Products, Inc.

"Pledge" is a registered trademark of S.C. Johnson & Sons, Inc.

"Post-it" is a registered trademark of 3M.

"Premium" and "Nabisco" are registered trademarks of Kraft Foods.

"Pringles" and "Potato Crisps" are registered trademarks of Procter & Gamble.

"Progresso" is a registered trademark of General Mills.

"Purell" is a registered trademark of Johnson & Johnson Consumer Companies, Inc.

"Q-tips" is a registered trademark of Chesebrough-Pond's USA Co.

"Quaker" is a registered trademark of the Quaker Oats Company.

"ReaLemon" is a registered trademark of Borden.

"Reddi-wip" is a registered trademark of Con Agra Foods, Inc.

"Revlon" is a registered trademark of Revlon Consumer Products Corporation.

"Resolve" is a registered trademark of Reckitt Benckiser, Inc.

"Reynolds," "Reynolds Wrap," and "Cut-Rite" are registered trademarks of Reynolds Metals.

"Rubbermaid" is a registered trademark of Newell Rubbermaid Inc.

"S.O.S" is a registered trademark of the Clorox Company.

"Sambal Oelek" is a registered trademark of Huy Fung Foods Inc.

"Saran" and "Saran Wrap" are registered trademarks of S.C. Johnson & Sons, Inc.

"Scotch" is a registered trademark of 3M.

"7-Up" is a registered trademark of Dr Pepper/Seven-Up, Inc.

"Shout" is a registered trademark of S.C. Johnson & Sons, Inc.

"Slim Jim" is a registered trademark of Con Agra Foods.

"Smirnoff" is a registered trademark of United Vintners & Distributors.

"Smucker's" is a registered trademark of the J. M. Smucker Company.

"SPAM" is a registered trademark of the Hormel Foods Corporation.

"Spic and Span" is a registered trademark of Procter & Gamble.

"Spray 'n Wash" is a registered trademark of Reckitt Benckiser Inc.

"Star" is a registered trademark of Star Fine Foods.

"Stayfree" is a registered trademark of McNeil-PPC, Inc.

"SueBee" is a registered trademark of Sioux Honey Association.

"Sun-Maid" is a registered trademark of Sun-Maid.

"Swiss Miss" is a registered trademark of Con Agra Foods.

"Tabasco" is a registered trademark of the McIlhenny Company.

"Tang" is a registered trademark of Kraft Foods.

"Thai Kitchen" is a registered trademark of Simply Asia Foods, LLC.

"3M" is a registered trademark of 3M.

"Tide" is a registered trademark of Procter & Gamble.

"Tidy Cats" is a registered trademark of the Ralston Purina Company.

"Tropicana" is a registered trademark of Tropicana Products, Inc.

"Tupperware" is a registered trademark of Tupperware Worldwide.

"20 Mule Team" and "Borax" are registered trademarks of United States Borax & Chemical Corporation.

"Uncle Ben's" and "Converted" are registered trademarks of Uncle Ben's, Inc.

"USA Today" is a registered trademark of Gannett News Service.

"Vaseline" is a registered trademark of Chesebrough-Pond's USA.

"Vicks" and "VapoRub" are registered trademarks of Procter & Gamble.

"WD-40" is a registered trademark of the WD-40 Company.

"Welch's" is a registered trademark of Welch Foods Inc.

"Wesson" is a registered trademark of Hunt-Wesson, Inc.

"Wilson" is a registered trademark of the Wilson Sporting Goods Co.

"Windex" is a registered trademark of S. C. Johnson & Sons, Inc.

"Wish-Bone" is a registered trademark of Unilever.

"Wonder" is a registered trademark of Interstate Brands Corporation.

"Wrigley's," "Doublemint," and "Wrigley's Spearmint" are registered trademarks of Wm. Wrigley Jr. Company.

"Ziploc" is a registered trademark of S.C. Johnson & Son, Inc.

Index

Underscored page references indicate boxed text.

Adolph's Meat Tenderizer, 284
Ajax Oxygen Bleach Cleanser, 319
Alberto VO5 Conditioning Hairdressing, 45, 273, 327
Alka-Seltzer, 270–71, 296, 306, 334
Almonds, 210–11
Altoid Mints, 283, 285
Aluminum cookware, 289
Angel food cake, 104, 105
Angostura Aromatic Bitters, 177
Apples, 5, 6, 82–83, 83
Appliance tips. *See specific item*
Aprons, 32
Aqua Net Hair Spray, 20
Arm & Hammer Baking Soda
    appliance and gadget tips
        barbecue gadgets, 49
        can openers, 53
        coffeemakers, 54
        coffee percolators, 55–56
        dishwashers, 56–57
        electric skillets, 59
        fire extinguishers, 60
        freezers, 61
        garbage disposers, 63
        microwave ovens, 65
        ovens, 68
        pressure cookers, 71
        refrigerators, 72
        stoves, 76
        toaster ovens, 80
        toasters, 79
    cleaning tips
        butcher blocks, 292
        casserole dishes, 296
        coffeepots, 300
        cooktops, 301
        countertops, 304
        cutting boards, 308
        dishes, 309
        drains, 310
        enamel pots and pans, 312
        floors, 313–14
        highchairs, 317
        nonstick cookware, 319
        plastic containers, 321
        pots and pans, 323
        silverware, 326
        sinks, 327
        tablecloths and napkins, 332
        teapots, 334
        walls and wallpaper, 336

    cooking tips
        baking powder, making, 87
        beans, 89
        brown sugar, 100
        cabbage, 102
        cake batter, 105
        chicken, 128–29, 132, 134
        coffee, 140
        cookies, 142
        cranberries, 147
        cream, 204
        eggs, 152, 159
        egg substitute and, 110
        fish, 163
        fruits, 169
        gravy, 174
        lima beans, 189
        meats, general, 194, 201
        meringues, 203
        milk, 204
        molasses, 207
        onions, 213
        pancakes, 217
        sugar substitutes, 258
        tea, 260
        turkey, 262
        vegetables, 264
        waffles, 265
    cookware and tableware tips, 35, 42–43, 45
    deodorizing tips, 36, 42, 57, 63, 72, 163, 292,
        308, 334
    healing remedy tips, 271, 277, 283
    rubber gloves and, 42
    vegetable cleaning and, 30
Arm & Hammer Super Washing Soda, 57
Arthritis, 269
Artichokes, 23–24, 24, 83–84, 84
Asparagus, 24, 24, 84–85, 85
Athlete's foot, 269–70
Aunt Jemima Corn Meal, 291
Aunt Jemima Original Pancake and Waffle Mix, 213
Aunt Jemima Original Syrup, 258, 260
Avocados, 6, 6, 85–86

Bacardi Rum, 236
Backache, 270
Bacon, 15–16, 86–87, 87
Bad breath, 270–71
Bakeware, 32. *See also* Cookware
Baking powder, making, 87
Baking soda freshness test, 87–88

Bananas, 7, 7, 88, 89, 105
Band-Aid Bandages, 17
Barbecue gadgets and barbecuing tips, 49–51
Barbecue sauce, 89
Bay leaves, 181
Beans
    Bean Croquettes, 90
    cooking tips, 89–91, 89, 256, 256
    lima, 89, 190
    shopping for and storing, 24, 25
    string, 256, 256
Beef
    Delicious Brisket, 194
    ground beef, 196
    hamburgers, 177–80, 178–79, 180
    liver, 190
    meatballs, 197
    meatloaf, 191–93, 192
    steak, 199–201, 200
Beets, 91
Berries. See also specific type
    in cakes, 107
    cooking tips, 91, 91
    shopping for and storing, 7, 7
Betty Crocker Devil's Food Cake Mix, 112
Betty Crocker Potato Buds, 190–91, 252
Beverages, making, 91–92. See also specific type
Birds Eye Baby Peas, 282
Biscuits, 92
Blenders, 52
Blisters, 271
Blue Bonnet Margarine
    cleaning tips, 299
    cooking tips, 181, 262
    food storage tips, 22, 25
Body odor, 271–72
Bon Ami
    appliance and gadget tips, 65, 71–72, 79
    cleaning tips, 299, 301, 304, 313, 323, 328
Bottles, 289–90. See also specific type
Bounce sheets
    appliance and gadget tips, 65
    cleaning tips, 296, 318, 323
    deodorizing tips, 36
Bounty Paper Towels
    appliance and gadget tips, 49, 51, 53, 70, 72, 80–81
    cleaning tips, 290–91, 320, 324–25, 336
    cooking tips
        asparagus, 84
        bacon, 86
        cakes, 104, 109
        cheese, 125
        chicken, 130, 132, 136
        cookies, 141
        corn, 145
        cucumbers, 148
        eggplant, 151–52
        eggs, 157

    fish, 160–61, 168
    fruits, 169
    greens, 242
    ham, 176
    meats, general, 194–95, 199
    mushrooms, 209
    mussels, 210
    onions, 213
    potatoes, 231–32, 235
    rice, 237
    rolls, 97
    soufflés, 249
    soups, 251
    vegetables, 264
    cookware and tableware tips, 33–35, 42–43, 47–48
    deodorizing tips for garbage cans, 36
    food storage tips, 7, 14, 17, 24, 26, 29–30
Bouquet Garni, 181
Bratwurst, 92
Bread
    baking tips, 92–98, 94, 96
    biscuits, 92
    corn, 94
    dough, 94–97, 96
    Garlic Bread, 95
    reheating, 97
    rolls, 97–98
    shopping for and storing, 10–11, 11
    sweetbreads, 259
    yeast, 98
Bread bags, 94
Breadbaskets, 94
Breadcrumbs, 11, 98–99
Bread machines, 52–53
Breakstone's Cottage Cheese, 123, 177, 221
Breakstone's Sour Cream, 108, 234
Broccoli, 99–100, 99
Broiling meats, 128–31, 160–61, 194–95
Broom sweeping tips, 291
Brownies, 101
Browning meat, 195
Brown sugar, 20, 100
Bruises, 272
Brussels sprouts, 101
Bubble Wrap, 291, 318
Budweiser, 92, 134, 158, 197–98, 200, 247
Bundt cakes, 108
Burner grates, stove, 77–78
Burners, stove, 77–78
Burns, skin, 272–73, 287
Butcher blocks, 292
Butter, 102
Buttermilk, 204

Cabbage, 102–3, 103
Cabinets, 292–93
Cake pans, 32
Cake plates, 32, 116–17

Cakes
    Angel food, 104, <u>105</u>
    bakeware, 32
    baking tips, 104–17
    bananas in, 105
    batter, 105–7, <u>107</u>
    berries in, 107
    Bundt, 108
    candles on, 108
    chocolate, 109, <u>113</u>
    cooling, 109
    cutting/slicing tips, 109, 116
    dates in, 110
    freezing, 111
    icing, 112–15, <u>114</u>
    layered, 116
    pound, <u>115</u>
    raisins in, 117
    sauces for, 117
    sponge, 117
    storage tips, 21, <u>21</u>
Calgon Water Softener, 54, 76, 304, 323
Campbell's Beef Bouillon, 174, 252, 264
Campbell's Beef Broth, 198, 259
Campbell's Broth, 83
Campbell's Chicken Broth, 134, 158, 189, 190–91,
    237–38, 252, 262
Campbell's Chicken Noodle Soup, 273
Campbell's Condensed Beef Broth, 202
Campbell's Soup, 201
Campbell's Tomato Juice
    appliance and gadget tips, 61
    cooking tips, 158, 189, 191, 198, 201, 238, 256
    deodorizing tips, 61
    healing remedy tips, 274
Canada Dry Club Soda
    appliance and gadget tips
        bread machines, 52
        coffeemakers, 54
        electric mixers, 67
        food processors, 60
        juicers, 64
        ovens, 68
        refrigerators, 73
        rice cookers, 75
        teakettles, 78
        toaster ovens, 80
        toasters, 79
    cleaning tips, 293–94, 297, 301–2, 304, 313–14,
        328, 331–32, 337
    cooking tips, 91, 132, 139, 165, 217, 265
Canada Dry Ginger Ale, cooking tips, 176, 195
Candle wax removal, 293
Candy, 117–18, <u>118</u>
Can openers, 53
Cantaloupe, 118
Carpets, 293–95
Carrots, 25, <u>25</u>, 118–19, <u>119</u>

Cascade detergent
    appliance and gadget tips, 72, 77
    cleaning tips, 306, 310, 323–24, 328, 332, 334–35
Casserole dishes, 296–97
Cast-iron cookware, 33–34, 297–98
Cauliflower, 120–21, <u>120</u>
Celery, 26, 121–22, <u>121</u>
Cereals, 122
Chapped lips, 273
ChapStick, 314
Cheerios, 65, <u>122</u>, 174, 200, 252
Cheese
    Cheese Croutons, <u>126</u>
    cooking tips, 123–27, <u>128–29</u>
    cutting/slicing tips, 127, <u>127</u>
    grating, <u>124–25</u>, 125–26
    grilled cheese sandwiches, 126
    hardening, 127
    mold prevention, 1–3
    sauce from leftover, <u>129</u>
    serving, <u>129</u>
    shopping for and storing, 1–4, <u>2–3</u>
    straining homemade, 127
Cheesecake, 108–9
Cherries, 8
Chestnuts, 211
Chicken
    broiling, 128–31
    cooking tips, 128–36, <u>130</u>
    croquettes, 131
    defrosting, 131
    deodorizing, 132
    frying, 132–33
    marinating, 133
    mousse, 134
    plucking, 134
    roasting, 134–35
    safety issues, <u>16</u>
    sautéing, 135
    seasoning, 136
    skinning, 136
    stewing, 136
    storage tips, 16, <u>16</u>
Chicken of the Sea Tuna, 158, 277
China dishware, 34, 299
Chives, 13
Chocolate
    cakes, 109, <u>113</u>
    cooking tips, 136–39, <u>137</u>
    hot, 183, <u>184</u>
    storage tips, 21, <u>21</u>
    white, <u>138</u>
Clabber Girl Baking Powder
    cooking tips, 94, 111–12, 132, 156, 165, 169, 224,
        232
    healing remedy tips, 272
Clairol Herbal Essences Conditioner, 285
Clams, 139–40

Cleaning tips. *See specific item*
Cleanser cans, 299
Clorox Bleach
  appliance and gadget tips, 52, 54
  cleaning tips, 289, 307–8, 310–12, 315, 319, 321,
    328, 330, 335
  cooking tips, 170
  cookware and tableware tips, 42
  deodorizing tips, 289, 302, 330
  disinfecting tips, 42, 289, 302, 308, 330
  food storage tips, 30
Clorox Bleach jug for funnel, 35
Coca-Cola
  appliance and gadget tips, 78
  cleaning tips, 300, 307, 311, 324, 328, 332
  cooking tips, 89–90, 92, 101, 147, 176, 200, 202,
    229, 262
  healing remedy tips, 275, 280, 285
Coca-Cola bottle, 42
Coffee, 140–41
Coffee filters, 53
Coffee grinders, 54
Coffeemaker, 54–55
Coffee percolators, 55–56
Coffeepots, 300–301
Colds, 273–74
Colgate Regular Flavor Toothpaste
  appliance and gadget tips, 52, 76–77, 79
  cleaning tips, 299–300, 302–3, 305, 313–14, 316,
    326, 328
  cooking tips, 166, 171, 213
  deodorizing tips, 166
  healing remedy tips, 272, 278
Collard greens, 141
Colman's Mustard Powder, 166–67, 210, 308, 321–22
Comet cleanser, 332
Con-Tact Paper, 13, 22, 23, 336
Conair Hair Dryer
  appliance and gadget tips, 49, 61–62
  cake icing and, drying, 112
  cleaning tips, 293, 307, 311
  for Con-Tact Paper removal, 45
  cooking tips, 112, 185, 232, 242
Confectioners sugar, 112–13, 142, 150, 174, 206, 218
Constipation, 275
Cookies, 22–23, 141–44, *144*
Cooking tips. *See* Recipe Magic; *specific food*
Cookware
  aluminum, 289
  cake pans, 32
  casserole dishes, 296–97
  cast-iron, 33–34, 297–98
  cleaning tips, 289, 296–99, 312–13, 319, 322–26
  electric skillets, 59
  enamel, 312–13
  nonstick, 40, 319
  usage tips, 40–42
Coolers, 302

Cool Whip, 278–79, 285
Cool Whip container, 14, 53
Copper items, 303
Corn, 145–46, *145*, *146*
Corn bread, 94
Corned beef, 195
Corn syrup, 146
Cottage cheese, 123, *123*
Countertops, 304–5
Country Time Lemonade, 57, 248, 260
Coupons, grocery, 19
Crab, 147
Cranberries, 8, 147, *147*
Crayola Chalk, 45
Crayola Crayons, 4, 156
Cream cheese, 123–25
Creamettes Spaghetti, 104, 108, 116
Crêpes, 147–48
Crisco All-Vegetable Shortening
  appliance and gadget tips, 49, 73
  cleaning tips, 292, 332
  cooking tips
    biscuits, 92
    bread, 92–94
    Bundt cakes, 108
    cakes, 18
    chocolate, 136
    cookies, 141
    corn bread, 94
    gravy, 174
    meringues, 203
    pasta, 219
    peppers, 224
    potatoes, 235
    sauces, 245
    soups, 253–54
    tomatoes, 261
    waffles, 265
  cookware and tableware tips, 32–33, 35, 42, 47–48
  healing remedy tips, 273, 281, 286
Croquettes, 131, 162–63
Croutons, *126*, 241–42
Crystal glassware, 305–6
Crystal vases, 306–8
Cucumbers, 148, *148*
Cupcakes, 149
Custard, 150
Cutex Nail Polish Remover, 44, 79–80
Cuts, skin, 275–76
Cutting boards, 35, 308
Cutting/slicing tips, 109, 116, 127, *127*

Dairy products. *See specific type*
Dandruff, 276
Dannon Yogurt
  cooking tips, 91, 124, 172, 175, 190, 204, 208,
    224, 241, 254, 267
  healing remedy tips, 287

Dannon Yogurt container, 38
Dates in cakes, 110
Dawn Dishwashing Liquid
  appliance and gadget tips, 49–50, 52, 56, 60,
    62–64, 69, 71
  cleaning tips, 296, 298, 302, 311, 324, 332
  cooking tips, 170
  deodorizing tips, 62
  food storage tips, 25
Defrosting food, 131, 163, 195–96
Dehydrators, 56
Deodorizing tips
  Arm & Hammer Baking Soda, 36, 42, 57, 63, 71,
    72, 163, 292, 308, 334
  Bounce sheets, 36
  Bounty Paper Towels for garbage cans, 36
  Campbell's Tomato Juice, 61
  Clorox Bleach, 289, 302, 330
  Colgate Regular Flavor Toothpaste, 166
  Colman's Mustard Powder, 166–67
  Dawn Dishwashing Liquid, 62
  Domino Sugar products, 167, 171, 335
  Dynasty Sesame Seed Oil, 163
  French's Mustard, 290, 331
  Heinz White Vinegar, 62, 66, 150, 163–64, 167,
    214, 290, 319–20, 331
  Jif Peanut Butter, 164
  Listerine, 73–74, 167
  Maxwell House Coffee, 62, 66, 73, 164, 167
  McCormick Pure Lemon Extract, 73
  McCormick Pure Orange Extract, 74
  McCormick Pure Vanilla Extract, 66, 74, 302
  Morton Salt, 42–43, 64, 132, 164, 167, 308, 335
  ReaLemon, 42–43, 64, 66–67, 74, 132, 164, 167,
    210, 308, 320
  Tidy Cats, 36, 63, 74
  20 Mule Team Borax, 63–64, 74, 330
  Uncle Ben's Converted Brand Rice, 61
  USA Today newspaper, 63, 74–75
  Wonder Bread, 75
Deviled eggs, 154
Dial soap, 272
Diarrhea, 276–77
Dishware
  cake plates, 32, 116–17
  casserole dishes, 296–97
  china, 34, 299
  cleaning tips, 296–99, 309–10
  pewter, 321
  wooden, 47–48
Dishwashers, 56–59, 58
Dishwashing liquid, 35
Disinfecting tips
  Clorox Bleach, 42, 289, 302, 308, 330
  Heinz White Vinegar, 42, 308, 330–31
  Listerine, 42, 308, 330
  Morton Salt, 330
Dixie Cups, 36, 152, 206

Dixie Paper Plates, 34, 40, 66
Dole Pineapple products, 112, 123, 135, 177, 262
Domino Sugar products
  cleaning tips, 335
  cooking tips
    bread, 95
    brownies, 101
    brown sugar, 100
    cake icing, 112–13
    cakes, 116
    cauliflower, 120
    cheesecake, 108
    cookies, 142
    corn, 145
    doughnuts, 150
    eggs, 152, 160
    fish odors, 167
    garlic odors, 171
    grapefruits, 173
    ham, 177
    mangoes, 190
    mayonnaise, 191
    meats, general, 195
    meringues, 204
    onions, 213
    pancakes, 218
    pies, 224–25
    potatoes, 229
    rolls, 97
    salt, 243
    sauces, 245
    soufflés, 249
    strawberries, 255
    sugar, 258
    syrup, 259
    tomatoes, 262
    waffles, 265
    whipped cream, 206
    wine, 267
  deodorizing tips, 167, 171, 335
  food storage tips, 1
  healing remedy tips, 276, 280, 282
Doughnuts, 150
Downy Fabric Softener, 296, 314, 318, 324
Drain boards, 310
Drains, 310–12
Dried fruit, 8, 150–51, 151
Drip plates, stove, 77–78
Drip trays, refrigerator, 75
Dynasty Sesame Seed Oil, 163

Easy-Off Oven Cleaner
  appliance and gadget tips, 50, 69, 77
  cleaning tips, 296–97, 324, 328
Efferdent
  appliance and gadget tips, 66, 78–79
  cleaning tips, 289, 297, 299–301, 307, 311, 316,
    322, 324, 328, 330, 334–35

Eggbeaters, 59
Eggo Waffles, 196
Eggplant, 8, _8_, 151–52, _152_
Eggs
  brown, _5_
  cooking tips, 152–60, _153_, _155_, _156_, _157_
  deviled, 154
  freshness of, 154
  frying, 154
  hard-boiled, 154–55, _155_
  marking for identification, 4, 156
  omelets, 156–57
  peeling, 157–58, _157_
  poached, 158–59
  scrambled, 159
  shopping for and storing, 4, _4_, _5_
  spills, cleaning, 160, 312
  substitutes, 110, 160
  usage tips, _153_
  whites, beating, 152–54
  yolks, 160
Electric can openers, 53
Electric mixers, 67–68, _67_
Electric skillets, 59
Elmer's Glue-All, 38
Enamel cookware, 312–13
Epsom Salt, 286
Eye care tips, 277–78

F

Facials, 278–79
Fire extinguishers, 60
Fish and seafood. _See also specific type_
  broiling, 160–61
  cleaning, 161
  cooking tips, 160–69, _161_, _162_
  croquettes, 162–63
  defrosting, 163
  deodorizing, 163–64, 166–67
  flavoring, 165
  frying, 165
  grilling, 165–66
  marinating, 166
  mousse, 166
  patties, 167
  poached, 167–68
  sautéing, 168
  shopping for and storing, 16, _17_
  smell on hands, deodorizing, 166–67
  sticks, 164
Flatware, 313
Fleischmann's Yeast, 95
Floor cleaning tips, 313–15
Flour, 22, 110, 168–69
Flu, 273–74
Food. _See specific type_
Food poisoning, 280
Food processors, 60–61

Food shopping supplies, 19–20
Food shopping tips. _See specific food_
Food storage. _See specific food_
Foot care tips, 279–80
Formula 409 spray, 332
Forster Clothespins
  cooking tips, 169, 204, 260
  food shopping tips, 19
  food storage tips, 10, 23, 94
  as recipe holder, 19
Forster Toothpicks
  appliance and gadget tips, 53, 60
  cooking tips
    bacon, 86
    brown sugar, 100
    cake icing, 113–14
    cakes, 104
    carrots, 118–19
    chicken, 131, 135
    fish, 161, 168
    garlic, 171
    herbs and spices, 181
    lamb, 187
    meats, general, 194–95
    oranges, 216
    sausages, 247
    stuffing, 257
    vegetables, 264
  food storage tips, 6, 20
Freezers, 61–63
Freezing food, 17–19, _18_, 111, 169, _180_
French fries, 231–32, _233_
French's Mustard
  cleaning tips, 290, 331
  cooking tips, 190–91, 235, 241
  deodorizing tips, 290, 331
  healing remedy tips, 273, 284
French's Mustard squeeze bottle, 23, 114
Frisbee, 142
Fruit of the Earth Aloe Vera Gel, 271, 284
Fruits. _See also specific type_
  Candied Fruit Peels, _218_
  cooking tips, 169–71, _171_
  dried, 8, 150–51, _151_
  shopping for and storing, 5–10, _6_, _7_, _8_, _9_, _10_
  sticker label removal from, 9
  washing tips, 169–70
Frying food, 132–33, 154, 165, 231–32, _233_
Funnels, 35

G

Gadgets. _See specific item_
Garbage cans/pails, 36, 315
Garbage disposers, 63–64
Garlic, 13, _95_, 171–72
Gatorade, 277, 281, 285
Gatorade bottle, 13, 23
Gelatin, 172, _173_
Gelatin Salad, 242

Gillette Foamy, 50, 294, 304, 337
Ginger, 182
Glad Flexible Straws, 17, 186, 224, 255, 274, 277
Glad Trash Bags
    appliance and gadget tips, 51, 70, 78
    for apron, 32
    cleaning tips, 290, 325
    cooking tips, 95, 149
Glass, cleaning up broken, 291
Glassware, 37, 305–6, 316
Gold Medal Flour
    cleaning tips, 303, 320, 328
    cooking tips
        artichokes, 83
        bacon, 86
        bread, 92–93, 95
        cakes, 105, 109–11
        cheese, 126
        chicken, 131–32, 135
        chocolate, 136
        cookies, 142
        dried fruit, 150
        eggplant, 151
        flour substitute, 169
        fruits, 170
        gravy, 175
        hamburgers, 177
        meats, general, 201, 203
        onions, 213
        pies, 225
        potatoes, 231–32
        potato pancakes, 235
        raisins, 237
        sauces, 245
        soups, 253
        sour cream, 254
    healing remedy tips, 275
Gold's Horseradish, 241
Grains. See specific type
Grandma's Molasses, 100, 218, 258
Grapefruit, 9, 173, 173
Grapes, 174, 174
Graters and grating tips, 37, 124–25, 125–26, 316
Gravy, 174–76, 176
Greens, 242–43
Grilling food, 49–51, 165
Ground beef, 196
Gum removal from hair, 280–81

Halitosis, 270–71
Ham, 176–77
Hamburgers, 177–80, 178–79, 180
Hand care tips, 281
Hand cleaning tips, 166–67, 316–17
Hard-boiled eggs, 154–55, 155
Headache, 281
Healing remedy tips. See specific malady
Heartburn, 282

Heinz Apple Cider Vinegar
    cooking tips, 90, 189
    food storage tips, cheese, 1
    healing remedy tips, 269, 272, 277, 282
Heinz Ketchup, 89, 198, 218, 297, 303
Heinz Red Wine Vinegar, 171
Heinz White Vinegar
    appliance and gadget tips
        coffeemakers, 55
        dishwashers, 57
        freezers, 62
        garbage disposers, 64
        microwave ovens, 66
        oven racks, 69
        ovens, 68
        pressure cookers, 71
        stoves, 77
        teakettles, 79
        toasters, 80
    cleaning tips
        aluminum cookware, 290
        butcher blocks, 292
        carpet stains, 294
        casserole dishes, 297
        cast-iron cookware, 298
        coffeepots, 301
        copper items, 303
        countertops, 304
        crystal vases, 307
        cutting boards, 308
        dishes, 309
        drain boards, 310
        drains, 310–12
        floors, 314
        garbage pails, 315
        glassware, 316
        pots and pans, 324
        silverware, 327
        sinks, 328–29
        sponges, 330
        sports bottles, 331
        Thermos bottles, 335
    cooking tips
        baking soda freshness test, 87–88
        beets, 91
        bread, 92
        broccoli, 99
        cabbage, 102
        cauliflower, 120
        chocolate cake, 109
        corned beef, 195
        doughnuts, 150
        eggs, 152, 154, 158
        fish, 161, 163–64, 166–67
        fruits, 170
        gelatin, 172
        meats, general, 193–95, 202
        oil, 212

Heinz White Vinegar
  cooking tips *(cont.)*
    onions, 214
    pies, 225
    potatoes, 230–31, 234
    salad dressing, 241
    salt, 245
    shrimp, 248
    soufflés, 249
    sour cream, 254
    sour milk, 205
    vegetables, 264
    wine, 267
  cookware and tableware tips, 35, 42
  deodorizing tips, 62, 66, 150, 163–64, 167, 214,
    290, 319–20, 331
  disinfecting tips, 42, 308, 331
  healing remedy tips, 284
  for vegetable washing, 30
Herbs and spices. *See also specific type*
  cooking tips, 181–82
  shopping for and storing, 13–14, 14
Hershey's Caramel Topping, 252
Hershey's Chocolate Syrup, 88, 138
Hershey's Cocoa, 109, 114, 136
Hershey's Milk Chocolate Bar, 108, 140, 149,
  287
Hershey's Milk Chocolate Chips, 137
Hershey's Semi-Sweet Chocolate Chips, 115, 144,
  207
Hiccups, 282
Hidden Valley Ranch Dressing, 254
Highchairs, 317
Holland House Sherry, 248, 253
Honey, 22, 182, 183
Honeydew melon, 183
Honey Maid Graham Crackers, 225
Hot chocolate, 183, 184
Hot dogs, 196
Huggies Baby Wipes
  appliance and gadget tips, 53, 55, 60
  cleaning tips, 292, 304, 317, 333, 336
Hunt's Tomato Paste, 175, 186, 198, 246, 252,
  278
Hunt's Tomato Sauce, 191
Hydrogen Peroxide, 170, 329

Ice cream, 184, 185
Ice packs, 282–83
Icing cakes, 112–15, 114
Indigestion, 283
Insect bites, 284
Insomnia, 284
Itchy skin, 284–85

Jams and jellies, 185
Jar label removal, 37–38
Jar opening tips, 38

Jell-O products
  cleaning tips, 311–12
  cooking tips, 104, 112, 124, 134, 166, 197, 225,
    236
  healing remedy tips, 269, 283
Jet-Dry, 55
Jet-Puffed Marshmallows
  cooking tips, 100, 108, 149, 185
  food storage tips, 20
Jif Peanut Butter
  appliance and gadget tips, 80
  cleaning tips, 293, 322
  cooking tips, 88, 114, 121, 164, 175, 183, 246
  cookware and tableware tips, 37
  deodorizing tips, 164
  healing remedy tips, 280, 282
  for jar label removal, 37
Johnson & Johnson Cotton Balls, 43
Johnson's Baby Oil, 59, 321, 329, 331
Johnson's Baby Powder, 43, 333
Johnson's Baby Shampoo, 35, 309
Juicers, 64
Juices, 186

Karo Light Corn Syrup, 138, 206, 260
Kellogg's Corn Flakes, 98, 131, 162–63, 192
Kellogg's Frosted Flakes, 142
Kellogg's Rice Krispies, 177
Ketchup bottles, unclogging, 186
Kingsford Charcoal Briquets, 73
Kingsford's Corn Starch
  baking powder and, making, 87
  cleaning tips, 294, 326, 333, 336
  cooking tips
    baking powder, making, 87
    bread, 96
    cake icing, 114
    cake sauces, 117
    chicken, 132
    chocolate, 138
    custard, 150
    eggs, 157
    egg substitutes, 160
    gravy, 175
    hot chocolate, 183
    pudding, 236
    salt, 245
    sauces, 246
    soups, 253
  healing remedy tips, 271
  rubber gloves and, 43
Kitchen magnets, 317
Kiwifruit, 186, 186
Kiwi Shoe Polish, 293
Kleenex Tissues, 21, 34
Kleenex Tissues box, 20
Knives, 38
Knobs, stove, 78

Knorr Beef Bouillon, cooking tips, 97–98
Knox Gelatin, 190–91, 206, 250
Knudsen Buttermilk, 127, 142
Knudsen Cottage Cheese, 123, 177, 221
Knudsen Sour Cream, 108, 224, 234
Kool-Aid, 58, 68, 92, 114
Korbel Brandy, 135, 150
Kraft Grated Parmesan Cheese, 249
Kraft Real Mayo, 38

Lakewood Papaya Juice, 2–2
Lamb, 187, 210
Land O Lakes Butter
  cooking tips
    artichokes, 84
    bananas, 88
    bread, 93
    cake icing, 114
    cakes, 106
    cheese, 127
    chicken, 129
    cookies, 142
    cranberries, 147
    eggs, 157
    fish, 161, 168
    jams and jellies, 185
    meringues, 204
    mushrooms, 209
    oil, 212
    onions, 214
    pasta, 219, 221
    pies, 225
    potatoes, 229, 232
    raisins, 117, 237
    rice, 238–39
    salads, 241–42
    sauces, 246
    soups, 249, 252
    syrups, 260
    turnips, 263
  healing remedy tips, 285
Lasagna, 221, 222
Lay's Potato Chips, 98, 131, 163, 249
Lea & Perrins Worcestershire Sauce, 303
Leftover food, 14–15, 129
L'eggs Sheer Energy Panty Hose
  appliance and gadget tips, 73
  cleaning tips, 309, 317, 322, 326
  cooking tips, 85, 90, 127, 145, 167–68, 181, 218, 242, 250–51, 262
  cookware and tableware tips, 42, 46
  food storage tips, 13, 28
  healing remedy tips, 285
Lemons, 187–88, 188
Lettuce, 26, 27, 188–89, 189
Lima beans, 189, 189
Limes, 187–88, 188
Linen, 40, 332–34

Lipton Recipe Secrets Onion Soup Mix, 175, 192, 200, 214, 239
Lipton Tea, 275, 281
Lipton Tea Bags, 201, 202, 273, 277
Listerine
  appliance and gadget tips, 73, 75
  cleaning tips, 304, 308, 315, 329–30
  cooking tips, 167, 215
  cookware and tableware tips, 42
  deodorizing tips, 73, 75, 167
  disinfecting tips, 42, 308, 330
  healing remedy tips, 269, 275–76, 279
List, grocery, 19
Liver, 190
Log Cabin Maple Syrup, 196
Lubriderm, 281
Lunch boxes, 317

Mangoes, 190
Manischewitz Potato Starch, 175, 246, 253
Marinating meats, 133, 166, 196–97
Marshmallows, 22
Martini & Rossi Dry Vermouth, 136
Mashed potatoes, 232–33, 233
MasterCard charge card as scraper, 292, 302, 309
Maxwell House Coffee
  appliance and gadget tips, 50, 62, 66, 73
  cleaning tips, 312, 320, 324
  cooking tips, 89, 92–93, 140, 164, 167, 176–77, 187, 215, 246–47
  deodorizing tips, 62, 66, 73, 164, 167
  healing remedy tips, 281
Maxwell House Coffee can
  appliance and gadget tips, 50
  cooking tips, 86, 104, 257
  cookware and tableware tips, 46
  food storage tips, 13, 22–24
Mayonnaise, 190–91
McCormick Anise Seed, 106, 117
McCormick Bay Leaves, 22, 168, 248
McCormick Black Pepper, 186
McCormick Black Peppercorns, 182, 248
McCormick Caraway Seed, 187, 245
McCormick Cinnamon Sugar, 107, 173
McCormick Cream of Tartar
  appliance and gadget tips, 71
  cleaning tips, 289, 299–300, 305, 320, 329, 334
  cooking tips, 87, 152, 159, 249
McCormick Curry Powder, 91, 96, 123
McCormick Fennel Seed, 90, 271
McCormick Food Coloring, 125, 165, 219, 232, 235, 239
McCormick Garlic Powder, 186, 227, 241–42
McCormick Ground (Cayenne) Red Pepper, 286–87
McCormick Ground Cinnamon, 132, 140, 258, 320
McCormick Ground Ginger, 274, 286–87
McCormick Ground Nutmeg, 101, 263
McCormick Ground Rosemary, 187

McCormick Ground Thyme, 241–42, 248, 276
McCormick Ground Turmeric, 156
McCormick Imitation Maple Flavor, 259
McCormick Oregano, 98
McCormick Paprika, 242, 245
McCormick Parsley Flakes, 248
McCormick Powdered Arrowroot, 176, 246, 253
McCormick Pure Almond Extract, 140, 210–11
McCormick Pure Lemon Extract, 73
McCormick Pure Orange Extract, 74
McCormick Pure Vanilla Extract, 66, 74, 106,
    206–7, 281, 302
McCormick Stick Cinnamon, 258
McCormick Tarragon Leaves, 136
Measuring cups and spoons, 38–39
Meatballs, 197
Meat grinders, 65
Meatloaf, 191–93, _192_, _193_
Meat mallets, 39–40
Meats, general. _See also specific type_
    broiling, 128–31, 160–61, 194–95
    browning, 195
    cooking tips, 193–203, _197_, _199_, _200_, _202_
    defrosting, 195–96
    Delicious Brisket, _194_
    freezing, 17–19, _18_
    grease splatter prevention, 199
    marinating, 133, 166, 196–97
    mousse, 197
    roasting, 134–35, 197–98
    safety issues, 193–94
    sautéing, 199
    shopping for and storing, 15–19, _16_, _17_, _18_
    stewing, 200–201
    tenderizing, 201–3, _203_
Meringues, 204–5
Microwave ovens, 65–67
Milk and cream
    buttermilk, 205
    cleaning tips for spills, 330
    cooking tips, 205–7
    cream, 204–5
    shopping for and storing tips, 5
    sour milk, 205
    substitutes, 206–7
    whipped cream, 206–7
Miracle Whip
    cooking tips, 82, 116, 130, 135, 153, 241
    healing remedy tips, 285
Mixers, electric, 67–68, _67_
Molasses, _28_, 207–8
Mops, 318
Morton Kosher Salt, 139, 157, 217
Morton Salt
    appliance and gadget tips, 50, 56, 60, 64, 68, 77
    cleaning tips
        butcher blocks, 292
        carpet stains, 294

        casserole dishes, 296
        cast-iron cookware, 298
        china, 299
        coffeepots, 301
        copper items, 303
        countertops, 305
        crystal vases, 307
        cutting boards, 308
        eggs, 312
        enamel pots and pans, 313
        hands, 316
        pots and pans, 324–25
        silverware, 327
        sinks, 329
        Thermos bottles, 335
        wine stains, 337
    cooking tips
        apples, 82
        artichokes, 84
        broccoli, 99
        Brussels sprouts, 101
        cabbage, 103
        cake icing, 114
        cantaloupe, 118
        cauliflower, 120
        chicken, 130–31, 135
        chocolate, 138
        chocolate cake, 109
        clams, 139
        cream, 205
        cucumbers, 148
        eggs, 153–55, 157–58
        fish, 164, 167
        flour, 169
        fruits, 170
        garlic, 171–72
        gelatin, 173
        greens, 242
        ground beef, 196
        hamburgers, 178
        honeydew melon, 183
        juices, 186
        lettuce, 188
        meats, general, 194, 199
        onions, 215
        onion salt, 182
        pancakes, 219
        pears, 223
        pecans, 212
        pies, 225
        potatoes, 231, 234
        pumpkins, 236–37
        shrimp, 248
        soups, 252
        spinach, 255
        sweetbreads, 259
        turkey, 263
        vegetables, 264

watermelon, 266
whipped cream, 205
cookware and tableware tips, 41–43, 47
deodorizing tips, 42–43, 64, 132, 164, 167, 308, 335
disinfecting tips, 330
food storage tips, 1, 4–5, 30–31
healing remedy tips, 270, 274, 278–79, 279, 286–87
for spills, 42–43, 160
Mott's Apple Juice, cooking tips, 82, 88, 105–6
Mott's Applesauce, 106, 212, 278–79
Mousse, 134, 166, 197
Mr. Clean Magic Eraser, 297, 301, 325, 334
Mr. Coffee Filters
appliance and gadget tips, 66
cooking tips, 101, 118, 124, 142, 170, 185, 212, 250, 260
cookware and tableware tips, 33–34, 40
food storage tips, 9, 101
healing remedy tips, 277
Muffins, 208, 208
Murphy Oil Soap
appliance and gadget tips, 76, 80
cleaning tips, 293, 294–95, 314, 331, 333
Mushrooms, 27, 27, 209–10, 209
Mussels, 210
Mutton, 210

Nabisco Original Premium Saltine Crackers
appliance and gadget tips, 65
cooking tips, 98–99, 131, 167, 179, 192, 197, 235, 257
food storage tips, 24
healing remedy tips, 280
Napkins, 40, 332–34
Nausea, 285
Nestea Iced Tea Mix
appliance and gadget tips, 77
cleaning tips, 290, 293, 307, 320, 331
cooking tips, 202
Nestlé Carnation Condensed Milk, 189–90
Nestlé Carnation Evaporated Milk, 34, 159, 192, 251, 254, 264
Nestlé Carnation Nonfat Dry Milk
cleaning tips, 327, 333, 336
cooking tips
bread, 93, 96
cauliflower, 120
chestnuts, 211
chicken, 133
corn, 145
fish, 163, 165
milk substitutes, 205–6
pastry, 222
pies, 225
potatoes, 232–33
healing remedy tips, 271, 279

Nestlé Coffee-mate Creamer Italian Sweet Crème, 191
Newman's Own Olive Oil & Vinegar Dressing, 166, 196, 209, 241
Niagara Spray Starch, 40
Nonstick cookware, 40, 319
Nuts, 210–12, 212

Odor removal tips. See Deodorizing tips
Oil, cooking
cleaning tips, 320
cooking tips, 212–13, 212
substitutes, 116
usage tips, 23
Omelets, 156–57
Onions, 28, 28, 213–16, 214, 215
Onion salt, 182
Orajel, 272
Oral-B Dental Floss cooking tips
cake batter, 116
cheese, 127
cheesecake, 109
chicken, 130, 135
cookies, 142–43
jams and jellies, 185
mushrooms, 209
rolls, 98
soufflés, 250
turkey, 262
Oral-B Toothbrush
appliance and gadget tips, 52–53, 56, 61, 64, 81
cleaning tips, 306, 316
cooking tips, 145
Oranges, 216–17, 216
Orville Redenbacher's Gourmet Popping Corn, 228
Oven mitts, 40
Oven racks, 69–71
Ovens, 68–71
Oysters, 217

Pam Cooking Spray
appliance and gadget tips
barbecue gadgets, 50
can openers, 53
dehydrators, 56
dishwashers, 58
eggbeaters, 59
electric mixers, 67
freezers, 62
oven racks, 70
ovens, 68
refrigerators, 74
rice cookers, 75–76
slow cookers, 76
waffle irons, 81

Pam Cooking Spray *(cont.)*
  cleaning tips, 292, 298, 325, 329
  cooking tips
    biscuits, 92
    bread, 96
    cake icing, 110
    cereals, 122
    cheese, 126
    chocolate, 139
    cookies, 143
    corn syrup, 146
    custard, 150
    dried fruits, 151
    eggs, 159
    fish, 162, 166
    fruits, 170
    honey, 182
    lasagna, 221
    meats, general, 200
    molasses, 208
    pies, 226
    rice, 239
    syrup, 260
    waffles, 265
  cookware and tableware tips, 33, 35, 37, 41–42, 44, 47, 47–48
  for greasing measuring items and plastic containers, 38–39
  healing remedy tips, 281, 286
  for jar label removal, 38
Pampers, 295
Pancakes, 213, 217–19
Parson's Ammonia
  appliance and gadget tips, 51, 68–70, 78
  cleaning tips, 290, 307, 314, 325, 333, 335
Pasta
  boiling, 219, 221
  cooking tips, 219–21, 220, 221, 222
  draining, 221, 221
  lasagna, 221, 222
  shopping for and storing, 11, 12
  types of, 12
  usage tips, 220
Pastry, 222
Peaches, 222, 223
Pears, 223, 223
Pecans, 212
Peppers, 182, 224
Pewter items, 321
Philadelphia Cream Cheese, 121
Phillips' Milk of Magnesia, 288
Pies, 224–27, 226
Pillsbury Softasilk Cake Flour, 110, 168
Pine-Sol, 320, 333
Pineapple, 9, 9, 227, 227
Planters Walnuts, 103, 120
Plastic bags, grocery, 20
Plastic containers, 40–41, 321–22

Plastic wrap, 41
Play-Doh, 336
Playtex Living Gloves
  cleaning tips, 291, 318
  cooking tips
    artichokes, 84
    bacon, 86
    cheese, 126
    chicken, 130, 135
    fish, 168
    hamburgers, 179
    meats, general, 198
    mussels, 210
    onions, 215
    peppers, 224
    pineapples, 227
    potatoes, 229
    turkey, 263
  cookware and tableware tips, 34, 38, 46
  healing remedy tips, 281
Pledge furniture polish, 310
Poached food, 158–59, 167–68
Popcorn, 227–28, 228
Pork chops, 229
Post-it Notes
  appliance and gadget tips, 58
  food shopping tips, 19
  food storage tips, 15
Potato chips, 23
Potatoes
  baking, 229–30
  cooking tips, 229–36, 230, 232, 233, 234, 236
  French fries, 231–32, 232
  frying, 231–32, 232
  mashing, 232–33, 233
  peeling, 234, 234
  potato pancakes, 234–35
  potato salad, 235
  sautéing, 235
  scalloped, 235, 236
  shopping for and storing, 28, 29
  sweet, 259, 259
  usage tips, 230
Potato pancakes, 234–35
Potato salad, 235
Pot holders, 41
Pot scrubbers, 322
Pots and pans. *See* Cookware
Poultry. *See* Chicken; Turkey
Pound cake, 115
Pressure cookers, 71
Pretzels, 23
Pringles cans, 11, 13, 22, 23
Progresso Breadcrumbs, 133, 143, 191, 236, 250
Pudding, 236
Pumpkins, 236–37
Purell Instant Hand Sanitizer, 51, 272, 276, 305, 327

Q-tips Cotton Swabs
  appliance and gadget tips, 52, 61
  cooking tips, 154
  cookware and tableware tips, 37
Quaker Oats
  cooking tips, 180, 253
  healing remedy tips, 269, 275, 279, 281, 285
Quaker Oats canister, 11
Quaker Yellow Corn Meal, 94, 133, 139

Raisins, 117, 237, <u>237</u>
Range hoods, 72
ReaLemon
  appliance and gadget tips, 54, 58, 64, 66–67, 71
  cleaning tips
    aluminum cookware, 289
    butcher blocks, 292
    coffeepots, 301
    copper items, 303
    countertops, 305
    cutting boards, 308
    flatware, 313
    floors, 314
    graters, 317
    nonstick cookware, 319
    plastic containers, 322
    pots and pans, 325
    silver, 327
    sinks, 329
    Thermos bottles, 324
    wooden spoons, 337
  cooking tips
    apples, 82
    artichokes, 83–84
    asparagus, 85
    avocados, 85–86
    bananas, 88
    beets, 91
    bread, 96–97
    broccoli, 100
    cabbage, 103
    cake icing, 114–15
    cantaloupes, 118
    celery, 121
    chicken, 130, 132, 135
    collard greens, 141
    corn, 146
    dried fruits, 151
    eggs, 155, 158–59
    fish, 162, 164–67
    fruits, 171
    garlic, 172
    gravy, 176
    honeydew melon, 183
    juices, 186
    lamb, 187, 210
    lettuce, 188, 189
    meats, general, 196

    meringues, 204
    mushrooms, 209–10
    mutton, 210
    onions, 215
    pastry, 222
    pies, 226
    potatoes, 231, 234
    rice, 239
    scallops, 247
    sour cream, 254
    sour milk, 205
    sweetbreads, 259
    turkey, 263
    vegetables, 264–65
    whipped cream, 207
  cookware and tableware tips, 42–43
  deodorizing tips, 42–43, 64, 66–67, 74, 132, 164,
    168, 215, 308, 320
  food storage tips, 18, 30–31
  healing remedy tips, 270–71, 272, 274–75, 280,
    282, 284
Recipe cards, 20
Recipe Magic
  Bean Croquettes, <u>90</u>
  Candied Fruit Peels, <u>218</u>
  Caramel Corn, <u>228</u>
  Cheerios Treats, <u>122</u>
  Cheese Croutons, <u>126</u>
  Classic Meatloaf, <u>193</u>
  Colorful Rock Candy, <u>118</u>
  Delicious Brisket, <u>194</u>
  Garlic Bread, <u>95</u>
  Glazed Walnuts, <u>211</u>
  Homemade Cough Syrup, <u>274</u>
  Homemade Ice Cream, <u>184</u>
  Low-Cal Lunch, <u>123</u>
  Stewed Rhubarb, <u>238</u>
Reddi-wip
  cooking tips, 141, 192, 205, 233, 254
  healing remedy tips, 287
Refrigerators, 72–75
Resolve Carpet Cleaner, 333
Revlon Nail Polish
  cleaning tips, 299
  for marking measuring cups and spoons, 41
  for plugging salt and pepper shakers, 44
Reynolds Cut-Rite Wax Paper
  appliance and gadget tips, 53, 63, 67, 81
  cleaning tips, 302
  cooking tips
    bacon, 87
    cake icing, 115
    cakes, 106, 111–12
    chicken, 135–36
    cookies, 143
    corn, 146
    eggs, 154
    fish, 168

Reynolds Cut-Rite Wax Paper
  cooking tips *(cont.)*
    flour, 169
    garlic, 172
    herbs and spices, 182
    ice cream, 185
    pancakes, 219
    rice, 239
    soufflés, 250
    whipped cream, 207
  cookware and tableware tips, 33, 41–42, 48
  food storage tips, 2–3, 15–16, 19
  for meat flattening, 39–40
Reynolds Parchment Paper, 56, 143
Reynolds Wrap
  appliance and gadget tips, 51, 67, 69–70, 80
  cleaning tips, 322, 326
  cooking tips
    bananas, 88
    bread, 93, 97
    brownies, 101
    cakes, 105, 111–12, 117
    celery, 122
    cheese, 126–27
    chicken, 131
    cupcakes, 149
    eggs, 154–55
    fish, 161, 164
    ham, 177
    hamburgers, 180
    meats, general, 194–95, 198
    onions, 216
    pies, 226
    potatoes, 229–30
    rolls, 98
    vegetables, 265
  cookware and tableware tips, 32–33
  food storage tips, 10–11, 15–17, 19, 26, 28,
    93–94
  for funnel, 36
  scissor sharpening and, 44
Rhubarb, 238
Rice, 13, 13, 237–40, 240
Rice cookers, 75–76
Roasting meats, 134–35, 197–98
Rolling pins, 42–43
Rolls, bread, 97–98
Rubber gloves, 43

Salad dressing, 241
Salads, 29, 241–43, 243, 244
Salsa, 243
Salt, 243
Salt and pepper shakers, 44
Sambal Oelek Chili Paste, 246
Saran Wrap
  appliance and gadget tips, 61, 74
  cleaning tips, 306

  cooking tips
    bananas, 88
    brown sugar, 100
    butter, 102
    cakes, 116
    cantaloupes, 118
    clams, 139–40
    cream cheese, 124
    ham, 177
    hamburgers, 180
    lemons, 188
    limes, 188
    meats, general, 202
    oranges, 217
    pies, 226
    pudding, 236
    rice, 239
    sauces, 246
    watermelon, 266
  cookware and tableware tips, 39, 41
  food storage tips, 2–3, 7–11, 15, 17
Sauces, 117, 129, 245–46
Sausages, 247, 247
Sautéing food, 135, 168, 199, 235
Scalloped potatoes, 235, 236
Scallops, 247
Scissors, 44
Scotch Packaging Tape, 20, 23, 291, 299, 318
Scotch Tape
  appliance and gadget tips, 74
  cooking tips, 154
  cookware and tableware tips, 41
  food storage tips, 9–10
  shopping supplies, 20
Scotch Transparent Tape, 143
Scouring powder, making, 326
Scrambled eggs, 159
Scrapes, skin, 275–76
Seasonings. *See* Herbs and spices
Serving spoons, 44
7-Up, 202
Shaving tips, 285
Shelf liners, 45
Shout detergent, 72, 77, 295, 305
Shrimp, 247–48, 248
Sifters and strainers, 46, 127
Silverware, 45, 326–27
Sinks, 327–29
Skin care tips, 286
Slim Jim, 231
Slow cookers, 76
Smirnoff Vodka, 44, 182
Smoking cessation tips, 286
Smucker's Strawberry Jam, 260
Snow cones, 248–49
Sore throat, 286–87
S.O.S. Wool Soap Pads, 298
Soufflés, 249–50

Soups, 250–54, <u>251</u>
Sour cream, 254
Sour milk, 205
SPAM, 87
Spices. *See* Herbs and spices
Spic and Span, 333
Spill and stain removal tips. *See specific brand*
Spinach, 29, 255, <u>255</u>
Sponge cakes, 117
Sponges, 330, <u>330</u>
Spoons, 44, 337
Sports bottles, 330–31
Spray 'n Wash, 69
Stainless-steel appliances, 331–32
Stain removal tips. *See* Spill and stain removal
    tips
Star Olive Oil
    cleaning tips, 321, 325, 329
    cooking tips
        beans, 91
        butter, 102
        chicken, 133
        cookies, 144
        fish, 165
        garlic, 172
        meats, general, 202
        pasta, 219, 221
        salad dressings, 241
        waffles, 266
        wine, 267
    healing remedy tips, 275, 278
Star Wine Vinegar, 127, 181
Stayfree Maxi Pads, 275, 278
Steak, <u>200</u>, <u>202</u>
Steel wool pads, 46
Stewing food, 200–201, <u>238</u>
Stoves, 72, 76–78, 301–2
Strainers. *See* Sifters and strainers
Strawberries, 9–10, <u>10</u>, 255, <u>256</u>
String beans, 256, <u>256</u>
Stuffing, 257, <u>257</u>
SueBee Honey
    cooking tips
        apples, 83
        breads, 96
        cakes, 106–7, 117
        coffee, 141
        dried fruits, 151
        onions, 216
        potatoes, 231
        salt, 245
        sugar substitutes, 258
        tea, 260
    healing remedy tips, 273, 276, 279, 283–84,
        286–87
Sugar
    cinnamon, 258
    confectioners, 112–13, 142, 150, 174, 206, 218

cooking tips, 258
shopping for and storing, 23
substitutes, 117, 258
Sun-Maid Raisins, 121
Sweetbreads, 259
Sweet potatoes, 259, <u>259</u>
Sweets and treats. *See specific type*
Swiss Miss Milk Chocolate, 141
Swiss steak, 201, <u>203</u>
Syrup, 259–60

Tabasco Pepper Sauce
    cooking tips, 92, 147, 228, 246
    healing remedy tips, 270, 274, 288
Tablecloths, 332–34
Tableware. *See specific item*
Tacos, 260
Tang
    appliance and gadget tips, 55, 59, 69
    cooking tips, 107, 117, 144, 156, 249
Tea, 260
Teapots, 46, 78–79, 334
Tenderizing meats, 201–3, <u>203</u>
Thai Kitchen Coconut Milk, 246
Thermos bottles, 334–35
3M Sandpaper, 38, 44, 76
Tide detergent, 70, 78, 291, 295, 309
Tidy Cats, 36, 51, 63, 74
Toaster ovens, 80–81
Toasters, 79–80
Tomatoes, 29–30, <u>29</u>, 261–62, <u>261</u>
Tomato sauce, 246
Tongue burn, 287
Tropicana Juice products, 190, 219, 227, 241,
    286
Turkey, 262–63, <u>263</u>
Turnips, 263
20 Mule Team Borax
    appliance and gadget tips, 57, 59, 63–64, 75
    cleaning tips, 295, 297, 299, 313, 314–15, 325,
        329–30, 333, 337
    deodorizing tips, 63–64, 75, 330
    food storage tips, 36

Ulcers, 287–88, <u>288</u>
Uncle Ben's Converted Brand Rice
    appliance and gadget tips, 54, 61
    cleaning tips, 290, 307, 331, 335
    cooking tips, 235
    deodorizing tips, 61
    food storage tips, 44
    healing remedy tips, 270, 282
USA Today newspaper
    appliance and gadget tips, 63, 74–75
    cleaning tips, 322
    cooking tips, 87, 198, 222–23
    deodorizing tips, 63, 74–75
    food storage tips, 10, 29–30

Vaseline Petroleum Jelly
  appliance and gadget tips, 51, 71, 72, 75, 80
  cleaning tips, 315, 331–32
  cookware and tableware tips, 38
  healing remedy tips, 274
Veal, 203
Vegetables. *See also specific type*
  cooking tips, 264–65, <u>265</u>
  shopping for and storing, 23–31, <u>24</u>, <u>25</u>, <u>27</u>, <u>28</u>,
    <u>29</u>, <u>30</u>
  washing tips, 30–31, 141
Vicks VapoRub, 280

Waffle irons, 81, 335
Waffles, 265–66
Walls and wallpaper, 336
Walnuts, <u>211</u>
Watermelon, 10, <u>10</u>, 266, <u>266</u>
Wax removal, 293
WD-40, in barbecue charcoal fire, 51
Welch's Grape Jelly, 260
Wesson Oil
  appliance and gadget tips, 52, 71
  cleaning tips, 292, 329, 335
  cooking tips
    bread, 93, 97
    butter, 102
    cakes, 107, 111
    cheese, 126
    chestnuts, 211
    chocolate, 139
    cookies, 144
    eggs, 158
    gravy, 175
    greens, 242–43
    meats, general, 195, 198
    onions, 216
    pasta, 221
    potatoes, 231, 234
    rice, 239
    string beans, 256
    turkey, 263
    veal, 203
  cookware and tableware tips, 33–34, 37, 43, 48
  healing remedy tips, 286
Whipped cream, 206–7
Whisks, 47
White chocolate, <u>138</u>
Wilson Tennis Balls, 270, 315
Windex, 295, 327, 332, 334
Wine, 267, <u>268</u>, 336–37
Wish-Bone Italian Dressing, 133, 166, 196, 210
Woks, 48
Wonder Bread
  appliance and gadget tips, 54, 61, 65, 69, 75
  cleaning tips, 291, 295, 305, 319, 336

  cooking tips
    broccoli, 100
    Brussels sprouts, 101
    cabbage, 103
    cauliflower, 121
    chicken, 131
    cookies, 144
    fish, 161, 165
    gravy, 176
    meats, general, 195
    oil, 212
    pork chops, 229
    rice, 240
    soups, 251
    stuffing, 257
    turkey, 263
  deodorizing tips, 75
  food storage tips, 20–21, 26
Wooden salad bowls, 47–48
Wooden spoons, 48, 337
Wounds, skin, 275–76
Wrigley's gum products, 11, 22

Yeast, 98
Yogurt, 267

Ziploc Freezer Bags, 201
Ziploc Storage Bags
  appliance and gadget tips, 71
  cleaning tips, 318
  cooking tips
    bacon, 87
    bread, 97
    butter, 102
    cake icing, 115
    cakes, 107, 112
    chicken, 133
    chocolate, 139
    clams, 140
    cookies, 144
    cream cheese, 125
    cupcakes, 149
    eggs, 154
    fish, 166
    grapes, 174
    greens, 242–43
    kiwi, 186
    marinades, 203
    meatloaf, 193
    meats, general, 196, 203
    mushrooms, 210
    onions, 216
    oysters, 217
    pancakes, 219
    pastry, 222
    popcorn, 229

potatoes, 233
soups, 250
steak, 200
stuffing, 257
waffles, 266
walnuts, 211–12
whipped cream, 207
wine, 267
cookware and tableware tips, 46
as coupon organizers, 19
food shopping tips, 20
food storage tips
apples, 5
artichokes, 23–24
asparagus, 24
berries, 7–8
brown sugar, 20
carrots, 25
celery, 26
cheese, 1, 4
cherries, 8
dried fruits, 8
eggplants, 8
frozen food, 17
herbs and spices, 13–15
lettuce, 26
mushrooms, 27
spinach, 29
strawberries, 10
watercress, 31
for funnel, 36
for gloves, 43
grating food and, 37
healing remedy tips, 283

About the Author

Joey Green—author of *Joey Green's Cleaning Magic, Joey Green's Fix-It Magic, Joey Green's Gardening Magic,* and *Joey Green's Amazing Pet Cures*—got Barbara Walters to put a wet Pampers diaper on her head on *The View,* made Jay Leno shave with Jif Peanut Butter on *The Tonight Show,* conditioned Meredith Vieira's hair with Cool Whip, got Katie Couric to clean her diamond ring with Efferdent, and showed Diane Sawyer how to polish furniture with Spam. A walking encyclopedia of quirky yet ingenious household hints, he has been profiled by the *New York Times, USA Today,* and *People.*

Green, a former contributing editor to *National Lampoon* and a former advertising copywriter at J. Walter Thompson, is the author of more than 45 books, including *Marx & Lennon: The Parallel Sayings, Contrary to Popular Belief,* and *The Zen of Oz: Ten Spiritual Lessons from Over the Rainbow.* A native of Miami, Florida, and a graduate of Cornell University, he wrote television commercials for Burger King and Walt Disney World and won a Clio Award for a print ad he created for Eastman Kodak. He backpacked around the world for two years on his honeymoon and lives in Los Angeles with his wife, Debbie, and their two daughters, Ashley and Julia.

Visit Joey Green on the internet at
www.wackyuses.com